The Empress Frederick Writes to Sophie Her Daughter

Victoria, Princess Royal and Later Queen of the Hellenes; Letters of German Royalty, 1889-1901

By Empress Victoria

Published by Pantianos Classics

ISBN-13: 978-1-78987-204-0

First published in 1955

The Empress Frederick

From the Portrait by Franz von Lenbach

Contents

Introduction..*v*
Editor's Note... *vi*
Familiar Names..*viii*

Chapter One - The Thirty-One Years Before the Letters...... 11
   I - 1858-1860 11
   II - 1861-1871..15
   III - 1871-1887 20
   IV - 1887-1888 24
Chapter Two – The Letters 1889-90... 32
Chapter Three – The Letters, 1891.. 51
Chapter Four – The Letters, 1892 75
Chapter Five – The Letters, 1893 98
Chapter Six – The Letters, 1894 119
Chapter Seven – The Letters, 1895...139
Chapter Eight – The Letters, 1896 160
Chapter Nine – The Letters, 1897 181
Chapter Ten – The Letters, 1898 202
Chapter Eleven – The Letters, 1899...222
Chapter Twelve - The Letters 1900-1901 245
Chapter Thirteen - Aftermath 264
Bibliography 268

Introduction

By Her Majesty Queen Helen, Queen Mother of Roumania

My mother, Queen Sophie of the Hellenes, greatly treasured all the letters written to her by her mother, the Empress Frederick, over the years between her marriage in 1889 and the Empress's death in 1901.

When my mother left Greece on her second exile in 1921, she took the letters with her and carefully preserved them, not only because they were a precious link with one she loved, but because she had in mind that they should one day be published. She considered that existing books about the Empress did not do her justice. They played so much on her frustrated role in public affairs and on her unhappy relations with Prince Bismark, and with her son. Prince William, that her underlying womanly qualities were lost sight of.

My mother felt that the letters written to her, if published, would reveal the Empress differently, not only as a woman who was enlightened and tolerant, but as a fond and devoted mother. But because they contained much that was too intimately personal for print, my mother decided to try herself to edit them for publication.

While in exile from 1924 onwards, she set to work on the formidable task of arranging the correspondence and deleting unsuitable passages. But there were over 2,000 letters, totalling a million words, and she had made but little progress when, in 1931, she passed away.

Because I knew how much my mother wished to have the Empress's letters published, I made up my mind, when she died, to see that her wish was fulfilled. But for some years, circumstances held me from action. Then came the second world war. The letters were kept at my house at San Domenico, near Florence. When the fighting broke into Italy and spread towards the north, I was in Roumania, and my sister, Irene, Duchess of Aosta, who also lived near Florence, fearing for the safety of the letters, took them to her own house.

But soon afterwards she was arrested by the S.S. and taken to confinement in Germany. During the fighting north of Florence in 1944, her house was bombarded and looted. When she returned there after the war, it was with little hope that the letters had survived. But she learned that her servants had found some of them strewn about the grounds and had saved them. In a cellar were the rest, in their heavy metal box, which the looters had forced open, but with probably no time to destroy the contents.

When I went back to Florence after the enforced abdication of my son, Michael, King of Roumania, I asked Air Vice-Marshal Arthur Gould Lee, who had already written my son's story in *Crown Against Sickle,* to undertake the task of editing the letters for publication. It is with gratitude that I extend my warmest thanks to him for his patient perseverance in this lengthy work.

The Empress Frederick has always been a wonderful tradition and inspiration in our family. Although she died when I was only five years old, I have clear recollections of her, deriving from our family visits to her beautiful home, Friedrichshof, near Cronberg. I can still remember driving with her in her carriage, and also that she used to hear me say my prayers of an evening. I remember too, quite clearly, like a photograph in my brain, seeing her lying ill during our last visit. I can still see the large bed and the lovely darkened room, and I even remember the look she gave me, which I only long afterwards realized was full of pain. I still feel myself looking out of a window and seeing soldiers and horses in the space in front of the house, around the fountain, and being told they had come to take my grandmother away. That must have been the day of the funeral. But then memory fades away.

Children are very sensitive to atmosphere, and though we were kept away from everything, we all realized and felt the desolation that permeated and clung to this beautiful place my grandmother had created with so much love, dedicating everything in it to the memory of her beloved husband.

This book will, I am sure, reveal to its readers some of those qualities in the Empress that prove her to have been a great and good woman, as she is to her descendants, who still venerate her example, and was to those of her day who really knew her.

Helen
Queen Mother of Lorraine
1955 London

Editor's Note

That the German Empress Frederick, eldest daughter of Queen Victoria, was one of the great tragic figures of the nineteenth century is doubly true. The wrecking of her life was a tragedy not only for her, but for millions of others of lower degree, for had Fate permitted her husband, with her at his side, to reign for even a decade, twentieth-century history might have run to peaceful evolution instead of world-shaking wars.

Because of her unpopularity in Germany, which was nourished by those who regarded her democratic aims as a threat to Prussian and later Imperial German ambitions, a distorted view of her character prevailed until, in 1928, her Letters to Queen Victoria were published by Sir Frederick Ponsonby. This correspondence, while confirming some of her temperamental shortcomings, vindicated her as a woman of high ideals and principles.

But these letters ranged over more than forty years, and were selected with one object, which was to show that she had been unfairly judged over her conflict with Bismark and her son. The emphasis necessarily placed on her political involvements, and on her many tribulations and her indignant reactions to harsh treatment, inevitably resulted in the overshadowing of her qualities as a kind, warm-hearted woman. She emerged as a figure deserving of pity rather than sympathy.

The Letters to Princess Sophie present her in a different light. They are not the confidences of a troubled daughter to a revered parent, but the counsels of a fond mother drawing on her dearly bought experience to guide her newly married child living in a distant land. Covering only eleven years, and written almost daily, except when she and Sophie were together, they portray her in detail against the day-to-day happenings of her family and social life.

Because these letters are not carefully compiled self-appraisals for posterity, but the spontaneous expression of her inmost thoughts and feelings, they reveal her personality more truly and more intimately than any objective description could achieve. Indeed, for that reason, as we read them, we may sometimes feel that we are trespassing into the secret places of her heart. But we need not be ashamed, for it is these unsuspecting words which prove her to have been, in spite of some feminine foibles and prejudices, a woman from whom it is not possible to withhold our respect and affection.

Her long stream of letters not only takes us into her own and her daughter's private lives, but also into the lives of other regal figures, some of world-important stature. She presents them as ordinary human beings, with inelegant familiar names and plebeian weaknesses, and though she does not often strike a note of deliberate humour, she sometimes does so unconsciously. We may be sure she would have looked indulgently upon our smiles.

It is not only in the subjects of her letters that she exposes every facet of her complex nature. She shows herself in her handwriting, with its characteristic firmness and vigour, [1] and in her unhesitating style. The expression of her thoughts runs always fluently, and yet accurately, for in all the letters to Princess Sophie there are incredibly few erasures and corrections. She uses simple unaffected language, in which shapely passages alternate with slang, and sometimes, oddly, with phrases that seem to belong to our Americanized diction of to-day. For she and her daughters corresponded always in English, the habitual tongue in the family. Usually she even anglicized the names of places and people, and her practice has been followed in the Editor's commentary.

The letters and extracts presented in this volume amount to only a tenth of the whole. Rigorous selection has thus been necessary, and this has ruled out any attempt to touch on contemporary affairs, except those in which the Empress was in some way concerned. The Editor's object has been simply to unveil her personality, and the range of her interests, against the developing story of her family's fortunes during her twilight years. As far as possible he has let the Empress herself speak, and has kept his commentary to the minimum consistent with clear understanding. In the earlier years of the letters he has had to include a due proportion of explanation in order to introduce the background and the people mentioned, but in general he has tried to avoid pointing out the obvious, and has left the reader to draw his own conclusions.

In amplifying the Letters, he was able, when necessary, to refer to most of Princess Sophie's letters to her mother. And in clearing up a number of obscurities, he was fortunate in having the gracious assistance, until her death in 1954, of the Empress's daughter, Princess Margaret, Landgravine of Hesse, who is 'Mossy' in the Letters.

The Editor has examined every letter that the Empress wrote to her daughter, and in many of them, as can be understood, occur passages that cannot for various reasons be published. If he may end on a personal note, it is to express his sensibility at being privileged to read these intimate writings, to look into a woman's unguarded revelation of her soul, and to find there only goodness, love and courage.

[1] Her letter of 16th May 1899, of which the first page is given in facsimile later in the book, is the one that contains the paragraph quoted, written when she had just learned that she was suffering from cancer.

Familiar Names

These are the pet and family names that appear most frequently in the Letters. Further details and later titles are given in the Index.

ADOLF	Prince Adolphus of Schaumburg-Lippe.
ALECK	Alexander, Landgrave of Hesse.
ALFRED (UNCLE)	Duke of Edinburgh and Coburg.
ALICKY	Princess Alix of Hesse, Tsarina of Russia.
ALIX (AUNT)	Alexandra, Princess of Wales.
AMAMA	Queen Louise of Denmark.
ANDREA	Prince Andrew of Greece.
ANNA (AUNT)	Anna, dowager Landgravine of Hesse.
APAPA	Christian IX, King of Denmark.
ARTHUR (UNCLE)	Duke of Connaught.
BERNHARD	Prince of Saxe-Meiningen.
BERTIE (UNCLE)	Edward, Prince of Wales.
CHRISTLE	Prince Christian Victor of Schleswig-Holstein.
CHRISTO	Prince Christopher of Greece.
DAVID	Prince Edward of York.
DETE R.	Baroness von Reischach.
DONA	Empress Augusta Victoria.
DRINO	Prince Alexander of Battenberg.
DUCKY	Princess Victoria Melita of Edinburgh, Grand Duchess of Hesse.
EDDY	Duke of Clarence.

ELLA	Grand Duchess Serge.
ELLENE	Princess Helen of Greece.
ENA	Princess Victoria Eugénie of Battenberg.
ERNST (UNCLE)	Duke of Saxe-Coburg-Gotha.
ERNIE	Grand Duke Ernst of Hesse.
FEO	Princess Feodora of Saxe-Meiningen.
FISCHY	Prince Frederick Charles of Hesse.
FOZZIE	Crown Princess Sophie of Greece.
GEORGE (UNCLE)	Duke of Cambridge.
GEORGIE	Prince George of York.
GEORGIE (BIG)	Prince George of Greece.
GEORGIE (LITTLE)	Prince George, Princess Sophie's eldest son.
HELEN / LENCHEN	Princess Christian of Schleswig-Holstein.
LIKO	Prince Henry of Battenberg.
LITTLE BEE	Princess Beatrice of Edinburgh.
LORNE	Marquis of Lorne.
LOUIS (UNCLE)	Grand Duke of Hesse.
LOUISCHEN	Duchess of Connaught.
LOUISE (AUNT)	Grand Duchess of Baden.
MARIANNE (AUNT)	Princess Frederick Charles of Prussia.
MARIE (AUNT)	Duchess of Edinburgh.
MARY (AUNT)	Duchess of Teck.
MAY	Princess May of Teck, Duchess of York.
MESSI(E)	Miss Angelica Contostavlos.
MINN(E)Y, MINOLA	Princess Marie of Greece.
MISSY	Princess Marie of Edinburgh, Crown Princess of Roumania.
MOSSY	Princess Margaret of Prussia, Princess Frederick Charles of Hesse.
NICKY	Tsar Nicholas II of Russia.
NICKY (GREEK)	Prince Nicholas of Greece.
SANDRO	Prince Alexander of Battenberg.
SERGE	Grand Duke Serge Mihailovitch.
SIGIE	Prince Sigismund of Prussia (dec.).
SITTA	Princess Helen of Greece.
SOPHIEKINS / SOSSIE	Crown Princess Sophie of Greece.
SWEETIE / TINO	Crown Prince Constantine of Greece.
TODDIE	Prince Waldemar of Prussia.
TOOTSEYMAN	Prince Alexander of Greece.
VICKY	Princess Victoria of Prussia, Princess phus of Schaumburg-Lippe.
VICTORIA	Princess Victoria of Battenberg.
WALDIE	Prince Waldemar of Prussia (dec.).
WILLIAM / WILLY, WM.	Emperor William II.
YAYA	Princess Frederick Leopold.

THE EMPRESS FREDERICK

Table of *Forebears, Descendants and near Relations, as on her death in 1901.*

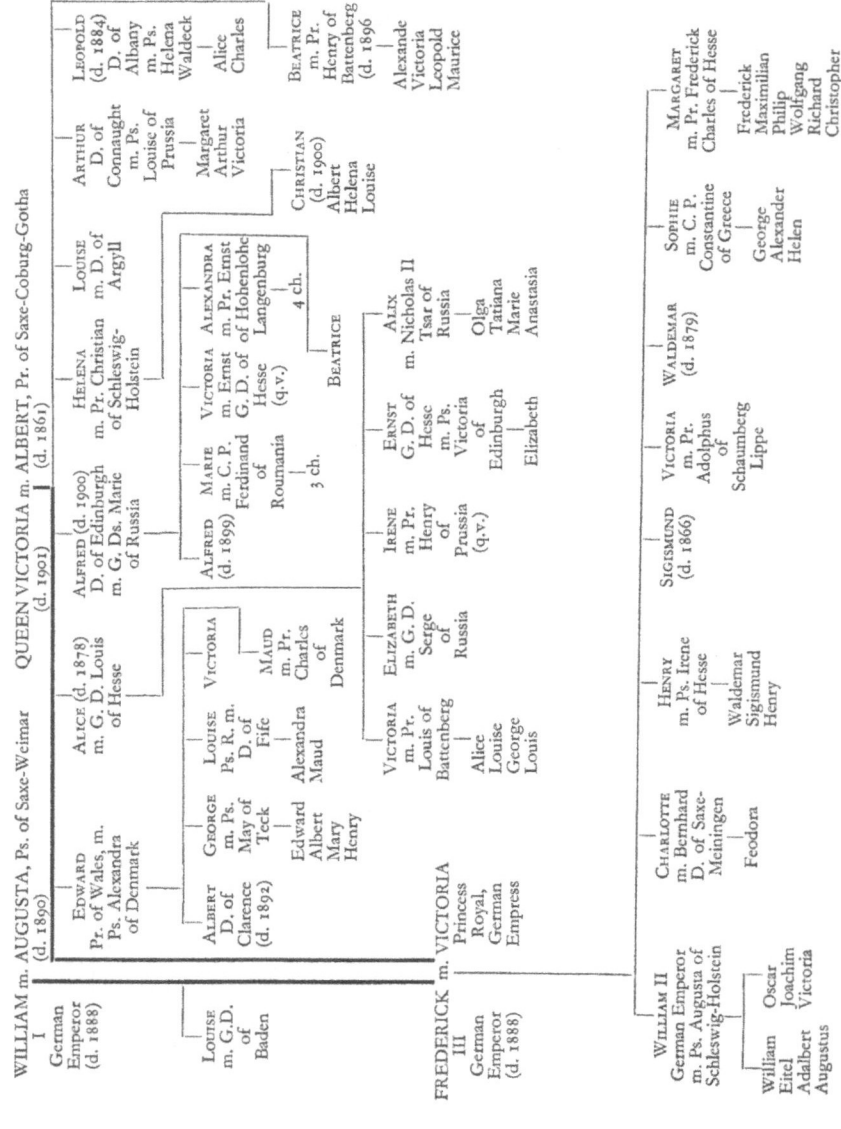

Chapter One - The Thirty-One Years Before the Letters

I - 1858-1860

When in January 1858, Victoria, Princess Royal, set out from London for Berlin with her newly wedded husband. Prince Frederick of Prussia, she shed many tears at leaving the mother she loved and the father she idolized. Queen Victoria accepted her daughter's departure with maternal resignation, but Prince Albert felt it deeply, for she was his favourite child, whom he had taught to be the reflection of his own good and earnest self.

But if the separation were sorrowful, there was only joy and satisfaction over the marriage, for it was a love match, the happy culmination of the designs of the Queen and her close friend. Crown Princess Augusta, Frederick's mother.

Tall and handsome, gentle and modest, young Fritz had won the heart of the warm-natured and intelligent Vicky when she was only a girl of fifteen, but their wedding was delayed until she reached womanhood. Two months after her seventeenth birthday she was a bride. From that day until their lives ended, no other woman existed for him, nor any other man for her.

Although overcome at leaving her parents, and the home where she had known only happiness. Princess Frederick's spirits were high, for the future was bright with promise. No young wife could ever have looked forward with greater confidence to a happy and useful existence. In the course of time, her husband would ascend the Prussian throne, in succession to his uncle King Frederick William IV, and his father. Crown Prince William, and even if her new country was of only secondary importance compared with her native Britain, she held her father's faith that it was destined one day to unite and lead the whole German people.

In Berlin, she was an instant outward success, for the general public, although far from friendly towards the English, could not resist her appealing youth and beauty. Her petite girlish figure made her seem even younger than she was, and her self-possessed though modest air, her pleasing voice with its slight English accent, and her frank and ready smile, won the popular approval. Elated by her welcome, she wrote to her father that she was happy and proud to belong to her new country.

During the weeks that followed, she was warmly acclaimed by both the civilian community and the army, and Prince Albert wrote of his pleasure that she had so quickly won such 'golden opinions'. Although inwardly shy, she tried to show with quiet composure that she intended to obey his injunction to 'dedicate the whole energies of your life to the people of your new home'. She realized that Destiny had called her to a great task and, despite her youth, she accepted the challenge in good heart, for she knew that her father's sage training had fitted her to take her place, in the fullness of the years, among her country's leaders.

But before long she discovered that her path was not to be so smooth as she expected. Among the aristocratic caste around the throne stood an influential pro-Russian element that did not welcome an alliance with the British Court. These men had never approved of Crown Princess Augusta's liberal outlook, nor of the progressive views she had instilled into her son, and a proper corrective, they thought, would have been for him to wed a member of the autocratic House of the Romanoffs. They looked coldly on the eager English princess, and especially on her democratic notions, for these were things they despised and feared.

Although at first disturbed and bewildered by this rebuff. Princess Frederick allowed it to touch neither her love for her husband nor her resolution to serve the true interests of the Prussian people. But she was a high-spirited girl, and hostility, so far from subduing her, provoked her to retaliation.

There were many things in Berlin and in Prussia that she could criticize, for she had come from the most materially and socially advanced country in Europe to one barely emerging from mediaevalism. In place of the constitutional and other freedoms of Britain, she found an autocratic monarchy that refused the people any effective voice in government, a peasantry and workpeople in a condition of near-serfdom, a society almost wholly indifferent to social welfare and advancement, and a womankind kept strictly to *Küche, Kinder und Kirche,* and permitted no standing in public or professional affairs.

To Princess Frederick, this attitude towards women was archaic and absurd, for her father's instruction had given her a learning and intellect much higher than those of many of the uncultured men around her who held the reins of power. As a woman, her education placed her decades ahead of her time. Even in enlightened Britain she would have been regarded as a bluestocking. In the Prussian Court her erudition, her reforming ideals, and her political awareness, were regarded as intolerable in a woman, and especially in a young one.

It was not only the spheres of government and welfare that were backward in outlook, for in her personal surroundings were many antiquated ways that she found irksome and unpleasant. Not the least of these was the punctilious and interminable Court ceremonial, which derived from and sustained the conception of the King ruling as the omnipotent embodiment of the State.

Princess Frederick was the less impressed by this ritual because of its contrast with the rough and often primitive standards of domestic life among even the noblest families. She took long to recover from the shock of arriving at her bridal abode in the Berlin Old Schloss to find the fustily ornate apartments lacking every modern convenience, including bathrooms and lavatories, and the domestic offices resembling stables, where the servants slept in their clothes on straw on the floors of the kitchen. The half-demented King would allow no alterations to the Schloss, and Prince Frederick could not persist in argument, for the House of Hohenzollern demanded unquestioning obedience to its head, even when he was out of his mind.

Inevitably the young princess's indignant objections to such quarters, and her distaste for the hidebound conventions of the pompous Court, awoke resentments among even those nearest to her. These feelings were deepened by her impulsive comparisons with the more civilized and cultured life of the British Court, her preference for certain British products and usages, her spells of acute homesickness, and her habit, which she was never able to lose, of referring to England as 'home'.

Such actions crystallized the fears of the ruling caste that she would always be 'the Englishwoman', a label used with a similar feeling of dislike and contempt as the word 'Boche' by the British and French in the first world war. Her disinclination to submit to the role of royal *hausfrau* and frank disapproval of Prussian social abuses, confirmed suspicions that, as Princess Augusta had attempted in the past, she intended to intervene in politics.

Her chief personal handicaps were her youthful self-assertion and her unguarded tongue. At home she had always said what she thought without anyone taking things amiss, but in Berlin her lively comments, whether spoken seriously or in fun, were viewed grimly. Distrust and opposition deepened among the unbending reactionaries of the Court, and especially in the Junkers group represented by crafty Otto von Bismark. [1] They made up their minds that 'the Englishwoman' must never be allowed to meddle in State affairs.

This was a line of attack that could be exploited to the full, for while to pillory her for her liberal views might have won her adherents, to condemn her as an Englishwoman intriguing for her native country ranged every Prussian against her. Before long, the theme was taken up by a subservient section of the Press, and inevitably it began to be accepted by the more credulous elements of the population.

At first Princess Frederick was not dismayed, for she was sure that these were all temporary difficulties which she would eventually vanquish. Unhappily she was mistaken, for the clash was fundamental and permanent. Both her own frank nature and the outcome of events were against her. Despite her faith, zeal and cleverness, she not only failed to dispel antagonism, but as the months passed, steadily strengthened it.

Her position was greatly worsened by the unfortunate consequences of the birth of her first baby in January 1859. The accouchement was so difficult that she was not expected to live, and her obituary notices were actually issued to the press. When at last she and the baby struggled clear of danger, the infant boy's arm was found to have been so seriously injured that it remained paralysed. And because, at Queen Victoria's desire, she had been attended by a British doctor, the public blamed first him and then the distressed young mother for this disability to the heir to the succession.

In all the unpleasantness that followed. Princess Frederick possessed the unfailing consolation of her husband's love and understanding. It seemed as though the more she suffered in the position to which he had brought her, the deeper became his affection, and the more stubborn his efforts to protect her. Yet even this devotion was criticized as evidence that her influence over him was so strong as to wean him from the rigid traditions of the dynasty.

Her detractors forgot that Prince Frederick had acquired his progressive outlook from his mother, and that it had not been changed even by his service in the Prussian Army, to which he was devoted, and in which he had already shown the qualities that were to make him a distinguished military leader. He was an experienced prince of twenty-seven, not a callow weakling to be easily swayed against his better judgment by an untested girl of eighteen.

The truth was that in their attitude towards great social and political ideals for the future they were as one, for just as he was determined to further his mother's enlightened aims, so she saw herself as her father's disciple for the spread of a new social conscience. Regardless of the attempted interferences of those near them, they remained united in their purpose. And despite their many set-backs, their mutual trust and affection deepened, the felicity of their married life went on undisturbed.

In July 1860, their second child, Charlotte, was born. Two months later, in company with her mother-in-law. Princess Frederick took the two infants to Coburg, where her mother and father were on a visit. Queen Victoria was enraptured to see William, her first grandchild, and so began that strange affection between the strong-willed Queen and her headstrong grandson that was to endure, with fluctuations, until she died in his arms forty years later.

As by now the Queen and her Consort were aware of their daughter's difficulties, it was strange that they did not take the opportunity of warning her against exciting Prussian antagonism by a too-openly expressed attachment to England. Queen Victoria later insisted that the Prince of Wales' bride. Princess Alexandra of Denmark, should forget her nationality when she married into the British Royal House, but it never seemed to occur to her that her daughter should accept a similar abnegation on entering the House of the Hohenzollerns. Similarly, Prince Albert, who had given his daughter much wise advice since her marriage, never sufficiently impressed on her the need to touch political and public matters in Prussia only with the greatest tact and prudence.

And so Princess Frederick, undismayed by opposition, went on working openly for the things she believed in, and showing little patience with the dour, complacent and usually reactionary opinions of those about her. She was attractive, accomplished, quick-witted, and brilliant in conversation, yet she gained but few really faithful adherents, for the reason that she tried to win people's heads rather than their hearts.

It was her great tragedy that in her mettlesome character there was something that created opposition from even those who might easily have been drawn to her side. This blemish existed largely in her inability to dissimulate or compromise. Transparently and often aggressively honest, she had no notion of how to stoop to duplicity, and was always shocked and indignant when others used it against her. When persuasive charm was needed she thought only of proving that she was right. She lacked the subtle feminine wiles that alone might have won over a crude, suspicious and touchy people.

To-day it seems incredible that a whole society of Prussian aristocrats should react so intolerantly towards a young girl simply because she was English, and a little naive about her aims to better their country. A child in politics as in life, she could hardly have been treated more seriously had she been a mature Machiavelli. Among all those around her, there was not one to see that she was only a well-meaning novice, still malleable to tactful handling, and well worthy, for the future benefit of Prussia, of being persuaded to the discretion demanded of her high station.

There were understandable reasons why no sympathetic link existed between her and the pro-Russian Queen Elizabeth, but it is strange that there was no continuing understanding with Crown Princess Augusta, who well knew from her own past efforts at reform what troubles her daughter-in-law was laying up for herself. In spite of their common interests and affections, which at first did keep them in amity, a gulf eventually developed which intriguing courtiers lost no opportunity to widen.

And so, without help and advice from those who might most readily have guided her, Princess Frederick continued on her long journey to disillusionment and bitterness.

[1] The name Bismark is spelt throughout as written by the Empress in the letters.

II - 1861-1871

When, in January 1861, the mentally-deficient King Frederick William died, and his brother, who had acted as Regent since the end of 1858, ascended the throne, the hopes of the new Crown Prince and Princess that they had moved nearer to the realization of their aims were presently checked by two momentous happenings.

The first, in the following November, was the sudden death, three weeks after Princess Frederick's twenty-first birthday, of her father, the adored source of her inspiration. 'Utterly crushed and heart-broken' by the shock, she could not even attend his funeral, for she was expecting her third child. Without him she was lost, for no one, not even her husband nor her grief-prostrated mother, could take his place. From then on there was no one to act as mentor, to guide her impetuous nature, or to mediate wisely and diplomatically on her behalf.

The second blow, which came in March of 1863, was an ominous stiffening of the autocratic rule that she and her husband had hoped to moderate. Their chagrin and disappointment at this step were all the greater because the hour might have been theirs. The new King, quarrelling with Parliament over the vital constitutional issue of whether it could refuse to vote funds required for army reforms, refused to give way, called his son, and announced his intention of abdicating. But Frederick, swayed by loyalty to his father and the dynasty, and disliking Parliament's belligerence, refused the succession under such conditions.

His motives were good but his devotion set the course of history on the downward path. For the King, alarmed at what he regarded as the beginnings of revolution, appointed as Minister of State the one man he could trust to act firmly, Count von Bismark. By this decision, Prussia and Germany were committed to autocracy, and Europe and the world to calamity. By it also was the life of Princess Frederick committed to tribulation and tragedy.

Like the Crown Prince and Princess, Bismark believed that Prussia's destiny was to bring the Germanic peoples into one great federation that would stabilize Europe. But he did not share their visions of unity achieved by peaceful democratic progress. 'It is not with Speeches or with parliamentary resolutions that the great questions of the day are decided', he had asserted in his inaugural address, 'but with blood and iron'.

The new Prime Minister's quickly demonstrated contempt for such constitutional procedure as existed provoked Prince Frederick to declare his disapproval. And when Bismark later closed both Houses of Parliament and curtailed the freedom of the Press, Frederick, after vainly protesting to his father, publicly disassociated himself from the Premier's actions. Ordered to recant, he offered to give up the succession.

The King frowned on this gesture, but the breach remained, and he blamed Princess Frederick for it, for he knew she strenuously supported her husband. And when, in the autumn, Bismark induced the King to dissolve Parliament and govern without it, and Frederick again protested, his father put him firmly aside and established Bismark as his unchallenged adviser.

These events confirmed Bismark in his dislike of the English dynastic alliance. He declaimed against 'petticoat government', especially by one who was, he declared, obviously the instrument of the Queen of England. He set out deliberately to injure the Crown Princess's position, chiefly by his control of sections of the press, which consistently presented her as a potential enemy of the State. Inspired insults by minor officials at last provoked the Crown Prince and Princess to leave Berlin for a time on a visit to Queen Victoria.

But even in London they were embroiled in Bismark's disturbing activities, this time the dispute over the duchies of Schleswig and Holstein, which were coveted by Prussia, claimed by Duke Frederick of Schleswig-Holstein, and owned by Denmark. While Queen Victoria favoured Prussian aims, and the

Crown Prince and Princess stood for the Duke, the Prince of Wales, who had married Princess Alexandra in March, strongly supported his wife's country. These opposing sympathies created deep emotional divisions in the Queen's family.

When later, in January 1864, Bismark decided, despite the Crown Prince's remonstrances, to settle the problem by war, the Prince as an army officer, had no option but to accompany the allied Prussian and Austrian invasion forces. His action deeply angered the Prince of Wales, and at first Princess Frederick sympathized with her brother's attitude, but as the war progressed, and especially when the British public and press roundly condemned Prussia's action, her feelings changed. Influenced too by her husband's presence in the field, she became vigorously pro-Prussian and wrote to her mother criticizing the unfortunate tendency of the British to interfere in what did not concern them. When Denmark submitted in June, she was jubilant.

That she had suddenly become a fervid patriot widened the breach with her brother, of whom she was sincerely fond, but did little to improve her position in Berlin, for the Bismark press still accused her of being the tool of Queen Victoria. She reacted indignantly, for she did not realize that she was being drawn, like almost everyone else in Prussia, into unwitting support of Bismark's ruthless *Realpolitik*.

The next move was inevitable, for Prussia could not hope to achieve leadership of the German states until she had established precedence over her rival and recent ally, Austria. Although the Crown Prince was against further war, he saw that Bismark was animated by the realistic desire for a swift conclusive decision, and gradually his opposition weakened. For his wife, the situation was more difficult. She wanted Prussian ascendancy, but she dreaded a conflict in which several of her relations, including her sister Alice, married to the Grand Duke Louis of Hesse, and her cousin, the King of Hanover, as well as her uncle, the Duke of Saxe-Coburg, would be ranged on the side of Austria. In her alarm, she asked Queen Victoria to intervene, but events moved too quickly.

Then as the two countries moved towards war in the spring of 1866, she became involved in affairs of life and death within her family. Her fifth child, Victoria, born in April, was christened in May, on the day before the Crown Prince left to take command of his troops. Hostilities opened in June, and as the fighting developed, the Crown Princess became daily more anxious over her husband's dangers. Suddenly her worries were engulfed in her grief at the death of her 21-months-old son, Sigismund. Heartbroken, she was at first too stunned to respond to the news of her husband's great victory at Sadowa, the critical battle of the war.

The seven weeks' campaign, ending with complete Austrian defeat, saw the Crown Prince enshrined as the idol of the army and the hero of the nation. Princess Frederick's sadness at the loss of her child fused with exaltation over her husband's success. Soon she wrote to her mother, 'I am now every bit as proud of being a Prussian as I am of being an Englishwoman'. She devoted herself to organizing nursing for military hospitals, and after the campaign ended, formed the National Institution for Disabled Soldiers. So changed was her outlook, that for a time, she showed but lukewarm sympathy over the fate of those relatives who had chosen the wrong side.

The four years that followed were among the most rewarding she was ever to enjoy. Her enemy, Bismark, occupied with his preparations for the next stage of his stupendous scheme, relaxed his antagonism. Her husband, now reconciled to his father, encouraged her to busy herself not with politics but with philanthropy, social welfare and the arts. She opened the Victoria House school for nursing sisters, which won European fame for its work, founded various educational and other institutions for women, and indulged in those artistic and literary tastes which, almost completely lacking in Queen Victoria, were so strongly marked in her. Girlhood aptitudes for sketching and painting were revived, and under the guidance of well-known artists, working in her own studio in her Berlin palace in Unter den Linden, she reached more than amateur competence in both painting and sculpture. Another artistic interest, which she cultivated over many years, was the discriminating collection of antiques, furniture and *objets d'art*, by which her home became one of the most distinguished in Berlin.

But these activities were only supplementary to the ever-growing cares of bringing up her family of four. In 1868, the loss of Sigismund was assuaged by the birth of a sixth child, a son, Waldemar. It was but natural that the two babies should absorb her more closely than the others, and she deeply resented the accusations of mischief-making gossips of Queen Augusta's retinue, that she was neglecting the three eldest children for hypocritical social welfare work. In fact, in these early days, the relations between them were as close as in any normal family. The only source of concern was William's useless arm, for which she persistently but vainly sought a remedy in both Germany and England. He could take little active part in sports and exercise, and she saw with compassion that he grew increasingly sensitive over his disability. But she did not want to foster self-pity, and taking the course of acting as though no disability existed, treated him in the same way as his brother, Henry.

What had become the comparatively even flow of her domestic life was then disturbed by the shadow of another war, this time with supposedly puissant Imperial France. In 1870, Bismark's plans came to a head with his doctored Ems telegram, which provoked France to take the role of aggressor and declare war. As Bismark anticipated, all the German states united under this menace. Like almost the whole population, Princess Frederick feared that her apparently unprepared country would be overrun by the army that still basked in the glory of the Napoleonic conquests, and once more she appealed to her mother to persuade England to intervene. But again she was too late, for Bismark had made certain, the machinery of war was set irrevocably in motion.

The strain of this period followed close on the birth of Princess Frederick's seventh child, on June 14th. A week after the opening of the war, in July, the Crown Prince returned from his command at the front to his home, where amid traditional pomp and ceremony, the infant was christened Sophie Dorothea Ulrica Alice. Early next morning, before his wife awoke, Frederick stole quietly away on the journey back to his troops.

As the campaign developed, the Crown Princess found herself far more worried over her husband's risks than ever she had been during the Austrian war, for against the French, prolonged fighting seemed certain. But her apprehensions were quickly dispelled as one German victory followed another, among them the Battle of Worth, where her husband's forces defeated McMahon's Army of the Rhine. Princess Frederick expanded with pride, and when, in September, the French failures culminated in the crowning disaster of Sedan, her elation was unrestrained. Yet, despite her outbursts of patriotism, which overflowed her letters to her mother, she was still suspect to the Prussian Court and Berlin press, which, because she had spoken of pity for the vanquished, alleged that she shared the Prince of Wales's known sympathy for the French.

Even her efforts to help the war-wounded were rebuffed, for her candid criticism of unsanitary conditions in field hospitals offended the high-ranking officers responsible, and she was told by the King not to interfere. But she persisted in her work, which eventually won her at least the respect of the hospital staffs and the affection of the wounded. The press and other attacks on her intensified when, during the delays and hesitations over shelling Paris, she was accused of exerting a pro-French influence over her husband, who had advised against a bombardment on military as much as humanitarian grounds. But she ignored these insinuations in her excitement over the dramatic events that followed the French collapse.

For the dream of German unity was realized. On 18th January 1871, King William assumed the leadership of an Imperial German Empire of twenty-six states, and was proclaimed Emperor. Bismark was appointed the Imperial Chancellor, and invested in the rank of Prince. Ten days later Paris capitulated, and the war ended with France as a shattered, humiliated republic, and Prussia and the Germanic states as a mighty Empire, the second Reich, garlanded with the new provinces of Alsace and Lorraine.

Princess Frederick watched this stupendous climax with joy and hope. Germany was united, the future offered the promise of fulfilment. The Emperor had already passed his allotted span, and himself declared he could not last much longer. Before many years had passed she would stand by her husband's side as Empress of a State whose power and influence might rival even that of England. When that day came, she could forget the hurts of the past and devote her energies to those great altruistic purposes that never ceased to consume her.

III - 1871-1887

It was fortunate Princess Frederick could not know that in the years immediately following the end of the war with France, she was to reach the zenith of her life's contentment. Certainly, from the beginning, her course had seldom run smoothly for long, but it had always led upwards, with her national position slowly consolidating and her family life happily expanding with the years. But soon she was to start on the downward slope, when blow after blow was to strike against both her regal eminence and her dearest affections, until, dazed and bewildered at the harshness of Fate, she was to stumble into the subdued twilight of her life.

There was little to indicate this sombre destiny as her country settled down to the enjoyment of its new greatness. As the months passed, her standing with the mass of the German people improved. Her war service to the wounded and disabled was recognized, and the benefits of her welfare work admitted. She was the hope of all those who longed yet to see Germany surrender to the democratic impulses that swept spasmodically through Europe.

She was happy, too, when, in July 1871, a visit to London brought reconciliation with her well-loved brother and his wife, who in return, came to Berlin later in the year for William's confirmation.

With these bettered conditions went her ample domestic felicity. She could indeed count many blessings. Her husband had passed safely through three wars to earn from the people the reverential title, Frederick the Noble. The love and trust between them had strengthened over the years. Their union had been well blessed with children, for although one boy had been lost to them, another daughter, Margaret, was born in April 1872.

With three boys and four girls, the time had arrived, it seemed, when long devotion to the older children would be rewarded by the deepening affections of their adolescence. But although she little knew it, the sands were already shifting under her feet. Oblivious as always to the underhand things, she did not see the rift opening between her and her three eldest children.

It had begun through the indulgence shown to William by the Empress Augusta because of his deformity. By contrast, his mother's way of appearing to ignore his handicap seemed to him wanting in tenderness. His boyish confidence once won, he had become susceptible to mischief-makers of the Empress's salon, who suggested firstly that his mother had little fondness for him because of his paralysed arm, even though she was responsible for it by insisting on an incompetent English doctor, and secondly that she had herself declared she could never love her three elder children because, in obedience to rigid Court tradition, she had not been allowed herself to nurse them.

Although wounded by these pernicious suggestions, the three children did not disclose their resentments to their mother. But William inwardly developed a complex identifying her with his defect, while nourishing the resolution that, in spite of it, he would one day lead Germany to great glory. These notions were encouraged by his tutor, whom the Crown Princess trusted implicitly, but who was secretly in sympathy with Bismark's political conceptions.

Until William reached the age of twelve, his mother retained some degree of control over his upbringing, but then, like her second son, Henry, later, he was taken from the home influence to the normal 'gymnasium' training. There he was, unknown to her but with the tutor's willing aid, indoctrinated with Bismarkian ideas, which led him to a contempt of his father's liberalism and an ever-increasing dislike of his mother's love and admiration for English institutions.

This deliberate weaning away of her son's loyalties and affections was in keeping with the atmosphere of mutual distrust and antagonism which lay upon the inner circles of the Court and the select few who ruled the country. It was indeed astonishing that so many of the leaders of the new State, who could have helped each other so much, were instead almost continually at loggerheads. The trouble started at the top, for the Emperor and Empress, whose marriage had never rested on love, were now little more than outwardly polite to each other. The Emperor blew hot and cold over his son, and was still suspicious of his daughter-in-law's supposed political intriguing. The Empress was seldom kind for long to Princess Frederick, and she detested Bismark. He in turn was hostile to them both, attacked them in his press, and provided sly mischief to prevent their combining against him. Behind them all was William, quietly developing the megalomania that was eventually to drive him against every one of them in turn, save the Emperor.

All these years, the Crown Princess had never been able to understand the animosities her candour brought her. She tried to adjust herself to them, but her fiery reactions to calumny made it difficult for quarrels to be resolved. Yet she was incapable of hating anybody for long, and was even able to say many good things of Bismark. And eventually her enemies, assuming that the old Emperor would not live much longer, began to restrain themselves at the prospect of her becoming Empress.

In June 1878, it seemed at last as if her day had come, for the Emperor was wounded in an attempt on his life, and at the age of 81, was not expected to recover. For a time the Crown Prince and Princess were treated with deference by Court and government sycophants, but these, when the aged invalid started to recover, soon edged carefully away. The Emperor resumed the throne in December, amid the cheers of the Berlin populace, and the Crown Prince and Princess returned to their normal secondary sphere.

It was during this period that Princess Frederick suffered two family afflictions that nearly broke her spirit. In December 1878, her sister, Alice, died tragically of diphtheria, contracted by kissing her sick son. A few months later the Crown Princess's fourth son, Waldemar, died suddenly, also from diphtheria. His loss overwhelmed her with grief for a long time, and the memory of his boyish image remained vividly with her for the rest of her life.

Other kinds of change in her family were taking place with the passing years. In 1878, Charlotte had become the bride of Prince Bernhard of Saxe-Meiningen, to whom, a little over a year later, she bore a baby girl, Feodora, the Crown Princess thus becoming a grandmother at the age of 39. Then William announced his intention of marrying Princess Augusta, daughter of the Duke of Schleswig-Holstein, once the central figure of the Danish quarrel. The Crown Princess liked her future daughter-in-law, and recommended her to Queen Victoria, who in turn approved of William's choice. The wedding took place in February 1881, and Dona, as the bride was henceforth known in the family, gained general regard by her good looks and modest demeanour.

With the two eldest children married, and Henry away under military training, the Crown Princess turned all her maternal affections on the others, Victoria, Sophie and Margaret, known in the family as Vicky, Fozzie and Mossy. All three were to give to their mother a love and devotion that did much to balance the later coolness of the others.

But her abounding energy needed a wider outlet than these remaining family responsibilities. Her first interests were still in the social and political scene, and she continued to work persistently and quietly for the spread of liberal and progressive ideas. But, like her husband, she had come to realize the futility of trying to challenge Bismark while the Emperor was still alive. She avoided contact with political figures, and turned more and more towards men and women of art, science and culture, and to that not over-large element of society which strove to improve the lot of the manual workers and the sick and needy.

She gave herself unceasingly to charitable enterprises of every kind, but especially those concerned with hospital work and nursing, and the care and training of women, young girls and children. She created and inspired organizations for improving the position of women, especially those which supplied higher education for the professions and commerce. She tried to help improve living and working conditions for industrial labour. And her artistic bent moved her to encourage the application of arts and crafts to industrial purposes.

Her devotion to all these worthy causes was not spasmodic, or concentrated within a few short years, but maintained, often against apathy or resistance, over three decades. In all her efforts, she had her husband's unfailing encouragement and practical help. And when in January 1883, on the occasion of their silver wedding, the German people presented them with monetary gifts totalling £42,000, the whole sum was devoted to furthering her good works.

This anniversary reminded the nation that in spite of their frequent doubts of 'the Englishwoman', she had given faithful service to Prussia and to Germany. The ordinary people saw that here was a perfect marriage, based on a tender enduring love and understanding, and for a time public opinion softened at the contemplation of this unswerving mutual devotion over the stirring times of the past quarter century.

Occupied by her social and artistic undertakings as well as by her family's upbringing, Princess Frederick now usually contrived to keep clear of open dissension with Bismark, who after long years of unchallenged power, had become the complete despot, inflamed by any opposition. Although his ruthless methods still excited her private indignation, she expressed it in writing only to her mother. Such measures as his repression of the Catholic priesthood, his upholding of the mediaeval privileges of the landed aristocracy, his opposition to every democratic urge, and his harshness towards unrest among the workers, all inspired her anger, but left her impotent, for they were backed by the Emperor.

Similarly his complicated juggling of alliances to maintain an external political equilibrium dismayed her. His fundamental principle of antagonism to France and Britain, and good-neighbour relations with Russia, was repugnant to her, both because she was English and because she detested the Russian political system.

During the winter of 1873-4, when she and her husband had visited St. Petersburg for the marriage of her brother, the Duke of Edinburgh, to the Grand Duchess Marie, only daughter of Tsar Alexander III, the contrast between the fantastic riches of the Imperial Court and the wretched poverty of the common people had deeply shocked her. She concluded that Russian foreign policy derived entirely from the personal ambitions of an unfettered ruler and a callous and selfish oligarchy. 'The Russians cannot be trusted', she wrote to Queen Victoria, 'keep an ever-watchful eye...'

But her doubts of Bismark turned to approval when, while still adroitly retaining Russian goodwill, he formed and strengthened the Triple Alliance of Germany, Austria and Italy, which was aimed entirely against France and Russia. And after the Russo-Turkish war, she recognized his skill when as 'honest broker' at the Congress of Berlin in 1878, he shared in the creation of the new Balkan state of Bulgaria, and in the nomination to its throne of Prince Alexander of Battenberg.

Yet it was through Alexander that there began one of her most serious quarrels with the Chancellor. For her daughter Victoria and the dashing young Prince fell in love. An early marriage was agreed upon by the delighted Crown Princess and her husband, with the full approval of Queen Victoria, whose youngest daughter Beatrice was married to Alexander's brother, Henry. But unfortunately, because Alexander spiritedly resisted Russian control of Bulgaria, the Tsar took a violent dislike to him. Bismark, whose relations with Russia were far too delicate to risk friction over what he regarded as an immature love affair, flatly refused to countenance the match. The Crown Prince and Princess protested indignantly against his veto, but in vain, for he was upheld by the Emperor.

When later, Prince Alexander, still boldly pressing Bulgarian nationalist aims, was kidnapped by Russian officers in the streets of Sofia, taken to Russia and forced to abdicate at the point of a pistol, Princess Frederick hoped the road to her daughter's happiness might now be clear. But Bismark, balancing precariously on his political tightrope, was determined not to run the slightest risk of offending the Tsar. He induced the Emperor to forbid the marriage, and in his action was supported, to Princess Frederick's distress and anger, by her son William.

Ever since his own marriage, William had shown more and more openly his antipathy for his mother and his lack of filial respect for his father. His attitude was shared by his wife, and to a lesser degree by his brother Henry, and his sister Charlotte and her husband. In the sharp quarrel which followed his opposition to the wedding, he told his mother brazenly that he was on the side of Bismark and her enemies of the Junkers clique.

Soon she was to realize that these men not only regarded her son as a better potential upholder of the Bismarkian principles than his father, but that they had brought the Emperor to the same way of thinking. Their flattery had fired William with vainglorious illusions, and a readiness to take his father's place in the Emperor's councils. Without reference to Prince Frederick he was sent to represent Germany at notable international conferences and celebrations.

The Crown Prince was disturbed at these assaults on his position as heir-apparent, but because the Emperor had authorized them, he could do no more than make his protest. He did not want another grave breach now that his father was so old, and he could bide his time, for when the Emperor's long life ended, it would be he who would succeed, and not William. But he realized that he could not afford, when he came to the Imperial throne, to lose the help of the man who had done so much for Germany. He let Bismark know his attitude, and for a time the disharmony between the two men seemed to lessen.

But all their wise personal adjustments for the future were soon to be put aside by the beginnings of the illness that within eighteen months was to bring not only a terrible death to the Crown Prince, and pitiable tragedy to his anguished wife, but to Germany a ruler whose path was already set for calamity.

IV - 1887-1888

In January 1887, Crown Prince Frederick developed hoarseness, with a slight swelling of the larynx, at first thought to be of no consequence. A month later the eminent doctors in attendance diagnosed a malignant growth, which they proposed to remove surgically, in an extremely dangerous operation. But Bismark intervened, and with the Emperor's approval, insisted on consultation with the best throat specialist to be found.

The doctors suggested among others, an Englishman, Dr. Morell Mackenzie, of whose name and existence Princess Frederick was until this moment in ignorance.

Mackenzie sent a fragment of the larynx for pathological examination by the eminent Dr. Virchow, and the result was negative. The German doctors still advocated the removal of the swelling, but until malignancy could be proved Mackenzie was against a very risky operation, which at best would leave the patient dumb. He was supported by the Crown Prince and Princess, who naturally turned to whoever offered hope.

This situation provoked the professional resentment of some of the German medicos, whose anger and doubts were conveyed to an already restive public. At once the usual storm of accusations burst out that 'the Englishwoman' had insisted on an incapable English doctor, and that she did not want an operation because if the Crown Prince became incapacitated by dumbness he could not, by the laws of the Hohenzollern dynasty, succeed to the throne. In fact there was no such, law, but the lie had a lead, and like many other lies told against her, was never overtaken.

Confirmed in his views by a second negative analysis by Virchow, Mackenzie pronounced hope for a cure in two months. Under his treatment. Prince Frederick improved sufficiently for the Emperor to permit him, with his family, to attend the celebration of Queen Victoria's Jubilee. On June 21st, Princess Frederick, driving with her mother and the Princess of Wales in the historic procession to and from Westminster Abbey, watched with pride and thankfulness her stalwart husband, in eagle-crested cuirassier uniform, riding among the escort of princes, outstanding even in that glittering cavalcade. Neither she, nor any of the thousands who acclaimed this splendid figure, could believe that death rode with him.

Many regal personages had come to London for the Jubilee. Among them was Constantine, Duke of Sparta, the tall handsome eldest son of King George (brother of the Princess of Wales) and Queen Olga of the Hellenes. Princess Sophie, attractive, lively, outspoken, met him at Marlborough House, and the two formed an immediate attachment, which soon led to their engagement.

Crown Prince Frederick, with his wife and three youngest daughters, stayed on in England for Mackenzie's treatment. There was pressure from Germany for them to return, for the old Emperor was growing feeble, but instead, seeking quietude and a kinder climate to maintain the improved condition, they went in September to the Tyrol. From here, still pursuing mildness and warmth, they moved to San Remo, where they settled in the pleasantly situated Villa Zirio. But soon the progress that had seemed so reassuring was arrested, and Mackenzie had at last to admit that the swelling was malignant.

The Crown Prince took his death sentence with unflinching calm, and rejected the dangerous operation for the removal of the larynx which, in the opinion of the German doctors, offered the only chance of prolonging his life.

The news that his condition was hopeless greatly angered the Berlin public and press which, forgetting that the stricken son might die before his father, now accused the Crown Princess of opposing the operation because she wanted her husband to live only long enough to ascend the throne and make her Empress. Such evil accusations should have been dispersed before the evidence of her suffering. To know that her husband must soon die was anguish enough, but she also had to bear William's and Henry's bitter accusations that their father's life 'is lost through the English doctors and me', as she wrote Queen Victoria.

Against this background, she did her best to keep up before her husband an unflagging hopefulness. She sat with him through every day, placing ice-bags against his throat, nursing him continuously, and trying never to expose the fears that devoured her. Even this, that she gave him encouragement, was held against her as evidence of an unfeeling heart.

The Crown Princess, 1884 - From the portrait by Heinrich von Angeli.

On his side. Prince Frederick wanted to believe that he would recover, but often he would reveal his bitter sadness that he must die with his life task not even begun, and his wife left at the mercy of their enemies. He saw the dangers that would threaten Germany if his headstrong son took the reins too soon. He knew that during his absence from Berlin, William had drawn close not only to Bismark but to Bismark's son, Herbert, and to others preparing for a grandiose Teutonic future. Already in November, the Emperor had delegated part of his authority to his grandson, a measure that wounded the Crown Prince immeasurably, for he was not even consulted.

As the weeks passed and his condition fluctuated, so his wife swung between hope and despair. Her torment was made the worse by unceasing press attacks as well as by her loneliness, for except for her three youngest daughters and a handful of friends and visitors, the world seemed to reject her. Only to her mother could she pour out her feelings, and from the Queen's sympathetic letters she renewed her courage.

Christmas came, and the New Year that held only dread. Within a few days. Prince Frederick's condition grew more acute, and in order to prevent suffocation, the throat had to be cut open and a canula inserted. From then on, a doctor was in attendance day and night.

Even in this desperate condition. Princess Frederick did not entirely give up hope, and she and her husband clung to the dream of a future, in the faith that between them they could keep death at a distance for many years to come. Alone in this nightmare they passed the first months of 1888.

In Berlin, the Emperor's strength at last began to ebb, and William, expressing no sympathy for either his father or his mother, was already receiving the adulation of the Court. To an appalled world he seemed to be callously awaiting the result of the race for death between his father and grandfather.

The Emperor died on March 9th. When the news came to the Villa Zirio, the three daughters, and the aides, ladies-in-waiting and doctors assem-

The Emperor Frederick III.

bled in the drawing-room to greet the new Emperor and Empress. The two entered, the Empress vainly trying to hold back her tears, the Emperor wearing uniform and orders, his tall, bearded figure firmly erect. He could not now utter a word, and after acknowledging the obeisance, moved to a table and wrote out the proclamation of his accession, which was read out for him. Then he turned towards his wife, removed his Order of the Black Eagle and invested her with it. Turning to Mackenzie, he wrote on the pad, 'I thank you for making me live long enough to reward the valiant courage of my wife.'

So pitiful a scene deeply moved those who were there. This Emperor and Empress whose accession should have taken place in the capital of their Empire, amid the pomp and ceremonial of a nation, stood under a modest roof on foreign soil, saluted only by a handful of people of the household. For long years the two had prepared for this first day of a reign that would bring new freedoms to Germany, but instead there could be only a brief impotent span, shadowed always by the curtain of death.

Despite his wife's pleas that he should wait until the winter ended, the Emperor decided to travel, whatever the risk, from the mild Riviera to the frozen Brandenburg plain, and there take on his hopeless task. The next day they were on their way to Berlin, where they arrived at eleven o'clock at night, in a heavy snowstorm.

The old Castle at Charlottenburg was chosen as a residence because of its quietness, but the abrupt change of climate and the stresses of active life — for the Emperor insisted on assuming his full responsibilities of consultation with his Ministers — bore heavily on his dwindling reserves of strength. Nominating Bismark as Chancellor, he proclaimed his aspirations for future enlightened government in a noble statement which evoked only amusement from those who knew it would never be put into effect.

To the Emperor's sorrow, the doctors would not let him leave the Palace to attend his father's funeral. There had been many differences between them, but now he saw that the dead patriarch of the nation had won, for he had made the mass of

The Empress in 1889.

the people believe that his dynasty's autocratic rule was right and inevitable. The dying Frederick and his wife well knew that all their ambitions for a Germany moulded to democracy had now no hope of fruition. Those around the throne looked upon them, in the Empress's words to Queen Victoria, as 'a mere passing shadow, soon to be replaced by reality in the shape of William'.

At first Bismark, who thought that the Emperor would last out another year, was comparatively mild towards the Empress, but his attitude changed when, in the desire to secure their daughter's happiness, she and the Emperor reopened the project of marriage to Prince Alexander. Again supported by William, Bismark strongly resisted the proposal. And when he heard that Queen Victoria, then staying in Florence, intended to visit Berlin to see her dying son-in-law and, as he thought, insist on the marriage, he threatened to resign. He did not know that the Queen had telegraphed her daughter that the marriage should not take place without William's consent.

The Queen arrived in Berlin in April, where in a distressful meeting she persuaded her daughter to relinquish her plan, or as the Empress saw it, to sacrifice Victoria's contentment to political expediency. But her submission brought little relief, for although the Queen received Bismark, and won his promise to treat her daughter kindly, she had barely returned to England when he resumed his customary hostility.

The Emperor tried to continue with his duties, but his ministers' obstructiveness wore him down quickly. With grief and bitterness, the Empress saw them all waiting impatiently for her husband to die.

Through all these dark days, the only moment of relief came in May with Prince Henry's marriage to his cousin. Princess Irene of Hesse. The Emperor, though very weak, insisted on joining the religious service, but the sense of tragedy that overhung the congregation gave the ceremony a sombre hue.

Early in June, the Emperor moved by steamer along the Havel to the Potsdam Neue Palais, which he renamed Friedrichskron. He wanted to die in the house which was his birthplace, and which held so many tender memories of his married life. Here in the home they had shared so long, the Empress tried to keep up an appearance of good spirits, but when in the privacy of her room, she gave way to her grief. He was unsuspecting, and she told later how 'he used to ask with the greatest surprise, "Why are your eyes so red?"'.

An occasion on which she needed all her self-control was when Princess Sophie, on her birthday, visited her father in the sickroom. He gave her a nosegay, and his kind blue eyes bestowed his silent blessing. It was the day before he died.

When he realized his last moments were near, he sent for Bismark. As his wife and the Chancellor stood by his bedside he placed their hands together and gazed at them in a speechless appeal for reconciliation. In only a matter of hours the uncompassionate Bismark showed how little this episode affected him.

Next morning, the fifteenth of June, as the end approached, a cordon of hussars surrounded Friedrichskron. As soon as the Emperor had drawn his last breath, even as the Empress knelt sobbing by his bedside, guards were placed on every door, and orders given in the name of the new Emperor that no one, not even his mother, might leave. The building was then searched thoroughly for documents, diaries, letters and other records which William knew had been written by his father and mother over the years. But he was too late, for the ones he wanted had been taken to Windsor at the time of the Jubilee visit. Everything else was seized and taken away.

Despite the Empress's certainty of her husband's wishes, the funeral procession and service in the Potsdam Friedenskirche were held without public ceremony. Overcome by her son's inhumanity at the moment of his father's death, and by the knowledge that the service would be attended by those who had caused both her husband and her such intense suffering, she could not bring herself to go, but drove instead with her three daughters to a simultaneous service in a modest church at Bornstedt, near Potsdam, where she and her husband had long owned a country house. But when the congregation had gone from the Friedenskirche, she came to watch the coffin being placed in a temporary tomb, where it would lie until a mausoleum was built.

The days and weeks that followed were among the most wretched the Empress had ever endured. She was consumed with her grief, and dazed by persecutions crueller than she had ever known before, the doubly hard to bear because her husband was no longer there to share and lighten them. Her wounds were all the deeper because most of them came from the eldest son who should have protected and sustained her. Instead, he showed utter indifference to her feelings. He had not only ordered a post-mortem examination of his father's body, but had publicly honoured the doctors whose published statements indicted Mackenzie, and by implication also her. He even cancelled the name Friedrichskron when he took over the Neue Palais as his residence. He transferred his mother to the Villa Leignitz, the smallest of the Potsdam Royal residences. He ignored his father's recent proclamation, and announced his intention of following the autocratic policies of his grandfather.

His example was followed by those near him. Bismark and his son spoke contemptuously of the dead Emperor as 'an incubus' and 'an ineffectual visionary', epithets that fired the Empress to fierce indignation. When she asked Bismark to visit her, in order that she might seek his help, he sent the reply that he was too busy with the new Emperor. He and his newspapers spared her no humiliation, and forgetting his original intervention at the start of her husband's illness, he acquiesced in the lie that it was she who had first asked for an English doctor.

In September, a fresh storm of trouble broke out on the publication by a Professor Geffken of extracts from the late Emperor's 1871 war diary, which showed Bismark to have assumed credit for the conception of the German Empire that should have gone to the Crown Prince. Geffken had taken his information from the diaries fifteen years previously, but now the Empress was accused of improperly showing him State Papers, whose publication her son pronounced to be high treason. Soon the Bismark press declared that during the war, both the Empress and her husband had been guilty of treachery by passing military information to the French, through the Prince of Wales.

The Empress's trials were not over, for the following month she was involved in the bitter fight that broke out when Morell Mackenzie, provoked by the recent attacks on his professional conduct, published his account of the Emperor Frederick's illness. The recriminations of the German doctors provided more openings for the Empress's enemies to place on her the responsibility for her husband's death.

During the three months' period of Court mourning, the new Emperor plunged into a succession of ceremonies and tours, among them visits to the Courts of St. Petersburg, Stockholm, Copenhagen, Rome and Vienna. He ignored the Empress Frederick's protests at these levities, and when Queen Victoria asked him to show more respect for his father's memory, and to behave more considerately towards his mother, he answered pertly that 'it is far better we Emperors keep firm together', and as for his mother, he could not agree that she had anything to complain of.

Very angry at his attitude. Queen Victoria invited the Empress to stay with her in England. Determined to show her grandson and the world that in Britain his mother was officially regarded as equal in importance to herself, she met her at Tilbury with a Guard of Honour, and accompanied her back to Windsor.

But indignant as she was with William, the Queen realized that there must be no further deepening of the rift between mother and son, and during the visit she tried to soften her daughter's anguish and resentment. For a time after the return to Germany in February, relations improved, but new causes of friction soon arose. William's offences were now due less to intention than to thoughtlessness, and indeed he made occasional filial gestures, especially in public, but the Empress's wounds were too deep to be healed so easily, and the pain was the more quick because it had come from one she still loved, in spite of everything.

For a time, life seemed to hold only emptiness. All those years during which she and her husband had fought for what they considered right had vanished like smoke. 'We tried hard to...prepare for the time in which we should be called to work for the nation. We had treasured up much experience! Bitterly, hardly bought! That is now all wasted.'

Gradually she realized the hopelessness of her position. She heard that Bismark had said 'it did not matter how they treated me, it would make no difference in the relations between Germany and England'. She was cut off from most of her friends, because if they spoke up for her they met trouble from the ruling clique. She saw that the forces against her were too strong, and wearily she submitted to the inevitable.

Eventually despair merged into an unwilling resignation, broken by flashes of contention, for much of the old fire was still there. She knew she had to fight on for the sake of her three youngest daughters, whose love and sympathy during this black period had helped so much to give her the strength to endure. And now she turned gratefully to the two things that provided distraction, the project of making a home of her own, and the engagement between Sophie and Crown Prince Constantine.

She believed that Bismark had deliberately set out to make her life so intolerable that she would be forced to live out of Germany, but after her first prostration had passed she refused to entertain the idea. She was a German, her children were German, and their home should be in Germany. But she could no longer endure to live entirely in her Unter den Linden palace in Berlin, and after a wide search saw an estate near Cronberg which she liked immediately. The house needed major reconstruction, and a year or more must pass before she could occupy it, but she bought the property and put the work in motion, then directed her attention to the forthcoming marriage.

She took Sophie to Copenhagen to introduce her to the King and Queen of Denmark, parents of King George of Greece and of Princess Alexandra of

Wales. Staying at the Castle of Friedensburg were 'Tino', as the 21-year-old Prince Constantine was familiarly known, and some of his brothers. The Empress wrote to Queen Victoria about the strong physique of the young Greek princes, and of their cheerful friendly spirit. She learnt something of the conditions of the Court to which her daughter would go, of its simplicity and its happiness, and also of its difficulties in a poor and primitive country, and among a people only sixty years free from Ottoman subjection, unstable but fiercely proud and independent.

In October 1899, she went to Athens for the wedding and was there received with the greatest kindness by King George and Queen Olga. A glittering array of relations of the bridal pair included, in addition to the Empress and her family, headed by the Emperor William and the new Empress, the King and Queen of Denmark, the Tsarevich of Russia, and the Prince and Princess of Wales with their two sons. Princes Albert and George.

The wedding ceremony took place on October 27th in the long and elaborate ritual of the Greek Orthodox Church, then after a brief Protestant service, a family luncheon followed, and in the evening a grand gala dinner. To the Empress, these and the subsequent celebrations, together with the consideration of her hosts, coming after the persecutions of the past years, were a reminder of almost forgotten serenities. Released from the restraints inseparable from her position in Germany, she took the opportunity to travel without ostentation, receiving everywhere a friendly welcome. The visit, her first to Greece, inspired an affection for the country and an interest in its affairs which, deepened by her daughter's responsibilities as Crown Princess, was to fill much of the emptiness of the coming years.

After four inspiring weeks in Athens, the Empress and her daughters. Princesses Victoria and Margaret, started on the return journey in a vessel lent for the trip by Queen Victoria. Never previously separated for long from Sophie, the Empress's opening letters are charged lengthily with the emotions of losing her. The first, dated November 23rd, is written 'on board H.M.S. *Surprise,* lying off Patras'.

Chapter Two – The Letters 1889-90

'My own darling Sophie,

I hardly know *what* to write, I am so miserable. Can it be that I have parted from my own dear little Fozzie, and that the terrible moment I have been dreading for so long has come and gone? Our tears fell fast as rain when you left us, my poor Mossy, and Vicky too, quite wretched. If beloved Papa were here, I should have to console him, I am sure, but he would also comfort me with his love and kindness.

Darling Sophie, we do not grudge you your happiness, your darling husband, your new home and country, and your bright future (please God). We must not complain. Heaven has smiled upon you, and given you dear Tino, whom I love with all my heart, and placed you amongst kind people and in so charming a family, so amiable and united, with a sweet mother-in-law, and a father-in-law who is sure to be a great aid and protection to you. God bless you my Sophie, my loving tender thoughts will be with you... are the photographs of your dear little person in your wedding dress done, and in your Greek costume? ...Once more. Goodbye (oh, that horrid word), *Auf Wiedersehen.*'

In her first replies, Princess Sophie does not find it easy to express how she feels over the parting.

'I also miss you dreadfully, it seems too odd not to have you anywhere, and I cannot believe that I am really writing to you darling Mama. I have not written you since years. I am sure my idiotic letters will bore you very much, for I cannot write properly.

It was too disgustingly awful, that saying goodbye the other day, and I never thanked you half enough for all your trouble and care for me. I am so touched by all you have done, and hope you know how grateful I am and always will be. I cannot tell you how intensely happy I am here with my Tino, and how I enjoy this dear little house, the lovely English furniture....'

In this, as in all her earlier letters, she signs herself, 'Your loving and obedient little child, Sophie'. The *Surprise* calls at Corfu, Palermo, Capri, and other notable places, but though absorbed in these new sights and encounters the Empress's mind is on the nineteen-year-old daughter left behind in a strange half-civilized land. For Greece, after centuries as a neglected province of the Ottoman Empire, was still immature politically, and undeveloped in social and cultural life. The Empress had found Athens charming and interesting, but lacking in modern amenities, and populated by a necessitous and backward people. Such enlightened society as existed revolved almost entirely around the Court, small and unpretentious as it was.

King George and Queen Olga were warm-hearted parents-in-law, and their elder children were lively and congenial companions. The Empress knew that Sophie would be at home with them all, but she also knew that her daughter, despite her background of the ceremonious German Imperial Court, or perhaps because of it, was inexperienced and shy. Her first need was for good friends outside the Royal Family. On December 2nd, the Empress writes from the *Surprise,* lying off Palermo.

'Have you seen dear Madame T. again? I hope you will make friends with her. She is both so excellent and intelligent. Next to her, no lady pleased and attracted me so much as Madame S. I am sure she too would be a charming acquaintance for you to have. I know how difficult it is in your position to see more of one person than another without giving offence or raising jealousies, still it is also very necessary to have a few nearer acquaintances, the very best and nicest, if one can. One learns a lot from them and remains in contact with the outer world, and this, if I were you, I would strive to do by cultivating the acquaintance of these two nice ladies. Your dear Mother-in-Law likes them so.'

The Empress and her two daughters stayed at the Grand Hotel, Naples, for nearly a month, meeting old and new friends, and sightseeing. She drew pleasure not only from the museums and palaces, but from the simplest excursions. 'We have been out in a char-a-banc to Pozzuoli, and took lunch with us. I looked for shells on the beach, which still amuses me as if I were a baby.' Coming after Athens, this second experience of freedom and normality pointed to the way to mend some of the emotional stresses of the past two years. But after a fortnight came a message from the past, from the hands of the Marshal of the Emperor William's household.

'I received a letter from Herr von Lynker...This he found in a box which he had taken from our Hofmarschall. I opened it without thinking of anything particular. Suddenly a letter drops into my hand, directed by beloved Papa and still sealed. It looked as though it had just been written. You can imagine the many bitter tears I shed! This letter was written to me containing all his wishes and directions in case of his death, about his funeral. You remember that nothing of the kind was ever found at Friedrichskron, and I felt so certain he must have written *something*, as he was so careful and tidy and particular. Of course the wishes expressed are what I *knew*, and to which William refused to listen or attend. To my dying day I can never forget that, and find it hard to forgive it. It was so brutal and so cruel!'

The shock of receiving the letter sends her back to her former melancholy.

'This is Xmas Eve, I can hardly believe it, and struggle hard to be a little cheerful. I long for beloved Papa, for my Waldie, my home and for you, my own Sophie. And the bitter, bitter change in my existence comes upon me with all its force, and all its cruel and sacred recollections of the happy past, gone never to return. My thoughts fly to the little Chapel near the Friedenskirche, so cold and sad and silent now. I dare not think of Friedrichskron tonight, all lit up and full of gay people, and we, whose home it was, driven out and banished by the angel of death; and the rooms where so many bitter tears were shed and such hours of agony gone through, now ringing with laughter and merriness. The thought drives me mad.... Oh, my Sophie! May you never know what it is to grieve as I grieve, and suffer as I do, it is too terrible.'

Princess Sophie is moved by her mother's distress, and her letters carry consoling words. '...a lump came into my throat, I could not help crying. It is too selfish that I should be so happy here and that you should be sorry and sad. Do try to cheer up! Poor darling mother, it is too hard for you. I pray God will help and bless you.'

Fortunately for the Empress, she was gifted with a precious faculty which usually came to the rescue during her spells of depression — her unfailing and active interest in everything and everybody around her. Soon she resumes her visits to art galleries and hospitals. In January, she moves to Rome, where King Humbert and Queen Margharita (godmother to Princess Margaret):

'...were most kind, as always. They received us at the railway station and took us to the hotel. They asked so much after you and Tino, in such an affectionate way.... The Queen's eyes fill with tears when she speaks of dear Papa.'

The Empress loves Rome, but after a few days of exploration, her hopes of 'spending a peaceful winter in this heavenly town and pleasant climate amongst kind people, enjoying a certain amount of liberty...', are broken by the news of the sudden death of the Empress Augusta in Berlin.

'How very very sad this is! Your poor Grandmama was taken very suddenly and as it seems, thank God, without pain, suffering or struggle. ... I dread having to go through a funeral again, in the same place, after a cold precipitate journey, as from San Remo ...but I cannot forget that she was Papa's mother, and that she had many virtues and had sometimes been very kind to me. I will try not to remember all that was so hard and bitter, and all I had to endure in thirty years.'

From Berlin she writes, on January 12th, after the funeral,

'Your poor Grandmama fell asleep so quietly that nobody could tell the exact moment when she ceased to breathe. She looked wonderfully well and peaceful in her last sleep. She reclined as if resting before a large party, in her golden train with ermine, her hands folded, with her bracelets on, and her hair done as usual, and a golden wreath, and a great tulle veil arranged in folds over her head, neck and shoulders — no trace of illness or suffering on the pale countenance we beheld for the last time....'

In the capital, as she had feared, she returned to her previous outcast existence. 'It is a most dismal and trying time for me. I know there are many who are glad I am back, but I also know how many wish me away.' She saw little of the Emperor. 'I have only seen William and Dona at the funeral ceremonies, but neither of them have taken any notice of me since.' A few weeks later she writes in the same vein. 'Willy often drives past me when we are walking, but he never stops the carriage to ask how I am or to speak to me. He never takes any notice.'

After the liberties and sunny skies of Greece and Italy, Berlin weighs heavily on her. She writes of her husband's favourite charger, which had carried him in the Battle of Worth in 1870.

'...the Siegnitz garden, where we walk up and down in dullness and melancholy every day as we have nothing else to do. The weather is so cold and wretched, the sky so dull, dark and dreary, and there is so much that gives me pain and annoyance that I am in very bad spirits...The only change in the little garden is a square mound with a faded laurel wreath. Under it rests our faithful old "Worth". If we were ancient Germans instead of Christians, we should fancy him in another world, carrying his beloved Rider to meet all the heroes gone before. There is much poetry in the strange ideas of our forefathers. As a child, I could not fancy Heaven quite without animals, the dear pets to which we get attached on earth, I thought, must go where we went.'

In the manner of the times, the Empress was meticulously conscientious in remembering and observing the birthdays and other anniversaries of her numerous relations, living and dead. These she noted in her letters, no matter how distracting her current worries and preoccupations.

'...On the 10th of this month, February, it would have been your dear Grandmama of England's Golden Wedding Day — fifty years since she was married at the Chapel Royal at St. James' Palace. We, her seven remaining children, are going to give her a beautifully bound prayer-book for the Mausoleum at Windsor or the little Chapel at Osborne.'

Among the happenings that gave her 'pain and annoyance' was the publication of hostile books and pamphlets, one by her father's brother, Duke Ernst of Saxe-Coburg-Gotha. 'There is a great deal most unpleasant about Uncle Ernie's abominable pamphlet in the newspapers.' It maligned her husband and herself, and revived the charges of treachery during the war with France. These slurs were disproved when the Emperor's War Diary was published in 1922 and the Empress's Letters in 1928, but at the time they were believed by the majority of the German people.

The galling atmosphere created by these attacks was made worse for the Empress when her son denied her certain patronages.

'I have been inexpressibly annoyed and offended at the patronage of the Red Cross and Fatherland Women's Association passing into Dona's hands, who knows nothing of taking care of the sick and wounded. For years and years I have reckoned on being the Empress Augusta's successor in these things. William simply tells me that Dona had arranged with the Empress Augusta already last year that she was to be her successor in everything, therefore simply ignoring me and leaving me out. I feel this a great want of respect and civility. Of the Empress Augusta, poor thing, I think it is very unkind, as it was I, her son's wife, who helped her with these things in '64, '66 and '70. But as you know she turned away of late years from Papa and me and took up with Dona and William.'

As the winter months pass, she is diverted more and more from her troubles in Berlin to the new and unfolding background of her daughter's life in

Greece. She devours her letters eagerly, even though Sophie still feels, 'I am sure my letters bore you very much'. Her mother replies fondly, with thoughts of the newlyweds happy in their rented home in Athens.

'My own Sophie darling, my precious child, I was delighted to get your dear letter yesterday. How *can* you say it would be a bore! It tells me just what I want to know, that is, how you spend your day. I can fancy you sitting in that pretty little room ...and Tino, sitting in an armchair deep in a book: and Blackie curled up, with his pretty shiny glossy coat looking very soft and his beautiful long ears lying on the chair.

'I am sure you must feel rather lonely in the hours that Tino is at his regimental training, I know I did when I was 17, and had to stay here when Papa commanded a brigade at Potsdam....The other day you asked me for books for Tino. Has he seen "The Life of Gneisenau"? And that of Clausewitz? Also of Bayen? They are most interesting. Has he read the Memoirs of Roi Joseph, brother of Napoleon? ...the Correspondence of Marie Antoinette? ...of the Empress Catherine of Russia? ...the books of Lecky and of Huxley ...and two very interesting novels called "Donovan" and "We Two", by Edna Lyall? What a mercy that Tino is so fond of reading, I could never get William or Henry to read.

'Of course I shall look for water-colours for you, and also for the Indian and Japanese cane-couches. It gives me great pleasure to look for anything that you may like. You could make such a snug corner on the balcony, outside your sitting room, with a tent lined with that plain red cotton stuff they call Turkey cotton. Then some pretty rugs and carpets and comfortable lawn tennis chairs and flower pots. I could make it so nice.'

At the beginning of February, the Empress learns that her daughter is expecting a baby, and from then on the letters are seldom without some mention of the coming event. At first, her references are coyly oblique. 'I am beginning to knit some very small counterpanes, and some *very tiny* shirts I wonder for whom?' But then she turns openly to practical preparations.

'I shall soon have to look out for a good English baby-nurse for you, as it takes months to find one. Do you and Tino and the dear Queen agree to that? You must also have a first-rate trained nursery maid to help the nurse in case she were ill, and whom she can trust. Then you will want a good nursery housemaid because there is a deal to do in keeping the rooms, etc. Your house is so small that I have been puzzling in my head how you can organize a nursery close enough to your room. You will want a night nursery and a day nursery, a little room where the nurses have their meals and a place for ironing and drying clothes and doing a little cooking, warming up milk, etc., and a place for the nursery maid to sleep.'

A few days later she returns to the question of a nurse, on the choice of whom Sophie has expressed decided views.

'I will tell P. that you will not have an old or ugly nurse but I cannot recommend having a young and pretty one, as that would be a continual bother and trouble to you. She would be thinking of herself, and you would soon find it an inconvenience. Well-mannered, well-spoken, well-dressed, fresh, wholesome, clean-looking, with a nice expression, is what we must look for, but especially a steady, experienced, intelligent, trustworthy person, who knows her business and whom you can feel sure of and safe with — who is strong and healthy and also has a little knowledge of sewing and making children's clothes, and also who will not quarrel with those under her, though she must understand and keep her own authority, as she has the responsibility. Forgive me suggesting all these things, but they ought to be thought about in time. I *have* a bit of experience now. Of course, I do not wish to meddle and interfere, but it is my duty to advise the first time.'

The paragon eventually chosen is 'not at all pretty, but not so ugly as the poor "Crocodile [*one of the Empress's own nurses long before — Ed.*] She looks quiet and nice and seems thoroughly good and trustworthy.'

The Empress goes on to consider the subject of doctors, and asks Sophie to urge on Queen Olga that an English doctor be chosen because, 'It is a well-known fact that confinements are better understood and better managed in England, that English ladies keep their health, their looks and their figures better than German ones.' But Queen Olga has other views, and a few weeks later the Empress writes, 'I had an answer from your dear Mama-in-law about the doctors, etc. How *could* I be angry? ...Of course, I am rather sad, but I have no right to oppose their wishes in any way. However I hope and trust all will be well.'

She now discloses that, at the time of the wedding, she had quietly provided her daughter with a London-trained midwife, Frau von E.

'The doctors and nurses at Queen Charlotte's Hospital told me she managed most difficult cases admirably, and that I need never be afraid, as even if the Doctor could not arrive in time she would be quite able to act. This was my reason for engaging her for you to go to Greece. Of course I could not tell you what her real profession was when you were a young girl, so I had to invent the name and function of housekeeper, so that you might have her always near at hand — accidents happen very easily. I had first intended to put her at the head of an institution here, to teach a branch of my Victoria Sisters. Then you married, so she went with you; but I could not tell you why.'

The Empress little knew that her action was to save probably her daughter's life as well as the child's, in exactly the contingency she foresaw.

Princess Sophie's letters describing the Athens climate, and her outings to the summer palace and estate which the King owns at Tatoi, a few miles north of the capital, provoke the Empress to contrast her bleak surroundings in Berlin.

'How delicious it sounds to hear you speaking of violets, blue sky and sunlit hours — here in the dark cold north, where all is so dull, monotonous and sad, at least to me, Berlin is like a prison, and I long for other air and surroundings.

'I hardly ever set eyes on Willy or Dona, they never visit me. They never inquire after me or try to see me ...although I am their mother and they are two steps from my door, and know what a hard and bitter trial it is to live on without beloved Papa, missing him so cruelly as I do every day and every hour. Of what happens I never have one word from them. For the first time since I was a girl of 17 I stand aloof ...and all that goes on at Court and in the political world distresses me and makes me very anxious.'

It is possible that her son's indifference was due in part to preoccupation over his growing difficulties with Bismark. The Chancellor was the established autocrat, but he had trained the Emperor to be an autocrat too, and they clashed head-on over what Bismark considered William's unrealistic measures to deal with socialist agitation. Although allowed no part in the official scene, the Empress always had a good notion of what was happening, but she was surprised when on February 19th, Bismark, for so long her implacable enemy, paid her a visit with his wife, and hinted that all was not well. Then on March 18th, came the announcement of his resignation. The Empress learned that on the 17th, after a heated argument with the Emperor, he had threatened to resign, as he had often done before, but this time William had insisted on his doing it.

That Bismark had at last received a dose of his own medicine might justifiably have given the Empress cause for exultation. But she had long grown past such littleness, and received him civilly, and even kindly when he paid her a call of farewell. He was replaced by General Georg von Caprivi, who also called formally on her. To Sophie, she wrote little about their visits, or on the possible consequences of her son's precipitate action. It was not only that she looked upon Sophie as still a child in political matters, but she was not sure whether her letters were not being examined. On March 24th, she wrote:

'All the events which have been happening here lately have distressed me very much and the way things have been carried out seems to me imprudent. I parted in peace and amicably with Prince Bismark. When people are in misfortune I gladly forgive and forget what I have suffered at their hands. I hope Caprivi will do well, it is a very difficult task for him, but he is a very honest, straightforward and respectable and reliable man, which is a great thing. He is the most energetic and determined of all our generals, but whether he understands politics I do not know. Few generals do.'

When Sophie urges her mother to comment on the significance of Bismark's fall, she replies, in April:

'...your Mama is afraid to write her opinions on politics by post, or she would have a great deal to say on all that is going on here which must fill her with anxiety and alarm for the future. The mistakes of the last 20 years are now bearing their fruit, and the way in which this result is being treated and handled does not betray wise prudence or a profound knowledge of the state of things, nor appreciation of the problems to be solved, nor of the different forces in Germany which might so well counter-balance each other if they were only allowed to do so, and if liberty instead of state interference and dictatorship were allowed. I fear you will not understand this, my Fozzie, but Tino will, I am sure.'

That a man who was not her enemy had taken Bismark's place made little difference to her situation, for her son and his wife were just as much against her as ever the Iron Chancellor had been. She attempted no change in her way of life, and continued to devote herself to social and welfare matters, and to the interests of Sophie and her new family. Of these, because of his artistic interests, she had a special regard for Prince Constantine's brother Nicholas, later to be the father of Princess Marina, Duchess of Kent.

'I have been busying myself with finding something to offer your dear Mama-in-law as a souvenir. Modern things that everyone can have seem rather meaningless from me to her. I have found a cut stone which we call bloodstone, though it is dark green, with a Byzantine Virgin and saint on it. It is wonderfully rare, and pronounced by the museum to be a most valuable piece and authentic. I hope she will like it. Most likely you will think it hideous but in reality it is most interesting, and Nicky would appreciate it I am sure. For Nicky I have collected a portfolio of old engravings. I thought it a better present than a modern watercolour, which he can find anywhere, whereas these ancient engravings increase in value and become rarer every year, now there are so many museums and private collections who want them.'

It is to be doubted whether these presents were, so far as Sophie was concerned, adequately appreciated, for a month later, referring to an exhibition held in Athens, the Empress wrote:

'I am sure the exhibition of Byzantine ecclesiastical objects was interesting. I am not aware that being "old, ugly and dirty" excites my imagination. It is the beauty and interest of ancient objects that attracts me. They may be ancient and archaeologically interesting without being in the least beautiful, these of course have less charm for me. I hope you will tell Nicky how valuable his prints are or else it might be thought that they were only "old, dirty and ugly".'

However demanding her other correspondence, and however busy her day, the Empress seldom allowed one to pass without her letter to Sophie. Sometimes it was only a brief note, sometimes a thick wad of a dozen pages, sometimes there were two or more letters in the day. She was grateful that this link existed. '...when one is separated from those one loves best on earth, then one blesses ink, paper and the art of writing, the telegraph, steamers and railways'. Her letters began: 'My own Sophie, darling', or 'Sophie love', with, in fonder moments, 'my precious child' added. Sometimes she used a nickname, Sophiekin, Fozzie or Sossie. Her letters ended usually, with many blessings, kisses and embraces, 'ever your own fond and doting Mama'.

Sophie began and ended her letters no less affectionately. The months of answering her mother's copious flow of correspondence had now trained her to fluency, but she found difficulty in keeping pace, and in March wrote: 'I hope you are not angry with me for only writing once a week, but in doing so I have more to say, and if you don't object I'll write every Wednesday. You're much too kind to write so often and such long letters to lazy old me.' In her reply the Empress is slightly pained:

'About writing once a week, do as you please my pet. I do not want it to be irksome and troublesome and a bore to write to your own Mama. I hope you will feel some day that it is a *comfort* to you to write to your Mama as *I* do when I write to *mine*. But I should be quite unhappy if it were to be a burden on you. I am quite satisfied with a little line now and then when you feel inclined, though the more I hear the better pleased I am, as I feel the separation from you so much and cannot get accustomed to it.'

She goes on to point out how Sophie could find more time for letter-writing:

'*What a pity* it is you have no gentleman of your own, as private secretary and man of business, to manage your own affairs and your own money — your bills and letters. Some day I am sure Tino will feel the need of one also, and such a person could manage both your private affairs which do not belong to your Hofmarschall Assistant. When the household and the family increase you will find that it is too much for your Hofmarschall alone if it is to be done properly. It wants somebody who writes and speaks German, French and English perfectly. You would find it an immense help, and learn a lot, I am sure. Of course it is not my business, still I can only tell you what my opinion is.'

She suggests, too, that for 'your charities, a married lady of education and experience would be of immense use to you, as you are young, and charities are hard work, as I know by experience'. While in Athens, she had seen that apart from Queen Olga's few charitable patronages, there was an almost unlimited scope for good works such as she had devoted herself to in Germany. Sophie was anxious to follow her mother's example, but needed constant advice. The Empress had to make her first suggestions with tact, in order not to trespass into the recognized domains of the Queen, and so she begins tentatively. 'I have collected the reports of the different institutions which I have founded, and of those of which I am patroness, for your dear kind mama-in-law. I thought it might interest her to have them in her bureau, to see what I have been doing these 31 years.'

The Empress keeps a maternal eye on every aspect of Sophie's day-to-day existence. 'I am so very glad that the Day of Independence went off so well. The dinner and Cercle afterwards must have been rather trying for you. I am sure you looked a Duck with your turquoise diadem on, and the turquoises round your dear little neck.' The *Cercle* was the ceremonial circulation of the royal personages among their guests. From this elevated level the subject descends abruptly. 'I trust the drains and water-pipes are all right in the old house at Tatoi. I think a sanitary engineer ought to look over them once before you go there — often one's life depends on all these things being in order.' Preparations for the coming event are frequently mentioned. 'I shall be able to give you all the baby things you will want', she offers, but when the list of requirements prepared by Frau von E. arrives, her good housewifery prompts the reply: 'I think the quantity is too great. As you know, things are only worn for 3 months for a baby, and most of them put by when the short clothes are put on. I am afraid in your climate especially the moths would eat them up.'

Towards the end of March, Sophie's letters on the Attic spring again provoke contrast with the prolonged grip of winter in Berlin.

'I can fancy how beautiful spring must be in Athens. Here we have a mild day now and again but the trees are all like black broomsticks and the very beginning of the tips of the buds are only now appearing. Nothing but a grey flat sandy waste of smoky chimneys is to be seen around Berlin, and one pines for the tints, the smells, the sounds of spring. In England the bushes are all green, I hear.'

Not for another fortnight can the Empress report that 'The little buds are beginning to come out now, and one sees a faint light green veil over the stems and branches of the trees, which I think such a pretty colour, so soft, especially in the evening.'

Early in April the Empress and her two daughters move to Romberg, and take up residence in the old Schloss. No time is lost in inspecting the new home at nearby Cronberg emerging slowly in the style of an English country house.

'I am always impatient to rush over to Friedrichshof to watch the work going on. The trees and bushes planted last year are all in a satisfactory state and all the grounds looking much more tidy. The new road is nearly finished. We had a consultation yesterday about the heating and lighting which is, alas, always an expensive thing.'

The timely inheritance of a large fortune from a recently deceased friend, the Duchess of Galliera, whom the Empress had befriended, had provided the means for this veritable castle. Into its design and decoration, and later of its furnishings, as well as the layout of the grounds, the Empress put all her considerable artistic taste, without interference from anybody other than the eminent architect, Ihne. It was, in that sense, more than a home, but an assertion of her creative self. The name of Friedrichshof was suggested by Princess Victoria, for the Empress looked upon the house as in the nature of a memorial to her husband, and had the inscription *Frederici Memoriae* carved over the main porch.

Friedrichshof stood in an estate of some 250 acres, within easy reach of the fashionable spas of Romberg and Wiesbaden. That the Prince of Wales came to the district periodically to take the waters was one of the considerations that had swayed the Empress's decision to live there. Another was its proximity to Darmstadt, where Queen Victoria occasionally appeared to see the children of her late daughter, Alice, in whom she took a tender interest.

The Queen paid a visit towards the end of April, and the Empress writes on the 23rd, which is Princess Margaret's birthday:

'Your dear Grandmama has arrived at Darmstadt, and we are going over tomorrow to see her. I am quite excited at the very thought...For Mossy's birthday, I gave her a silver mirror, in which William and Dona joined. We were a very large family party yesterday, and in the middle of it, the Empress of Austria arrived. It was a sad meeting — I felt most deeply for the poor thing. She was so very nice to me. Her house at Corfu seemed a great pleasure to her, and she invited me to come and stay with her there.'

The Empress visits her mother several times, but there is no letter describing their talks, other than the injunction:

Tray write to Grandmama of England, she is longing for a letter from you. She said "Sophie never writes to me". For her birthday on the 24th I think Tino and you ought both to write. Can you not send her some photos? I am sure she would like it so much.'

In a letter half-way through May, the Empress refers to the efforts which the young Tsarevich Nicholas of Russia is making to win the hand of Princess Alix of Hesse, whose father is against the wedding on religious grounds, although another daughter, Elizabeth, had already married the Grand Duke Serge.

'The weather is lovely here again now. We have had such storms and they have done much damage, 300 trees were blown down and up-rooted, some of the largest and finest. It is a very sad sight when they are all lying around with their roots up in the air. Dear George of Wales will be starting with his ship for the West Indies very soon. Eddie [*Prince Albert — Ed.*] has returned to his regiment at York. Alicky has again refused, and this time for the last time and good and all. I regret it very much and hope she may not regret it later.'

On Sophie's birthday the Empress, sending her blessings, tells how her last act at night ...

'is to pray God to bless her and protect her, keep her free from cares, trials and sorrow, and make her life a glad one. Till now my prayers have been heard, you have been blessed with a good kind husband and a happy home of your own, and the crowning happiness will be the dear little baby you are expecting.'

Sophie's bliss contrasted with the lack of it vouchsafed to her elder sister, Victoria, who had never recovered from her broken romance with Prince Alexander of Battenberg. The Prince, now Count Hartenau, had, in reaction to his treatment by Bismark and the old Emperor, cut himself adrift from his former associations by marrying a professional singer, with whom he lived happily in Austria. The luckless Victoria had fretted for long over her lost love, for no other affection had replaced it. Now suddenly, the situation was changed by the appearance of a suitor. The manner in which events developed throws a light on how, in those days, husbands were sometimes found for Hohenzollern princesses. In early June, the Empress writes:

'This week Adolf of Schaumburg-Lippe comes to Wiesbaden, and will most likely visit us. What will come of this I do not know. He is not clever, and I believe that he has learned but very little, as his parents gave him no opportunity, but he has the highest praise from those who know him as being most trustworthy and good, and having a high character, and being very popular with his comrades. ... I think one can call him good-looking, with an amiable expression. This is all I can say about him. Perhaps he and Vicky will fancy each other, perhaps not, we must wait and see.'

Four days later, the Empress is able to break the glad news.

'Since I last wrote to you Mossy will have told you that our darling Vicky has engaged herself to the Prince of Schaumburg-Lippe. Let us hope that it may be for her lasting happiness, and that she may be repaid in her married life for all the sorrow and bitter disappointments she has gone through. He is a little stiff and shy and awkward, and this I am sure will wear off when he mixes more in society. Much polish and outward refinement he has not, but he is so civil and polite and he makes a good impression.

'We have been through a great deal of anxiety and excitement in these last few days. I wrote yesterday to Willy, who particularly wished this marriage, and begged of him to telegraph his approval directly, but he has not yet done so, which puts us on tenterhooks. Adolf rushed away to his parents yesterday and is to return late at night.

'Dear little Mossy was an angel, such a good kind sensible little sister. So many tears flowed yesterday that the celebration was really more like a funeral. Today, darling Vicky looks rested and her face wears a peaceful and satisfied expression, which is of course a great comfort to me. It was so difficult to know what to do and what to say. Urge her or advise her I could not. She had to decide for herself and I think she was wise, as such a chance having offered itself she might regret later not having availed herself of it. Of course, many will say that it is not a grand or a brilliant marriage for Papa's daughter, but happiness and great riches do not always go together. From what I hear of him, he will do his utmost to make her happy. Still of course it is a great and serious step to take, and one which always makes a mother's heart tremble.'

The Empress returns to Berlin, from where she replies to Sophie's letter on the engagement.

'I can fancy how excited and how pleased you are about our darling Vicky. Yes, I am very grateful that she has found a nice good and kind husband whom all speak well of, though you can understand that it gives me pain to think of the one who was such an exceptional creature to whom she ought to have belonged, and who was so shamefully ill-used and persecuted and calumniated, and for *no use* and *no reason.* He is one of the many victims of Bismark's hate and violence into which William entered and of which William made himself a *tool!* But all that is past and gone, though I can never forget all that happened, the injustice and intrigues which so profoundly disgusted me.'

On June 15th, the anniversary of the Emperor Frederick's death, which Sophie does not fail to honour, the Empress replies:

'It was such a comfort to receive your dear telegram this morning. I knew your thoughts would be here, where it hardly seems possible to me, even now, that two sad years have elapsed since that dread hour, that I have lost for ever what I held most dear on earth, that my children are deprived of the best father, and the country of the one man who would have been such a blessing to it...his hopes and aims were noble and pure and good...oh, that the love and peace he sought to spread would penetrate some hearts and make them feel what wrong they have done...I try to be brave I assure you, and not to think of myself, but oh! the longing for one squeeze of dear Papa's big hand, for a kiss, for the sound of his voice or his step, is so heavy, it takes all courage out of me. To face life and struggle on without him seems too hard, too incomprehensible.'

In Berlin, the Empress has many social and official engagements to fulfil. Of one she writes:

'General Caprivi dined with us last night...Heligoland is Germanized, and Germany has agreed about different lands in Africa which are to be under

British sway. I think the arrangement is a good and useful one for both sides.'

All through the spring the Empress has been making plans for going to Greece for her daughter's confinement. Earlier she has written dubiously on whether to bring the two sisters, for Vicky 'cannot bear the heat, and then I thought it might be embarrassing at such a moment for our Mossy, who is still so young'. Now she arranges to arrive in Athens in August, after spending a few weeks in England with her mother. But first she visits the little town of Bückeburg to meet Adolf's parents. On June 27th she writes:

'We have been most kindly received here. In spite of the rain a great many people had assembled and garlands were hung out and flags, etc. We had a gala dinner and illuminations in the garden and bands playing. The old Prince and Princess, who are a most attached couple, and in a few years will celebrate their golden wedding, are delighted with Vicky. She looked very pale and tired, poor thing. Adolf was beaming, he seems his parents' favourite. Everybody seems overjoyed at the engagement. The old Prince, in spite of his strange rough manners, is a clever and excellent man.'

From Bückeburg, the Empress, accompanied by Adolf and the two girls, continues to England, crossing the Channel in the Royal yacht, *Victoria and Albert*. At the end of June she writes from Windsor Castle:

'We arrived yesterday morning in proper time at Gravesend, after an excellent passage in the dear yacht. Dear Uncle Arthur [*Duke of Connaught — Ed.*] met us at Queensborough....What it was for me to see him again after not seeing him since the Jubilee, you can imagine, my Sophie! I found dear Louischen [*Duchess of Connaught — Ed.*] looking marvellously well, and as beautiful as her three dear children, such nice little things. Everyone asks after you and wants to know how you are, and dear Grandmama was full of questions about you. Adolf pleases everybody here and is so nice. Vicky is still in a state of mind about his beard and his clothes and his servant, who has very untidy German ways, but I tell her that will come all right.

'I hear our great Sir Morell Mackenzie has left for a 6-weeks voyage in the Mediterranean.... Athens will be one of the places touched at, and I hope you will send for him to see him, it would give him so much pleasure, and me too, and we ought all of us to lose no opportunity of showing him our gratitude for his invaluable services to dear Papa, all the more because of the shameful way he has been treated by others. His health is very bad I hear...'

The Empress has a busy time preparing for the voyage. Writing early in July, she answers Sophie's suggestion to exclude a certain lady-in-waiting from the party.

'Darling Fozzie, you must not be unreasonable, it is all arranged that Countess Bruhl goes with me, and I cannot upset it. We leave next week and I have hardly a moment's time to myself. There is so much to do and look after in

London, your layette, your nurses, Vicky's trousseau and future home, and the things I want for Friedrichshof, so many people to see and that wish to see me, and so much I have to leave undone. You have no idea of the worries and difficulties. I suppose by the 19th August we may hope all your troubles will be over.'

In mid-July, still writing from Windsor Castle, she is able to announce:

'After a great deal of deliberation and much thought and discussion we have at last settled on going all together. Your dear Grandmama gives us the yacht and we embark at Portsmouth and run direct to Gibraltar, there take the *Surprise* and go to Piraeus. I shall most likely arrive on the 29th or 30th July, as you telegraphed. Dear Grandmama with her own dear hands worked a little quilt in crochet work for the baby. I told her how much you liked her presents. Goodbye my darling Fozzie, may we meet safely, and all go well for you, my darling. I am really only afraid we shall be a bore to your parents-in-law, and such a large party. We tried to reduce it and found it very difficult, please explain all this to your father-in-law. I could not bring less than one lady and one gentleman, of course, and with the servants it mounts up to 13 persons.'

To the modern mind the Empress's party may seem large, but compared with the formidable suites, sometimes amounting to a hundred, that accompanied the Emperor William on his travels, her thirteen erred on the side of modesty. The careful timing of the trip came to nothing, for while still at Gibraltar, news came that a boy had been born prematurely on July 19th. The elderly Court *accoucheur* was late, but fortunately Frau von E. rose to the occasion, and more than justified the faith placed in her.

Queen Olga returned to Athens from Russia two days after the confinement, but the Empress did not arrive until the end of July. The anxieties of the journey were soon dissipated in the presence of her daughter and the baby, who, on August 18th, was christened in the first name of George. At the end of the month, the Empress started on her return journey and sent her first letter from the *Surprise* while at Corfu.

'How my heart does ache at having parted from you. How quickly those 4 weeks have passed, like 4 days! I only feel it must often have been a great burden to your dear kind parents-in-law to have us as guests for so long. It is always a strain and a fatigue to try to entertain others, and they really were so kind and hospitable to us. I am much grateful. It was an immense comfort and relief to me to be with you, and watch you prosper day by day in recovery, and to see that little angel baby. How I love that little thing, and how sad I am not to be able to see it unfolding like a flower, to hear its first coo and first laugh, and watch the first beam of intelligence in its eyes, all the delights in store that repay a mother for all she has gone through.'

The yacht calls at places of interest on the Dalmatian coast while *en route* for Venice, where Adolf meets them.

'We were sorry to leave our "Surprise", and all the kind, merry British faces that surrounded us, good-natured and kind, as sailors usually are. To Vicky, Venice falls flat after the games of "Quoits" and "Halma", and the excursions aboard the "Surprise", but she is delighted to have Adolf. I am sure you will like him, as one feels what a true honest trustworthy creature he is, which after all is the *first* thing in life. To be brilliant and quick and amusing is very nice indeed, but it is not always coupled with all the most sterling qualities on which one's safety depends.

'The sea-bathing here in the morning is delicious. I could not help smiling when you wrote that Tino's dear Mama would not go into the water because she was too stout. I do not think I can boast of being much thinner, but my love of the water makes me go in all the same! I have rummaged a great many shops here to find things for Friedrichshof, but there are not one half of the nice pieces (old ones) to be found as formerly, the different museums and the Americans carry everything away.'

After three weeks, the party leaves for Germany. From Berlin, the Empress now discloses that Margaret has formed an attachment for the charming, handsome Prince Max of Baden.

'...Berlin, which to me is only a tomb or a prison, but for Mossy, contains Max, and this makes it a paradise. I am unhappy about it. I wish she liked anyone else, because I am afraid Max does not care for her, nor dream of marrying, and it is pain to me to think Mossy should set her heart on what perhaps she cannot have, and then live the next years, the heart of her youth, under the gloom of disappointment, but you see I am powerless to do anything.'

In a few days occurs the ceremony of transferring the Emperor Frederick's coffin from the Chapel at Friedenskirche to the Mausoleum which has been built, partly to the Empress's design, at Potsdam. The service 'simple, short, but solemn, impressive and touching', revives all her inmost sorrows. She writes to

'...my own absent darling, the only one of his children still on earth who did not stand round the stone which closes the vault, and has forever hidden the precious coffin from view....Oh, how I miss darling Papa so cruelly, and in the morning on waking, his empty pillow, his silent and empty rooms, make me so wretched. It is no use to grieve and to mourn, but one cannot help it. How unfeeling I should be if I did not suffer this pain.'

The tone of her letters suddenly changes when a telegram announces that Sophie and Tino will come to Berlin for Victoria's wedding.

'What a joy to think you will start in a week. I am so impatient to have you and Tino, you do not know. You shall have the little rooms upstairs you like, though they are not half good enough and not proper for you, my darling, to whom I would wish to give the best of all I have. The preparations for the wedding take up a great deal of my time, and a great deal has to be done in a short while.'

Early in November, Prince Constantine and Princess Sophie arrived in Berlin, where there assembled representatives of the families concerned, among them members of the British Court. The several days of festivities that preceded the wedding included banquets at the Schloss, and a gala performance at the Opera. The Empress Frederick gave a banquet for her birthday but did not join in the other celebrations. The wedding took place on November 19th, in the spacious chapel of the Schloss. For once the Empress put off her widow's weeds, and wore a dress of pale lilac.

All the harmony that the wedding created was suddenly dissipated when Princess Sophie informed her family that she intended to enter the Orthodox Church, the religion of the Greek Royal Family and people. The strongest objection to her decision was taken by both the Emperor and his wife, who rebuked Sophie severely. A violent quarrel developed, which spread to others of the family, and provoked much ill-feeling, which the Emperor capped by threatening Sophie that if she carried out her intention he would never allow her to return to Germany again. In an atmosphere of strain the Crown Prince and Princess left for Greece on December 19th, and for the Empress, the usual pain of parting was swallowed up by her indignation at her son's action, as her letters show.

'I am Still so unhappy about that ridiculous and wretched business. William, who is not much fonder of the truth than Charlotte, has it seems represented everything falsely to Aunt Helen [*Princess Christian — Ed.*] who told Reischach [*the Empresses Lord Chamberlain — Ed.*] that *I had ill-treated William until he cried!* ...William is convinced that I had tried to persuade you to become Greek. He is so firmly convinced that I am always in some "intrigue" against him. Of course, such ideas are put into his head by others, but he must be very green to believe such absurd nonsense. I am sorry for him, as he is quite taken in very often.... Poor Mossy's eyes are swollen out of her head with weeping.'

Her next letter is from the Schloss at Kiel, to which she has fled to escape from William after giving him a piece of her mind. She is staying with Henry and Irene, and on December 21st writes:

'Oh, if only William and Dona behaved differently, my life would be less sad. I try hard to get on with them, as a cruel fate has put them at the head of the family and the State, but am for ever exposed to disagreeable things. ... It is very sad I can be of no use to him, he does not want my advice or care about me one rap. Of course it would be far better for me to go away from

Berlin and not return, but I cannot be banished from the spot where my darling husband and two sweet children lie buried, nor leave the home for good and all where we spent so many years together, and where now recollections haunt every nook and corner, nor can I abandon the many institutions and works of charity of which I am the patroness and who constantly want me, so all these considerations make it impossible for me to leave Berlin altogether. Besides, it would look as if I were afraid of them if I gave up my rights, and as if they had succeeded in frightening or driving me away, as was intended in the days of Bismark.

'William appeared yesterday morning at the railway station when I left, and tried to be civil and unconcerned, but no words passed. The country was buried in snow between Berlin and here, and now the sky is dark and grey and a dismal wind howling. Henry and Irene were so nice, and the Schloss looks so clean and well-kept and comfortable. They are so happy and their home so peaceful and harmonious because they are away from Berlin, and mischief-making....'

Her letter next day returns to the subject of Sophie's conversion:

'I am still frantic with all that has happened these last days. Henry and Irene are quite of our opinion. I think you had better say a little word to Grandmama when you write, as it is sure to reach her ears in a very different form and she should hear the truth. I am sure she will listen to all you say. What will your father-in-law say? Perhaps he will laugh and hardly believe that a man can be so foolish and childish when he is 32 years of age, and holds so high a position.'

Her Christmas Day letter, after recording her gratitude for the several presents from her children, continues:

'You will have a dinner at the Palace today, for the King's birthday. I am sure they are mighty glad to have you both back again. Please do not forget to let a photo be done of baby, also one of yourself in the Greek costume which I suppose you will wear on the 1st January ball...Henry and Irene had a Christmas Tree yesterday evening...it was a quiet and peaceful Xmas Eve. At dinner, we solemnly drank the King's health in champagne, standing up. Please tell him. Many, many loving Xmas wishes to you and beloved Tino and the sweet baby. Many kisses, many blessings. P.S. The wind is something terrific here. The harbour is quite frozen over to the other shore, and the boats, all caked with ice, lying immovable, like so many dead things. Oh, what a vile climate is the north of Germany in winter!'

The Empress had herself written to Queen Victoria regarding William's threat of exile, which would prevent Sophie coming to see her.

'I have had a letter yesterday by messenger from your dear Grandmama, and I thought you might like to hear what she says, which is as follows: "I cannot say how grieved and distressed I am at what has happened, and which was so entirely unnecessary and uncalled for. I think it was all Dona's love of interference. I hope and trust that it will blow over and that nothing will prevent your dear children from often coming to see you at Friedrichshof or Berlin. I quite understand all you say, I myself do not understand such narrowmindedness. I could not, even though I may be against a person changing their religion. If they do it willingly out of conviction and without compulsion, I could not blame them or be angry with them for it." You see, dear Grandmama thinks just as we do, and as every sensible Christian and tolerant person must.'

The last letter of the year exposes the real resentment that lies in her heart, that she will not submit to being treated as a 'has-been'.

'William and Charlotte do not want me at Berlin...I am not old enough only to watch people living, and to be quite passive myself, and yet I am given to understand every moment that I belong to the past, and that the official Germany of today has nothing to do with me. I hope to become philosophical enough in time not to care, but it is very, very difficult, I am too thin-skinned....'

Chapter Three – The Letters, 1891

The first letters of the New Year are concerned chiefly with the situation created by the Emperor's ban on Princess Sophie. Writing from Berlin, the Empress quotes from letters sent to her by Princess Victoria, then on her honeymoon in Cairo, from King George of the Hellenes, and from Queen Victoria.

'I had a letter from Vicky in which she says: "I am utterly bewildered and distressed about this row. Good gracious, have they gone clean mad? To think of sweet Sophie and Tino having these disagreeable scenes makes me boil with indignation. The audacity of Dona to speak to Sophie like that! May not Sophie do as she pleases about her Church, now that she is married in Greece and belongs to another people and family? It has quite spoilt my Xmas, thinking of you and them."'

'It was most kind of the King to let me have copies of what he wrote to William and also of William's really *preposterous* telegram. It makes me quite furious, and yet I am obliged to laugh. He seems to be copying Peter the Great, Frederick William I, Napoleon or some such conspicuous tyrant. To a free-born Briton, as I thank God I am, such ideas, so little in harmony with the XIX Century and personal liberty and independence, are simply abhorrent; and this my own son! Your father-in-law, who has quicker wits and sharper brains of course has the best of the argument, and I admire him for being so gentle and moderate, in spite of such provocation.'

'I heard from my dear Mama, and she says, "The tone of the King of Greece's Letter to William as well as to you I think admirable, so kind, forbearing and dignified. Pray when you write to him tell him so, and that I deeply deplore what I think most *inconceivable* conduct on W's part. I think however that it will blow over, and that it should not be mentioned. William will see in time the great mistake he has made." Perhaps you will kindly tell this to your Papa-in-law, it may interest and please him.'

The Empress Augusta has given birth to another baby, an event which provides grounds for a partial truce.

'General Caprivi dined with Mossy and me, and afterwards I had a little talk with him. He was exceedingly sorry for all that had happened, but tried to excuse William as best he could. William lunched here yesterday and was quite amiably and civilly inclined. Of course I avoided *all* thorny subjects. I visited Dona in the afternoon, she was on her sofa. I offered to hold the baby during the christening, but Dona informed me that *William* did not wish it! I only asked to please them, and thought it excessively rude to answer thus.'

The Empress duly attends the christening, where:

'...the heat was suffocating. The baby screamed a bit, but not for long. He is called Joachim. Not *one* of their children is called after me, Victor would have been so nice. Sweet Mossy looked such a Duck holding the baby. And yet such ceremonies make me very sad now at the Schloss, the tears and sadness rise and I look round in vain for beloved Papa's dear face and fine tall figure, so broad and strong and handsome. The christenings of you all came so vividly before me, and I cannot believe that all the terrible things I have been through are reality and not a bad dream...It is just on 33 years ago that I arrived here in Berlin, a young bride, very shy and uncomfortable, and yet it seems to me like yesterday.'

In Athens, Princess Sophie and her husband live in a private house, for which the Empress, always watchful over such matters, thinks they pay more than enough. She inquires about the official residence which the Greek Government is building.

'How is your future Palace getting on? I hope the garden will be *very* pretty, and that you will have shutters and *marquises* so as to keep off the sun, and nice bathrooms and other comforts, and just a few visitors' rooms. *Salons* they are *sure* to give you enough of, every German architect thinks of that, but the rest is usually grievously deficient, such as the bedrooms, the servants' rooms and the offices downstairs.

'I am so glad you are going to give dinners. I am afraid it is a bore for you, but still it is so good that people should get to know you and that you should show them civilities. For Tino's position and for yours it is so important — also that you should create a little circle of acquaintances to invite now and then for a cup of tea in the evening. I am sure there must be some distinguished men at the university, and amongst the wealthy men who have done much for the town, also young rising people. It would increase Tino's influence, and is worthwhile making the sacrifice of being a little bored now and then. It will make you enjoy your quiet evenings at home all the more!'

The Empress returns to this theme a few weeks later, when she also writes of two of her enlightened crusades.

'Poor Sosikin! To have a subscription Ball and Ladies' audiences. I pity you, but yet I am glad, as it is so necessary, and the shyness (which I rather like to see) will wear off in time though I still to this day suffer very much from this malady, and hate going out, much as I wish to be civil and put people at their ease.

'I am very glad you have been to such a good seminary for young ladies, and the Lady Superintendent is so nice, indeed I should like to make her acquaintance. Here, I am doing all I can that we should have a *real* Ladies' College, rather like Newnham or Girton or Holloway. This has been my endeavour for *years* and *years*, and dear Papa was deeply interested in it and always encouraged me and the Ladies who helped me. Wm. was told by a gentleman the other day that there was a great movement in Germany in educational circles for this idea, but he said he would not hear of it, that women's education was unnecessary. If women remain only a sort of upper servant, the whole of the nation *must* suffer. But *selfish* men are silly enough to think that they can trample more easily on *ignorant* women.

'I *sincerely* rejoice to hear that you are trying to do some work for improving and reforming the prisons. The one I saw at Nauplia gave me the creeps. I will make it my business to collect all the information I can for you on the subject. It will be a real good work which your Mama and you will be doing, and I can only hope that you may be energetically supported. I belong to a society in Germany for the *employment* of prisoners when they leave prison. To *save* and *improve* evil-doers, not only to punish their offences, must be the end and object of prisons and prison administration.'

Eager that her daughter shall initiate some of the social and educational institutions that Greece so sadly lacks, the Empress is constantly on the lookout for ideas to pass on, as the following extracts show.

'I have been today to hear the amateur chorus sing. Is there a good amateur Chorus at Athens? Would it not be great fun to get up one and have all the good music one is fond of? I always think it such a pleasure and interest.'

'I am sending you a new German cookery book prepared by my wish, to be taught from in the girls' schools. Could you not have something of the kind prepared in Greek, for your schools? Of course with the special national dishes of Greece, etc., and simple and wholesome things added. It would be an excellent thing for the institutions where poor girls & orphans are trained.

'I send you today the report of the society for teaching schoolboys to carpenter and carve and do bookbinding, etc., of which I am patroness, and which has really very good results, though it met with great opposition at first. The schoolmasters have gone through a regular course so as to be able to teach the boys of an evening. Have you anything of the kind in Greece? It is so very useful. The boys are so fond of it; it makes them clever with their fingers and keeps them out of mischief; it is an interest, occupation and amusement at the same time. Aunt Alix [*Alexandra, Princess of Wales — Ed.*] has also a class at Sandringham and the children did such neat things in copper and brass.'

'Could not a class for gardening for girls be attempted or do you think it would not take on in Greece, and not be useful and that they could not find employment afterwards? I think it excellent. Women could open little shops and be "seedmen and florists" and keep nursery gardens.'

The Empress turns to two subjects she is to harp on many times, that Sophie should get to know Greece, and particularly a small property at Manolada, in the Morea, which her husband owns.

'Have you made any plans for travelling a little in Greece, for seeing the provinces, and especially Manolada, before the weather gets unbearably hot? One hears it said so often, what a good thing it would be if you and Tino showed yourselves in the country. I know the people long for it, and what pleasure it would be to them and of what *importance* it is. *Do* think of it. The Government you have got now is *not* a blessing, and for your Father-in-Law it must be very trying and a great anxiety. For all who love Greece and earnestly desire her welfare and prosperity it is a painful thought that things are not quite what they might or should be at present. At any rate the more the Country learns to know the King and the Royal Family the better, and especially Tino and you. Forgive me saying this, but I am such an anxious Mama, and the good of my children I have so deeply at heart. It is no wish to meddle in your affairs.'

The Letters now mention a projected visit to Paris which the Empress is making with the Emperor William's approval to test the possibility of a later visit by himself. This point, however, if she knew of it, she does not discuss. She had been to Paris several times since 1871, and had always been well received. On this occasion, she went as the patron of an art exhibition soon to be held in Berlin, with the object of personally thanking some well-known French artists who had promised to show their paintings. With Princess Margaret and the usual suite, she arrived in Paris on February 19th, and the first few days passed smoothly in visits to studios and picture galleries, and in shopping expeditions.

'I am very glad to be at Paris again, as it contains so much that is interesting, and yet to me all is so sad now, seeing places again where I spent happy days and hours in former times. I trust my Mossy enjoys herself. I do not take her everywhere I go, as I do not think she would care for private galleries and collections as much as I do. But of course I enjoy everything doubly when I have her with me.'

But then she unthinkingly pays a visit to Versailles, scene of the French humiliation in January, 1871.

'Our visit to Versailles on a most lovely day was very interesting, and yet very mournful to me, the places where beloved Papa stayed so long during the war, etc., and where he helped to decide the fate of Germany. All the relics of past grandeur there are quite exquisite and I could have passed many hours roaming about and looking at everything.

'We have again been into different studios. Whenever I saw anything particularly lovely, I thought of you and wished I could send it you. Things are most expensive here, almost more so than in London. The *best* things I mean. There are such *clever* amateurs and collectors and such good judges of what is really *good* here that the objects, being so much *recherché*, are very expensive.'

Engrossed in her artistic explorations, the Empress did not realize that her trip to Versailles, and others to St. Cloud and nearby battlefields, had caused an outburst of resentment, expressed in violent attacks by the chauvinist press and politicians for insulting the French nation. Upset and angry she left for England on February 27th, but suppressed her feelings in the letter she wrote from the packet-boat in Calais harbour.

'During the latter part of our nice stay at Paris the worst part of the press got up a cry against the Exhibition, and tried to give the question a political aspect, and to work themselves, or rather the public, up into excitement on the subject. It was very absurd and is much to be regretted, as it will do harm and make bad blood. If you read and hear about it, you need not attach too much importance to it. Most likely it will subside after a few days, and people will see how foolish the outcry was.'

But the clamour did not subside. The French painters withdrew their support from the exhibition, the Berlin press reviled them and all Frenchmen, and the Parisian press replied in kind. In her letters from Windsor Castle, the Empress resents the way a few politicians...

'...got up such a row in the nasty papers on the occasion of my innocent visit to Paris, which had no political character at all. It is to be deplored that all Paris and France have to give way, against their *own* wishes and feelings, to an impertinent set of mischief-makers who do *not* represent French public opinion one bit, and against whom the Government, Society and the Bourgeoisie and all peaceable people have not the courage to stand up. It is really very sad. I trust this unpleasant outburst will have no serious consequence, i.e., that in Germany they will not take any measures of retaliation against what was a piece of folly.'

Her interest in French art was genuine, and to her, the visits were but harmless outings. She did not understand the French character, nor realize how bitter were their memories of the war. The only result of her visit was a worsening of Franco-German relations. Her failure was not only a mortification for her, but an epitaph to her last participation in even semi-official affairs.

Anxious to forget this disagreeable experience, she sets out to enjoy herself in her more sympathetic surroundings. 'Dear old Windsor looks as splendid as ever, and I am so glad to be here. Today we went to see a most splendid Horse Show at Islington. Really it was a pleasure to see those fine animals so beautifully kept. Afterwards I visited Bedford Ladies' College, which I thought so interesting.' She comes for a few days to Buckingham Palace for shopping excursions.

'Yesterday we dined with Uncle Bertie [*Edward, Prince of Wales — Ed.*] and Aunt Alix at Marlborough House. I had not been to a large dinner there since the Jubilee. How I thought of when Tino and you were there. After dinner we went to Burlington House and looked at the Exhibition of old pictures; it was all lit up, and tea was provided. There was no one there but the family and our ladies and gentlemen, so that we could quietly enjoy looking at the pictures. Only (for me) it was very late and the gaslight hurt one's eyes frightfully. Still I liked it very much.

'I have chosen three bonnets, or rather hats (as only girls wear the bonnets) for darling baby. I send you for him some little "smocks" to wear out-of-doors over his frocks, or indoors in the morning, without or instead of a frock, as I think them so pretty. I also send a couple of pinafores which seemed very smart and pretty to me.

'Now about your present for Tino. I have found at the splendid watercolour exhibition, 3 pictures which I can propose to you: a tiny one, a peep down an English lane, sweetly painted, for £14, one of ships, also quite lovely, for the same price, and one which I like best of all, it is a girl with her hands folded in prayer and looking up, in the dress of a Byzantine saint. It is excellent, and costs £12, because the artist is not yet very celebrated. Will you let me know by telegraph which to have? The last is a subject which would also delight your mama-in-law, in case you children have nothing for her birthday, or perhaps the King might like to give it to her. I was charmed with it.'

In England, the Empress, as always, is content in the company of her mother. But after three weeks, the time comes for the Queen to leave for the Riviera. 'Alas, my stay here in dear beautiful old Windsor is coming to an end, and in a few days Grandmama will have left. Yesterday, I unveiled a little statue of dear Grandmama at Eton, erected by the boys over the archway leading into the new school building.' She recalls, on March 20th, that:

'I was confirmed this day thirty-five years ago, here at dear Windsor on a day like this. How it all comes back to me! What a privilege I consider it to belong to the Church of England! I am so much attached to our Prayer Book and our services, though in thought I am very much a *German,* and feel how much humanity owes to the spirit of scientific research and courageous independence of thought in which Germany excels, and to which the horrid, narrow-minded *Court* and society of Berlin is so opposed. But you are too young to have heard of all this.'

When 'beloved "Gan-Gan" is gone off to Grasse', the Empress stays with the Prince and Princess of Wales at Sandringham. On March 28th, she writes:

'Yesterday was my own Waldie's [*Prince Waldemar — Ed.*] *Todestag* [*death-day anniversary — Ed.*] and my heart ached *bitterly.* I went to the sweet little Church with Auntie and opposite my pew is the Tablet with beloved Papa's medallion. So good and so like his dear noble face, so manly and calm. It was indeed so nice and good of Uncle Bertie to erect this little monument to our dear one's memory in the dear little Church where they worship every Sunday.'

From Sandringham she goes to Buckingham Palace, where she spends a few more days.

'How much I thought of you when I visited Alma Tadema's studio yesterday. *He* would be the man to advise about decorating your house at Athens. He has *such* taste and art, and such an eye for the beautiful and simple. I wish you could see his home, it would delight you. I went to see dear Sir Morell Mackenzie's hospital, and he came to dine with me at the Palace. I was so glad to see him, kind dear man.

'How nice that you saw the Empress of Austria, she is really so kind, to *me* she has always remained a *true* friend, like Queen Margharita of Italy, and I love her very much. She has a sore trial and a heavy affliction to bear, which makes me feel all the more sympathy for her.

'Bernhard [*Prince of Saxe-Meiningen — Ed.*] wrote me a rude and nasty letter, meant to wound me and make a hit at you over your change of religion, and I do not think it very becoming as an answer to a Birthday Letter. Really, what I have to stand from him and from your brothers sometimes is *not* to be told! Now their father is not there to keep them in order or to protect me, they think they can say and do *what* they like, and are ungrateful and *rücksichtslos* [*inconsiderate — Ed.*] Henry often does not mean it, but the others intend it.'

The next letter, written on Board Royal Yacht, *Victoria and Albert,* off Sheerness', ends:

'We are here waiting to cross over to Flushing early to-morrow morning. I am all impatience to see my Vicky, and yet I cannot tell you what it costs me to leave Home, where I have so many kind friends and all are so good to me. P.S. Oh, England is such a jolly place, it spoils one so for living elsewhere.'

At Bonn, she stays with Victoria and Adolf in their first house. Straight from Athens, the last of the honeymoon visits,

'Vicky could almost only talk of you, of baby, and of your home, of all your kindness to her. She does not know how to say enough of the pleasure of seeing you and your sweetness to her. I liked to hear that so much, my Sophie. Grandmama telegraphed from Grasse that the poor housemaid (such a nice woman) whom she had taken with her had died. What a sad occurrence!

'It was a great wrench to leave the dear beautiful yacht yesterday, all kept so clean and arranged to such perfection, and to plunge into the discomfort of a German hotel. The vile tobacco smell everywhere, the iron stairs, the hard beds and coarse linen, so narrow that you cannot turn round, and everything slipping off! However one puts up with all that with pleasure to see Vicky darling. She was touching, brought me a beautiful bouquet to the hotel. We dined with her last night. She was so amusing, and I often wonder how I can get on at all without her. If only she is happy. ... P.S. If we all live, and the manoeuvres take place in July, Vicky will come to Homberg.'

Princess Victoria has had her house furnished in English style. 'She is much pleased, but S. and W. [*two of her staff — Ed.*] fight against everything that is English, and of course, Adolf is thoroughly German in his ways, so I fancy Vicky has a hard time of it to get things done nicely.'

From Bonn, the Empress goes on to the Schloss Romberg. 'It was bitterly cold on arriving here, a keen north-east wind and drizzling rain...', but in spite of the weather she at once inspects Friedrichshof, only to find that the work has been slowed up by months of frost and snow: 'When the mortar will not bind on account of the cold, and no spade or pick-axe can get into the ground, nothing can be done.'

Princess Sophie encloses a copy of a letter she has sent to William to explain that she is changing her religion out of conviction, and not for 'worldly or political considerations of any kind'. In the course of a long reply, the Empress outlines her broad and tolerant attitude towards religion.

'...your letter to William — I am afraid your kind and nice words will be lost on him, as he has absolutely *no heart*. It is perhaps not his fault, and therefore one ought not to be angry with him, but it is a fact. There is no sentiment in his nature, so I fear he will not answer your letter lovingly and sensibly as he should. He is, besides, not *learned* enough to understand that our Christian Religion has centuries ago divided into branches, of which each one naturally considers itself the true one, the purest and the best. In *each* we may do God's will, we may follow our Saviour's example, we may find strength in difficulties, comfort in sorrow, and light to guide us aright. To which of these branches we feel most drawn, and which forms of faith appeal to us, is a matter of our conscience and our individuality. One way is as good as the other. *All* human Doctrines are imperfect, each has its advantages and disadvantages. But in the whole of Christ's teaching breathes *his spirit* of tolerance for the beliefs and the creeds of others.

'...I may regret that your *expression* of religious conviction will not be the same as mine, but I am glad you make the change if that expression gives you *more* than what you had before. In England *no one* thought it strange or unnatural or had a word of astonishment, criticism or reproach. Everyone wishes and hopes it will be for your happiness.

'With William it is *not religion* that vexes him, it is his silly vanity and pride of being "head of the family", and *their* being obliged to bend to his will. It makes him think the Prussian Church the only right one. Do not torment yourself, dearest child. ... I think we ought to strive to seek the points of *union* and *similarity,* and not those that *separate* us from our Brothers in other Churches.

'"In my Father's House are *many* Mansions,' says the Bible, and also, "There are many folds, but *one* Shepherd". Whether you lift up your soul to God in a Greek Church or a Latin or a Protestant one is the same to the one Spirit, whom all adore, and whom all try to seek each in their different way. That you should long to feel united with your dear Husband and your Child is quite natural....'

In a later letter, she replies to an appeal which, in the circumstances, does Sophie every credit.

'My darling, you say I am to forgive Willy. Of course I forgive all his hasty words, and try to forget them, but I *cannot* forgive or forget all his *deeds* of the last four years against his Parents and their friends unless he *asks* me to do so, and shows me he regrets them and tries to behave better. *I* am the sufferer, not he ...and *he* is the offender, let him ask and wish for forgiveness and he shall have it, but *not* in the way he goes on now!'

As the Empress foresaw, William was not affected by his sister's appealing letter. His unbending reply impelled Sophie, who had now entered the Greek Church in a ceremony that she describes as 'very emotional', to telegraph openly with her usual frankness, through the post offices at Athens and Homberg: 'Received answer. Keeps to what he said in Berlin. Fixes it to three years. Mad. Never mind. Sophie.'

But her mother does mind, and writes back in great indignation, with many underlinings. 'It is really too unheard of. It is a piece of *tyranny* and *injustice* which fills me with *contempt,* indignation and disgust...It is a piece of despotism from which every right-minded person *must* turn away with pity and derision...a step which simply *prevents* your coming to *my* House...*This* I shall and *will not* swallow ...you are *quite* at liberty to do as you like, you are not *his* subject, but King George's.' Then after several such pages, she pauses to reflect.

'Of course I must be very careful. But I am *thoroughly* determined to have *no* discussion with him and *no* correspondence with him on the subject. I shall *only* answer him if he speaks to me, which I suppose he will *not*. I must also be very careful about carrying out my threat of this autumn, i.e., of not putting my foot into his house or receiving him in mine. This is *exactly* what he would particularly like and wish, and if he could get rid of me for three years from Berlin he would be only too delighted and say, as he did then: "Pray do, you are quite welcome, and I do not care a rap."

'He has then the power to annoy and persecute me by saying he wishes Mossy to be at Berlin in the winter. Of course a violent struggle and fight would ensue, as to give up my child not even *he,* who thinks he can do *everything* he plans, would make me, unless by main force. So you see I shall have to be very calm and think well over what I must do.'

The truth was that the Emperor was indifferent to his mother's reactions, as to those of almost everybody. He had, after dismissing Bismark, proclaimed that he was the embodiment of the State, and as such, his will must be unquestioningly obeyed. His mother and his sister were not exceptions to this doctrine.

The death of Field Marshal Count Karl von Moltke, military strategist of the wars against Austria and France, evokes a sincere panegyric.

'We have just heard of old Field Marshal Moltke's death. Poor dear old gentleman, he has had a happy and respected old age, without illness, and has died from a seizure of the heart. He was a *most wonderful* man, and your beloved Papa was quite devoted to him, and always thought his opinion on strategic matters better than anyone else's in the world, *even* at his *great* age, because his head had remained so wonderfully clear, and his brain seemed to work on with the regularity and precision of a well-ordered and balanced machine. He was a *just* man, free from vanity, ambition, spite or jealousy, simple and upright, caring very little for all the fuss made over him. Alas, Alas, William consulted him very little or not at all in these last three years. Moltke is a *great* loss. I hope you will not forget him.'

It is mid-April, and Princess Sophie writes once more of the delights of the Greek spring, and of how attractive Athens might be made were fresh water available for gardens.

'How charming to hear you speak of green fields and high corn, and flowers and all the beauties of early summer. Here nothing has come out yet. Yes, indeed if Athens had only water in plenty it might be made as delightfully green and pleasant as Nice or Cannes or Florence, and trees might be planted in quantities. What a pity that a company with foreign capital could not do it at first, and then the Greek State buy the waterworks whenever they have the money to spare. Berlin waterworks were made by an English company and then bought by the town. When one has not the money oneself it is a great advantage to let foreign capital work for one.'

The Empress tries to find an appointment for one of her numerous *protégés*.

'Do you think that Athens would be a place for a *good* master of music, leader of orchestra and master of organ and pianoforte? Is there any place one could give such a man? For instance, to begin to form a School of Music, to teach instrumental and vocal music — choir and orchestra — and have a regular "Conservatoire"? Would the town of Athens, or the Government, or a large society of amateurs *found* such an institution? Greek composers would be sure to spring up from such a school — music in general and singing in particular would spread in Greece ...there must be countless young people anxious to learn piano, violin, violoncello, etc. who have not yet the opportunity. Good concerts would be sure to pay, I should think. Perhaps your dear Mama-in-Law might like to see such a thing started.'

With thoughts of the coming summer, which in Athens can be sub-tropical, the Empress writes, '*You,* my precious child, *ought not* to remain *all* through the greatest heat in Greece. You ought to have fresh air, mountain air.... *Your* health must not suffer from Wm's caprice.' Then when Sophie announces her intention of visiting Western Europe, but wonders whether her brother's ban will prevent her coming to Homberg, the Empress is 'enraged and furious', and threatens that 'if he attempts to prevent my seeing you here, I shall *protest* and make a *row,* and then it will get public...It is really dreadful to think that he fancies he can do *all* and *everything* he likes!' She proposes to write to Caprivi, and goes on bravely: 'I will be quite calm and keep my temper...I will tell you in a few days what happens in the matter. In the meantime, it makes me quite wretched.' A week later she reports:

'I have nothing much to tell you except that Uncle Bertie writes he has seen a certain letter to you which he thinks "pompous, ridiculous and unkind". He thinks all cannot fail to come right. Grandmama writes to me she has received your letter containing William's to you, and is quite shocked. She means to write to him. Alas W. has made some very awful speeches at Bonn and Dusseldorf which are so imprudent that they made my hair stand on end. It is most unfortunate. Charlotte is coming here at Whitsuntide, I wish I could look forward to her coming with unmixed pleasure, but that I cannot, considering that she and Bernhard take the *reverse* view of what *I* do on almost *every* subject, and abuse me right and left behind my back.'

No reassurance comes from Caprivi, or the other intermediaries whom the Empress has tried to persuade to approach William. 'I hardly dare to propose to you to come *here,* as I really *cannot* take the responsibility of saying *what* he might not do.' She suggests meeting at 'St. Moritz, or one of the surrounding places which are not quite so expensive'.

But in the end, the Crown Prince and Princess risk everything and come to Heidelberg. Prince Constantine visits the Empress first, then Sophie and the baby follow, and they stay undisturbed with her for several weeks. It is possible that the Emperor was deterred from ill-disposed action because he did not want to risk prejudicing the success of his first State visit to London. While he and his Empress were receiving a public welcome there, the Empress Frederick enjoyed a spell of contentment, especially over the company of the baby, until her visitors left on July 7th.

'Oh, this parting is really too dreadful. I thought my heart would break last night, and have not slept one wink. I am thinking of you continually in the train. I don't dare to go into the nursery, silent without that sweet baby. It used to be my joy to see the angelic little thing in his little blue flannel crawling on the carpet as far as he could and showing his little fat arms and lovely little neck, those sturdy round legs and those little pink toes. I was never tired of watching all his pretty ways, his bright merry eyes sparkling with pleasure and intelligence, and his two bewitching little dimples, and the struggles to get on his little legs...11 o'clock, you must be just leaving Munich. I hope you had a pleasant rest there. I am sure sweet Baby was glad to get out of the train and get washed and crawl a little bit. I can fancy my sweet Sophie walking in the streets of Munich in her dainty yachting costume and Tino looking most dear in his grey suit and Goldman hat, his hair fresh cut and a cigarette in his mouth.'

Sophie sends her telegram of arrival, and the Empress pictures her at Tatoi, 'dining under the large poplar trees, with the wind rustling the dry leaves. It is a great comfort to have been to the place and to be able to see it all in one's thoughts. Here at Romberg, the young moon has been so lovely and bright these last two evenings. I am sure it has shone down on Tatoi from your bright heavens in full beauty, and that we were gazing at it at the same time as you were.'

In letters that follow, her mind is still on Tatoi and Manolada.

'I am indeed so glad you enjoy dear Tatoi so much and are feeling that it does you good. The hours of meals that the dear King insists on must be a great trial, as luncheon at 11 and dinner at 3 completely spoil one's day and one's appetite. I pity you that! What a relief that Tatoi is not so hot as last year and that you have had a bathe in the lovely blue sea. Two bathes a week are not too much, they will strengthen and refresh you and do you good. You should learn to swim, I am sure there is *someone* who could teach you.

'I think so often of Manolada. You might build a house there later and lay out gardens and a kitchen-garden, orchard and flower garden, and set up a cow-house, dairy and laundry. Perhaps Tino could sell a little land to the railway that would bring money to begin to build and lay out roads, etc. What an interest and pleasure it would be to you and how delighted the people in the country would be to have you there.'

She devotes almost a whole letter to another suggestion for Prince Constantine.

'It is a pity a large *pottery* is not started near Athens, so that you might have *all* shapes and sizes of vases and jugs and pots of brilliant colours *cheap,* and also tiles for the walls and floors. ... I am *sure* it would *pay,* and then washing basins and baths, etc., would not be so scarce. A drawing and modelling school has of course to be attached to such an establishment, and it wants a chemical laboratory for trying the *colours* and the g*laze,* etc., and also an artistic director.

'What a thing it would be for Greece if Tino got such a thing started somewhere where the clay is found, perhaps near Manolada! It wants *no* engines, no machinery, no steam! Only sheds to work in and others to dry the clay, and ovens to bake. The principal thing is that the objects should be cheap, and within reach of everyone. *Tiles* for floors, stoves, walls of houses (inside) and churches are so suited to the country and climate. Do not think me gone mad, but I think it would be so nice and so useful. The Government could give a little subvention at first. One could begin in a very small way and go on increasing as the demand for it becomes greater.'

It is mid-June, and the Empress sends her blessing for the baby's birthday, wondering, 'if you will arrange him a birthday table and a cake with one candle'. And she remembers something. 'I always forget to say that I implore Tino on my knees *not* to tumble and shake and lift Baby about *too much.* It is rather dangerous with little children, as any jerk or slight wrench *may* give them...an injury for life.' She then details all the possible consequences of careless handling and explains exactly how the baby should be held. She recalls that 'This day last year we left England on our way to Greece', and continues:

'Oh, dear, when I think of our arrival at Gibraltar, my joy and yet my terror and anxiety when I heard of baby's birth, and thought you might not have everything you wanted and all the comforts I wanted you to have. What a state of mind I was in! What impatience to get on! What fears lest my child might not be doing well on account of the heat. My fright lest the doctor might not have been the right one, good or skilful enough. I shall be eternally grateful to Frau E. that she took such good care of you. Pray tell her so.'

During the recent visit of the Crown Prince and Princess to Homberg, the Marshal or Lord Chamberlain of the Empress's Household, Baron Hugo von Reischach, had done everything in his power to make their stay agreeable. Now comes his reward.

'...I spied your letter on the breakfast table upstairs, my precious Sophie, as soon as I came into the room. Hot with riding as I was, I made a dash for it, as you may fancy. Mossy instantly plunged into hers, and there we sat, both with the coffee and the omelette getting cold. 1,000 thanks and kisses for your dear letter and the pleasure it gave me.

'I received the big one with Tino's official letters conferring the decoration on Reischach...thank Tino so much. I am so glad that my Hofmarschall's first Grand Cordon is the Greek one, and I shall feel quite proud when he puts it on over the much-loved *Garde du Corps* uniform on great occasions...I gave it him myself, and in Tino's name. He was exceedingly pleased and touched and grateful.'

The Empress is in weekly correspondence with her mother. Queen Victoria, to whom she usually writes less on domestic affairs than on political. But Sophie and her family are not forgotten. 'Grandmama writes enchanted about the photos I sent her, and said "He must be a beautiful child!" In every letter. Dear Grandmama writes how anxious she is you should pay her a visit next year. Who knows, perhaps you will be able to do so.'

Visitors to Homberg keep the Empress well occupied. 'There are many of my English friends and acquaintances here now, but as I do not go down to the *Kurgarten* during the season, I see only those that I ask for luncheon or supper, or who specially come and see me.' But many do make a special journey to call on her, and in addition there is a constant flow of her numerous relatives, close and remote. One of these is the famous old Duke of Cambridge, cousin of Queen Victoria. 'Uncle George came up to pay me a visit today and was rather depressed, he talked about having arranged his grave at Kensal Green Cemetery in London, and of having built himself a little mausoleum, etc. Otherwise I thought him looking well.' [*The tomb is still there today — Ed.*]

Another visitor was the Empress's niece, Victoria, eldest daughter of Princess Alice of Hesse and wife of Prince Louis of Battenberg. 'Victoria Battenberg has been here for two days, with her two dear little girls and looks well. She is so amiable and pleasant to have with one, so full of spirits and "go". Little Alice is quite lovely. The tiny one is very pretty too.' She is deeply impressed by the beauty of Alice, who is destined years later to marry Prince Constantine's brother, Andrew, and become the mother of the Duke of Edinburgh of today. '...one can hardly take one's eyes off little Alice's face, it is so interesting and picturesque. If she remains so, she will be one of the prettiest girls in Europe.'

The Prince of Wales also comes to see her. 'Dear Uncle Bertie looks quite well, and seems in good spirits, he asks so much after you and Tino and baby...We have not talked much about Willy's visit to England. Uncle is so kind and knows how it irritates me to think of it all, so he says nothing.' Her brother stays several weeks at Romberg, and the Empress draws comfort from his company. When the time comes for him to go, 'Tomorrow dear Uncle Bertie goes, alas, which makes me quite melancholy, as I do so enjoy having little glimpses of him from time to time. His kindness is so great to me who am so utterly neglected by others who owe me at least gratitude even if they cannot give me affection.'

Occasionally comes a visitor whom she does not welcome, such as Bismark's son, Herbert.

'Princess Bismark is here and I shall invite her tomorrow and be obliged to ask her son H. to dinner, which is a bitter pill to me. His behaviour towards Papa and me passed all bounds, and to have to be even superficially civil to such a person is "gall and wormwood" to me, and I feel a hypocrite all the time. I cannot avoid asking him, as he is staying with his mother, and they have both written their names down in my book.'

The Empress is becoming worried over Victoria, who is dieting for her figure, and also fretting at her husband's absences on prolonged army manoeuvres. The doctor considers 'she does not eat enough or have the right things. One cannot persuade her, you know, to live off that foolish regimen. She still refrains from milk, sugar, butter, bread and sweets. Please do not tell her I wrote this, as it will only make her worse....' But a week later she notes that,

'Vicky was mighty delighted because Adolf rode over from his quarters for two hours. The manoeuvres seem hard this year, and unnecessarily long, longer than they have ever been, quite exhausting for officers, men and horses, and a trial to the wives and families. It was never like this before.'

The two girls went on their horses to watch a phase of the manoeuvres, but the Empress would not accompany them.

'I dearly love a ride, and especially a good scamper over a stubble field, but I can never again appear on horseback where there are troops, it would be too painful to me. The army beloved Papa loved so much, served in so long, led in battle so many times, of which he was the head for three short months, I cannot bear to see belonging to another who has so little acted as a son. It is a bitter feeling but I cannot help it.

Princess Victoria was not left alone for long: 'You will have heard from Mossy about Adolf's accident. It might have been very bad, the horse fell upon him on the pavement of the village street, broke the stirrup and crushed his foot very much. Now he has to be up on the sofa and have it bandaged, etc.... Vicky is delighted to have him home.'

Princess Sophie writes about the progress being made on her official house, and her mother replies:

'I think Z's idea of building a ballroom detached from the house is a very good one. You will find it a grand convenience. Only a passage and cloakroom must not be forgotten, with a little room for ladies to retire and arrange their toilettes. And how about the supper room, for the buffet? It would be nice to have it next door to the ballroom or you would always have to pitch a tent each time. Of course you will have electric light without any trouble as it is already in the town, which is a great advantage, both for cleanliness and purity of air. I am sure you will think it fun arranging your own house.'

The Empress expounds lengthily on the risks to health from insanitary conditions of living. She explains how to guard against tuberculosis, and continues: 'Typhus, diphtheria and cholera are propagated by standing water, bad sewers, imperfect drains and a careless arrangement of the W.C. That is why I am always so anxious these things should be in perfect order.' She explains fully how the sinks and lavatories should be constructed with air-tight jointings, external vents, adequate flow of water and so on. 'If I were you, I should inquire into these details in your new house, and see that they are properly carried out. You should get the English journal, "The Builder", as well as "The Gardeners' Chronicle" and "Agricultural Gazette". I am very much interested in all building, engineering and gardening work, also in agriculture. To many people it is a hideous bore, I know.'

She explains how she is embodying all these sanitary precautions at Friedrichshof and describes the progress being made. '...the park and little garden are quite finished now, and look very nice. I went up on the top of the tower for the first time, and saw the view, which is really lovely, so extensive....'

'I am very busy now about the electric light', she adds, and describes a visit to an Exhibition of Electricity, where her interest is intrigued by the then new notion of power transmission. 'I hope to be spared the necessity of having an engine-house of my own, which would be a very disagreeable expense.' Soon she writes:

'Yesterday I had a great discussion at Friedrichshof on the lighting of the place by electricity. The head electrician of the Exhibition at Frankfort, came to explain that a great central electric station at Bockenheim is going to be established and that they could transmit the electric power from there by means of a cable, which as now proved can carry the current to a considerable distance. This would of course be of great convenience and one would pay for the light in the same way as one pays for the water. It would have interested Tino very much, I am sure. Tatoi could be lit from Athens, according to the same system.'

During September came two close bereavements. Prince Constantine's young sister, Alix, the Grand Duchess Paul, then expecting her second child, was taken ill while visiting a remote country property in Russia, where only a village midwife was on hand. The child was born, but the mother died. At the news the Empress wrote:

'Oh, how dreadful is this! ...The thought of the King wrings my heart. How he doted on his child. How all Athens loved and adored her. Sweet lovely young thing, so good, so pure, like an Angel. *You* have lost a sweet sister and friend, my darling Sophie. ...May God console the afflicted ones. My thoughts and prayers and tears are with them. I know my own misery when my sweet sister Alice was snatched from us, and I not allowed to go to her and attend her myself. She was to me what Mossy is to you, when we were girls we were always together. Such wrenches are quite terrible and one never finds the world what it was before.'

'Who will look after the sweet little babies?' she asks. 'Oh, what a sad Christmas this will be for all the dear ones, what melancholy will hang over Athens and dear Greece. That sweet young flower! Gone! Oh, how uncertain is life, and how jealously one clings in fear and trembling to those one loves.'

The Grand Duchess is buried in St. Petersburg and the King and Queen attend the funeral. The Empress feels they will need some memorial to their daughter in Greece. 'Once, your parents-in-law intended building a little church near that pretty spot from which one overlooks the house at Tatoi. I am sure they will carry out that plan now in memory of darling Alix, When the time comes, if it should come, I must send something to put into it as a remembrance.' In course of time the chapel was built, and around it, in what became a family cemetery, were later buried the members of the Royal House.

The Empress's second bereavement was in Germany, for Prince Adolf's sister also died after a brief illness following her confinement. Again sympathy reaches out to the stricken husband and parents, and to Adolf, who is greatly distressed. 'How amazing', reflects the Empress, 'that both my sons-in-law should lose their sisters in confinements at the same time.'

During the past few months, although the Empress was scarcely aware of it, the ill-feeling between her and her eldest children had begun gradually to lessen. The change was partly in them and partly in her. It had shown itself even in January, when she had written that the Emperor's arrogance over Sophie's change of religion '...makes me quite furious, and yet I am obliged to laugh'. That she could laugh at him was a big step towards an easier relationship.

The Emperor still held aloof, but in September visits were paid to her which showed an improving spirit. In her letters to Sophie, pride forbids her to enlarge on her feelings, but in oblique ways she exposes her pleasure, and her readiness to respond at the first advance. At this time, the Emperor and his brother were experimenting with beards.

'Charlotte and Bernhard were here for a night and the best part of two days. Dona came yesterday. She was very grand and stiff and cold and condescending at first, but became much nicer afterwards. Perhaps it was also partly shyness. William has never thought of coming near me. This is my third summer here, but he has never paid me a visit. Henry comes on Tuesday. His beard does not improve him. Sisters think it does, but Dona also thinks it suits both brothers very badly.'

A fortnight later however, William did pay her a visit. Unfortunately, there is no letter to describe what passed between mother and son at this first comparatively friendly encounter for many years. After he had gone the Empress wrote:

The Empress with princesses Victoria and Margaret, and standing, Sophie with crown prince Constantine.

The Darmstadt Group

Taken at the Hesse-Edinburgh wedding in 1894: includes the following, frequently mentioned in the Letters:

Seated: Emperor William, Queen Victoria, Empress Frederick.

Standing, First Row: Tsar Nicholas (Nicky), Tsarina (Alicky), Princess Louis of Battenberg (Victoria), Princess Henry of Prussia (Irene), Duchess of Connaught (Louischen), Duchess of Edinburgh (Aunt Marie).

Second Row includes: Prince Alfred of Edinburgh, Prince of Wales (Bertie), Princess Henry of Battenberg (Aunt Beatrice), Princess of Hohenlohe-Langenburg (Sandra), Princess Bernhard of Saxe-Meiningen (Charlotte).

Third and Fourth Rows include: Prince Henry of Battenberg (Liko), King Carol I of Rumania, Crown Prince Ferdinand, Grand Duke Serge, Crown Princess Ferdinand (Missy), Grand Duchess Serge (Ella), Duke of Connaught (Uncle Arthur), Duke of Edinburgh (Uncle Alfred).

Kneeling: Princesses Beatrice and Feodora.

'I thought you might like to have one line to hear that everything went off all right yesterday except that I had a nervous headache, which made everything feel doubly irksome to me. At nine last night W. left in his railway train (of I don't know how many carriages) and Henry and Irene went as far as Bockenheim. Wm. had skimmed through the electric exhibition in the morning at Frankfort. The beard does not become him badly, but he has grown so fat and heavy, and has much less colour in his face than he ought to have. He seemed to admire Friedrichshof's situation, grounds, house, view and everything, only of course it was only a superficial visit.'

The Emperor, in writing to Queen Victoria, said far more about the house than about his mother. 'This autumn. Mama showed me her new house at Cronberg, which is a marvel of good taste and arrangement. The extensive grounds are laid out with great skill, and show what an excellent landscape gardener she is. I think the whole property is the most delightful site imaginable, and Mama very much to be envied.' [Quoted in the Kaiser's *My Early Life*— Ed.]

It was now October, and for some time the Empress had been in doubt about where to spend the winter months. She was torn between reluctance to leave Victoria, who was 'so unhappy as there are no signs yet of her having a baby . . .', and the design of visiting either Sophie or Queen Victoria. In August she had written:

'Of course if I can manage it, I will come to you, but I must also see my own dear Mama, who I cannot forget is no longer young, and also that you are at the two opposite corners of Europe. Still, I will try and make it all fit in if I can, and hope Reischach will say there are no financial difficulties, for you know that has to be considered also.'

In the end her hopes came to nothing and so she proposes to spend a month at Trento, in the Italian Tyrol. But Princess Margaret, who still clung to her girlish attachment for the unresponsive Prince Max of Baden, prefers the Berlin social life in which he moved. She had already written to Sophie about her unexciting existence at the Schloss Homberg, and her disinclination to go abroad. Sophie sympathizes, at which her mother is stung to protest.

'I am not at all angry with you about what you say about Mossy going with me. From a distance however, my own Fozzie, you cannot judge of our arrangements. I cannot go back to Berlin direct now, as I cannot be exposed to discussions as to whether or not I am to pay visits to Friedrichskron while the Court are there. It would be expected, and I cannot and will not do it. So it is best to avoid it. Mossy will have a time to amuse herself...you need not fear that her wishes and tastes are not consulted. She is really not much to be pitied for having to stay under her Mama's roof and share her life. When she is once married, she will, like you, be free from her tiresome Mama, who is such a bore and so dull, and likes the "hideous mountains" and enjoys seeing "ugly countries" such as the Alps, and "tiresome towns" such as Rome and Venice and Naples, where according to my Sophie's judgement there is nothing to see.'

When the Trento visit is decided, Sophie returns to Margaret's support, but the Empress points out that:

'It will be charming in the Tyrol, I am sure. What you are pleased to call a "rotten" journey will be a treat, but of course if dear Mossy is set against everything and told that it is cruel and a bore, etc., she will end by thinking that she is a martyr when she goes on a trip with her Mama. This does not make it very pleasant for me, nor is it the way to be unselfish. If darling Papa had lived she would be the centre and the pet of a brilliant Court. This we cannot help, and the sorrow which has fallen upon me and robbed me of everything has of course cast a gloom over the life of my darling girls, and most on Mossy's because she is alone with me. But please God there are many bright days in store for her, and in my house there are always many people coming and going, and I think she can hardly complain of being dull.'

The journey starts next day, and from Munich the Empress writes: 'The "rotten" journey has begun, till now it has been full of interest, and our Mossy in good spirits. How Tino would love the beer here.... Give him my love.' But from the next stop, at Innsbruck, she has again to expostulate over Sophie's renewed sympathy for Margaret.

'Please, Fozzie darling, do not lament so much about Mossy and me travelling. An autumn trip in one of the loveliest countries in Europe is surely no hardship. It is rather hard for me to be considered such an old bore that Mossy is deeply to be pitied for having to be with me. You have so much influence on our Mossy that you should use it not to set her against my arrangements, and make her dissatisfied, and think herself ill-used, but to encourage her. Everywhere where Max is not and everywhere that you and Vicky can't be with her, she will find dull, and is determined to dislike, this I really cannot help. I do all I can to make her happy.'

Two days later she writes from Trento. 'We are comfortably established here in the Hotel Trento, which is clean and quiet, and the scenery is lovely.'

'We had a beautiful drive yesterday and a most glorious day. I never saw a more beautiful enchanting spot than along the Lake of Caldonazzo. The groves of enormous sweet chestnuts covering the high hills down to the water's edge, and foaming waterfalls sparkling over little mossy stones, all covered with clinging creepers: the rugged alps behind and the snow-covered peaks in the distance: the little lake as clear as crystal: the country so fertile and the villages so picturesque, the grass so emerald green: the contrast between the rugged giant peaks and this garden below, buried in vines, flowers in every corner, apples, pears and plum trees, is so striking and lovely. I am never tired of gazing and thinking how fair some parts of this earth are, and others how dreary and ugly.'

A week later, she has almost settled into a routine:

'...The evenings here are so beautiful when the sun is going down and the blue twilight creeps up the hills, and the moon rises. I always feel so sorry to come indoors and yet it gets so cold and chilly. I enjoy the hour by the lamp and fireside between tea and dinner which I spend with adored Mossy. She either plays the piano, and I reading, or she writing to you, or her journal or some other letter, while I write my letters. To see her sweet face each time I look up is a joy to me...'

But although the Empress is content in her peaceful corner, her thoughts are always with Sophie and the baby, whose progress she notes approvingly. 'I am so glad to hear that dear baby can walk with anybody holding him by the hand', and a few weeks afterwards, 'What good news that sweet baby can cross the room alone'. But she is anxious when babyhood ills arrive.

'Darling Fozzie, I am so distressed to hear that sweet baby has not been quite well, poor dear little man. It fidgets and worries one to death when anything is the matter. What I went through when you had bronchitis as a baby I shall not forget, nor with Henry who had an inflammation of the lungs, and my own sweet Waldie the cramp so badly. Oh dear, I was driven nearly wild, because after having lost my Sigie [*Prince Sigismund — Ed.*] I remained so nervous and frightened and did not like to show it to dear Papa, who was always even more nervous than I was. But the climate of Athens, thank God, is far, far better for children than that of Berlin, which is downright dangerous in winter for little things. I hope your little pet is all right again now and that you are quite easy about him.'

Periodically she asks Sophie whether she feels well, and urges her to look after her health and take exercise.

'I am so glad you like swimming now. Perhaps you will like riding again too some day, and get all your nerve back. It comes and goes in an unaccountable manner and is purely physical. You ought to begin again with a very small horse or pony, a quiet safe animal, and all your confidence would come back again quite naturally.'

Sophie explains that she does feel well and does take exercise, but the Empress writes, 'I am indeed glad to hear that you are feeling so much better and stronger, but I don't call an hour a long walk. ... I hope that you will feel strong enough soon not to find two hours too long to take exercise. I hope you will go up and down the Lycabettus without fatigue.' The Lycabettus is a steep cone-shaped hill, 950 feet high, in the centre of Athens, a good climb at even a leisurely pace.

The Empress thankfully notes the anniversary of Sophie's wedding.

'These lines are to wish you joy on your dear wedding day. May God bless and protect you both, dear ones, and your sweet baby. You are all three the joy of your Mama's heart. I can see my Fozzie now, in the Cathedral, standing with her white train and gown and wreath, with her taper in her hand, looking such a sweet, and what an agony it was for me to part from my child, and yet how happy and thankful I was to think that she would have such a dear husband as Tino, and now you have your little darling to rejoice over.'

Her mind is always on the alert to help and advise her daughter and son-in-law in both their home life and their official responsibilities. She recommends more informative books to Tino, such as the three volumes of Talleyrand Memoirs, and heavy tomes on the Jewish problem, 'an important and dangerous question which is treated (especially by Germans) in a most prejudicial way. I think it cannot fail to interest Tino, though perhaps not the sort of reading for you'. She sends copies of useful journals such as the Lancet 'because they contain a resume of some of the interesting lectures held at the Congress of Hygiene'. For Sophie she sends 'a little paper on art work at home. ... If you find it a bore my sending these things, pray say so. I only think it might be agreeable if I called your attention to anything which seems remarkable.'

She again urges them to widen their friendships.

'I am sorry you do not form a circle of acquaintances at Athens with whom to keep up more or less intercourse. Often you would hear something new and interesting. One's intelligence goes to sleep and one has no chance of increasing one's knowledge or developing one's own opinions, if one does not come in contact now and then with the outer world, though life *en famille* must remain the principal thing. I think in our way of life. Princes and Princesses ought to be in contact with men of culture and intelligence. It also gives an influence which may be greatly for good, especially in Tino's and your case. For me, an old thing whose work has stopped, it is no longer necessary, but as long as beloved Papa lived I strove to bring all those who one could learn from in any way in contact with him, and I think it was good and useful, and increased the sphere of his interests. But even now, I like the old friends of former days to come and see me now and then, and in all matters of charity and art and science, I try to continue active. One may do a little wee bit of good here and there in a humble way to help one's fellow-creatures.'

At the beginning of November, the interest of the Letters suddenly switched from Greece to England, for the Prince of Wales's second son, Prince George, went down with typhoid fever while Princess Alexandra was on a visit to her parents in Denmark. On November 21st, the Empress writes: 'Thank God dearest Georgie is doing well, comparatively speaking, but of course it is still very anxious work. Poor Auntie Alix is travelling back day and night...' A week later, the crisis is over. 'We hear dear George is well under the circumstances, and was delighted to see his Mama....' In these letters, the Empress mentions that 'Mary and May of Teck have been staying with Grandmama and she praises them so much.' Mary is Queen Victoria's cousin, the Duchess of Teck, and her daughter May is destined to become Queen Mary. The Empress extends her stay at Trento until her birthday has passed.

'I purposely avoid spending my birthday at Berlin. I should have to give a dinner or go to one, which are equally disagreeable to me, and receive congratulations from people who do not wish me well and whose faces I am glad not to see, though many would be really and sincerely kind and sympathizing. Last year, dear Vicky's wedding helped me over the day, but this year would have been too sad....'

Soon preparations are in hand for the return to Germany. 'We are packing our things now, but do not travel tomorrow so as not to give our servants trouble on Sundays.' Once more the Empress takes exception to Sophie's poor view of the holiday.

'My Sophie, what you persist in calling a "rotten" journey (not a very pretty word) is now coming to an end. It has been a rest, and has done Mossy good. The fine mountain air makes me sleep better and feel stronger, that was why I came. I think you might realize that I am no longer quite young, and after the shocks I have sustained, must do what is good for me. For darling Mossy's sake I am now going to Berlin, where you well know I live in a sort of imprisonment, without air or exercise to speak of, and where my position is most painful and difficult....'

Back in the capital, at the beginning of December, 'Mossy is of course delighted to be here, and arranges her things and potters about in her rooms.' But the Empress is depressed, and her feelings are not helped by the prevailing conditions. 'Berlin is not in cheerful mood ...there is so much distress this year among the lower classes, and also in the middle classes, who have lost so much money in Argentine and Chile, and now with the failure of the banks. The times are sad, and the influenza is raging, and the thoughts of war strike terror in every one.'

Then after a short period of alarm at the news that King George had suffered a mild attack of small-pox, which spurs the Empress to a stream of letters on the precautions that Sophie must take, including vaccination, isolation, and a thorough disinfecting of the King's rooms, the Letters reflect a more cheerful note from England, the engagement of Princess May to Prince Albert.

'We are much excited and delighted at the happy event of May Teck's engagement to dear Eddy. May he be very happy, he so fully deserves it. Aunt Mary Teck will be in the 7th heaven, for years and years it has been her ardent wish, and she has thought of nothing else. What a marriage, and what a position for her daughter! I hope you and Tino will go to the wedding in England.'

In the letters that follow there is frequent reference to the coming event. 'Grandmama writes that Eddy's wedding is to be early in March, but she says nothing about our being invited.' Her doubts are soon resolved. 'Dear Grandmama writes to me today that Eddy's wedding will be on the 27th February, and that she wants me to come, and hopes you and Tino will come too.'

For Queen Victoria and the Prince and Princess of Wales, December closes promisingly. 'Thank God, Georgie is recovering and they seem very happy at Marlborough House, and the engagement of Eddy is a great source of satisfaction.' And for the Empress too, the year ends on an unaccustomed note of gratification. On Christmas Day, William and Augusta come to her for luncheon.

'...and I had some presents from them. Willy tried to give me pleasure by arranging that the old Burg at Cronberg [*which adjoined the Friedrichshof estate — Ed.*] should pass into my hands and become my property. I had tried to arrange this with the authorities, but difficulties were made, and I gave it up as I did not like the bother and annoyance and it was not worth while. I told William in the autumn that I much regretted this, and now he has arranged this as a Xmas gift for me, at which I am of course much pleased. It is an object of no earthly use or value to the State or indeed to any one, but for me it is very agreeable to prevent its being turned into a restaurant, and in time, in later years, I might even do it up a little. [*She completely restored it — Ed.*] Anyhow I was glad that for the first time William tried to give me pleasure, which of course makes me value the thing much more.'

Chapter Four – The Letters, 1892

During the opening weeks of the New Year, the most exciting topic of correspondence is the prospect of a meeting at the approaching wedding in England.

'Your dear letter of the 1st has just arrived and I am so very overjoyed that you will most likely go to England that I really do not know what to do with myself. ... As Uncle Bertie, Aunt Alix and cousins came to your wedding at Athens, it is only right and fair you should both go to Eddy's. About baby, I shall certainly tell Grandmama, if you are not afraid of bringing the little angel at that time of the year. About your going to Buckingham Palace or Marlborough House, there will be heaps of time to arrange that.'

But a capricious Fate now intervenes, for Prince Albert is taken ill at Sandringham, where his fiancée and the Duchess of Teck are staying during the celebration of his birthday. On the 13th, his condition has become dangerous, and the Empress writes:

'Now we are in fresh anxiety about darling Eddy. He seems to have caught a chill at the funeral of poor Victor Hohenlohe. He has the influenza, which developed into an inflammation of the lungs. All this I only learnt yesterday, but I had a line this morning from Grandmama saying his doctor was not uneasy. I trust all will go well. Poor Uncle and Auntie have had such many trials and so much anxiety lately. I think this will not make any difference about the wedding, and that Eddy will be quite well and strong again before then...Whilst I am writing, a telegram comes from Grandmama saying they are still very anxious about Eddy and the news is not so good from Sandringham this morning. It worries and torments me very much. Poor Eddy, I do trust he will pull through all right. It is so dreadful to be constantly cast from one anxiety into another, dreading and fearing what may come, trembling for those one loves. Such is Life, such is its uncertainty, and we are weak and helpless creatures.'

Prince Albert expired the following day. The Empress writes that evening, and the next morning:

'...Our sweet darling Eddy. That dear boy, so gentle good and affectionate, so dear to his parents, how truly awful this is! For our family and our nation it is a great blow, I cannot tell you how deeply I feel it. To think that dear Uncle Bertie's kind home should have to suffer such agony, and sweet Aunt Alix to be sorely tried. Oh, this horrid influenza, how many people old and young it has carried off. The poor young bride! What a terrible ending to her short happiness and to all her bright hopes. My poor Mama! She dotes on Eddy, he is her favourite grandson. Coming so close after Georgie's illness, it is too terrible. I wanted to go off directly, but Grandmama says I had better wait and come later.'

'I could not finish last night. I was so bewildered and had such a headache with crying, and had so many telegrams to write. My thoughts are always at Sandringham with those dear ones in their misery, which daily will seem greater to them. At first one is too stunned with the shock to take in all that has happened. It dawns on one in all its true force by degrees. My beloved father was only 40, Auntie Alice and Uncle Leopold [*Duke of Albany — Ed.*] little over 30, and now dear Eddy, 28...No one can help grieving for a dear young man in the flower of his age, born to so great a position, so precious to his family. What a difference for poor Georgie, now suddenly hurled into quite a different position, still weak after a long and serious illness. Eddy had the same doctor and the same nurses, and every care that could be imagined, but the inflammation was too violent...'

The Empress does not attend the funeral. On the 21st she writes:

'Darling Uncle Bertie telegraphed to me yesterday, "Heartfelt thanks for you and your dear girls' sympathy on this terrible day, it has been most trying, but ceremony impressive beyond words. God bless you all. Signed Bertie, Alix." My poor dear Mama telegraphs, "We are well. You know, they would not let me go to the funeral, which I shall never cease regretting."'

Two weeks afterwards, the Empress suffers another loss:

'...While I write I just hear that our dear kind Sir Morell Mackenzie is dead. It is such a shock, he was such a true devoted friend to me, and shared the bitterest and darkest hours of my life. He was so devoted to dear Papa, and never was the same again after dear Papa's death ...the shameful attacks and intrigues against him were too great a strain on him. His health was always delicate. I cannot say how much I feel it. I was much attached to him and thought him a most remarkable and eminent man. I shall find but little sympathy here, where so few people understood him and so many minds were purposely poisoned against him.'

The dashing of the eager expectation of seeing her daughter is a great disappointment, and she tries to work out how they can meet during the spring and summer. Then, after a brief reproach, for Sophie had not always her mother's flair for remembering anniversaries — 'So many thanks for your letter received yesterday. It was written on my wedding day, but I suppose you forgot the day' — the Empress is alarmed in February to learn that her 'precious child' has been taken ill with the dreaded influenza. But she soon begins to recover.

'You cannot think how much it worries and torments me, at such times one feels how terrible it is to be separated by so great a distance. ... I must go to Greece either in spring or autumn, only as I am not going to England, I must see my dear Mama, when she is at Darmstadt. It is now almost a year since I last saw her, and at her age I don't like being so long separated, especially after the sorrows we have now been through, which have tried her so much.'

'Thank God, at last the telegram from Tino says you have no more fever, and yours to Mossy says you are well. Telegrams are blessed inventions. ... I have been trying to do a pastel of our darling Mossy for you, but alas it is very bad and would not succeed, perhaps because I was so anxious that it should, but I shall try again, so you may have what I promised you.'

The Empress's letters to Greece went through the ordinary post, and as she had not yet put aside the wariness born of Bismark's long and close watch on her activities, she still wondered whether her correspondence was not inspected. Her comments on the German political scene were thus rare, brief and cautious, but they did expose her concern at what might befall Germany under a rash and inexperienced ruler advised by men whom, apart from

Caprivi, she did not trust. In February, after the Emperor, in an imprudent speech at Brandenburg, had threatened those who opposed his political notions, she wrote:

'Here matters are most unsatisfactory. I do not like to trust to paper all I think. All I always feared and expected comes true, bit by bit.... Alas, William made a speech which I fear will do harm and make mischief and which was a mistake. You will read it in the papers. We had riots here ... a good many unemployed workmen were hanging about the streets, singing, making a noise and marching up and down, but it was nothing serious ...still, one can never quite tell whether they mean more than one sees. The unemployed are of course hungry and miserable. Potatoes are bad, scarce and dear, bread is dear, socialism is rampant, so it is difficult to distinguish between a common row and disturbances of a more organized and serious kind. To see the people scampering across the Linden, and the police after them with drawn swords, banging away and hitting quite innocent people, was not a pleasurable sight, I assure you.'

Meanwhile, events in Greece were also giving cause for concern. Since 1882, economic and social development had been due chiefly to the constructive work of Tricoupis, the first real statesman that modern Greece had yet produced. His chief opponent, Delyiannis, was a clever jingoist politician, who, now in power, had run the country into debt by mobilizations and other belligerent gestures against the Ottomans. The constitution of Greece gave the sovereign specific power and responsibility to intervene in the political situation when the country's interest so demanded. In the past. King George had known many difficulties over Delyiannis and his reckless policies. Now, to halt the decline into insolvency, the King asserted the Royal prerogative and dismissed him, in spite of his having a majority in the chamber. Such was the situation when the Empress wrote, on March 3rd:

'I am so sorry to hear affairs are in a ticklish state in Greece just now, and that the King has difficulty in forming a new Government. I cannot regret that the Delyiannis Government should leave, but it makes matters rather complicated that they should have had a vote of confidence in the Chamber, and I can understand M. Tricoupis not wishing to undertake the formation of a Cabinet in the face of this vote. I do hope all will go straight and without too much trouble.'

King George had no alternative but to approve of an election. Its issue seemed uncertain, and Delyiannis promised to be intractable if returned to power. The prospects were not pleasant for King George, and the Empress voiced her apprehensions.

'I am so anxious about your affairs in Greece. There is rumour that the King is so sick of it all that he meant to abdicate if Delyiannis manages to get the election in his favour. On my knees I would implore your father-in-law not to do such a thing. If even in a fit of annoyance or despondency, which would only be too natural, he were to think of doing so, it would be such a mistake for everything and everybody, and mar the effect of his long, beneficent and successful reign, so full of sacrifice and patience and abnegation. It would be bad for the dynasty, for the country, for the principle of constitutional monarchy, for stability, and everything! He must not give in! The people look to him, and such a man as Delyiannis is really not worth so serious a step.

'For Tino and you it would be dreadful, as it is so necessary for you to see more of the world and gain more experience before so heavy a responsibility is laid on dear Tino's shoulders. ... It is very presumptuous of me to say this, but you know I am devoted to the King, and attached to Greece. So I may be excused for expressing my opinions so freely.'

The supporters of Delyiannis stage disturbances in the streets of Athens.

'You can imagine how horrified I am that these horrid rows should have done you harm, and that you should have to lie up on the sofa. How very unpleasant the disturbances must have been, and how I feel for the King, please tell him so with my love and say how much I think of him. Delyiannis's behaviour is really outrageous.'

Princess Sophie is impressed by her mother's opinions, or perhaps it is Prince Constantine who recognizes the authentic voice of experience. They feel that the King should know her views. The not ungratified Empress answers: 'Of course, my darling Sophie, I leave it quite to you to show what you like to your dear father-in-law, only in writing to him of course I should have expressed myself more respectfully, you know!'

The elections went against Delyiannis, but for some time there was much tension in the capital. This was unfortunate for the Empress, for she had planned to visit her daughter, but with memories of the unhappy consequences of her mission to Paris, she feared that some malign interpretation might be placed on her presence in Athens during such a crisis. Sophie's protests draw the answer:

'How can you think for a moment it is my wish not to come to you now, whereas it is a dreadful disappointment. But you are quite right in saying that others have spoken to me, they have indeed, and pointed out the difficulties, and said it was most inadvisable. You know I am not so headstrong and obstinate as not to listen to advice when I see that it is sensible and kindly meant. They tell me Caprivi would not like my going to Greece just now, as it might look odd, and as if Germany wanted to demonstrate. My wishes, my heart and my sentiment all say "go", but I *must* say, my reason tells me it would be wiser and better to put it off for a quieter time. How can you call your poor Mama "unkind"? The very thought of your fretting to see us, and longing for us, torments me dreadfully.'

Her further efforts are not successful, and it is clear that she has at long last learned something of the meaning of discretion.

'I have tried my utmost to go to Athens, and God knows with what a heavy heart I have had to abandon it. ... I had even the promise from Grandmama that I should have the "Surprise". Grandmama and Uncle Bertie thought it so natural that I should want to go. You say I should not listen to other advice. My darling Sophie, that is not easy. If I am told that it would not be tactful of me, that the moment is not opportune, that it would meet with opposition here, that it is unwise of me, etc., what could I do? Should anything go wrong, it would then be easy to say, "she would not listen to advice". I do not shirk responsibilities where I alone am concerned, I do not even ask for advice, but in this case I really did not dare push my wish and desire further.'

Concern over events in Greece was suddenly distracted by the grave illness of her dead sister Alice's husband, the Grand Duke Louis of Hesse, her closest and most trusted friend in Germany. A week later he died, and once more she has to write of:

'...this new misfortune to our family. Poor Uncle Louis, so kind and affectionate, so much beloved by us all. Those poor children! Alicky, without Parents and home, Ernie so much too young and inexperienced for his position, poor Victoria who doted on her father and was his pride and his support. I am glad indeed that they were all together and could help one another in this sorrow. I hear my poor Mama is overwhelmed with grief, she was so particularly fond of Uncle Louis, doubly so for poor Alicky's sake.'

She attends the funeral at Darmstadt, and for some time afterwards finds it difficult to return to her normal routine in Berlin, which, in any case, does not often occasion enthusiasm.

'I have a great many people to see...I must give audiences to those who write their names in my book, and those who knew me formerly.... Yesterday evening I gave a dinner to the French Ambassador...I still have got the Turkish, Austrian, Spanish Embassies to see...I have got heaps of appointments for institutions that I must visit this next week, and then I hope and trust the winter's work will be finished. Willy and Dona were here to luncheon. He looks particularly well and bright and merry, in tearing spirits, which really astonished me considering how much reason there is to be serious. She is expecting No. 7 in the autumn. I am glad for her, but how difficult it will be to provide for all these princes someday!'

Time could always be found for welfare organizations such as a convalescent home for mothers — 'How I thought of you when I saw all the mothers sitting in a row with their babies on their laps' — and a childrens' holiday institution. 'Yesterday evening I had to go to a large meeting ... it was suffocatingly hot, but the people were so kind and civil, and received me so well, that I was quite touched and gratified. The undertaking is getting on well. Last year 25,000 children were sent from the different towns of Germany, at the cost of 1 million marks, to the country for a holiday of 4 weeks, and received milk, medicine, baths, etc.'

In spite of her many interests, the Empress still dislikes Berlin, except for the one place of devotion, her husband's tomb at Potsdam.

'...this Berlin, where my life is one of duty and often fatigue, and certainly without a pleasure. I endure it because my Mossy goes out every night now, and seems to like it very much, but it is not unnatural that I shall be glad when this time is over. I suppose Mossy told you we took the Sacrament in the dear Mausoleum. I cannot tell you what a peaceful and comforting impression it made on one, and how glad I was to have this opportunity. I find it hard to tear myself away from that sacred spot.'

Her habit of expanding her letters with questions to draw out lengthy replies prompts Sophie to a comparison to which exception is taken. But this melts into pleasure over her changing artistic taste.

Friedrichshof: The Main Entrance

'I am *much* flattered to be compared to Aunt Louise of Baden! [*the Grand Duchess, sister of the Emperor Frederick — Ed.*] The difference, you see, is that she asks questions because it is a habit and she cannot help it, because it is her way of making conversation, and because she loves meddling in other people's affairs and making herself important. I do not quite think that my reasons are the same! I have a child that is far away and that I love very much, and about whose health I naturally feel very anxious. She is very young and I don't know whether she is always very wise, and at any rate she has not much experience, so for my peace of mind I ask questions....

'Fancy your beginning to like "old things", by that I suppose you mean really good things that are pretty in shape, design and workmanship, and no more made nowadays. What can be so lovely as the things so often found in Greece, the fragments of sculptures and stone and metal and the vases, urns, glass and coins. I am sure you could get together most beautiful things. When I was collecting, you used to call everything "old dirty rubbish" and "nasty old horrors", do you remember? There are very few modern things that one can always admire, still there are some, even of the simplest, that are good in colour and form, and will always please an educated eye. I am very glad to hear that you are longing to see my things again. With what pleasure I shall show them to you. Tino always seemed to me to have a good deal of taste, and Nicky too. ... I inherited my taste from my dear father.'

Pursuing the aim of developing Sophie's artistic judgment the Empress goes to some trouble to find her a present that would be educative. Half-way through April she writes:

Friedrichshof: The Hall

'The picture is on its way to Greece, please do not unpack it, as it is a joint present from us for your birthday. (Of course, unless you specially want to unpack it sooner.) ...the frame I had copied from an English one. I feel that the more you look at the little picture the more you will like it. It was for a long time in my room and I found that I looked at it with growing pleasure instead of getting tired of it, and this is always the best praise for a work of art. Often one is much struck and captivated at first and cares less after a while.'

The picture did not meet with the hoped-for appreciation, but the Empress accepts her setback indulgently. 'I do not think the figure in the drawing is out of proportion, the little lady is supposed to be very tall. The drapery is charming, is it not? The whole composition is restful and full of poetry and the light charming.'

The duty months in Berlin are ending and the Empress looks forward to seeing Friedrichshof. But first she goes to Bonn to stay with Victoria — 'it is a great rest and pleasure to me after Berlin'.

'I write you a few lines on Easter Morning. I own I think this neighbourhood quite charming. We go to Church here (a very ugly one) crowded with people and the sermon very long and most wearisome. How I should love to see baby playing with Christo [*Prince Constantine's youngest brother, Christopher — Ed.*] they should be photographed together. How poor Vicky and

Adolf long for a baby, I see a shadow of sadness pass over their faces when they look at the photo of you and baby. "Oh, how I envy Sophie", says Vicky. But they are very happy together and their little menage is so harmonious and peaceful.'

The stay at Bonn offers an opportunity of doing a little sightseeing along the Rhine.

'Yesterday we had a delightful day ... in the afternoon we made an expedition, crossed the Rhine, which was as rough as the sea, in a sailing boat and went up to the Drachenfels. The view was quite lovely. Then we looked at a large castle, built by some rich man a little lower down the hill, called the Drachenburg. It is a building which would have pleased poor King Louis II of Bavaria. Purporting to be Gothic, not very pure or correct in style but very gorgeous, with good frescoes of mediaeval subjects all over the walls. The Castle is situated in one of the loveliest spots I have seen in Germany. The Rhine winds its way so majestically through the fruitful well-cultivated plain, and at the back are the hills, with pretty valleys.'

The Empress with Queen Victoria

After a week at Bonn, the Empress goes to Homberg, where she at once tackles Friedrichshof. The grounds are nearly completed, but, 'The inside of the house is still very backward and unfinished and I must try and hurry the people a little ...but in general from the outside the house really looks very nice, and inside the light seems excellent, and the heating is satisfactory, and there are no draughts. It will be as dry as a bone, which in this climate is a great thing.'

The Empress wonders whether she can improve her temporary home at Homberg, 'the untidy, ramshackle, tumbledown old Schloss which we are so fond of, in spite of its neglected half-finished and dilapidated state'.

'I hope this year one can make the Schloss at Homberg a little more comfortable, so that when you come (if you do) it may be nicer than last year. But the Crown will hardly spend a penny on the old place, and my money I keep for Friedrichshof, as you will understand.'

An approaching visit by Queen Victoria now absorbs the Empress's attention. The Queen, who had been staying in company with Princess Beatrice and her husband at Hyeres, made the return journey by way of Darmstadt in order to talk to her orphaned grandchildren.

'Tomorrow we go to Darmstadt to see Grandmama', writes the Empress on April 27th. 'I can hardly believe that I am about to see her again after so long a while.' Two days afterwards she describes the visit:

'Yesterday we were at Darmstadt. You can imagine what an emotion it was for me to see my beloved Mama after all that had happened. I found her looking sad and aged, and less able to move about than when I saw her last, but her dear face is not changed, and I found her as fresh and vigorous in mind, as full of interest, as ever. The two blows of darling Eddy and Uncle Louis have been all too much for her, and she is quite weighed down by them. She asked so much after you and with such affection.

'Poor Uncle Bertie and Aunt Alix are still in great grief, I hear. ...Darling Auntie Beatrice and Liko [*Prince and Princess Henry of Battenberg — Ed.*] it was a great pleasure to me to see, they are looking very well.'

Also at Darmstadt was the eldest of the bereaved family, Victoria, of whose girl the Empress again says, 'Her little Alice is, I think, the most beautiful child I almost ever saw.' After a few days the Queen continues the journey to England, and the Empress takes her affectionate leave. Returning home through Frankfort, she calls to see 'Aunt Anna', the widowed Landgravine of Hesse, whose second son, 'Fischy was there, dear boy, I like him so much. He looks rather frail, but I think will grow stronger.' The 24-year-old 'Fischy', otherwise Prince Frederick Charles, was soon to burst importantly into her family affairs.

For several months the Empress has made periodical inquiries about the progress of the new Palace in Athens. Now, Princess Sophie, in doubt over its layout, sends drawings and plans, and seeks advice. In reply go several long letters filled with detailed comments and proposals, extracts from which indicate that the Empress was both practical and far from Victorian in her decorative taste. She suggests:

'...that the doors be of polished wood or prettily painted cream colour, and the other woodwork in the rooms done cream or in pale soft greenish hue, in others pale soft bluish. The walls should be pale yellow stucco or pale grey, or only painted a soft tone. Pictures would look very well hung up on them.

'Marble being cheap and very beautiful in Greece, all that can be made of marble should be. The hall should have a marble floor, and the banisters also, but have as little ornamentation in the shape of figures as possible. I should certainly omit the "angels" and winged griffins of the bannisters, and also the wall painting.'

'Are you going to have a library and a billiard-room which could also be used as a waiting-room in which gentlemen could wait who come to see Tino? In the library he could give his audiences. Upstairs you would only want a boudoir and he a study, and you would not receive people at all on that floor, and keep it quite private to yourselves, for you and baby, and go downstairs for meals. There would be no smell of dinner on your floor, and the servants would not have to go upstairs to clear away. If you give a party, ball or concert, you would have the buffet close at hand in the dining-room. I think it would be doubly nice to have the dining-room and drawing-room opening into the hall, on the same level, as it is at Marlborough House, for instance, where the hall can be used as a drawing-room and for music.'

'The lamps for the electric light are very ugly. You would do best to choose these for yourself, the simplest and prettiest are the English ones. The furnishing is a great expense, but surely need not be done all at once. Not the most expensive things are always the most beautiful and useful. One needs to have seen and compared a great deal to choose and decide wisely. I do not find it easy for myself either.'

'You say nothing about the offices, kitchens, cellars, wood-cellars, larder, store-room, linen-room, china and glass pantry, plate-room, sculleries, kitchen, ironing-room, washing-room, servants' hall, housekeeper's rooms, your wardrobe room. The hotter the climate the more roomy the offices ought to be, as things spoil so fast and servants suffer from the heat. Of stables, coach-houses, etc., you say nothing, and I suppose the drainage and the water supply still depend on the vexed question of the water being brought to Athens and laid on throughout the town.'

Princess Sophie does a tour around some of the Aegean islands, among them Tenos and its famous shrine. In her letter lies a clue to her lack of enthusiasm for indiscriminate travel in Greece. Replying, the Empress refers again to one of her favourite reforms.

'...Your long letter written directly on returning from your trip to the islands. Poor child, to be tormented by the bugs! It is really too bad! I had heard of the island of Tenos, but never of the church nor of a "Madonna" to which the legend is attached of having miraculous properties.... How much I wish you would travel over all Greece. ... I am so glad you are going to begin Greek lessons again. I took the little dictionary you gave me, and tried to learn a few Greek words, but I am too stupid, and cannot remember them.

'I send you for your own and your mama-in-law's study and perusal an account of an American prison and reformatory. It is a very important question, as much so as the question of hospitals and lunatic asylums. Many eminent and excellent men have devoted their energies, their time and money, to rouse the attention of the public to a better understanding of the manner of treating criminals. Every effort of that kind in Greece is sure to be a blessed and beneficial thing.'

For a long time the Empress has made uneasy references to Princess Margaret's unreciprocated liking for Prince Max of Baden, for she seemed to have no eyes for anybody else. Now, unexpectedly, a wooer appears, the previously mentioned Prince Frederick of Hesse, who to complicate matters, is a close friend of Prince Max.

'Our distress and perplexity is great. Poor Fischy seems to have fallen deeply in love with Mossy and has proposed to her, and seems in a dreadful way. What on earth is to be done? We all like Fischy so much that it distresses me dreadfully to think that we are causing him pain. He has not made a formal demarche or asked me, but he came over to luncheon yesterday, and certainly I dreamt of nothing, guessed nothing, and saw nothing, but that he seemed rather absent and cold and a little constrained and stiff in his manner. If I had only had the faintest notion of his feelings I should not have asked the poor boy here, nor have let Mossy go to the Opera at Frankfort. I am quite at my wits' end what to do. I always thought Fischy would want to marry Alicky or one of the Wales cousins. I also imagined he had guessed Mossy's sentiments for Max, as they are such friends. Please speak to Tino and put your two young heads together and think of what can be done, for it is very cruel to Fischy to keep him dangling, and very bad for Mossy to be so anxious and troubled and worried....'

A few days later the love triangle is made easier, for Prince Frederick's sister calls to explain.

'Elizabeth came to see us yesterday, and was most nice...and she told us of course a great deal we did not know. She said her brother was sincerely devoted to Mossy with heart and soul, and that ever since the Ball this winter he had had no other thoughts than her, and to marry her. She told me that with his shy, modest and retiring nature he had never dared to make up to Mossy, he had suffered much, and was quite wrapped up in her, and had spoken to her at the opera the other evening without telling Elizabeth or his mother. It seems he has two confidants in the world, his sister and Max!

'He left Frankfort the other day without our knowledge, and went to Berlin to speak to Max and consult him. On the strength of this and feeling that he was free to try and win her for his own, he spoke to Mossy. Since then the poor boy is in a terrible state of feverish anxiety and uncertainty.

'This alters everything very much. For though Mossy cannot at once change her sentiment, yet she is too sensible a girl and has too much womanly delicacy and pride not to see that a man who feels only as a brother or cousin towards her, is not the one to fix all her affections and hopes in life on for ever. And that it is no use sighing for the moon. The only thing to be done now therefore is not to worry or press her but give her time to consider what is wisest and best...and giving Fischy an opportunity of winning for himself, by his own true love and devotion, an affection in return which thank God may and does spring up in a young girl's heart when she sees another young heart beating for her. There is such a thing as fate! This has all come of itself, it was none of our seeking, it was nobody's planning, there was no interference....'

The following day the Empress takes up the development of the romance.

'We have asked poor dear Fischy to go back ...poor Mossy cannot say yes or no. Fischy, as he loves her so much, will be ready to wait for her, and will understand her hesitation. But she too has suffered and it is not easy for her to realize that her love of three years has only been a dream, and that the hopes of it ever being realized have vanished. May Heaven reward her one day and send her true happiness and a happy home. It is something to be so much loved, in this world many a woman and especially a Princess passes through life without ever knowing what it is to be truly loved, and it would have broken my heart if that had been my Mossy's lot.'

A few days more pass, then the Empress is able to announce with relief that Margaret has made up her mind and said, 'yes'. She notes that the day is May 24th, 'my beloved Mama's birthday, God bless, protect and keep her for many a long year', and then refers to the welcome news that Sophie is proposing to visit her. 'The newspapers say you are going over to England to see Grandmama before coming here to see me. Of course I do not know whether this is true.' For once the newspapers are correct, but Sophie and her husband, after visiting London and Copenhagen, eventually arrive with the baby and stay at Friedrichshof until towards the end of July. The day of parting comes, and the Empress writes:

'My own sweet Sophie, can I believe that you are really gone! It looks the same, the sun is bright, the hills blue, the day fine, but all seems steeped in melancholy and the light and life and interest gone out of the place. My heart aches bitterly, and I thought it would break when I kissed the soft cheek of that beloved little angel. You cannot know, you cannot guess, my Sophie, how dear you are to me, how I dote on your Tino and how I am wrapped up in baby. My poor Mossy came to my bedside from 11-12, still in tears. It was such a comfort and blessing to be all together, and such a joy to see that sweet child, to watch his pretty ways and listen to his dear little talk and gaze at his beloved little face, the bright smile and dimples. I am thankful you have such a little sunbeam to call your own. Oh, what a terrible thought it is that every moment you are being hurried further and further away. But nothing can prevent my thoughts following you...'

At the end of the letter the Empress notes that her maid 'has gone and packed up my silver brushes among your things. I am afraid I must ask for them back, as they belong to a set, and my dear Mama gave them to me.' Two days later, she writes:

'...just as we were sitting down to our little supper under the chestnut tree on a most glorious evening, the young moon rising in a sky still glowing and pink from the setting sun (we are only 4, the 2 Reischachs and Mossy and I) and my heart so heavy, your dear telegram arrived from Brindisi. I can fancy you on board the steamer with pure sea air blowing around you. Poor Mossy has not smiled once since you left.'

Sophie duly reaches Athens. 'The King kindly telegraphed to me yesterday, and said you had both arrived safely.'

On August 1st, the Empress, as always, vigilantly observant of anniversaries, writes: 'First let me wish you joy for your darling Tino's birthday. May every blessing be upon him, health, prosperity, success and long life be his with all possible happiness, this is my fervent wish.' But for once she has made a slip, and her letter the next day begins, 'What a stupid I was! I sent all my good wishes and congratulations for yesterday, and it is today that is your darling Tino's (*our* darling Tino's) birthday. Please excuse this, all of you.' She goes on to mention a visit from her sister and brother-in-law, Princess and Prince Henry, whose Battenberg house had been damaged by fire two days previously:

'Aunt Beatrice and Liko arrived yesterday at 12.30. She was still quite shaken from the frightening fire, which destroyed rooms and part of the roof. It was a most lucky escape. Poor Aunt has lost ever3rthing she had with her, linen, hats, boots and shoes, boxes, shawls, jackets, all gone, also her bracelets and her beautiful pearls, her two watches, and her dressing-bag with silver tops, and all her souvenirs.

'It was in the night and the maid came in with a candle, and Aunt with her elbow pushed the curtain into the flame, the whole bed caught fire in a moment. Aunt had to run from the house in her nightgown and wake the people. Liko was away at the shooting box on the hills some distance off. The firemen from the village and the servants succeeded in putting it out. Aunt's poor maid became quite lightheaded with fright, and talked nonsense, and the next day wanted to jump out of the window.'

Continuing, the Empress refers to the engagement of her niece, Princess Marie, daughter of Alfred, Duke of Edinburgh, to Prince Ferdinand, the heir presumptive of Roumania. Four years previously the Prince had won some unpopularity in his country, as well as in strict regal circles, for engaging himself to one of the maids-of-honour of his aunt. Queen Elizabeth. Public disapproval having broken this romance, Ferdinand was now to marry the young and beautiful Marie.

'Aunt Beatrice is not at all delighted at Missy of Edinburgh's engagement, and thinks about Ferdinand as we all do. Neither my Mama nor Uncle Alfred seem much pleased. It seems Marie was perplexed and did not know what to do. There were different suitors, and this was thought the best way to solve the question. Still my family regret it. Missy is till now quite delighted, but the poor child is so young, how can she guess what is before her...?'

Events in England, where a general election promises the return of a Liberal administration, now excite the Empress's anxiety. She writes, 'Lord Salisbury's government is out, and Mr. Gladstone really coming in. I wonder what sort of a Cabinet he will get together. I pity dear Grandmama, as she is frantic to lose the people in whom she has confidence, and have to take those who she feels will be a great failure and make great mistakes.' The Empress trusts that 'Gladstone's hands will be so tied that he will not be able to introduce the so-called Reforms which would be so hurtful to the country'.

A fortnight afterwards, she sounds both reassuring and disturbing notes. 'I hear from dear Mama that Lord Rosebery will be Foreign Minister after all, which I am glad of, as he is the only one of that Party who is fit for it. I cannot help feeling anxious about the news from Afghanistan, no doubt the Russians thought it a good opportunity to push forward their troops now that the Cabinet has changed in England.'

In Greece also, the political situation once more engages the Empress's attention. The people's vote has again upheld the King, and she writes: 'May all now have a chance of getting straight, i.e., of steady improvement of the financial and material state of the country. I congratulate your Papa-in-law with all my heart, it is a triumph for him, most decidedly. I also wish you joy at dear Tino becoming a general.'

During the absence of his father, who goes to take the waters at Aix-les-Bains, Prince Constantine acts as Regent, and the Empress shows a lively interest in his work and in the new administration.

'I am so sorry Tricoupis is in low spirit, and has found things in such a mess, it is just what one expected of a Delyiannis administration, it must indeed be a very difficult task to *retrench*, and yet not to stop necessary work and necessary progress and development which costs money but also brings money, for instance the water-supply! I am sure it is right to make the students pay something at the university. Indirect taxes bring in most and are least unpopular and least felt by the public....'

'How is darling Tino getting on?' she asks in a later letter.

'Do matters seem to run smooth now, and the Tricoupis administration to go straight? Will Athens have her water supply? What a pretty town it would soon become if there were water everywhere and nice little gardens kept green and the place in front of the Royal Schloss laid down in terraces, steps, walks, flower beds and fountains, and how it would improve the air and keep down the blinding dust. I trust that will be done some day.'

In the course of time, as those who know their Athens of today will be aware, Constitution Square was laid out as the Empress pictured it. Prince Constantine's additional responsibilities as Regent inspire suggestions for his household staff.

'I always think that S. would be such a good Hofmarschall for you both, he is so careful and would carry all details out with great precision, as he does not mind working things out. He would also have the proper authority over the people and has seen a good bit of other Courts now, and has certainly the spirit of order. The great thing is to put no power into the hands of subordinates without proper and constant higher control. It is only tempting them to be dishonest, as they have not the same standards in many matters as a gentleman. I had such opportunities of watching that at the old Emperor William's Court at one time.

'I do not know what my Papa would have done with all his business and correspondence if he had not had G. M. Norman for years. My Mama has three gentlemen for her privy purse and her correspondence, indeed 4...Uncle Bertie has 2...I know you will allow me to say what I think without fancying I want to meddle in your affairs. I am only thinking of Tino's interests and yours, and telling you what management has succeeded the best with us.'

Prince Albert, and her never-fading affection for him, are again recalled a few days later.

'Aug. 26th, my beloved Papa's birthday. What a man that was, or rather what an angel, as good, as wise, as he was clever and beautiful. How I did love him, how I always miss him, and what grief it is to me that none of my children should have known him. What a comfort and support and help he would have been now. How happy we as children used always to be on this day.'

It is mid-August, and once more Homberg fills with visitors. 'There is a Mr. N. here, I wonder if he is any relation to the man who owns your house and asks such a large rent?' The Prince of Wales comes to take the waters, and his son George stays at the Schloss for a few days. 'Dear Uncle Bertie arrived yesterday looking much better and in better spirits. I went down to his house to see him, but he was taking his bath and could not receive us...' 'I try to see Uncle Bertie every day. His cure seems to agree with him ... he has bought all your newest photographs from Voights [*a well-known Homberg photographer — Ed.*] and put them up in his room, baby's and Tino's also of course. Today dear Georgie of Wales has arrived, looking much thinner, but so dear and bright. He is such a darling.'

But as in the year before, there are other visitors whom she does not welcome so eagerly. Her attitude reveals the great change in Prince Bismark's standing with the Berlin Court.

'Yesterday for luncheon I had to invite "Bill" Bismark and his wife, and the Princess (mother). I really could not help it. They wrote their names down and asked to see me. No intimation has ever reached us that the family are not to be received at Court. Of course at Potsdam it will be turned against me, that would not matter so much, as everything always is. I only hope that old Prince B's newspapers will not try to make much of this invitation. I am not a supporter or admirer or partisan of his in *any* way! He has often done me cruel wrong, and all the harm he could, but I should not think of being uncivil to his wife and other son. Herbert I should not again receive, if I could possibly help it, because I have the most utter contempt for him and despise him with all my heart. I think him bad and wicked, and the harm his friendship did to William in every way I hardly think can ever be set right....'

The Empress is alarmed at outbreaks of cholera which have spread across Europe and reached the port of Hamburg. Some of the nurses of her Victoria House hospital volunteer to work there, including one of her *protégées*, a Greek, Elizabeth P. 'I must now tell you', she writes in early September, 'that I seriously had the intention of joining them and going there too, but I have abandoned the idea for several reasons. If I could do any good you can imagine that I would have gone straight away, but I should only have given trouble and caused confusion.'

She urges that precautions should be taken in Athens in case the disease strikes there, and quickly proceeds to the pet project.

'It struck me that the cholera might be a good lever, i.e., a good argument, to use for the government and town of Athens to prepare their canalization and at last bring a water supply to the town. The fear of the horrible illness makes people more willing to spend money in adopting means of prevention, and undoubtedly, providing Athens with a suitable and sufficient water supply is one of the most important sanitary measures to be pushed. I think one ought to lose no time in bringing the idea forward.'

She writes lengthily on the need for an efficient nursing organization, and continues:

'Before I die I hope to have instituted a staff of good monthly nurses for the public as a branch of the "Victoria Haus", but we have not yet got so far. All improvement and progress is very uphill work and there is so much prejudice and ignorance to be overcome. The great thing is to hit on the right people to help one who have not the unfortunate idea that one can learn nothing from foreigners or other countries, and that the greatest patriotism consists in thinking that one knows everything better than everyone else, instead of comparing and studying and finding out in different countries what is done, so as only to choose the best to introduce into one's own country and avoid the mistakes made by others. Do you not think so? I hope you and Tino will send out busy bees into all lands to collect the honey of learning and experience and then store it all in the Hive at Athens.'

A few days on, she again urges that anti-cholera precautions be taken while Prince Constantine is still Regent.

'I am so pleased that Tino has spoken to the police and that attention is going to be paid to the sanitary state of the town of Athens. It is most distressing to think of the country's finances...There are so many rich Greeks in England. Why do you not write a letter and head a subscription list, which could be sent round to Greek ladies living abroad, asking them to contribute towards a sanitary organization at Athens? You want a few carts and wheelbarrows and brooms to take all the rubbish and dust out of the town. You want a few ambulances, stretchers and litters, etc., to carry sick people and also some tents and barracken to put them in...disinfectants...mattresses ...everything ready to meet the first epidemic.'

'Cremation for the dead' she points out, 'would be wise, but that requires to be carried out with great care, and in a manner that does not hurt the feelings of the poor suffering mourners.' As a result of all these promptings. Princess Sophie becomes patroness of a committee of ladies to prepare for the worst.

The improving relations between the Empress and her eldest son were shown in a visit which he paid her in September, for the purpose of discussing Margaret's wedding. A few days earlier, the Empress Augusta had given birth to yet another child, her first daughter, who, to the Empress's pleasure, was soon afterwards named Victoria Louise.

'I am very tired, I had not a moment to myself all day. William arrived at 8 in the morning and left at lo in the evening, and I was on the go the whole time. Down to the station to fetch him. The day was marvellously fine, the air sharp and clear and the sun bright. The people had decorated the town and as it was Sunday there were a good many about. After his bath we had breakfast and looked at dear Papa's monument. Then after luncheon we drove out to Friedrichshof, where they played tennis together, sister, Fischy, William and Reischach. After supper I took W. to the station. He was looking well and in good humour. Seemed delighted about the little girl. Dona is said to be very well.

'All serious subjects, alas, I had to avoid with W. I fear on great questions he is still very far from understanding me, and I should not agree with him. Still, all went off well. About Mossy's wedding...it seems that it would suit them all better if it could be in the second half of January, so for the present, my dear, the wedding day has been chosen so that the fêtes of the wedding and William's birthday will all be in one. This is simpler, more convenient and less expensive for the large Court.'

At the end of September, the Empress sets out, in company with Princess Margaret and her fiancé, for Italy. She does not enlarge on her object, which is to give the two young people a chance to get to know each other better. She writes her first letter from the Hotel Belle Vue at Cadenabbia, on the Lake of Como.

'Here we are in this lovely place, which makes me feel that we are no longer so far from you. There are heavy clouds and shadows hanging about.

Mossy does not like it because it makes her fringe come out of curl, and her feet tired.... This is my dear engagement day, 57 years ago. It seems to me like yesterday, and oh! how sore my heart feels, we were so happy then, dear papa and I.

'We left dear old Homberg on Tuesday evening. Everyone we knew almost came to the railway station to take leave. At Frankfort, Fischy joined us. The passage on the steamer from Como here to Cadenabbia, which lasted almost 2 hours, was too lovely.

It was a gloomy evening, and clouds hung low and the sheet lightning shot across them from time to time, but the lake, villas, gardens, villages were an enchanting scene, buried in flowers and creepers and mingled with steep rocks. The moon struggled with the clouds, and one little light after another came out on the shore, and reflected in the water.'

After a fortnight, the party goes on to Venice, and the Empress writes from the Casa Malcolm.

'Yesterday morning at Milan, the King and Queen and their two nephews paid us a visit at the hotel. It was pitch dark when we arrived here in a gondola. Gliding along in the dark with my Mossy and Fischy, how I thought of your wedding and of the day we spent here when we embarked. How fast time flies, now you have a darling baby! [*Next day.*] Another very fine morning.... This night I was not devoured by the mosquitoes, as I was the night before and also at Milan. We are very comfortable in this dear old Palace. There are so many nice things here to be had in the shops for your house, if a Greek ship were coming here, or a Russian vessel used by one of the Grand Dukes, or a dear English yacht, one could put things on board and save the expense of the carriage, but of that I see no chance at present. We trotted about on the Piazza San Marco yesterday and took a turn in a gondola.'

In the midst of her enjoyment of Venice, there comes on October 18th, the anniversary of her husband's birthday, and her next letter is a lament for him.

'My own darling Sophie, on this day, once so bright and which might have been a national holiday, I must write to you, his little daughter whom he loved so much. Oh, what memories crowd in upon me, how they seem to bear me along with them far away, back to the past. That the present and the future may bring all that is good for my darlings is all I can wish for. For me personally life can bring nothing more, nor lessen all the bitterness and disappointment I feel. I must try to be brave and unselfish but I cannot cease to mourn nor to grieve, nor to long for him who was my first object in life. How I should have loved to have seen him enjoy all the honours, the popularity and affections he so truly deserved, they never could have made him proud or vain, or inconsiderate towards others. He was taken from his country and his work at the very moment when he was most needed and wanted, and when he was most fit for so responsible a position.'

She soon returns to the scenes around her, but no matter how full her pleasure, her thoughts are seldom long away from Sophie.

'I saw a house of which the plan would do very well to be adapted for the castle in the air I am always building called Manolada! Do you remember how often you scolded me last year for bringing Mossy here? Now that is already a year ago and she is almost a happy bride and no more unsettled in her mind ...that is indeed a thing to be thankful for.

'Have you got a little goat-carriage for baby like you used to have when you were young? Or one of those quite tiny donkeys such as those at Naples, no bigger than a large dog, they would drag a little carriage for baby so well. It is such fun for little children....'

She writes approvingly when she learns that another of her suggestions has at last borne fruit.

'I am very glad that you have a Philharmonic Society and that the singing and choruses are being taken up in Greece. I hope someday there will be a school for music and vocal, instrumental, etc., and that you will in time have good concerts, and then the children will be taught to sing in the schools, and in the orphanages, etc., I am sure there must be some very fine voices in Greece, and the choral societies will form of themselves in the towns and villages. It should especially be encouraged in the regiments and among the soldiers. It is really so nice and cheerful for them.'

The Empress passes her days in a succession of outings, sightseeing, shopping and social visits, revelling as always in the freedom she finds everywhere except in Germany. One of these trips is to an old castle in the foothills to the north.

'The view is lovely. The mountains are on one side, the plain on the other, and dear Venice just distinguishable in the distance. The country is all covered with pretty villages, lovely church steeples (campaniles) vineyards, mulberry plantations and green meadows bordered by acacia hedges, and the river Piave, that comes down from the Dolomite mountains, winding along. I should have loved to have painted away.

'Last night was full moon and too glorious for words. After supper we went in the gondola just outside the Grand Canal, and all Venice seemed in a mist of blue and silver reflected in the calm waters, with the lights aglow like a fairyland dream. The boats were full of singers, and we enjoyed the sights and sounds in silence, but most thoroughly. I thought of how the sweet moonlight must be pouring down on the snowy Acropolis, which looks oh, so grand, so weird and so entrancing on a fine night.'

October 27th is the silver wedding of King George and Queen Olga, for which celebrations are held in Athens. For the Greeks in Venice there is a *Te*

Deum in the Orthodox Church, which the Empress attends. But —

'Alas, I have no clothes with me except black, so I shall have to go in black to the service, which I know is not the right thing, but I cannot help it, better I should go in black than not to go at all. ...Please ask your parents-in-law to excuse this breach of etiquette which is involuntary on my part. How well I can imagine the Cathedral at Athens today. My best wishes attend your dear parents-in-law.'

On the return journey to Berlin, a stop of a few hours is made in Vienna 'to give Fischy an opportunity of looking at the beautiful churches and buildings. Mossy sees this place with very different feelings from what she did last year, and would no longer think it a bore!' The Empress's aims in arranging her trip have been achieved, for back in Berlin, 'Sweet Mossy's big eyes filled with tears when she said goodbye to her Fischy. The separation, however, will not be very long.'

She continues: 'We arrived early in the morning. William and Dona came to breakfast. She is certainly not *en beaufe,* oh, dear!'. 'It is rather an extraordinary hour to pay a visit', she comments, when they come again to breakfast a fortnight later.

The Empress's birthday draws near. To her pleasure Princess Sophie has not forgotten: 'How am I to thank you and Tino enough for your lovely present which I found on my writing table yesterday morning. A sweet silver inkstand and candlesticks, which will look beautiful at Friedrichshof. I am so much delighted with it.' But Prince Henry is less considerate, and the Empress writes that she is '...intensely annoyed at Henry saying his shooting would interfere with his coming for my birthday. I think it selfish and ungrateful and am much hurt, as it shows how little I am cared for, that the chance of shooting a stag is put before seeing his mother.' However, when Henry does appear, all her resentment immediately vanishes. 'Henry has just arrived and sends you his best love. He is very anxious to see you again and trusts you will come, both of you, to the wedding. He is looking very well and I am of course delighted to have him. We went over to Potsdam yesterday to the Mausoleum.'

A week later she replies to the letter which Sophie has sent her in response to the 'stag' episode.

'You need not be afraid I should be angry with Henry, I really am not at all, only grieved to think that he should not try to arrange to be with me sometimes during the year, and feel it his duty to look after me a little. Fancy if baby were to grow up and take no notice of you, what would you feel? I know that Henry's heart is not at fault, and that it is thoughtlessness and he does not mean it, but I suffer from it all the same.'

The visit to Potsdam provokes a protest at the 'improvements' being made at Sans Souci.

'How you would grieve if you saw what havoc Eulenburg [*the Emperor's Master of Ceremonies — Ed.*] and Lynken are making of the beautiful Park of Sans Souci. Cutting down large trees that were perfectly healthy, now lying across the paths, being sawn up into pieces. All the shady walks are being made broad and light and straight, and all the beautiful and picturesque stone vases that had such lovely colours with time and moss have all been scraped, and look brand new as if they had just come out of a shop and stood about in some cafe or public tea-garden. I never saw anything so spoilt....

'It is, alas, the same with all the present regime do. They destroy, change, sweep away, and what they put in the place of the old is much too large, massive, expensive and showy. It makes me so sad. Of course, I am not consulted, as you can imagine. What Papa and I did at Charlottenburg they have all pulled to pieces. It was so pretty, and the only thing done in poor Papa's short reign, which out of respect and affection to his dear memory ought to have been carefully preserved. No one at the Court has one bit of taste or knowledge or feeling for art.'

The large army vote necessitated by the Emperor's bellicose policies inspires further protests.

'Caprivi made his grand speech in defence of his estimates two days ago. It was full of detail, it was as honest as possible and may ensure him getting the money, but politically I can only regret that the possibilities of war are so openly discussed in such detail, as it may produce the impression that Germany desired war, whereas it is the very reverse. I think the sum immense that has to be voted and it is a most unpopular measure. While it may be most necessary for the army it is certainly a misfortune for the country, as the money is not forthcoming for so many things which *are* necessary for the development of our prosperity, and the progress of our culture.'

Following on the death of the chief administrator of the hospitals of which the Empress is patroness, changes are made that arouse her ire.

'The present man, Z. I cannot bear, he is a servile creature, runs after William and Dona, flatters them, and takes an interest in those horrid deaconesses and none in my nurses. For years and years, as you know, I always had the loyal support of the town of Berlin for all my endeavours. Now, all my friends are put completely on one side, their names never appear on committee lists, they are not asked about anything. From the Court and the Government of course, we have nothing to expect, as they only support what is put forward by Dona and W. and by the blessed set of donkeys she has round her! I have belonged to the minority and to the losing side all my life and so it will remain until I die. Thank God I have the one satisfaction of feeling more than ever that my convictions, principles and opinions are the right ones. Though success be denied us, as I am deprived of the power and the means to further our institutions, yet I trust they will outlive me and do good when I am gone.'

In response to a letter from Queen Olga, the Empress makes suggestions for organizing a nursing service in Greece. She proposes to send back to Athens the trained nurse, Elizabeth P., to become matron of a hospital there.

'She would then I suppose have to train other sisters. You want three classes of nurses to be trained, nurses for the houses of the rich, district nurses, i.e., nurses that go out amongst the poor of the towns and villages, and hospital nurses who do the services in the hospitals. They must all be trained in the hospitals, and the matron must choose when the training is finished for which of these three branches of service she thinks them most fitted, and propose them to the Queen and the Committee, who must then sanction their taking up this special branch service.'

When Princess Sophie writes of her continuing efforts to engage in public life, and to do more entertaining, her mother replies approvingly.

'I am so glad to see you take so much interest in things of public life, institutions, etc., and that you have the wish and this ambition to be of use not only to your fellow creatures but also to your country. In that I am sure you will be Papa's and my own daughter and the granddaughter of my father, and you have the example of your dear mama-in-law always before you. I shall be too ready to help and assist you with any little advice or suggestions out of my own experiences that I can possibly offer you.

'I am also pleased to hear that you are going to give some dinners, it is a good thing, and I am sure you will get over your shyness and be a sweet amiable little hostess who knows how to make her guests feel at home, and that they will feel it a pleasure and privilege to be asked to your house. Receiving is a talent and an art like everything else, and does not come of itself, it wants cultivating and habit, and a little thought, and is not easy. I have no right to preach, I know how gauche and awkward I am in such things, not possessing any social talent at all! The perfection of a hostess was the Empress Eugenie, no one ever came up to that, and the next best is the Queen of Italy...Uncle Bertie and your Papa-in-law are the two best hosts I know.'

A delicate situation arises over the question of Princess Sophie's attendance at her sister's wedding. The three-year ban is not yet over, and the King of Greece, who has not forgotten or forgiven the Emperor's affront, is annoyed by an indiscreet paragraph in a Berlin newspaper. He forbids his daughter-in-law to accept the invitation. The Empress's protests fill letter after letter for several weeks.

'Now my Sophiekin, tell your Papa that I implore him on both knees not to prevent your coming here. I do not know what the stupid *Berliner Tageblatt* says, I have never seen it, but I do know what everyone else says. You know my Sophie that I am as proud and as susceptible for Greece, for your parents-in-law, for Tino and you, as for myself. Indeed I think I was more angry than any of you, but I have suffered so much by this unbecoming dissension in the family and am so anxious to see it ended and forgotten, once and for all.'

And in successive letters, she repeats and enlarges on her arguments.

'Surely the King is far above caring for what a vulgar newspaper says! I am quite in despair at his dear Majesty's attitude. ...Till now the fault has been on Wm's side, but now that he shows a desire to get out of a false position, the mistake would be on the side of those who do not meet him half way and with a good grace. Please, please listen to the voice of reason.'

The stream of appeals is suddenly halted when, in mid-December, Sophie announces that in any case she could not now undertake the journey. 'Of course, my child', replies the delighted Empress, 'if you have reason to suppose that you are expecting a baby, you must not travel ...the state of your health settles the question.'

Christmas draws near. '...yesterday ... I went to the Kinderheim [*children's home — Ed.*] at Bornstedt, and we had the party for all the little children and the Xmas Tree, and singing and repeating of hymns and poetry ... it was nice.'

Apart from this modest outing, the Empress spends a very quiet Christmas with Princess Margaret, who goes to bed with a bad cold on Christmas Day. The following evening, the Emperor and his wife, with her sister and her husband. Prince and Princess Frederick Leopold, come to dinner. Next day the Empress writes:

'Dona was very smart and inclined to be on a very high horse, and was grand and condescending, but presently she came down and was quite nice and amiable. Yaya was simple and natural, and I thought much improved in looks. That young couple get on much better together now.'

On December 30th, after discussing various personal matters and noting, 'How nice that darling baby speaks English, German and Greek already! I am sure he is a most intelligent little boy, bless his dear little heart', the Empress goes on:

'This is my last letter in the old year. I part with 1892 with very mixed feelings. This new year will carry away my Mossy from under my roof, and leave me without a child. But it will bring her new happiness, and for that I am so thankful. It will bring me a meeting with my darling Sophie and Tino and darling baby, and perhaps bring you new blessings so much longed for.'

Chapter Five – The Letters, 1893

The Empress has some important happenings ahead of her in 1893, for Margaret is getting married, there is to be a two months' visit to Queen Victoria, and in the summer comes a trip to Athens for the birth of Sophie's child.

That she must miss the wedding makes Sophie despondent, and her mother writes consolingly, 'Oh, I well know what a bitter disappointment it must be to you not to come, and no one can fret and grieve more than I do, but we must cheer up, you and I, life is a long sequence of sacrifices, trials and difficulties, and one but rarely gets what one wants. We must try and help each other on the stony road as best we can.'

She is very concerned that Sophie's confinement will occur during the heat of the summer. 'Why could you not come to Germany? You are not the reigning Queen, and the heir to the Throne is born. Surely the most important thing for the dynasty and Royal Family is that you should remain well and have a strong and healthy baby. Do talk it over with Tino.' She raises this issue several times in later letters, but without success, for Sophie remains in Greece. Meanwhile, she is having trouble with Frau E., for whom the Empress busies herself trying to find new employment.

'I quite see that she talks, and perhaps a good deal of rubbish, but she had her good qualities, and just think when baby was born, what would have become of you and baby if you had not had her? I cannot let her "sink or swim", i.e., let her find a place for herself, because I took her away from a very good practice, when she was doing well and earning money, so I am of course in a certain way responsible for her fate. I am sure she is very troublesome, but I am doing my best to find her other employment, as it would not be fair not to assist her. Of course I could offer her to come into my private service at Friedrichshof, where my people are not servants of the Crown, and have not the same rights for pensions, etc. If you have no objections, I will propose it to my gentlemen, as of course I can engage no one without first hearing what they have to say.'

In the end Frau E. is found suitable employment, but meanwhile there is the problem of obtaining a replacement. Sophie asks if a Mrs. P. is available.

'If you are positive you want to have her, I will let her know. Henry and Irene swear by her, so does Victoria Battenberg, but Dona says she drinks, and I am not able to discover whether it is true or not. She was overworked at the Schloss and kept in such terribly small rooms and was so bothered by C. that she may have taken more than was good for her, but I will find out once more before finally advising you.'

The Empress confirms that Mrs. P. does not drink unduly, but reveals that she does not want the appointment, as she is 'promised elsewhere'. Eventually Sophie finds a suitable woman in Athens, at which the Empress writes. 'I think your plan of taking Mrs. S's housekeeper excellent. It saves the bother of the journey, etc., but is she as good as you want? An American house is not an English house! Still, if you think the recommendations quite satisfactory I would certainly take her.'

The Empress turns to other affairs, for the programme for Margaret's wedding is formidable. 'There is a Court on the 14th, an investiture on the 18th, the Quadrille of the Dragoons on the 20th, also the Ball, and then something every day until the wedding on the 25th, then the Dinner and Gala Opera on the 27th, dinner at the British Embassy on the 28th, and on the 29th everyone disperses and returns home.'

But meanwhile, another wedding takes place, that of Sophie's seventeen-year-old cousin, Marie, to Crown Prince Ferdinand of Roumania.

'Wedell [*one of the Empress's gentlemen-in-waiting — Ed.*] returned from the wedding at Sigmaringen and said it was all well managed and arranged and that Missy looked very pretty indeed and also very happy. That the assembly was very brilliant and the cold nothing like what it is here. It must have been extremely difficult to put up so many guests in a tiny place like Sigmaringen. ... I think it very hard upon her, that she should be married off so young, and go so far away.'

In Berlin, the weather is severe, but the Empress makes the best of it.

'The cold here is still horrible and intense — it goes through the walls of the house as if they were paper. I have been skating on the pond at Bellevue, I get along again quite nicely, to the amusement of the little boys. The snow is so thick now that for once Berlin is not so horribly noisy, and my sitting-room is quiet, the rumbling, rattling, shaking and clattering traffic which almost drives me mad sometimes has ceased for a bit, which is a great relief.'

The guests are beginning to arrive, among them the bridegroom's elder brother, Alexander, Landgrave of Hesse. 'Poor blind Aleck was at luncheon yesterday. He is such a strange queer creature, so clever and gifted and talented and full of energy and life, but with an unfathomable disposition. He is so tyrannical and suspicious and has such a bad temper and is full of odd fancies and as changeable as the wind.' Then comes the first of the week's ceremonies, to which 'Fischy' unfortunately cannot go, as he is sent to bed with a sudden cold.

'Of course this was very hard for Mossy and her eyes filled with tears when she had to drive away with me to Court without him. She had been looking forward to going out with him so much, and I only went for them. The Cercle was interminable, and the driving away in the murderous cold out of the hot rooms with our low gowns and trains, the carriages feeling like ice, was really enough to kill one outright. For me it was painful as it always must be when I have to go to Court, and feel useless and put on the shelf.'

The wedding is on the anniversary of the Empress's own wedding day. Two days previously, after a long letter describing the wedding gown and going-away clothes, as well as the gown she will herself wear, she follows up with a second letter.

'In the midst of all this hurry and rush and running about I fear my letter will be very confused, and yet I should wish to write to you two or three times a day, so that you may know every trifle. I go through it all with a heavy heart, though it is a joy to me to see happiness on my sweet Mossy's face. Nearly all the guests have come, everyone has brought her a charming present, all put out in her sitting room and looking very imposing. Yesterday evening was the reception at the Schloss. The heat was enough to knock one down. Dona was not dressed to advantage, and wore the beautiful ruby necklace I gave her lower than her waist, which I do not think pretty.

'I have chosen the Crown present which William will give Mossy, a small but very perfect riviere of diamonds, and a pair of solitaires for her ears, and two small diamond brooches in the shape of bows, which I thought would be very useful. I hear Aleck gives something of the same kind, so she will be well set up with jewellery.'

That evening, the Empress finds time to dash off yet another letter. 'The hurry and scurry and rush is simply indescribable. I am sitting beside Mossy watching that she should not be disturbed for just one short quarter of an hour before dressing for the Gala Dinner. She is dead tired and quite worn out. Her room is never empty, the knocking at the door goes on constantly and she is never allowed a minute's peace.' The following day, the Gala dinner is summed up:

'The dinner was quite good and well arranged, the salons all lit with electricity, almost too light. The music was too loud. William has such a passion for a row (which I think dreadful) that there were deafening trumpets in the Garde du Corps on arriving at the Schloss, and drums at the bottom of the staircase, which almost knocked one's head off. Mossy looked most sweet in her white and gold train (the one out of my trousseau) and her little diadem. Vicky looked charming and so regal in her silver wedding train trimmed with sable, and her sapphires: Charlotte in her white and gold train with emeralds. The Cercle was very hot and fatiguing.

'Tonight is my dinner, and tomorrow the great day. I feel very low and sad, and I miss dear Papa so cruelly. I want to turn round every moment and say, do you remember what we were doing when I was your bride? One sweet moment I can look back on! But never can I forget the pain of parting from my home and parents, the dreadful moment of saying goodbye to my adored father.'

For the next two days, the Empress is for once unable to send off even a brief note. Then on the 27th, she writes:

'I tried in vain to write to you yesterday, but had not one moment. My eyes were so painfully swollen with weeping and I had such a headache, and was completely knocked up with the day before. My Mossy is really little Mrs. Fischy now! I can hardly believe it. She looks calm and smiling and happy, quite satisfied and at her ease.

'The struggle I went through on the 25th I shall never forget. I thought of my own wedding 35 years ago, and had a heart-sick longing for dear Papa, to be able to throw my arms around his neck and say, now we are alone, in the house together once more, as we were when we were bride and bridegroom. But all was silence around me.

'The wedding day was grey and dark and still very cold. Early we had breakfast together, and all telegraphed to you. Arrangements, telegrams, etc., took up the short time till our hurried luncheon, and then the answering of endless questions, of which of course in the bustle and excitement, a good many were forgotten. The dressing with trembling hands and flushed faces was a complicated business. I helped to put the pretty wreath on Mossy's sweet head, which suited her so well, and pin my wedding veil on, and put on the great diamond necklace of the Crown, which all the brides wear, and which I wore for Henry's wedding. She looked such a little love. Serious and grave but no tears.

'We had only just finished when the time for signing the civil marriage contract arrived, a little before four, in the long dining room, and heaps of people looking on. Then the driving away. Mossy and I in my gala coach with 6 horses. Getting in and out of the carriage very difficult with the bridesmaids carrying Mossy's train. At the Schloss, up the great staircase, with a noise of trumpets and drums enough to stun you.

'Dona and I and the hairdresser pinned on the little Crown, which I thought so became my darling Mossy. She held herself so well and bore herself with such natural dignity and grace that everyone was charmed with her. Then we moved slowly in procession to the Chapel, I between Willy and poor Aleck, whom I had to help to lead.

'In the Chapel, Mossy stood motionless before the altar, with Fischy looking very pale and grave. The music was very good. I do not like the weddings here as you know, I think them stately but stiff and mournful. Nothing but ceremony! Nothing joyous! I preferred yours infinitely. And most exhausting! From the morning at 8 until the night at 12, I never sat down except at meals, and was dead beat.

'The assembly was very brilliant and smart and the crush tremendous. When the church service was over, endless congratulations. Then the ceremonial Tafel, a splendid wedding cake, the food very bad, no speeches, room very hot. Then the Fackeltanz! [*ceremonial wedding torch dance — Ed.*]. Mossy looked so dear and made such nice pretty curtseys. The music played one march and one fackeltanz after another for 4 hours. I wonder the poor things did not drop. After that we got home and changed our clothes. Mossy looked a perfect dear in her white cloth dress, trimmed with silver braid and white bonnet and muff, a cloak with white ostrich feathers. We went to the railway station to see her off. It was a most awful moment for me. When I came home and realized she had gone, I cried my eyes out. Dona was really nice and kind to me, and showed me as much sympathy as she could, and

Willy tried in his way, I think.

'Yesterday was sunny and bright and I went over at 2 to see them at Potsdam and found them looking rested and happy. They and Vicky went with me to the dear Mausoleum The sun was shining and it looked so peaceful. It was my goodbye, as I shall see it no more before I leave for England. Yesterday evening the dear young couple returned here. All today has been taken up with State Ceremonies at the Schloss. The throng and crush was great. The dinner was very brilliant and very noisy. Then came the Gala Opera, from which I of course stayed away. Now I must end, I have not told you half, my Sophie, because I am so hunted about and so shaky and miserable.'

Several days passed before the commotion subsided. 'My house is like a restaurant. People keep dropping in for breakfast and luncheon. I never have one minute to myself.' And the Empress's gloom did not subside at all. 'No words can express how miserable I am this morning...my last one has gone, and now I am quite alone I am thankful Vicky is here with me. Her tears flowed as fast as mine last night.'

Accompanied by Victoria, the Empress travels to England, and on February 2nd, writes from Osborne:

'On arriving here it seemed like another world. The horrid cold, snow and ice and all the restraints and bothers of a town left behind, instead the sun shining, the sea pale blue, the fields all so green, the air soft, and the splendid evergreen laurels, oaks, etc., all over the place, reminding one of the south. The dear house here, so comfortable, smelling so sweet and clean, fresh flowers in all the rooms, and instead of nasty stuffy stoves, a bright little fire in the sitting room and in the bedroom. I am sitting in the same room as I had four years ago when you used to be scribbling to Tino next door, or having Greek lessons from B....

'Beloved Grandmama, thank God, is well, quite unchanged in face and voice, only much more infirm and unable to get about. What a joy and emotion to see her again. I have told her all about the wedding and how sweet my Mossy looked. Uncle Arthur and Louischen are here, also Louise and Lome [*Princess Louise, Marchioness and Marquis of Lorne — Ed.*] Beatrice and Liko, so that we are a nice family party.

'We have heard today with real grief of the terrible earthquake at Zante and all the damage done and the loss of life. I suppose that Tino or Georgie [*King George's second son — Ed.*] will be going there or the King himself. What a calamity it is! That lovely island, so celebrated for its flowers.'

In her subsequent letters, she refers frequently to her concern over the Zante disaster, and to the sympathy felt in Britain. She sets about to raise funds — 'I am trying to get up a concert in aid' — but abandons this idea in order not to clash with the national appeal launched by the Lord Mayor of London.

She writes of the changes in Queen Victoria's appearance.

'...I find dear Grandmama showing traces of age creeping on, which distresses me. She is more bent and can hardly walk at all. Her eyesight, which was so excellent, is getting a little dim both far and near, and she can read nothing without glasses. She has pain every night in her leg, and it is very stiff. Her mind and spirits are as bright as ever, and she takes the same interest in everything. Of course she is dreadfully annoyed and worried about Irish policy, and disapproves highly of this Home Rule Bill. It is a great trial to her to have everything upset again in Ireland when it had been steadily improving under the former administration.

'I breakfast and have tea with dear Grandmama in her room every day. Yesterday the others all went over to Portsmouth and I remained alone with her, and for lunch we had the three little dears of Uncle Arthur and three of Aunt Beatrice, They were really so well behaved and most amusing. Ena [*Princess Victoria Eugenie of Battenherg — Ed.*] is quite lovely. Grandmama hopes so much you and Tino and baby will come to see her one day.... To-day is the anniversary of her wedding. Beatrice and I are going to give her a lamp as a surprise!'

All the letters now dwell on her enjoyment of the beauties of the district, and of the company of her brothers and sisters.

'We had the most lovely day yesterday and I picked primroses peeping out from the green moss.... This morning I took communion with dear Grandmama, Uncle Arthur, Louischen, Beatrice and Liko and the household in the chapel here in the house. My Sophie was in my thoughts, may God bless her and watch over her. This afternoon we took a long walk along the sea, it was a lovely evening, so still and clear, such lovely lights and shades. Yesterday I had a ride with Aunt Beatrice. I rode Liko's enormous chestnut hunter, a beautiful beast, she had a very rough canter and pulled a wee bit but her trot was lovely...Alas, we leave here on the 17th and go back to Windsor, as dear Grandmama must be near the ministers on account of all the work that has to be done.'

The Empress now refers to the rumours that an engagement is pending between Prince George and his dead brother's fiancée. Princess May of Teck. Writing from Windsor on February 23rd she reports that:

'...yesterday Aunt Mary Teck was here with May whom I thought very nice indeed. Her position is most difficult and embarrassing. She is still in mourning for our poor darling Eddy, and the newspapers are constantly writing about her becoming engaged to Georgie, and the whole of the public seem to wish it ardently. Of course not a word has been mentioned in the family, but there is a universal feeling among them all that it is almost sure to take place sooner or later. There is much for it...I think it will seem very sad...but in many ways she is very much suited for the position, and everyone praises her.'

From Athens comes news from Sophie that stirs the Empress to a rhapsody on mother love.

'It is such good news to me too that you have felt some signs of Hfe. It is indeed, as you say, the greatest happiness a woman can experience, except that of nursing one's own sweet baby, pressing it to one's heart and feeling how it drinks and how much love one gives with every little drop, and how sweet it is to watch the little one fall asleep afterwards on one's own lap. That is the tenderest joy on earth. I always thought there is nothing to compare to it, and I do so pity the poor things who have never tasted this happiness.'

Sophie consults her mother about committee trouble in a hospital of which she is patroness. This is one of the Empress's favourite subjects, and in the course of a lengthy and authoritative reply, she says:

'No committee lady can give orders. The matron alone is responsible for the management of the nursing and nurses. The committee choose her, appoint her and invest her with these powers, but they cannot meddle with her work. If she does not give satisfaction, they can send her away. No one must interfere with her, she details the work to the different nurses, trains them, etc. Unless this is kept to, all discipline is upset, and the matron cannot then be answerable for proper nursing and proper management.'

As is her way, the Empress keeps an eye on the world political scene. In a lengthy letter on Balkan affairs, she shows a shrewd insight into current Russian policy, and a long-sightedness which time has proved no less acute. She writes still from Windsor Castle.

'Ferdinand of Bulgaria's bride [*Princess Marie Louise of Bourbon-Parma — Ed.*] is said to be quite charming, so good and intelligent, not at all pretty, but very *distinguée*. He wished to marry Carol Theodore of Bavaria's daughter, a sweet pretty creature, but I am sorry to say William interfered and spoilt the marriage. It is supposed the Russians said they would not have a German princess marry Ferdinand. I quite understand them not liking Ferdinand to consolidate himself by founding a strong dynasty, because from their standpoint it makes it more difficult to end the dynasty by paying assassins to murder or kidnap, as they did with poor dear Sandro. They consider themselves justified in adopting any measures, even the most criminal, to secure for themselves the future annexation of Bulgaria and Constantinople.

'Loving Greece as I do, I should consider this a great danger, as when it has succeeded in Bulgaria and Constantinople, and perhaps in Servia and Roumania, they may wish to try it in Greece. The Russians make a mistake if they think that these countries, which they helped to liberate from the Mussulman yoke, are anxious to be incorporated into the Russian Empire. Pray do not think I am anti-Russian, I am in no ways so, and wish we could be on best terms of friendship, but I think that though their form of government may suit them best, it would not be for the good of the countries who are already in possession of liberty to a greater degree. Please, pray keep this only to yourself and Tino, who I am sure understands what I mean, and knows I am for peace and harmony and settling all difficulties and differences amicably, drawing nations closer together and improving the understanding of each for the other. The Russian Empire is immense and very powerful and can do more or less whatever it likes. This question will most likely drag on when we are all dead and gone, and how it will resolve itself, no one can know.'

Moving with Queen Victoria for a few days in London, the Empress writes from Buckingham Palace about her shopping and other expeditions. Among her purchases are paintings, some for Sophie and some for Friedrichshof, for which she also buys stable fittings — 'Nowhere in the world do they make stable fittings and requirements as they do here...all very neat and plain, but so good and solid'. She again 'saw the horse show at Islington, which was quite beautiful'.

She meets others of her relations, among them the Princess of Wales. 'I saw Aunt Alix yesterday, sweet creature, and the two darling cousins of Wales, Victoria and Maudie, looking so dear and I am happy to say really much better. Auntie is going to the Mediterranean now in the *Osborne,* as a change for Victoria...she will come to Athens to see her brother, the King, and will take a box for me with things for you...'

Queen Victoria returns to Windsor, where, after a brief stay with the Duke and Duchess of Rutland at Belvoir Castle — 'What a grand noble imposing old place it is, so very interesting inside. We saw the "meet" on the morning we left, such a pretty sight' — the Empress soon joins her. Extracts from successive letters prove her continuing enjoyment of her stay.

'We have had a glorious day today and bright sunshine. We have been quite a family party. Uncle Bertie, Aunt Louise and Lorne, Louis and Victoria Battenberg.... Yesterday I had a delicious afternoon at Bagshot Park with Uncle Arthur and Louischen.... Grandmama gives dinners almost every evening, so I am always seeing people, ministers, diplomats, etc.'

'Yesterday evening Tennyson's "Becket" was given in the Waterloo Gallery. I went too, as it was such a serious piece and under dear Grandmama's roof, the first acting I had seen for 5 years. It was beautifully arranged and done, and very well acted. I was much interested, though as a drama it has many faults, yet the subject is very stirring, the language very fine.'

'I often go to the library here and look at the splendid prints and drawings and miniatures, all so beautifully kept. I am sure they would interest you. Alas, my visit to dear Windsor is soon coming to a close, and the parting with dear Grandmama very near. It has been a great comfort and treat to be here, and I trust that two whole years will never pass again between my visits.'

'Aunt Beatrice sends you her best love, and would be so delighted to see sweet baby. I should like to see him play with her children, they are such dears, so amusing and original and so quick and wide-awake. Ena less so than her brothers, but she has a charming disposition, so affectionate and full of feeling. She is so sensitive that I fear she will never find life easy. Little Leopold is my special favourite. "I love you, I do", he said to me yesterday, bringing me a bunch of white violets, "I picked them for you because I love you". Of course, I never get a chance of seeing my Berlin grandchildren, or knowing them, as I do these.'

The Letters contain references to the Emperor's current indiscretions.

'Charlotte had announced to me she was going to Cannes and now she telegraphs it has been forbidden by W. as it was in France, and so she is going to Naples. What utter rubbish to order her about in that way, also to object to Cannes on account of it being in France. There are other objections but not those, and I do not consider Charlotte as standing under W's orders, either. This sort of thing makes me so cross.

'At Berlin, things seem in a great mess about the army and navy bills. The immense sacrifices imposed upon the country are not compensated in other ways, and also poor W. is terribly unpopular and one mistake is made after another, so that I cannot wonder that the Reichstag is not inclined to vote these gigantic sums in a hurry, though I believe the army sincerely wants them.'

On March 20th, she writes, in a tone that holds dejection, and perhaps foreboding.

'I have had my very last drive with beloved Grandmama before she leaves for Florence. It was a glorious evening without a cloud or a breath of wind, and the dear old Park looked so fine. But I felt sad. At her age partings seem doubly melancholy, as you can imagine, and the thought of living far away from her in her old age is very painful. However I must be thankful to have seen her.'

After Queen Victoria's departure for Florence, the Empress returns to Buckingham Palace, from where her letters take up the tale of her rounds of visits.

'Dear London is looking its best, although of course the season has not yet begun. The new Imperial Institute in Kensington is a magnificent building, such as I have not seen a better, and Uncle Bertie is justly proud of it. Yesterday he took me to luncheon with others to Baron Ferdinand Rothschild, and then to the studios of Sir Frederick Leighton, who has some pictures that are too lovely, intended for this year's Academy.

'This morning I was at a service at St. Paul's which was so moving. Then I drove to White Lodge, Richmond Park, and had luncheon with Aunt Mary of Teck and her husband and sons. It is a charming house, such a view into Richmond Park. Then I drove to Sheen Lodge and had tea with Louise and

Fife, a delightful place with a very pretty garden. Uncle Bertie took me home, an enjoyable drive. This evening we dined at Marlborough House. Tomorrow Uncle Bertie goes to Sandringham and everyone is leaving town for Easter. Dear Victoria Battenberg has just been walking with me in the garden, she sends you her best love. P.S. Grandmama is delighted with Florence.'

April arrives, and with it the time to return to Germany. Throughout her visit, the Empress's letters have been a good deal occupied with her daughter's coming confinement, whether it shall be in Athens, the choice of doctors and nurses, and all the other preparations on which she places such importance. She spends her last two days at Cumberland Lodge, in Windsor Park, and her thoughts turn again to Greece.

'While the Easter sun is streaming into my cheery little sitting room, and the sound of Easter Bells is carried on the soft spring air coming in at the open window, I write to offer you my loving Easter wishes, praying for blessings on your dear head, and precious Tino's, who is as dear to me as if he were my own son, and on your adored little son. My thoughts are so much with you all. What you tell me about sweet baby amuses me very much, that he pointed to the blotting book and said, "Grandmama in there". Sweet blessed little man. I am longing to see him.

'I am horrified to think of more earthquake tremors, and your being so frightened, and having to go to the dentist, my poor darling.

'I am indeed very glad to spend Easter here with dear Auntie, it is so peaceful and restful in her pretty home, that she has made so comfortable and livable in. This morning at a quarter past eight we walked to the Park Chapel, which was beautifully decorated with flowers, and took communion with the congregation. This afternoon we go to St. George's at Windsor to afternoon service...Only tomorrow still in England. The day after, I embark for Flushing, so this will be my last letter. I must say goodbye now, my darling, and scribble my other letters.'

Back in Bonn, where she stays with Victoria, who had returned home after a week in England, the Empress writes:

'The parting from the loved ones in England was very hard, and I felt it so much, also leaving the dear beautiful yacht yesterday morning. Everyone had been so kind to me. Dear Uncle Bertie was touching. In this dear little house which Vicky keeps so beautifully, Adolf and she are kindness and hospitality itself, and it is so nice to stay with them and see how happy they are together and devoted to each other. If only they had a child, it is the one sad point in their lives and they feel it most terribly. I do all I can to comfort them. May they have a dozen, please God.'

A visit to Margaret a few days later produces news. 'I find our loved Mossy looking very well. Certain little signs make me think that something may be on the way, though one cannot yet be certain. Dear Fischy is certainly looking brighter and less pale, and they seem so contented and happy.'

The Empress discusses at some length the coming engagement of Prince George and Princess May, which she regards a little dubiously. She thinks that in the circumstances...

'the whole situation is a sad one. In many ways the marriage will be good.... May is an excellent girl, she has an excellent character, is steady-going and good, and as you know, she is very popular in England. Dear Aunt Mary is quite devoted to her children's interests and wrapped up in their future. May was born and brought up in England, she considers herself quite an Englishwoman, and this of course makes it a great deal easier for her. Many people in England are exceedingly anxious for the marriage, many are not.

'One thing I think good, which is that she is very strong and healthy, her brothers are fine strong young men, the eldest most remarkably nice, full of tact and good sense, and praised by everyone. To me, May was exceedingly nice, and her very great reserve wore off as we saw more of each other. I like her very much and fancy that in many respects, if not all, she will fill her position very well'

At last news comes that the Princess of Wales has arrived in Athens.

'I cannot say how glad I am that you have been able to see so much of dearest Auntie Alix and sweet cousins, two of the most delightful girls I ever saw ...and were also able to go on board the dear "Osborne". I am sure it reminded you of happy days gone by. That dear Victoria is an angel of a girl, so good and unselfish, so helpful and useful and true. Of all the nieces I have, I love her the best. And Maudie is a perfect duck and so bewitching. I long to squeeze her when I see her. I wish they would marry, they would make such excellent wives.'

Greek affairs continue to excite the Empress's concern. 'I am indeed distressed the King is so much worried about the finances. It is not to be wondered at.' She suggests ways in which the country's economy might be improved.

'If only the Salonika railway and the road through Greece were opened, and all the Indian mail and Indian passengers came that way, instead of by Brindisi, it would bring money into the country, and if foreign capital could be placed in certain undertakings such as the working of the marble quarries, the growing of olive trees, flower farms for perfume, and fruit gardens for preserved fruit, one might have more articles of trade for export, which would increase the revenue ...the neglect of centuries cannot all be repaired in a moment. I cannot help thinking that if more tobacco were grown, it might develop to a much larger article of export, as also currants, lemons, oranges. But to raise production, capital must be put into the land, and if capital does not exist in the country one must try and encourage it to come from elsewhere.'

The Empress goes now to watch over the work at Friedrichshof. The house is not yet ready for occupation, and she stays in the gardener's cottage. From here she writes early in May.

'Every day I find something to do in the garden, or the building or the grounds. The details that have to be watched and decided are endless. I can only begin furnishing in 2 or 3 months, that also will be a great business. My greenhouse and hothouses looked very nice, and fruit and flowers prosper wonderfully under the care of my two English gardeners. In some parts of the house they are laying the floors, others putting up the wainscoting, others staining the ceilings. The masons and carpenters make a dreadful deal of dust. I think the stables will be good, 50 times better than at the Berlin or Homberg Palaces, and I trust well-drained and ventilated. The house is really very light and cheerful and will be very comfortable. If I could only get the servants to be more clean and tidy and careful in their ways and habits.'

Interest in the Letters switches to Prince George and Princess May.

'The news has arrived that darling Georgie is engaged to May. He telegraphed it to me yesterday. May he be happy, darling boy, and she too. One can only think of the engagement with very mixed feelings, but with many prayers for their future, so important for their dear parents, the whole family, and the country. I am sure the very fact that Georgie is to marry May will give great pleasure in England. Aunt Mary Teck is overjoyed, as well she may be and Grandmama thankful that something is settled for Georgie. Still, over all, there is a mist of sadness and melancholy.'

A few days later, after announcing that she is 'to be godmother to Louise Fife's second little girl', she continues, 'I have had very nice letters from May and dear Georgie, they seem really very happy. I hear the wedding is to be in July ...and at the Chapel Royal, St. James', where Grandmama's wedding took place, and mine. Of course, St. George's at Windsor was impossible on account of poor dear Eddy, it would have been too painful.'

Internal affairs in Germany are frequently commented on, though usually briefly, as in the following.

'I am very sad at the dissolution of the Reichstag, which is a great mistake, and also at one of William's speeches, which alas is very unfortunate and much to be regretted in every way. He does not understand the A.B.C. of a constitution, alas, nor what the real position and duties of a monarchy must be in our days. It makes me so unhappy and anxious.'

In successive letters, the Empress discourses lengthily on King George's worries over the Greek financial crisis, and on the European political influences which hinder the negotiation of a loan. She refers Sophie to leaders on the subject in *The Times,* and sends her articles from German papers. After an exceptionally long and judicial appraisal of the whole Greek situation, she concludes:

'Perhaps all this will bore you my poor Sophie, you are not much given to politics. But the affairs of the nation to which one belongs of course are one of the principal and foremost interests and preoccupations in life. They cause one often much sorrow and anxiety but one cannot help being deeply interested in them. Tino will be able to explain to you what I mean. P.S. Cannot all the rich Greeks living in England France and Constantinople, Cairo, Alexandria, lend their country enough money to pay off what is due in June? Cannot the Greek Consuls ask them? I only wish my private fortune were such that I could give it, I would do so willingly.'

As the time approaches to go to Athens for the confinement, the letters bear more and more on Sophie's background.

'How amusing your reception of the new Ministers must have been. I am so glad you spoke Greek with them. It interests me much to hear about the finishing of the Corinth Canal. Perhaps the "Surprise" can take me though if it is to be opened on the 2nd of June...I am so pleased that you have opened a soup-kitchen for the poor. I am also very glad you are going to be patroness of what we call "almshouses". They are such a boon to the sick and aged poor. One wants a thorough good Matron to keep order and see that everything is clean, tidy and wholesome, a clergyman and a doctor to visit daily, some lady visitors from the committee, and a couple of inspectors, then it is sure to go on straight.'

'It must have been interesting to see Sarah Bernhardt, she is an extraordinary actress from all I have heard. I hope you did *not* make her acquaintance, as alas no *lady* can, she is so very bad, and has an awful reputation. It is a pity those immoral pieces are always given, such as those you saw. They do so much mischief and continually occupy the imagination with things and situations with which one can have compassion but which one would rather avoid seeing and hearing. The French stage is pernicious in this respect, but especially French authors of a certain kind. This poison is spread all over the world. The cleverness with which their plays are written, the interest and excitement they give, and the beautiful acting, all of course attract people.'

'All you tell me about baby is too delightful and I am all impatience to see him. I am so sorry he should forget his German, it seems such a pity after he had learnt it so well. Can you not speak it to him sometimes?

'I am so thankful your parents-in-law are so kind and indulgent about your not tiring yourself, or having to appear at official occasions, now that you must take care of yourself. How different from the Empress Augusta, who used to be so tyrannical to me on those occasions, downright cruel, because she was so angry and annoyed each time I had a baby, she thought it unnecessary, and used to torment me terribly when I was in your state.'

The Empress duly makes her way to Athens, and so misses the wedding of Prince George and Princess May in July. But this time she is with her daughter when a boy is born, Alexander. On August 15th, after a visit of six weeks, she sets off on her return journey in H.M.S. *Inflexible.* Her first letter, written while still within sight of Athens, reflects her usual emotions at separation.

'Oh, the pain of parting, I feel it more than words can say, and I struggle not to show it, but it half breaks my heart. ... It is always a treat for me to be on board an English ship, but I was almost too sad to enjoy it this time....'

She transfers to H.M.S. *Scout,* in which she makes her first trip through the Corinth Canal, which she suggests should be provided with locks to control the current. Then she joins the Surprise, and her thoughts go back to

'...my own angel lying on the balcony or on your bed, with that little sweet downy head and precious little pink face cuddled up to its dear young Mama, making all sorts of little soft contented noises.... This cabin is stifling hot, and the screw shakes a good bit, and my eyes are full of tears, so you must excuse the disgraceful writing. Perhaps you will think me foolish and sentimental to feel going away so much, but I cannot help it, I am not the gay light-hearted creature I was once. I only hope you will not miss your old Mama so much as she will miss you.... How many people do I see every day to whom I am indifferent, but from the ones I love the most I have to be parted. However, I take dear and precious memories away with me.'

The journey to Trieste in the *Surprise* is uneventful, and her letters dwell almost entirely on those she has left behind, and especially on Sophie and how she must look after herself and the baby. By the end of the month she is back in the Schloss Homberg, from which she writes of the death of Ernst, Duke of Saxe-Coburg-Gotha, her father's brother, who is to be succeeded by her brother, Alfred, Duke of Edinburgh.

'I feel Uncle Ernst's death very much and heartily forgive him the harm and mischief he did me, and only remember the happy days I spent under his roof years ago, when we went every autumn and winter to him. He was my only relation in Germany except darling Alice. It is another link with the past broken. For Uncle Alfred, this is a difficult time, he will have to give up dear old London for good, and devote himself to his German home and his new duties. But he will do it all so well, and Aunt Marie will love being No. i, and reigning Duchess, I am sure.

'Homberg is full of smart people. It is a great joy having dear Uncle Bertie near, he and I breakfast every morning together, either here or at his rooms in the hotel. There is not a kinder brother in the world, and I cling to him in my loneliness very much.

'I saw Lord Rosebery and had a little talk with him about Greece. Yesterday I had people to dinner and supper, which fatigued me, but as it is expected of me, it must be done. All the cousins come over from Darmstadt today, and Dona tomorrow, which I am not looking forward to. Charlotte and Bernhard left the day before yesterday. It does grieve me to see her so 19th century, thinking so much of her clothes and appearance, and smoking so much. She is looking well, but her complexion is so yellow, and she often smells like a walking cigar shop, which for ladies is not the thing. I shall never think it ladylike to smoke regularly and every day. She seemed most pleased to be here, and I thought him very amiable and good humoured. If they could only keep their little tongues and imaginations in order!'

Meanwhile in Athens, Sophie has become unwell, and for some time the Empress's letters fluctuate between confidence and apprehension. 'Thank God, the news about you are pretty good, and you seem to be getting on', she writes, then a few days later. 'My poor darling Sophie, I wonder whether you are allowed to read your letters...'

She writes to Constantine. 'I do thank you for sending me a telegram every day. You do not know in what a state of misery and anxiety I am to think of our darling having a return of fever and pain.' After a long letter of detailed advice on the medical and nursing precautions to be taken for the dry pleurisy which Sophie has now developed, she adds, contritely, 'You will think me a great bore writing so often, I am sorry, when you have all your duties to attend to, and no end of things on your mind.' But when later Sophie improves, though not enough to receive long letters, her mother begins one with unusual levity. 'Darling Tino, you will again see my tiresome handwriting, and wish your Mama-in-law "to Jericho", or in good old English, "to...*Hanover!*"

She is anxious about the upbringing of little George, who is clearly developing a will of his own, and writes to Sophie:

'He will be an intelligent, manly, independent boy, who can easily be led if one sets about it in the right way, but who cannot be driven by force, or by bullying, which would only sour his nature.... He has plenty of will and spirit, as a boy should have, but it would be easy to spoil his temper, and I think one must be gentle and patient with him, and not brusque or rough. Else he will turn obstinate, which would be a pity, as he is such an affectionate little man, and so fond of his Mama. I send him some reins to play horses and some wooden forms to make sand-pies with, which he is so fond of doing.'

The Empress's letters always contain news of what is happening to Sophie's sisters and cousins. 'Mossy now takes her work and lies down on the sofa, so good and dear, and Fischy takes a great interest in everything. She is looking well, and shows her condition very little as yet.' The other son-in-law, 'Adolf has been made a major, to Vicky's great delight, as he will not be worked so hard, and will have more time for her and to be at home and to take leave from time to time.'

They go on leave without much delay, and: 'Vicky writes to me that she enjoys herself very much, and finds the walking in the mountains delightful. She trots after Adolf up and down the rough mountain paths carrying his gun when he goes out stalking. How often I used to do that for my Papa when I was a girl in dear Scotland.'

Charlotte and Bernhard are on their way to Athens. 'How I envy them!' the Empress exclaims. 'It makes me mad that it should be they and not I who will see you.' She mentions also Crown Princess Marie of Roumania. 'Soon I should think we must hear about Missy. Aunt Marie and cousins are at Sinaia since summer, while Uncle Alfred is in the Tyrol.' A fortnight later comes the news that 'Grandmama and Uncle Alfred are much delighted at Missy having a son yesterday at Bucharest. Poor Elizabeth of Roumania will feel it very much, a son was always denied her. Dear Vicky always frets bitterly whenever any of the family has a new baby. How I wish she had one.' Of the new Duke of Coburg, she writes:

'Uncle Alfred has a great deal of trouble with his inheritance, as poor Uncle Ernst's money matters were in a dreadful mess, and he has had to cut down and reduce the expenditure in every way. With care and prudence and great self-denial things will come round in a few years, but there are tremendous debts to pay off. The fortune is in fact a very fine one, and if properly managed and looked after, ought to be very large.'

Whatever her preoccupations, the Empress seldom fails to take her favourite form of exercise, her daily rides, which sometimes last three or four hours.

'We have a fine bright day today, so that the rest of the hay will not be drenched and spoilt, and I can take a good ride. Tell Tino I have 2 new horses I think he would like. And I have a lovely new pair of carriage horses come from England, charming animals, very dark, but not black, they are quiet, good and easy to drive. You like to hear about the stables, so I tell you. M ... is so awkward putting me on and off my horse that he nearly drops me.'

The Empress keeps an observant eye on the situation in Greece — "The opposition papers are still very rude, I see' — and also on Mr. Gladstone's efforts to pass his Irish Bill.

'I hope dear Tino will read the Duke of Devonshire's speech in the House of Lords (in *The Times*). Nothing better can be said about the Home Rule Bill... So truly statesmanlike. I hope the Bill is what the Yankees would call "smashed up", and any rate it will be very difficult to put it on its legs again without taking very extreme measures.
'I have been sitting yesterday and today for my portrait by Herr von Angeli. It is the same as the profile you know, only full length, sitting in a carved wooden chair, with a book on my lap. Everybody likes it very much. He certainly paints better than ever.'

The tense condition of Greek affairs continues and some of her longest letters contain advice which she hopes Sophie will pass on to Constantine and the King.

'What difficulties your papa-in-law will have to encounter! I suppose the Chamber will be dissolved and then we shall see what the elections will do! If only the King never speaks again of abdication. It would be excessively bad for the monarchist principle that a faction with its newspapers and agitators should succeed in shaking the one stable element which nothing ought to shake and move.... What are 4 or 5 thousand excited politicians, newspaper writers and coffee-house frequenters at Athens? They are not Greece!'

But these political difficulties come second to the news that Sophie is only slowly recovering from her illness. T am still so impatient to hear you are no longer hot and feverish. ... I kiss your dear white forehead a 1,000 times, where all the little hairpins are in the fringe.' Sophie's progress is not helped by a new outburst of servant trouble, and by worry over the delays in the building of her house. The Empress sends a German interior decorator to look at it. 'I told him that as far as I knew the whole building had come to a standstill, Z...'s contract had come to an end, and the government had not renewed it, a new grant was wanted for the continuation of the building, and I did not know whether Tino had asked or was going to ask for the sum to complete the house.'

The Empress's own house is making far quicker progress than Sophie's, and she is already preparing to move some of her things from the Schloss Romberg.

'I am in the midst of packing and clearing out my furniture to go to Friedrichshof ...my books are being put in my library, and I find that I have not room for one 3rd of them, oh, dear, I don't quite know what to do.... The day before yesterday we had a trial of the electric light but it is not quite to our taste yet. The ground round the stable and cottage is being levelled now, and that will be the last work in the garden, then there will only be planting of trees and sowing of grass, and one more road behind the gardener's cottage to the village.'

The Empress is so busy over Friedrichshof that she sighs, 'My head aches with all I have to think of.' But she still keeps up her riding, and her local welfare interests, such as a visit to 'a home for poor ladies, who can live there on a small income ...much wanted, as the distress among people of better class is almost greater than amongst the lower orders'. And she has a constant flow of guests: 'The house is so full that there is hardly an empty room, which tires me very much and I find it difficult to manage all my writing and correspondence, of which I have so much...it is so dark today I am writing with candles.'

But in the midst of her preoccupations, her thoughts drift back to her last visit to Greece.

'The weather is gloomy, cold and rainy. If you knew with what longing I think of Tatoi, and summer, and the lovely nights, the window open, and the balcony of my bedroom, the splendid moonlight streaming in at the window, the wind sighing through the pines, the lovely stars in the sweet blue sky. Oh, how beautiful it was! The silver streak on the sea, and the group of dark cypresses standing up in front of the terrace. It seems like a dream. In the early morning at 4 or 5, how lovely the tints were on the landscape. I used to jump out of bed and look at the roof of my Sophie's little house in among the fir trees...'

At the beginning of November, she moves to her residence in the capital.

'Here I am again in old Berlin. It does seem very sad and melancholy, with no darling child, no Vicky, no Sophie, no sweet Mossy. Dear Papa's rooms empty and silent. I feel in lowest of spirits. It is not right perhaps, but sometimes one has not the strength to resist these memories.... William and Dona came to luncheon. I had not seen him since January, but I don't think he remembered this fact. Dona was looking very well in a very smart lilac velvet gown. In the afternoon I rushed to the new Victoria Haus, it is not finished yet, but will be a very nice place. They wish to have it ready for my birthday.

'I have had a fine business here today, rearranging the rooms with all the Potsdam things in place of the things gone to Friedrichshof, but it looks quite comfortable. You must excuse this short letter, the next one will be better, but there is so much bustle and confusion still.'

Her following letters are filled with chatty news of her activities and the changes she finds. She goes to Potsdam, where:

'...I went quite alone to our dear Mausoleum, and the sun was streaming in and made the tomb look quite lovely. It was so still and peaceful and I wished my Sophie had been standing by my side. The silver wreath you placed in the little chapel before you married is now hung up in the mausoleum...'

'We opened a new wing to the Bornstedt Kinderheim. There was a little ceremony and a few speeches. There is room now for 86 children...I am thinking of giving up the dear little Bornstedt house, as I shall want the furniture for the cottage at Friedrichshof. It seems a waste to have the Bornstedt house empty because I am there so little, it would make nice summer quarters for some of the gentlemen and ladies of the present Court. But it costs me a pang all the same, though I know it is more sensible.'

'I went to pay a visit to Yaya at Glienicke [*the Frederick Leopold palace at Potsdam — Ed.*] She was very amiable but looked very red and very ugly in the face, with a waist so squashed and pinched that it almost made my eyes water to look at it. Really I cannot think what she can be made of. She showed me her nursery and her three children, they seemed very flourishing. They had an enormous lot of playthings, almost too many it seemed to me. The house looked very well cared for and comfortable. Still, it seems like a dream to me that the young generation should be in possession of everything at one's dear old Potsdam and not only the *old* generation, but *ours,* dead and gone, disappeared, with only Aunt Marianne [*Princess Frederick Charles of Prussia — Ed.*] and I remaining, and lone widows. It seems like yesterday that we were the young people! I am glad that I do not live in the midst of it all, I don't think I could bear it. My new home is not so surrounded with the dear ruins of the past, which I cannot look at without bitter pain rising up within me.'

In November occur two deaths that carry the Empress back into the past, the first of a well-known British diplomat whose career had suffered because of his friendship with her and her husband, the second of Prince Alexander of Battenberg.

'Poor Sir Robert Morier's death has grieved me so much. He was the cleverest of all our British diplomatists, and a personal friend of mine for so many long years. The only British diplomat who looked upon German affairs exactly as I do. Prince Bismark never forgave that, and waged a little warfare against him, with his favourite weapon of calumny, etc. Poor Morier suffered much. He was ailing all this summer, but I much hoped to see him again. Grandmama telegraphed the news of his death to me yesterday evening. He did not long survive his great friend (and mine also) Professor Benjamin Jowett, master at Balliol College at Oxford. I have indeed lost many friends lately, and new ones are not easily made at my time of life.'

'You can imagine what a grief to me poor Sandro's death is...Here there is a deal of feeling shown, not a newspaper that does not speak in praise of him. Amongst officers, and indeed in the whole German Army, he was immensely and deservedly popular. Bismark's paid press is no longer there to sound a chorus of abuse and calumny, and now that Prince B's clique, headed by your brother W., no longer finds it profitable to attack him, the real public opinion comes out. Poor dear young man, such a splendid creature to die at 3 6. Of course, I had not had any great interest in the wife, but now poor thing I feel intensely sorry for her. To be left with 2 tiny children, one only three weeks old.... Poor Princess Battenberg had not seen her son for three years, as she was so frantic about the marriage.

'Late yesterday evening Vicky and Adolf arrived. It was their wedding day anniversary. Happy as she is with Adolf the death of the one whom she first hoped to marry cannot but make a deep impression on her.'

The time is now approaching for Margaret's confinement, but the Empress, who had made all plans to be at her daughter's side, is taken by surprise, for the birth is premature. On November 24th she writes from Prince Frederick's mother's home at Frankfort.

'Now what do you say to this! Here I am sitting by our darling adored Mossy's bedside, in Aunt Anna's house. Mossy looks sweet and blooming as usual, her pink cheeks like a ripe apple. By her side is the most tiny of babies you ever beheld...As this dear beloved little man insisted on coming a month before he had any business to appear in this world, of course he found nothing in order for him. His devoted grandmama heard the news that Mossy was ill yesterday morning at 10, telegraphed to you, collected her things as best she could, left everything in the greatest confusion, birthday letters unanswered, Xmas things unordered, packing up for Friedrichshof all undone, dashed to the station in anxiety, agitation and terror not to be described. Dear good-natured Vicky would not let me go alone, so she came with me. At Nordhausen, the news that a little boy was born reached us. How grateful I was, and yet how miserable not to have been with our angel Mossy. How I thought of Gibraltar and little Georgie's birth. At 10.40 last night, I arrived, dead tired, with aching head and aching back, but able to see my darling. The house was in a nice mess, I assure you, and the picture of discomfort. But all had gone well...I have 12 grandchildren now, 10 grandsons. If dear Papa could only see them!'

During the days that follow the event, the Empress's letters are taken up chiefly with the baby and his mother, and with King George's difficulties in Greece.

'...I am quite miserable when I see all the angry letters in the German, French and English newspapers, about Greek finances, and think how the Ministers make enemies instead of friends for their country, whereas Greece as a nation cannot help it in any way. Nothing makes people so angry as losing their money, and I fear things look very hopeless for those who have their money in Greek bonds. I see in the paper that Mr. R. [*recently a minister — Ed.*] has had a duel with somebody, but I did not make out about what...If the various parties would bury their differences and grievances, and unite more for the sake of the country at such a critical time of national trials and difficulties, that would be true unselfish and enlightened patriotism!'

The Empress is very cross with a Greek millionaire who had recently died and left...

'...his enormous fortune to a hospital and Greek church in Paris. I wish he had left it to Athens for the canalization and water supply, for public baths and wash-houses for the people, or for a Park between Athens and Phaleron, or for a good drawing and modelling school, or a school of music for the whole country. All these things are preferable to endowing already rich Paris. I own I am annoyed at this poor dead man having made his will in this fashion.

'I went over to Darmstadt on the sad 14th, and with Ernie and Alicky put a wreath on dear Auntie Alice's tomb on the Rosenhohe. It was so sad to go to the Palace after, and see Ernie and his sister quite alone in that big house, which was looking so bright and cheerful, pretty and comfortable and well kept, just as it did when Uncle and Aunt were there surrounded by their children, and now those two dear young orphans alone, and the voices and footsteps of those we loved heard no more within those walls.'

As the year closes, she contemplates her changing family scene, and refers to Sophie's promised visit in the summer.

'How much I shall think of you and the dear little ones at Xmas. Oh, that I had you all around me once more, but the old days are gone, my home broken up, my children dispersed, the eldest one hardly knows or remembers he has a mother, and the others are as happy without me. Still, I must be very thankful to be with my precious Mossy, and so I am, it is a constant joy to watch her sweet face, and have her little one in my arms. Goodbye, my precious Sophie. God bless and protect you and may you remain well and strong. 1,000 kisses to the sweet little people, tender love to Tino. P.S. I am impatient for 1894 to begin, because it will bring the time nearer for you to arrive.'

Chapter Six – The Letters, 1894

The first letters of the New Year contain news 'of Sophie's sisters and young relations. 'Mossy darling is recovering her strength very well, and only feels her feet and ankles weak.' From England, 'I hear May of York is expecting her baby in June. It will be a great happiness for the family. ... I hope she may have many children, and that they may be strong and healthy.' There is, too, another engagement to announce, that of the Grand Duke Ernst of Hesse and Princess Victoria Melita of Edinburgh.

'...Ernie and Ducky! Perhaps you are not astonished? If she were only not his 1st cousin, what could be nicer? She is a charming girl, bright and clever, with plenty of spirit, which is rather what he wants, and then it is so nice to think that it will not be a stranger in dearest Alice's place.

'Yesterday evening Missy and Ferdinand of Roumania came to see us, she looking sweetly pretty and quite a baby, and very transparent and delicate, and he, poor dear, more unprepossessing than ever. She seems quite happy, but she is so young and inexperienced and cannot compare people with one another. At sweet 18, she rejoices in life and change and beauty. She has all the buoyancy of youth, and luckily for her no very deep feelings, I suppose. She says her little boy is quite well.'

Half-way through January, the Empress returns to Berlin, where, 'my first day here was so busy that I hardly knew how to get through everything there was to do. I went to the Schloss and saw Dona and the children, and she came to me to luncheon with 3 of the boys. I have been to see the Victoria Lyceum, which has a new house now, far nicer than the old one, and hurried off to the Victoria Haus and found all in good order....'

The bustle continues next day. '...Willy and Dona came to breakfast. Later I had audiences of the Spanish and American Ambassadors...went across to Potsdam, and remained long in the dear silent Mausoleum...The rush and scramble of Berlin existence is not wholesome, but I cannot avoid it, as you know ...and now I shall have to trot out to this blessed Ordensfest [*assembly of the members of a knightly order — Ed.*] which I do so hate and abhor.'

The Empress's letters are still periodically taken up with Sophie's continuing feeble health. Sophie herself is worried as to the cause of her weakness, and writes frequently about it. The Empress asks the advice of various doctors, and sends back detailed information upon what is now thought to be a thrombosis in the leg, with advice on how to recover from it and prevent a repetition. The letters also touch frequently on Sophie's welfare work.

'There is a wide field and scope for improvement and philanthropy before you in Greece, and I am sure in some years great progress will be made. I send a little account of our Kaiser and Kaiserin Frederick's Children's Hospital for you to see what work has been done there.

'The new lying-in hospital you are thinking of founding would be best along that fine broad new road, somewhere near that convent wall ... I am sorry you found the almshouses so dirty and neglected and ill-arranged when you went to see them the other day.'

Greek financial difficulties form a constantly repeated subject for comment. 'It must all be a great worry to the King, and one wishes one saw daylight,' Referring to the attempts being made by Europe to put the country on its feet again, she writes of '...dear Greece, where the benefits of modern civilization now have to be introduced from other countries, whereas all these countries have built up their civilization on the teaching and knowledge of ancient Greece!' She continues:

'...Everyone here, newspapers and public, is convinced that on account of the financial difficulties Greece is in, the island of Paros is going to be sold to the Russian Government as a Mediterranean station for their Fleet, in case of war with Turkey. This I for my part do not believe. I know that there is some Russian property at Paros and that the Russians have already a strong hidden arsenal at Mount Athos in the convent, but very likely it is all a mistake.'

Efforts are now in progress to put on an appearance of closing the breach between the Emperor and Bismark.

'Everybody here today is in wild excitement, as Prince Bismark is expected to pay a visit to the Schloss. It is an exchange of courtesies which so far is very good, though of course many constructions will be put on this step which I fear may not be without their dangers. For my part, my feelings are divided, as I am inclined to distrust all sensational demonstrations.'

A couple of days afterwards, the former Chancellor pays a formal call on the Empress.

'It was strange to see Prince Bismark here. I think the occurrence was made a little too much of. At any rate he was very courteously received. His visit lasted about 8 minutes, we only exchanged some civil words, and then parted. I sat next to him on the sofa, and thought him unchanged, perhaps a trifle thinner, but he had more colour in his face than formerly, as now he is out of doors a great deal, and leads a country life. I do not think his visits will make his press and his party much less violent against the Government, but I do think they may calm the feelings of those who fancied he was ill-treated last year, and in this respect it was a good move.'

At the beginning of February, the Empress sets out again for a visit to England, and once more she writes from Osborne.

'I arrived at this dear place yesterday afternoon, after a 16-hour very rough disagreeable passage in the dear yacht. The poor Reischachs were both dreadfully sea-sick, and I too, and had a racking headache besides, and crawled into my bed at Flushing and never got up until we were under shelter of the Isle of Wight. The maids and the menservants were also ill, but it was by no means considered a bad passage for the time of the year.

'I found Grandmama looking well in the face, and seeming bright, but very lame and not able to stand and walk more than a very few minutes. She complains that you have never sent her photographs of Georgia and baby and that she is so anxious for them. She asked so much about your health. She is seriously thinking of going to Ernie and Ducky's wedding, which is to take place on the 19th of April at Coburg. I shall go too.

'Uncle Bertie and Aunt Alix came today and Victoria and Maudie. Dear Auntie Alix seems in much better spirits, and I have not seen her look so well for a long time. Uncle Bertie is going to sail his new yacht, the "Britannia", in the Mediterranean at the beginning of March, he is to try her to-day. Liko is still very sad about his poor brother's death.'

Successive letters describe the Empress's encounters with her various relations, the walks and rides with them, church services, the weather, the scenery, and all the things she revels in.

'It is such joy waking up in the morning and finding oneself here! Dear, dear place, how I love it, with all its charms and beauties and comforts and dear memories of bygone days...I have made great friends with Victoria Battenberg's 3 little ones. The boy is my godson, he is such a love. He is a grand baby, a most magnificent child. Little Louise is really lovely. She has such a sweet gentle expression and such beautiful features. Their room is next to mine and I often go in and have a nice play with them. Aunt Beatrice's Ena is quite a big girl now, and very dear, but no longer as pretty as she was. Poor little Leopold is much grown but he is rather delicate and an anxiety to them. Maurice is also a fine child. All these little people in the house make it very bright as you can imagine. I think sweet Victoria of Wales is looking very well, and dear Maudie, too, and very much "en beaute". I cannot help admiring them more than Ella or Alicky. They are more graceful and more natural, and so much more agreeable and bright. I think they are more clever too. How I wish they would marry. It does seem a shame for such nice charming girls not to have homes of their own. They would make such perfect wives and mothers.'

The Empress describes an accident to Princess Ena, who is thrown from her pony and sustains concussion. 'Grandmama, Liko and Aunt Beatrice are much tormented, and we are all so distressed ...she looks so pretty lying there with her fair hair over the pillow, but it is so grievous that she cannot take notice or open her eyes.' She goes on:

'Everybody teases me about my love for Greece, and says I have gone a little mad on the subject. It is only to chaff me.... Fancy your 2 dear little people going to communion and being so good, and tiny Georgie trying to sing with the choir! How is your house getting on? If only your papa-in-law would consent to put his kitchen garden somewhere else you might have the most lovely terrace and flower garden under your windows, with a lawn tennis ground and a place for the children to play.'

The letter crosses with one from Sophie about the delays in completing the house, to which goes the reply:

'It is indeed too bad that the government can find no funds to finish your Palace, though considering the state of the finances, I am not surprised that the money should be wanting. Would it not be better to borrow the money and finish the house ourselves, and have a written contract with the State that it will pay you back in a certain number of months or years while you pay the capital back by instalments? It would not cost you more than the rent you have to pay to N.P. for your present house, which is really getting too small for you now.'

The attachment that still persists between the Tsarevitch of Russia and Princess Alix has found mention several times.

'I hear (and only tell you in confidence) that Alix of Hesse has now decided not to entertain the idea of marrying Nicky of Russia, though he wished it deeply, and Ella [*Princess Elizabeth, the Grand Duchess Serge — Ed.*] took great pains to bring it about. Alicky likes him very much, but will not change her religion on any account, because her father did not wish her to do it, and in this case it would be unavoidable. I am very sorry for the poor girl, and I am sorry for Nicky, as I fear he had set his heart upon it.

'Ferdinand of Bulgaria's wife has been very ill indeed again and they were very anxious. It is a wonder her nerves are not more shaken, as the whole time before the baby was born she received threatening letters from Panslavist agents, telling her she would be murdered with her child, she would be assassinated if she had a son, one dagger was to pierce them both, which was not very pleasant for the poor thing.'

Writing still from Osborne, the Empress notes that 'The whole day yesterday was one of great anxiety about dear little Ena. She is still in great danger....' But a few days afterwards, she thankfully writes:

'Dear Ena is now clear of danger, but has to be kept very quiet. ...We leave for Windsor in an hour, but I must still send you a line from this dear place, which I am so awfully sorry to leave...looking this morning so bright and lovely. The other evening the moon was so magnificent that I did not find it in my heart to shut out its lovely light, and I sat and gazed and dreamed of how its rays were falling on the Acropolis and the Lycabettus and on your balcony, and thought of the lovely evenings at Tatoi when your dear Mama and I sat enjoying the entrancing beauty of the full moon shining over the silent trees and the plain and distant sea. In spite of the spiders and centipedes of which I was in such dread, it was glorious, and I should be miserable if I thought I was not to see that much loved scene again.'

In her next letter she urges, not for the first or last time, that Sophie should bestir herself to travel round Greece.

'I do wish you would visit Olympia and Nauplia and Manolada and Corfu, before it is hot. It would do so much good if you and Tino showed yourselves outside Athens, and make you so popular. So many, many people have told me how ardently it was wished. Your health has often prevented you, also the weather, but a little tour of 10 days or a fortnight would show you an immense deal and give you a greater knowledge of other parts of the country. It is *so* important, indeed I look upon it as a duty. Now you speak Greek so much better and are more at home in the ways and customs of the people you would not feel half so shy, and think what pleasure it would give to the hearts that would be won.

'It is indeed good news to hear you are really growing stouter, and drink so much beer. If you can tell me your cheeks are getting rosy too, I shall be quite delighted.

'I have seen some sweet pictures at the water colour exhibition which I think you would like, amongst others a little gem of still life, very light and pearly in tone, as if Alma Tadema had painted it. It was only £10, and I should certainly advise you taking it, as it is a lovely bit of colour, and one must have a still life amongst one's other pictures, too many heads and landscapes exclusively do not set one another off to advantage.'

From Windsor, the Empress goes for a brief stay with the Prince and Princess of Wales at Sandringham.

'York Cottage is very small, but most charmingly arranged, it would quite delight you, and you might take many a hint for your own house. We saw the kennels, the stables, the stud with all the yearlings, and the mares, the splendid kitchen garden and greenhouses. We looked at the farm, and then at the little technical school where the children of the village are taught to make charming things in wood and iron-work and brass and copper. It is impossible to find an estate in finer order than Uncle Bertie's, plantations, fields, roads, fences and walls, cottages and churches and all, so trim and well cared for.

'May came over to dinner and looked very nice, only a little pale, that is the only perceptible sign of her condition. Auntie has still on her table the photo of Eddy, together with May. "I cannot put it away," she said. "What *has* been, *has* been, though it *is* no more." I feel that she is right, but it is so painful to be reminded constantly of what *might* have been. Georgie looks quite happy and contented, and both Victoria and Maud are looking well, and Auntie Alix also....'

The following day the Empress wrote of how:

'This morning Uncle and sweet Aunt took me into the room where poor dear Eddy died, all is left just as it was, his dressing table with his watch, his brushes and combs and everything. His bed covered with a "Union Jack" in silk, and his photos and trifles and clothes, etc., in a glass cupboard opposite the bed. This room was his and Georgie's school-room when they were little, and there he died, poor darling. No one is to live in it again.'

She pays a visit to Cambridge University, which she much admires, and goes to see:

'...the 2 ladies' colleges, Newnham and Girton, which interested me immensely and I was not a little proud to see how worthy the buildings were of the learning that is taught to women within their walls. The lady students do great credit to the institution, and show that when proper opportunities are afforded for serious and methodical study, we need not be the more ignorant sex even though we are the weaker, and that though it is neither necessary nor desirable that we should copy men or try to take up their professions, yet we may enrich our lives and be of more use to our husbands and families, our households and our countries, by being thoroughly trained and possessing a certain amount of solid knowledge. There is so much work to do in the world that I do not see why women should not help as well as they can, and the better educated they are, the more fit they will be to do it. Of course there are 1000's of young ladies who cannot and will not study. Them I would certainly not force, as it would be a waste of time. 'Yesterday Mr. Gladstone resigned, but what is going to happen is not yet known. Most likely Lord Rosebery will take his place for the present.'

Back at Windsor, she describes, on March 4th, Gladstone's last call upon the Queen:

'Yesterday, Mr. Gladstone came to take leave of Grandmama. He was much moved. The end of his official days and of his political career! I thought the dear old gentleman very touching and very dignified. I am not as you know a supporter of many of his political plans and measures, and think him eccentric in many things, and narrow-minded in others, but he is a true *idealist*, and not one of those wretched opportunists who think that slyness and quickness are everything in this world. He has noble qualities and large-hearted sympathies. He retires a poor man and does not wish a title. As he walked away down the corridor I felt that another chapter of English history had closed, and that he was disappearing into the past. It was the *right* moment to go. The shoulders of 80 cannot bear the immense burdens of the affairs of so large an Empire. His eyes are failing, his deafness increasing, and he is no longer what he was, or able to stand fatigue, though his health is good. I feel *much* more sympathy with a nature like his than with one like Prince Bismark's. Mr. Gladstone loves the people, while Prince Bismark was utterly indifferent to them, to their hopes and joys and sorrows and trials. They were to him a political factor and nothing more.'

The next day's letter contains an assortment of family news.

'Dear Grandmama received Lord Rosebery, and tomorrow there is a drawing-room. I am going to a few exhibitions in London, and this afternoon with Aunt Alix to two studios.

'Dear little Ena arrived here from Osborne 2 days ago, and is doing very nicely, but she has to be kept very quiet indeed, and still looks pale and weak...Frogmore Gardens are in great beauty, the show of flowers in the conservatory would delight you. I am going to send 2 children's picture books to tiny Georgie, but they are so pretty, and the drawings so well done, that I fancy his Mama will care still more than her little son for them! ...Dona and her children go tomorrow to Abbazia. I don't think the place will charm, it is bleak and windy. The party will be 72 in number, which quite makes one laugh!'

The last letter from Windsor, a week later, mentions that 'little Ena is now almost right again', and goes on:

'Dear Gan-gan sends you her best love. How lame and infirm she is breaks my heart to see, but thank God she is otherwise well and bright, and her mind and intelligence and interest and power of work quite what they were. She makes very light of it all, which is wonderful. She is still so helpless that she often gives herself a twist or a rick in the effort of rising from her chair or getting in and out of the carriage. One of her Indian servants is cleverest about helping her about and she leans on him, but has a stick in her other hand...tomorrow is my last day with her and I feel the parting dreadfully. Six weeks a year is all I get. I wish I could stay longer and try to be of use to her. Her dear hair is quite white now, but it suits her so well, with her fresh complexion, and soft white cap, and smile which is still so young. Of an evening she *does* look charming, but it is sad to see her aged and helpless.

'Grandmama held a Privy Council yesterday and some of the ministers remained to dinner, also the Lord Chancellor, Lord Herschell. It is a very interesting time in politics just now. Lord Rosebery has a most difficult task to face, but being a very clever energetic man he will succeed, I hope, in keeping his Party and his colleagues together, and yet not try to carry out *all* Mr. Gladstone's programme, of which a great deal is simply impossible and would be dangerous. My heart is much more with the Liberals than with the Tories, as you know.'

She spends her last week at Buckingham Palace, from where she completes her shopping expeditions, has a final round of meetings with her many relations, and sees various other people, one of them the woman who is her great inspiration in her nursing work. 'In the afternoon, I paid Miss Florence Nightingale a visit, and found her unchanged.' Then she crosses to Germany. Back in Bonn, she writes on Good Friday, March 23rd, of staying once more with...

'...dearest Vicky and Adolf. Bonn is such a cheerful place that I don't wonder they are so fond of it.... The whole visit to England seems like a dream. Dear England! How I love it! I cannot help it! What dreadful Katzenjammer [*'fed-upness'*— Ed.]. I should have if I had to go direct from there to Berlin! But being with Vicky is such a treat. Adolf has become a staff officer and has given up the command of his *schwadron* since 3 days. Vicky is delighted, as now he will no longer be tied down, and will not work so hard nor spend so many hours away from the house, nor be so exhausted when he comes back. It was really perfect slavery. He is very sorry though to part from his men and to say goodbye to his comrades.'

From Margaret's home, Schloss Rümpenheim, she writes, among long descriptions of the house and its furnishings, 'I think Mossy's sweet baby such a pretty little dear. It has not Mossy's fine large eyes, but a sweet little face of its own, and is certainly more like Fischy than her.' She then goes on to Friedrichshof, which is now habitable.

'The first day I spent in my new abode was very fatiguing, and there will be weeks of work before everything is comfortable and in order. What will you say when you see all you used to call the 'dirty, ugly, horrid old rubbish' which I used to collect on journeys, to your utter horror and despair and contempt, now placed about the house? The villagers all turned out to receive me, with the schoolgirls in white dresses, and bouquets. They had put up a triumphal arch, and the bells were ringing. I was very touched.

'I don't wonder at the disappointing impression Lord Rosebery's speech made on your papa-in-law, but there is this to be said. Lord Rosebery is not quite a free agent, he took over Mr. Gladstone's policy and his colleagues and his party. But although he is a strong radical, at the same time he is very keen about upholding the strength and power, influence and honour of his country, and has that more in view than Mr. Gladstone had...But I do not think the present Government will last very long, and then there will be new elections.

'I hear dear Grandmama is delighted with her stay in Florence and has enjoyed herself very much indeed. Uncle Bertie's Britannia has won all the race prizes off the coast of the Riviera, and he says he had a very nice time there.'

Some days later she returns to the subject of Sophie's welfare work in Greece.

'I am very glad you found the almshouse in order and the inhabitants clean and happy and satisfied. A committee that quarrel are a great nuisance — you should have a "working committee", i.e. 2 or 3 persons chosen out of the large committee to meet every week, the large committee once in every 3 or 6 months.

'How nice it must have been to hear the singing at the new Conservatoire School of Music. In Greece music has so long been neglected, forgotten and put aside, but the taste cannot be wholly wanting in the Greek people, it must simply be dormant. Every town should have its choral and orchestral society, and in every school singing ought to be taught. I also hope to see a school for drawing and sculpture started one day.

'I am going over to Rümpenheim as it is Sunday to spend the day with the darlings. The bells are ringing, and the birds singing, all the fruit blossom out, and the early green beginning to cover the branches of the larch and birch trees, and it is a real spring morning.'

The Empress is informed that the Emperor William proposes to visit her for a night. Discussing this, she refers to the breach which still exists between him and Sophie over her embracing the Orthodox Faith.

'It does not suit me at all, as it will overwork my servants very much to get quite ready by that time. Although I do not wish to grumble, yet I cannot be expected to be overwhelmed and touched and enthusiastic about a visit which I consider a duty to me. And I am still *too* sad at heart, the hurts are too fresh in my memory. Still, I shall make the visit as pleasant for him as I can, as I think he is animated by better sentiments, and wishes in his way to be as friendly as possible to his Mama. But it is a very strange way.

'I wonder when you will ever meet him again. The initiative must come from *him* and not from *you*. If he invites you once to meet him when you are in Germany, of course you could not well refuse, but I would not take the first step, I do not think it would be right or dignified. Still, I trust an opportunity will present itself, as it is necessary that you should meet once again, and that he should end the foolish rupture which was of his making, though both he and Dona were instigated by Charlotte, as I now know, though I did not then.'

The next letter deals with the Coburg wedding, which Queen Victoria attended.

'Ducky looked very charming and *distinguée*. She had a plain white silk gown with hardly any trimming, and Aunt Alice's wedding veil, a light slender diadem of emeralds with a sprig of orange blossom stuck in behind. It all suited her charmingly. During the service Aunt Marie was very calm, but the tears rolled down Uncle Alfred's cheeks, and Grandmama's and mine too. The wedding breakfast was very well served and arranged. No one wore trains, but low gowns, diadems, orders, etc. Little Missy of Roumania was looking pale and thin, and is expecting No. II! William seemed quite in a good humour, and to enjoy himself a great deal...Grandmama looked so nice in her white cap and veil and diamonds. Nicky was there looking very handsome. I wish I could tell you that everything is settled about him and Alicky, they both much wish it, but the religious question still seems the obstacle.'

But the next day the engagement is announced, for the Emperor William, with the political advantages of such a match in mind, had persuaded Alix to overcome her scruples. The Empress did not then know of his intervention, for she writes:

'Alicky was quite radiant and beaming with joy. The moment Nicky arrived I saw by her face that she *would* — though it was so strange to refuse him first, and to swear to everyone that though she was very fond of him, she would never take him. Even my dear Mama thought she would not accept him, she was so positive about it. ... I could not help chuckling to myself that William did not think Alicky so very sinful to accept Nicky, and with him the necessity of conforming to the Orthodox Church. Of course, I made no remarks!'

She refers to the projected visit of Prince Max of Baden to Athens.

'Of course, no one knows whether he is free, and still looking for a wife, but ...Grandmama is so anxious that if he has not made up his mind to ask for one of your Aunt Vera's [*Queen Olga's sister — Ed.*] daughters, and does not think of your sweet Minny [*Prince Constantine's sister, Marie — Ed.*], he should marry one of the darling cousins of Wales. I wonder whether Tino or you could tell me when you have seen him whether you think such a thing possible? Victoria and Maud are two of the sweetest girls I have ever seen, and would be sure to make him happy, and how he would enjoy being often in England! Indeed, I wish he would, if he has no other plans. Uncle Bertie would like it very much, I know, only dear Aunt Alix dislikes us Germans so, and it is really not quite fair to generalize. Such a man as Max is not to be met with every day.'

The Emperor duly pays his promised official visit to Friedrichshof.

'William arrived with his suite of 18 people yesterday evening. The whole province had turned out, and express trains were run from Frankfort and Wiesbaden, which brought crowds of spectators, who were drawn up by the railway station and along the road up to my gates. The little town of Cronberg was charmingly decorated. Of course I should far have preferred an unofficial visit, and no uniforms and more peace and quiet. The weather has been as unfavourable as possible, cold, blowy, rainy and dark, so that nothing showed to advantage, which is very irritating. Still I think the visit is going off all right, and that in his way William enjoyed himself. His gentlemen seemed also to like being here, but all these great big noisy *aides-de-camp* are a great bore and trial.'

A few days previously news had come of another severe earthquake in Greece. In the course of her letters of sympathy, the Empress writes: 'It is too sad and shocking to think that 300 people have perished. The survivors will need everything, food, clothes, shelter, help and medicine. Poor things. You should send Elizabeth P. off to help them, with a couple of ladies.'

When Sophie's account of the disaster arrives, her mother comments:

'I am quite miserable about the earthquakes. Thank God you were all mercifully preserved. I think I should beg your Papa's large tent off him and live in camp until the period of these awful shocks is over. If I were to build a house in Greece, I should never build more than one story, I think the ancients built their houses low on purpose...Grandmama wrote to me so distressed about the earthquakes and asking after you so much. A great deal of courage and presence of mind seems to have been shown, and much resignation. It is strange that people should find comfort in religious processions, or imagine the course of nature once laid down by Providence in immutable laws more than half hidden to us poor mortals, and yet for the good of all, can be changed by appeals to Heaven. Such a simple belief has something touching and melancholy, but perhaps it consoles those in fear and distress, and enables them to have strength to fight against the dangers around them, and bear with resignation what is sent.'

On May 15th comes the telegram saying that Sophie and her husband are starting for their visits to their respective grandparents in Britain and Denmark, and also to Friedrichshof. Everyone is highly excited, the Empress most of all, as her letter shows.

'When your dear telegram arrived I jumped up from my chair in such haste that I upset it. Vicky was overjoyed. Mossy telegraphed in high glee from Rümpenheim.... What pleasure it will give dear Gan-Gan and Apapa. This letter I send to Venice. ... I pray and trust the sea may be smooth. I shall not sleep until you arrive.... I shall feel like an old hen gathering her chickens once more under her wings!'

After spending a few days with her mother, Sophie leaves the children at Friedrichshof while she and Prince Constantine visit Queen Victoria and the King and Queen of Denmark. They return for a while, but at last the day of departure for Greece arrives, and on July 15th, the Empress writes her usual letter of woe at the parting.

'I went into your empty room, and the flowers and little scraps of paper still strewn about all seemed dear to me. It is very foolish, I know, but I could not help sobbing my heart out. I sat on your sofa and in Tino's armchair, and

Kathleen the housemaid, with her broom in her hand, shed tears of sympathy. It was indeed such a joy to have you here. Thank you both my darlings for all your love and affection, and the life and brightness your young lives bring into mine.

'Would you remind dear Tino of a decoration for G., head of the Prussian Railway officials at Frankfort, who has been very helpful in your travelling arrangements at different times.

'I have read in the papers that there seems some chance of an agreement with the English and German delegates about the foreign bondholders, at which I sincerely rejoice, as the press here were adopting language which I think most violent and insolent, talking of sending Fleets to the Piraeus and occupying some islands, etc., until some promise is given of Greece fulfilling her obligations. I was much disgusted and it made me very angry, but the loss of money does make people savage! I feel certain that all this will eventually blow over, but it is very sad that the ministers should not have saved the country from falling into so disagreeable and painful a situation.'

On August 2nd she uses for the first time in the Letters Crown Prince Constantine's pet name.

'This is "Sweetie's" birthday, may God bless and protect him and give him strength for all his duties. Who can be more devoted to him except his little wife and his parents than I am? I cannot say all I feel on the subject, nor how very, very dear he is to me.... But I cannot fancy Tino dear with a beard! It seems such a shame to hide the dimples! But he will find it a great convenience not to be obliged to shave, in the meantime it looks all stubby and scrubby, I am sure. Georgie of York and Nicky of Russia and our Henry have grown beards, and I suppose Tino wishes to keep them company.'

Now that the Empress is firmly installed in her home, almost every letter contains mention of some visitor to whom she proudly shows the house and gardens, and especially the flowers in which she takes such joy, 'the roses splendid again in their second bloom'.

'King Charles of Roumania brought me a book he has just caused to be published of his place at Sinaia, Castel Peles, very handsomely got up with good woodcuts and etchings. The country must be too beautiful, glorious mountains and woods, like in the Bavarian Alps, but the house seems to me a gimcrack affair without style or taste, much reminding me of the hotel at Toblach, very large and costly and in a most beautiful position, but oh! dear, to think of 6 million francs spent on so ugly a building. I prefer unpretentious Tatoi out and out.

'Can you not send me a little photo of what the garden at Tatoi looks like now? Is there nobody among you all who takes photographs? Shall I send a list out of plants which would do for the terrace, bright flowers that are not expensive? Perhaps I could send you some seeds? Tatoi ought to be a bower of flowers, the soil is so good and can always be improved with manure from the stables and the cow house, and it is easy to water, as you have those streams which supply the ditches of the vineyard.

'William is at Cowes now being feted and enjoying himself. Unfortunately the Britannia has been beaten twice. She has won so often that it really does not matter, still it is most annoying.'

Selections from successive letters about this time, August, show how the Empress passes her days, and occupies her mind.

"The town of Cronberg is going to build a little hospital for "general" patients, both for surgical and all other cases. I have given the land, and I am going to pay for the nursing, and it will be under my patronage. I hope this will be a boon to the town and the very poor villages around.'

'My cows have got quite accustomed to grazing in the fields now with their bells on, and look very pretty. The calves are much grown and frisk and kick about on the grass. I never saw anything so beautiful and in such rich bloom as the heather this year, and the meadows are even more covered with wild flowers than they were in the spring before the first hay was cut. If we only can get a week of dry weather we shall have quite a fair second crop of hay. I come home every afternoon with a perfect armful of heather and wild flowers from the hedges and sides of the ditches, and baskets and pocket handkerchiefs full of blackberries and mushrooms. It is real fun going out to gather them — you see your Mama is still like a baby over these things!'

'How nice it is to hear you give such a good account of yourself. I am so glad you have some fun and amusement and society...Do not play too much lawn tennis and put yourself in too great a perspiration, as you will catch cold to a certainty. Do you think of keeping your neck uncovered and not wearing those tight high collars all day?'

'I fancy I can see sweet baby crawling along the rooms and pushing a footstool before him.... Fancy him dining with you! Indeed I agree with you that children are the greatest happiness in the world. I loved my babies to distraction especially those I nursed myself! But I love all babies, and dote on yours, as you know. It is *terrible* what one goes through when they are ill, and I will not speak of the agony when death snatches them from one's arms. I really nearly lost my reason twice. When they grow up and often give one *pain* and *sorrow,* it is hard, but few people are spared this in one shape or form, so that a parent's life is a perpetual school, as well as the child's. This I am sure you will find. How many things will dawn upon you now, that you will understand but never guessed before. What true mother would not wish to study and learn to be of use to her little ones, to protect them from harm and danger to body and mind? No detail seems unimportant, no care too troublesome, but that is the joy of being a mother.'

'Yesterday afternoon dear Uncle Bertie came over here from Romberg. It was very dark, and poured in torrents, so that I fear he cannot have had a good impression. Quite between ourselves I think Uncle Bertie and Aunt Alix had hoped that Victoria would marry Christian of Denmark, and are much disappointed that Victoria will not hear of it. What a pity...Uncle had received letters from Peterhof, and they did not sound quite favourable about the Emperor of Russia's health...but it is nothing that causes apprehension.'

'Alicky is in very good looks, but is in no hurry to marry, it seems. I think she is determined to wait until Ducky's baby is born, and she is well again, so that Ernie will be free to take her to Russia, but that seems a long time to wait, does it not? She is learning Russian and also has taken lessons with a priest.... Yesterday Charlotte arrived, and is looking in a decidedly anaemic state, which she herself admits. Sitting up so late, tight lacing, and especially constant smoking have done her a deal of harm. She ought to have a thorough cure, but instead of which she is going to rush off to Roumanja, which I think very odd...Henry is given command of the ship "Wörth", which Vicky christened for me two years ago.'

'...one feels that Greece ought really to have a foreign committee of finance control for some years.... But of course it would be impossible for the King to propose such a thing, and foreign powers cannot and ought not to propose it ...but wise men in Greece ought to demand it, as an *extraordinary* measure to meet an *extraordinary* situation. If it came from Greece, I cannot see that it would be undignified or humiliating. Greece after all has not been an independent state for much more than half a century. Administration is a very difficult thing, wants good tradition and long training, and it is really no shame to have made mistakes if one learns from them.'

'Yesterday evening we had a great treat. Joachim came with Robert Mendelssohn from Berlin, and we had Uzielli from Frankfort to accompany them. They played too beautifully. A concerto of Schumann's and one of Mendelssohn's and a sonata of Handel's. Never did Joachim play better or with more power and style. Aunt Lenchen [*Princess Christian — Ed.*] came to listen, and I asked some people in after supper to enjoy the lovely music, which one can really say was the best of the best, and sounded so well in the green salon.'

In September the Empress is concerned over an incident in Athens, when a number of indignant army officers invade a newspaper office.

'I fear my sympathies are quite on the side of the officers, still such a business is not in the interests of discipline, and I am afraid it is not quite the thing for officers to take part in politics. These vile newspapers that go on attacking the army and Papa and Tino make one savage, still one must not attach too much importance to them, and everyone that likes to answer them has a pen. Much evil comes from this liberty of the press, but also much good, and the absence of it is a great danger. Usually the good, sensible and useful people are too lazy and indolent to write against the nonsense, rubbish and untruths written by the professional newspaper scribblers, who have *no* conscience whatsoever, and only write for money, and whatever will create a sensation. Usually the press is quietly left to the worst hands, but a good press and a free one is an immense engine for good.'

German army manoeuvres are taking place in the neighbourhood, and several regiments are billeted around Cronberg. She rides down to see them when they leave after three days.

'The troops all leave Cronberg today. I have just heard them march off with their band playing at their head. I sent the men some beer yesterday, so that they should have a pleasant remembrance of the place. It seems they were received with open arms everywhere in the agricultural towns and villages round here, whereas around Frankfort the people grumbled and complained bitterly to have soldiers quartered on them. Of course it is hard for them, there is no doubt, but in the large factories near Frankfort the people are all rather socialistic, and hate soldiers, the army and everything military, and one cannot much wonder from *their* point of view.'

Periodically, when the Emperor makes one of his too outspoken speeches, his mother is stirred to brief remonstrance.

'W's speech at Konigsberg makes me quite unhappy, it is so mistaken and reveals an absolutist tendency which *for him,* and in the place he occupies, is most dangerous and gives rise to discussions which are not at all good. However I say nothing, but it grieves me much when such mistakes are made.'

A typical gossipy letter in October mentions a visit by King George of Greece, who comes to take the waters in the locality.

'Fancy my joy and astonishment when I had a telegram yesterday from Romberg from your Papa-in-Law saying he would be here this morning. I was so pleased.... His visit was very short, but all the same I enjoyed it very much. Alas there was a dense fog and your Papa never saw any view at all, and did not walk in the garden. I have seldom seen him looking so well and in such good spirits, and we had a nice little talk together.

'Yesterday evening news arrived that Missy had had a little girl at Sinaia. Poor thing, she seems to have had a bad time, I am very sorry...Do not forget I was promised one of baby's beautiful little curls whenever one can be spared, from the back where it will not be missed. ... I send an account of a bazaar at Balmoral. Later, some day, if you make a bazaar for your maternity hospital, I shall be very glad to assist you with a few things.

'Are the grapes gathered and the wine made at Tatoi? I wonder with the many fine cows you have at the farm that there is no dairy to make butter and cheese and cream. It would be really quite easy. ... Or if you started your own farm at Manolada!

'How is the trial of the officer's going on? I hope they were not punished much.'

October 18th, is the anniversary of the Emperor Frederick's birthday.

'On this dear never-to-be-forgotten anniversary I know your thoughts will be with me, and as mine are, dwelling on the beloved one whose birthday it was. Oh, how my heart does ache when I think of what might be were he still among us for the good and happiness and welfare of so many. What happy days and years we still might have spent together. How darling Papa would have loved Tino, just a son after his own heart. What a joy your sweet little ones would have been to him, how he would have loved to carry them about. How our dear old home would have been a gathering place for you all. It all makes me so sad. However we must not murmur, but cling to what is left, and think of him who was so good and kind. P.S. Grandmama telegraphed to me yesterday evening that the news of the Emperor of Russia from Livadia were not good, the weakness causes anxiety, and that Ella and Serge had left for the Crimea. It is very sad. Poor dear Aunt Minny! [*Marie, Empress of Russia — Ed.*]

During the past months the Letters have periodically mentioned Margaret's interesting condition, and on October 21st the Empress hastens to announce that:

'Thank God all is well, and I am sitting near Mossy darling's bed. She bids me tell you she had not an ache or pain, has slept well and likes her food, and is delighted with her little baby, who is a nice healthy boy and weighed over 7 German pounds when he was born. You can fancy how cruelly disappointed I was to be too late. The telegram that Mossy was taken ill, which was sent off at 4 in the morning, never reached me until a quarter to 8, together with the telegram that the child was born. That I was frantic you can well imagine. Train there was none at that hour. I flew downstairs and ordered my carriage and scrambled into my clothes, had no breakfast and tore off as soon as I could. In an hour and a few minutes we reached Frankfort, where we found Fischy's brougham, and came on directly, so that I was with Mossy darling before 11, and found her well.'

At the end of October, the German Chancellor General von Capri vi resigned as the result of political manoeuvrings.

'You will be surprised to hear that Caprivi has retired and Prince Chlodwig v. Hohenlohe has taken his place. In many ways I am very sorry. Caprivi enjoyed the respect and confidence due to a thoroughly estimable, honorable and excellent man, but I think in many ways Prince Hohenlohe will be preferred from the fact that he is *not* a soldier, and has had more political experience. I only fear that his health is too shaky and that he is too feeble altogether for the work and responsibility and anxiety. Still one must say, it is always a blessing that none of those short-sighted prejudiced Junkers has been chosen, which would have put everyone's back up, and made a lively opposition in the Reichstag.'

On November 2nd, the Empress writes of the ominous condition of the Emperor of Russia. Later in the day she continues:

'When I wrote to you this morning we were still in ignorance of the sad news that already yesterday the poor Emperor had passed away. For him a blessing and mercy that his troubles are at an end, but for dear Aunt Minny how cruel and sad and terrible. I do feel for her intensely and sincerely, who could understand what she is going through better than I do? May her children prove a real comfort and consolation to her, as I am sure they will.'

For some time her letters contain reflections on the possible consequences of this event.

'How sad that Nicky is so young in this most responsible position, enough to crush any one. May he have all the good and wise council he will want. He has a great mission, may he be rightly inspired to fulfil it. That unfortunate nation groaning and thirsting for the simplest elements of liberty, such as every other country now enjoys! Will Nicky be allowed to understand or know this? No one is *more* dependent than an absolute monarch, as if the truth does not reach his ears, all his decisions, even with the best intentions, may be wrongly taken. The last poor Emperor's life was always more or less in danger. This dear young man could escape all this, kill nihilism with one blow, and rest in safety, if only he could take up the plan his grandfather had prepared all ready. But who can tell him? [*Tsar Alexander II was assassinated just as he was about to introduce sweeping radical reforms — Ed.*]

'How hard for poor Aunt Minny to see another young Empress in her stead, with she still herself so much too young to be an Empress Dowager. It is a very difficult and painful position, at any rate for some years. However Nicky is such a good, dutiful and devoted son, he will make it easy for her, and she will not have to go through what I had to endure, and often still have. Alicky is sure to be very good to her, even though she has grown up without a mother, and been a little spoilt, which has made her a little vain and conceited and affected at times, but she is very kind-hearted, and when she becomes a little less indolent will, I am sure, do all she can to make matters easy for her mother-in-law.'

Further news follows from the Prince of Wales who, with his wife, has gone to the Crimea:

'Uncle Bertie telegraphed that he found Aunt Minny calm, which is indeed a blessing. Grandmama wrote to me that Alicky would be married, *en famille*, after the funeral, at which Grandmama seemed much upset as she hoped to see her again before her marriage. I think it the only sensible thing to do now she has become Grand Duchess Alexandra Feodorovna, and has joined the Russian Church. It is very sad to think of the young inexperienced heads now wearing Crowns. One can only trust they will do well. Nicky is so good and nice that he will be sure to do his best, and one's wishes, blessings and prayers attend him.'

Referring to the departure of the Grand Duke Ernst for Russia, together with many other relations of the new Emperor and his bride, the Empress adds:

'Poor Ducky will be left all alone at Darmstadt. She is looking lovely, but very pale, and her figure showing scarcely anything of impending events. She is such a dear and so sympathetic, unaffected, gentle and ladylike. She is looking very pulled, thin and drawn in the face, which usually denotes a little girl, as people say, but these sayings are mostly nonsense.'

On November 23rd, two days after her birthday, she writes from Schloss Rümpenheim:

'How I have struggled to find a moment to write to you these 2 last days, but with 270 telegrams and a couple of dozen letters to read and answer, I really did not know *what* to do. I knew you would forgive and excuse me.... My birthday repose with Mossy love was quite upset by William suddenly appearing without having been announced. I was in my bath, Fischy was in bed, and the surprise was rather too complete a one. However, it was kindly meant, and I think Mossy was pleased to have him. He was in a very good mood, and had never been at Rümpenheim before. Of course the luncheon was completely upset, we were expecting Charlotte and Bernhard, Vicky and Adolf, Aunt Anna and Ilia [*Princess Sibylla, "Fischy's" sister — Ed.*], they had all to be telegraphed *not* to come, as there was no room with William and his gentlemen. So they appeared for the afternoon and stayed to tea. I received many charming presents, some of which were for Friedrichshof. The bouquets I sent down to the cellar so that the servants may decorate the rooms and the dinner table for the christening today. Of course I was frightened for fear all this unexpected bustle should agitate Mossy dear, but she felt no ill effects, I am happy to say, nor darling baby either, whereas Fischy and I had racking headaches!'

The celebration of the new Tsar's marriage gives the Empress occasion to reveal her forebodings for Russia.

'Tomorrow is Alicky's wedding. I am sure she will be very glad when it is over, as her position in her new home must have been very awkward and difficult. It is all easier for her in many ways than for anyone else. She has no father or mother from whom to part, her sisters are married, one of them will always be near her, and had she stayed at Darmstadt it would have been with a sister-in-law at the head of the house, so I can fancy nothing more fortunate for Alicky than the lot which has fallen to her — though *I* should *not* like to live in Russia, and I am glad and thankful my Sophie does not live there, but in the free air of sunny Hellas. I would not change your position with hers, not for all the state and grandeur, the splendour, riches and jewels which hide the other dark side from view. I would not say this to a Russian of course, but you understand what I mean.

'The idea that the will of one person governs the whole of that vast gigantic empire is a fiction, and those who wield the power in his name are many of them not to be trusted, so that the lot of the people under such government is not to be envied. The horrors of Siberia still exist, the persecution of the Jews, the oppression of the Protestants. Will dear young Nicky, with the best and noblest and most humane of intentions, be able to alter this? Who knows?'

From Rümpenheim, the Empress goes to Berlin, where once more she finds that: 'the life has given me quite a headache again, and tries my nerves a good deal. There is always so much going on, and always at times when it is most inconvenient. The day before yesterday all the Hohenzollerns came ...yesterday Henry and Irene arrived between 6 and 7 in the morning ...then I had to go to two bazaars, they were intensely ugly and the air in the close room dreadful.' But a welcome guest arrives, her brother.

'Uncle Alfred arrived this morning, I am happy to say looking much better than I expected. Aunt Marie [*Duchess of Edinburgh — Ed.*] never came near me, but went straight on to Coburg. Since 1888 she has not paid me a visit, but has often been to Friedrichskron or to Charlotte's house. This I feel a little and think myself a bit neglected. Uncle Alfred is always so pleased to see me and I should be so glad to show them Friedrichshof.

'The sparrows are chirping in the yard as I am writing, just as they used to. It is less cold today so they are more lively, yesterday they all sat close together on the roof like little balls, looking very doleful because of the frost. I feed them almost every day.'

A few days later, the Empress describes how her brother rose to a pressing situation.

'Since I last wrote we have had a dreadful scare. Uncle, who was very tired, having spent 2 nights in the train, went to bed between 10 and 11. At 3 o'clock, the firewatch passed along the corridor, opened Uncle's salon door and found, as he says, all in order. At 4, Uncle awoke nearly stifled with smoke. He jumped up, and rushed into the salon, which he could hardly cross as the smoke was so dense, opened the window, called his servant, and sent him to rouse the house. He poured 2 or 3 jugs of water where the smoke came from, by the stove, and turned on the water in his bath to have some more ready. You know how quick and practical he is, being a British sailor, and accustomed to all sorts of emergencies. The fire wagons soon rattled into the courtyard and lit up the whole place with their torches. What a scene of confusion and smoke and water and mess, in our nice rooms, it was really wretched! They tore up the floor around the fireplace with their axes, and found that two of the beams had been smouldering for 2 days most likely. If Uncle had not been living up there and had not called for help the whole place might have been burnt down.'

Extracts from some of the letters from Berlin indicate the Empress's varied interests when staying in the Capital.

'Yesterday I was in the English Church, and the singing was so good. In the evening Passini and some other painters came and we had a long pleasant talk about their work.'

'Strange Aleck was here with Herr A. and they played to me, with no one else there but Countess H. They played beautifully and I enjoyed it much. In the afternoon W's brother, a doctor of medicine, came to see me and I talked to him about this new Serum against diphtheria, which in spite of much that is still uncertain and difficult to prove, already has been and will in future be *very* useful.'

'Yesterday evening I had tea for all the ladies of my different institutions, and we talked over affairs of schools and hospitals for a long while. They all begin to know each other so much better now, and to be less shy. To work all together is the only way. Things are getting on well, I am happy to say, the only thing wanting is money. The only decent building of all my institutions is the Victoria Haus, new and clean, and the only one otherwise well-kept is the Home for British and American Governesses.'

'Yesterday I received a Russian General, who with his staff, came to announce Nicky's accession. In the evening I went to distribute toys among the children in the Kindergarten. It was an enormous room, but the crowd, the gas, and the stoves made the heat tremendous.'

'Old Minister F. and Prof. H. spent the evening with me and we had much interesting conversation. The latter, although he is a professor, is a charming and agreeable man, even you, who are not partial to professors would be obliged to admit this, my Sophie.'

'Today, I was at Potsdam. ... I went to the dear Mausoleum and remained there all alone for half-an-hour.'

'Here I am not at all happy about politics and I cannot feel that the government are going the right way to work or doing the right thing, alas. But one has to hold one's tongue and can only deplore many a mistake. I fear they will find the difficulties immense, which dearest Papa would have known how to solve, as he was in touch with the best and cleverest heads in the country, whose opinion now is never even heard, much less considered. Let's hope some day time may bring a change in this respect, but I do not think it.'

'Yesterday was really a lovely winter's day, sunshine, and an attempt at blue sky, with all the trees and bushes under snow, looking like *sugar,* but today it is dark and foggy again. I am sending a ridiculous little book which I beg you to read with Tino, it is very vulgar, but now and then very absurd, and may make you both laugh!'

In a letter consisting mainly of a description of how to ventilate a room in winter without draughts from an open window, the Empress concludes with some paragraphs of advice about Alexander, who is cutting his teeth and seems generally out of sorts. In the evening, a postscript is added, 'Your telegram arrived, which was indeed a great comfort and joy to me, to hear that sweet baby has 3 little teeth through and is better and now seems jolly.'

Over the Christmas period she is engaged in her customary good works, and writes on the 24th and 25th.

'I went yesterday evening to the Children's hospital and had a touching Xmas Party — the poor little things in their beds, many so terribly ill, and the Xmas tree in the wards, with presents laid out on a table, or on the little beds. I had sent heaps of things.

'I went to the Darmstadt ' Kinderheim" where there was a very pretty Xmas tree, and a charming tableaux of the Adoration of the Magi. The Virgin Mary and the child were lovely, like a picture by Raphael. The little baby was quite good and hardly moved, only once it laughed and stretched out its dear little hands and gave a little cry of pleasure at all the lamps and lights.

'On Christmas Eve I went to the Christmas Party in the large hospital at Friedrickshain, and then to the Victoria Haus for all the nurses. It was so well arranged and every one pleased with their presents. The sisters all looked so nice, I wish you had seen them. Last night Vicky arrived, an hour late.'

Although it is the festive season Sophie has once more had trouble with her staff, this time the nurse, whom she is obliged to dismiss.

'You are frightfully unlucky, Sophie dear. I thought her a very good nurse, active, careful, punctual and with a very good and quiet manner...but perhaps she *was* too strict and severe with little Georgie. I did not dare say much, as I am always afraid you might think I wished to interfere in your affairs, whereas my only wish is to help you or be of use to you and those precious darlings. I thought it was wrong always to threaten the child with his Papa. "If you are not good I will fetch your Papa!" It makes children afraid of the father if he is always held up as a sort of croquemitaine [*bogey — Ed.*]. Early childhood is the sunny time of life, and later one ought to look back upon it with joy. We have to surround the little things with love and happiness and govern them with gentleness, patience and kindness.'

Her last letter of the year looks forward as usual to the next meeting.

'This is the last day of the year, my own darling. When I look back on 1894, the happiest days and hours were when I had you with me at Friedrichshof. Oh, may it not be too long before we meet again and I can clasp you to my heart, and have your darling children in my arms, and see dear Tino once more.'

Chapter Seven – The Letters, 1895

Early in January, the Empress reluctantly refuses Sophie's invitation to join her in Corfu.

'How intensely I should enjoy it, but I am going to England in February to see dear Grandmama, and shall remain there until she goes to the Riviera in April, near Nice, les Cimiez, the place is called. Then I shall return to Germany, to Friedrichshof. I could not well come back here to Berlin! So for this year at least, I could not go to Corfu. I think, after the Riviera, Grandmama hopes to visit Darmstadt, and from there will come to see me at Friedrichshof. I have no plans yet for the autumn, but perhaps we could arrange something. It is such a pleasure to turn all these possibilities over in one's mind.

'Henry dear and Irene have gone, so that now I am quite alone, but I find plenty to do. Yesterday Gen. v. Loe and Gen. v. Seeckt and the Colonel of my Hussar Regiment had luncheon with me...I hope the box of toys has arrived for your darlings, all right and safe, and that the things will amuse them. The little American organ will be a pleasure, I am sure.

'Nicky's birthday will soon be here, pray give him my love and good wishes. I often wonder your parents-in-law do not send him to Woolwich to the Artillery and then for a year at Oxford. He is quite the young man to learn, and to develop into a most accomplished Prince. A little while in a regiment here in Germany would also be most useful to him.'

She writes of the sudden illness of Queen Victoria's private secretary.

'You will have heard how very ill Sir Henry Ponsonby is. He has had a paralytic stroke, but I am thankful to say not a very bad one, and the doctors have all hope of his recovery, but what an upset and a shock for dear Grandmama, he is her right hand in so many things, and I do not know how she can replace him.

'William and Dona came to town yesterday and took up their abode at the Schloss. She called at the door with the children on her way from the station. William I did not see, as he came over from Potsdam in a sledge. It is still freezing and very dark and snow falls often...It is a great blessing for agriculture that everything is covered with snow, as the frost cannot do half the harm when the ground is covered.

'Today I have been with Fischy and Mossy to two museums, only for very short visits to show them some of the things that have been newly brought, and they were delighted. Henry and Irene do not care for museums, she cares only a trifle more than he does.

'There is a function at the Schloss for my Hussar Regiment, and then a big luncheon there. In a few minutes Charlotte will be arriving and Uncle Alfred comes later. I have not a spare corner, as you can imagine. ... I am much flattered that my relations so much prefer coming to my home than going to the Schloss! ...

This evening we all go to the British Embassy for dinner...I must end here, my darling, and go and see Mossy's dear children in their bath, and dress to receive Bernhard and Charlotte.'

Uneasy Greek political and financial affairs again engage the Empress's interest in successive letters. Of the resignation of Prime Minister Tricoupis, who is defeated by the problem of making Greece solvent, she writes, 'This is mean! The first time he resigned, he tried to throw the blame on the King, and now, on Tino...He wishes it to appear as if the Royal Family made it impossible for him to carry on the government.'

She praises Prince Constantine for reacting firmly to a provocative situation staged by the Prime Minister.

'You know how I hate despotism and absolutism, and how firmly I believe in good institutions to protect the country both from arbitrary government and from the caprices of the masses, but I think in the case of Greece, the institutions are faulty, and when the people look to the Crown to get them out of a mess the Crown must not shirk the responsibility, and must take such opportunity as presents itself in a fortunate and providential manner.'

On the renewed European pressure on Greece to pay her debts, she remarks:

'I am afraid I have not much pity for the German bondholders, their behaviour and language has been too rude, insulting and impertinent, whereas the French and English have at least brought forward their just claims in a proper tone and way. The modern Germans enjoy bullying and tall talk, and it does put my back up so.

'Of course I am very sorry for all who have lost their money, but I do not see that they are nearer getting it back by abusing Greece, though one must make allowances for their exasperation when they are told that the Greek Government does not care whether they lose it or not.

'The cold is still intense, we are quite ice-bound and snowbound and hardly leave the house. It is really grievous to think how much the poor suffer in this cold weather, it is even more important to get firewood for them than food. There is a deal of distress here just now, as always when the cold puts a stop to all work out of doors, and 1000's of men are suddenly thrown out of work. Charity does a good deal, but it is only like a drop in the ocean.

'Yesterday we drove to the mausoleum at Charlottenburg. It is sad how it has been spoilt by a very ugly figure of an angel (or archangel) in the first hall as one goes up the steps, and then 2 sarcophagi with reclining figures of grandmama and grandpapa, which are very indifferently done. The whole place is spoiled, to my taste, and it used to be *so* pretty.'

The Empress's journey to England is 'a terribly cold one...from Berlin to Flushing was all one sheet of thick snow. On board the dear yacht, it seemed milder than what we had left, but it was still cold!' From Osborne, she writes:

'In the Isle of Wight they have not had such a frost at this time of year for 40 years or more. Still it has not hurt the beautiful evergreens, and the air feels very different from Berlin. I found dear Grandmama very well, very lame alas, and her eyes failing her a good deal, which is a great trial to her.

'Poor Liko has dislocated his shoulder and wears his arm in a sling and cannot put on a coat. Little Drino [*Prince Alexander of Battenberg — Ed.*] is the liveliest and most intelligent boy I have seen for a long time. He reminds me of Andrea [*Prince Andrew of Greece*] in the way of picking up and learning. He and Ena play little duets together on the piano, and read stories to one another in the evening. How one misses poor Sir Henry...I fear he will never be again what he was, which is dreadful for poor Lady Ponsonby, and for Grandmama. Everyone asks after you and hopes that the political state of Greece will improve.'

Her first enjoyment of her surroundings persists over several letters.

'It is such a joy to wake up and see the sky and the sea from my bed, and the lawns and the trees...and to hear no carts and carriages rattling! I do so enjoy the air, liberty and peace of dear Osborne. As I grow older I love the country more and more, and it is so pleasant to share its charms with those one loves. In town one can never have any quiet, it is very nice for a short time, but not for long.

'I am so sorry you find the life in Athens so dull and monotonous, but surely there is so much of interest there, and you have time to study and cultivate many a talent, drawing and music for instance, if you took lessons, or even if you travelled in the country and made expeditions to different parts still unknown to you. I think it would be delightful, and before those elections it might do a deal of good! I wonder you do not make a little tour inland now, it is neither too hot nor too cold, and you are not expecting a baby. It would give so much pleasure to many. *I* should do it if I were Tino and you, and life would not seem dull then. P.S. Why do you not take some simple lessons in chemistry and physiology and some Samaritan lectures to teach you how to put on a bandage and what to do in case of accidents.'

The first public speech of the new Tsar, from whom she had expected so much, dismays her, for he pledges himself to the principle of absolute autocracy; and Sophie's views on the deficiencies ,of the Greek constitution evoke a monitory paragraph.

'Tell Tino how greatly I regret the speech Nicky of Russia has made! It has done him an immensity of harm, I fear, in the opinion of foreign countries, and will bitterly disappoint those at home who have been looking to him, longing and pining for reforms and improvements *so* long deferred. It was bad advice indeed that prompted him to make this speech. He need not have made any binding promises or programme, but he has crushed the hopes and perhaps the confidence and affection, which were so valuable for him to possess, of his many suffering subjects. I grieve at it.

'I am glad our views on politics agree, but I am *far* from thinking that constitutions are the root of all evil, quite the contrary. I am a strong and convinced believer in good constitutions, which shall alike protect the nation from the dangers of despotism, which in unworthy hands, i.e. in ignorant and injudicious hands, is the worst of evils, and also protect the government from the follies and blunders of the masses. A wise constitution is an intense blessing and safety, and ensures liberty to both the governed and the governing, if rightly and conscientiously observed. Your constitution is not easy to work with, and in many ways not adapted to the wants of the country, and I wish it were different. But to be without one would be impossible, and chaos and confusion would follow.'

Towards the end of February, the Empress moves to London, and writes daily from Buckingham Palace.

'Here is the usual rush and scramble, and the many people to see. At Marlborough House I found dear Uncle Bertie with rather a cold. Auntie Alix very well, also Victoria, but Maudie had hurt her foot skating with too tight a boot. Georgie and May came to see me, both looking in the best of health. For dinner there was Uncle Bertie and Aunt Alix, Victoria dear, who asked much after you, and Aunt Mary Teck, and Dolly [*Prince Adolphus of — Ed.*] Teck and his young wife. In the Afternoon I had a walk in Regent's Park, and went to a shop to buy some trifles. The shops are so beautiful here, they would tempt you very much.'

'Grandmama held a drawing-room. The children (Louischen's and Beatrice's) were delighted to watch the carriages driving up, and the glimpses of fashionable ladies with feathers, veils and diamonds, sitting inside, and the smart powdered footmen, all with flowers, or rather *bouquets* in their buttonholes. Grandmama, Auntie Alix and Beatrice, Louischen all looked so nice in their gala attire, and May too. A drawing room is a pretty sight.

'Lord Rosebery dined with grandmama yesterday evening, and so much praised what Tino had done, of course I was delighted, and we spoke together for some time. Grandmama tells me that Nicky and Alicky write to her often, and seem very happy. I only wish with all my heart that Nicky had not made that speech.'

'Last night there was some singing by Mr. Ben Davis with a lovely tenor voice, and Miss Clara Butt, who is very young, but 6-foot-high, and has a splendid contralto voice.'

'Does sweet tiny Georgie begin his letters? or to say a few bits of poetry or count a little? It is so nice to begin by degrees, with bricks and pictures, etc., without tiring the children. When they are intelligent and if done carefully it does them no harm. Tell me whether the illustrated fairy tale books I sent for you to keep or give Andrea ever arrived. I should so like to hear, and whether you thought them pretty?'

In her chat about the family, the Empress frequently indulges in matchmaking notions among her younger relations and friends, including even 15-

year-old Prince Andrew.

'Big Georgie must be the first to marry. I wonder whether he thinks of Sandra [*Princess Alexandra — Ed.*] of (Edinburgh) Coburg or of Fischy's sister Ilia? Princesses with large fortunes do *not* exist now any more, the before-named ones though not rich are not poor. Aunt Helen [*Duchess of — Ed.*] Albany is here with little Alice, who is a dear child and would be a nice little wife for Andrea someday. Uncle Arthur's Daisy, who is a lovely girl and taller than I am, would do for Nicky. There would be charming sisters-in-law for you! How you will laugh at the idea of these young men having wives of their own, but these are only passing ideas when I think of those dear charming young men at Athens.'

At the end of the month, the Empress goes with her mother to Windsor, and stays with her until she leaves for abroad. She writes on March 10th:

'The dear Windsor Bells are ringing out for memory of Uncle Bertie's wedding day. Formerly I used to think they sounded merry and festive, and made one feel so light-hearted. Now their music floats over the Chapel where darling Eddy and Leopold lie in their last sleep, and the sound makes me think of how Papa *loved* to hear them, and of *our* wedding day, and my heart aches. You can understand. Yesterday was the anniversary of the Emperor William's death. Ah! that day at San Remo, shall I ever forget it!'

Four days later, she is back at Buckingham Palace.

'I was very sad at parting with dear Grandmama yesterday morning at Windsor. She had a lovely day for travelling and I heard from Cherbourg that she had a good passage. How sorry I am I shall not go to Sandringham and see dearest Auntie Alix and cousins and make the acquaintance of the baby, but Uncle Bertie returns much later from the Riviera, and does not like me to go to his dear Sandringham without him.

'I am sure you will be pleased to hear that dear Ducky has a girl. They say it is a large child and that she had a very long and tedious time, but that she is doing very well indeed now. Poor Missy's little boy has been frightfully ill with diphtheria at Bucharest, and was in great danger, but thank God he is well again, poor little man.

'Your telegram arrived yesterday telling me to find a big picture for the price of the 2 small ones, and I consequently went to two water-colour exhibitions. The first was full of lovely things, but in spite of carefully looking round I could not find just what you wanted, as I am bent on your having the best for your money. Then I went to the other exhibition and saw some exquisite watercolour paintings of different gardens. I succeeded in finding a perfect *gem* of a picture, a dream of delicacy and refinement, so airy and pure in colour. You can hardly fail to be pleased.'

Towards the end of her visit, the Empress enjoys a brief trip to Yorkshire.

'I returned home last night after a most interesting visit to the Bishop of Ripon. I cannot describe to you how beautiful Fountains Abbey, Hall and Park are, really a dream of beauty in a valley, the short soft green turf covered with snowdrops. It was a bright warm spring day and I enjoyed it *so* much. The dear Bishop was so kind and I was so happy and comfortable in his house with his nice wife and children.

'Tomorrow I leave dear England but whether I go to Bonn or not depends on Vicky's plans. The Prince of Lippe-Detmald has suddenly died, and the brother who succeeds him is mad, and so Adolf will be Regent, and perhaps Vicky will have to settle at Detmald and leave her dear Bonn and her house and be much further off from me. I do not think she will like that...Lovely Princess Helene of Orleans is engaged to the Due D'Aosta, it is a very good marriage for both, and I hope they will be happy.

'I have today been to see the Scottish Exhibition in the Grosvenor Gallery. Some very good Raeburn portraits, who was a contemporary painter of Sir Thomas Lawrence and almost as great an artist. The other day I went to the Kensington Museum. The weather is quite beautiful and dear old London looking its best filled with carriages and fine horses and ladies with pretty toilettes, children in perambulators, etc. The quantities of violets and daffodils sold in the streets are certainly huge, and the flower shops, indeed all the shops, most tempting. One's money runs away in a very short time, alas. Really, dear old England is a most fascinating place and it is indeed hard to leave it. There is so much to be seen, and so many kind friends to see, that the time seems to pass like a dream and one cannot do half of what one intended. ...Grandmama writes that she is charmed with the Riviera and "Les Cimiez".'

The Empress has a very rough crossing to Flushing, and the *Victoria and Albert* has to wait outside harbour until the gale subsides. On board, she writes:

'I still feel most wretched from having been so frightfully sick — *un sentiment qui n'a aucun charme,* as Philip Flanders used to say — and so ill that I felt within an inch of expiring, yet I must write to you my darling Fozzie, even though with swimming head and aching ribs and shaking hand. I am so sorry Tino has the measles, how tiresome for you, I trust he will only have a mild attack, and that the children will not get it, nor you yourself, though you have had it already.

'The last day in London was one rush and scramble from morning till night. Poor Georgie was ill in bed with influenza, but May and Aunt Mary Teck came to see me, and Franz [*Francis, Duke of* — *Ed.*] Teck afterwards, and Aunt Helen Albany came and took me to the station, which was most kind and nice of her to come on purpose from Claremont.

'I am rather upset at Bernhard being made Commandante of the Silesian Armée Corps. I do so dread Charlotte making a fool of herself there. She is too foolish and imprudent, and makes so much mischief and gets herself and others into too many scrapes. It is an important place, a large town and large society and one requires to be very careful. Bernhard is *not* popular with his subordinates, as he is so irritable that he becomes easily so rude and offensive, and that grieves me, as he is really such a good creature and also a good officer.'

Safely back at Rümpenheim, she writes of the nation-wide celebration of Bismark's 80th birthday, which the Emperor has signalized by presenting the former Chancellor with a sword of honour.

'The fuss they made about Bismark's birthday is really too ridiculous and fulsome, and so exaggerated one really feels quite ashamed at the ostentations and pompous vulgarity and chauvinism displayed. I think it is very well for his advisers and acquaintances to celebrate the day, congratulate him and send him presents, why not? In the eyes of many he is a very great man, but this is really carrying the thing too far, and those who see the sad and painful consequences of his terrible system and the harm it has done to the country cannot but think that though he, together with many others, has achieved great things in foreign policy, etc., yet he is not the demi-God and national hero that certain parties now make of him. He was a man of rare energy, astuteness and shrewdness and ability, but not of lofty and noble aspiration. He was unscrupulous, false and tyrannical to a degree, and a bitter and vindictive enemy to any one who dared to oppose him or even disagree with him, or who he found in his way. No means were too bad to employ for getting rid of whoever seemed a hindrance, and he suspected and persecuted the most innocent people in a shameful way. He completely corrupted the public conscience and crushed *all* independence of character and opinion. We *suffered* under him for 25 years intensely.

'I wrote him a simple letter of congratulations, which he will receive today, but I was unable to fill it with flattery. I cannot join in a Bismark "culte", and think this adoration does Germany as much harm as good.

'Vicky dear seems terribly worried and anxious about the uncertainty of her and Adolf's future. The state of things is very complicated and unpleasant. The late Prince of Detmald appointed Adolf as Regent in his will, but the Counts of Lippe Biesterfeld consider *they* have the right of succession, and contest this will, and are getting up an agitation against it in the Detmald press and Land Tag. William telegraphed to Adolf to go at once to Detmald, which he did.'

For several months, the Empress has referred occasionally to what became known as the Kotze affair. A large number of scurrilous anonymous letters were sent to people prominent in Berlin society, and finally a member of it, a Herr von Kotze, was accused of writing them. The instigator of this accusation was a Herr von Schrader, a friend of Baron von Reischach. The controversy led to a duel between Kotze and Reischach, in which the former was wounded. As duels were officially forbidden, Reischach was given four months' confinement in a military fortress. The Empress writes:

'You will have seen in the newspapers that Reischach has fought a duel with Kotze, and wounded X. in the leg. I am very sorry indeed that it had to come to this, but thankful that Reischach remained unhurt. I do not see that it changes the affair in the least, because though the Court Martial have acquitted Kotze, the people who were convinced of his guilt have the same opinion still.'

The Empress's next two letters deal chiefly with Queen Victoria's visit to her grandchildren at Darmstadt, and to Friedrichshof.

'Yesterday we went to Darmstadt to see beloved Grandmama, it is always a great emotion for me to see her, and very tantalizing that the snatches are so short that I get of her dear presence. She is staying at the Alte Palace at Darmstadt. I think she would have far preferred to be in the Neue Palace, but now Ernie is married and has a baby it was hardly possible, as they have no lift and the top storey could not be used for her. It was warm and rainy and many people were out in the streets and all the flags flying. Dear Grandmama looked very well, but complained of much pain in her leg. We had luncheon together and I was so glad at last to present Fischy, whom she had never seen. Ducky was looking rather pale, but very pretty, the baby is a fine child and very pretty too.

'Today dear Grandmama is coming here, she arrives at 12 and leaves at 5. Goodbye, my precious Sophie, pray excuse this scribble and this haste, but today is *quite* a day apart from all others to me, and I feel all in a tremble and flutter, and quite excited. To have my dear Mama under my roof is a thing which has only happened *once before* to me, and that at Charlottenburg in those never to be forgotten days.'

'Dear Grandmama's visit here went off very well, only alas in the afternoon it poured with rain, which was too provoking! In the forenoon, Grandmama planted a tree, and just took a turn in her little garden chair through the flower garden and into the stable yard. I think she liked it very much, and said the next time she comes to Germany she would prefer to live here, and not at Darmstadt as she does not feel at home at the Alte Palace, or much like it.

'It was most annoying that we could not get out on the terrace, so really she saw very little view, and this will be for another time I trust. Grandmama was much pleased with Fischy and thought him very amiable. The children were all most good when they were presented, and looked sweet in their smart frocks.

'Yesterday Willy was at Darmstadt, and today he returns to Potsdam, he was looking rather pale, I thought. There was no opportunity of mentioning the duel, and I thought it much more advisable *not* to approach the subject.

'I wonder whether Tino will go to the opening of the Nord [*Kiel — Ed.*] Canal, where so many are going? I think it absurd to make an International and European business of it when it is so distinctly a German one, but however, you know how Willy loves splash and fuss and display on all occasions, and how even quite small events are turned into opportunities for ceremonies. It is his taste, which I cannot share. Nowadays people like show and noise, but one wearies of incessant performances of this kind, and they cease to make an impression.... Tomorrow Vicky and Adolf are to have a solemn reception at Detmald, the Regency having been accepted by the Land Tag.'

Once more the Empress's main interest switches back to Greece, where the recent elections do not promise well for the future.

'The result of the Greek elections is not very satisfactory, and old Delyiannis being returned is a great bore, and must be very disagreeable for your papa-in-law. One can only hope for the best.

'How very delighted I am that Tino has the inspection of the Army to do, and that these duties will take him about from place to place. Nothing could be better. I wish you could follow him and visit the places where he has to be, and receive people and see the ladies, it would do a lot of good, make you known and popular, and increase Tino's influence.

'Yesterday I went to an exhibition of the work of the art school pupils, and thought the things really very good, both the drawing and the modelling work. You ought to have the same at Athens, I am sure the young people would be very clever at it, with all their opportunities of seeing beautiful things.

'How heavenly Athens must be just now. Your description of the orange blossom perfume wafting into your open window makes my mouth water! Here, the cherry blossom is over, but the apple blossom is too magnificent, and the lilac just out, also the horse-chestnut, filling the air with sweetness. P.S. I suffer much from flushes, blood to the head, sleep very badly, have palpitations, etc., and still the nettle-rash.'

As the Empress had anticipated. Prince Constantine was invited to the Kiel Canal celebrations. Sophie and the children came with him, and while they were on their way, the Letters peter out into desultory topics.

'Mossy and I started off for Church yesterday morning but were so late that we were ashamed to go in, so we turned back and went to Homberg instead, to the English service in the afternoon...'

'At Berlin the Reichstag has thrown out the anti-socialist Bill, which was at once so stupid and mischievous that it is a perfect mercy it has not been passed. All sensible and cultured people made a stand against it. The Government had a thorough defeat, but it is really in their own interest for the future.

'I have a little donkey carriage all in order here, it is all ready for your dear children to use when they come.'

Crown Prince Constantine and Princess Sophie duly arrive, and leaving the children at Friedrichshof in the care of the Empress, set out for Potsdam to effect the reconciliation with the Emperor that the occasion offers. Sophie writes: 'At Potsdam all went off beautifully. William himself fetched us, and they were most amiable. Poor Dona looks so ill and miserable. Later we all went to church together.' After visiting her father's mausoleum, they go to Kiel for the celebrations, then to Copenhagen to see Prince Constantine's grandparents, and then to London. The Empress writes spasmodically, and usually about the children as the following selections from her letters show.

'Thank you so much for your kind dear telegram from Friedrichskron. I knew you would both think of me in our dear old home with all its sweet and terrible memories. I can hardly believe I shall never see it again, the dear old place. I could not bear to see it changed and inhabited, it would be too painful. The darlings are "as good as gold". Do try and rest whenever you can, take your iron and a little glass of brandy or liqueur, and do not stand about.'

Tray do not trouble to write when you are tired and want rest. I know what a fatigue it is to scribble. So many thanks for writing to me at all!'

'How glad I am to think you are at Windsor safe and sound. I am sure it gives you pleasure to be in England again, where dear Grandmama and every one was always so kind to you. You will have seen a great many friends and relations. Grandmama telegraphs to me "I think Tino charming", so you see how pleased she is. Your dear Dots love playing out of doors, and under the chestnuts in a cool spot, because it is very hot. The pony and the donkey and carriage usually appear of a morning. I think Georgie will soon ride quite well.'

'I can again begin by saying that your dear children are very well, and have enjoyed a morning's wild strawberry picking in the woods. The sun is very powerful, but there is a pleasant fresh breeze moving. I hear it is as hot again in England as it was in Jubilee time. How it will remind you of those days, and beloved Papa, and all our sorrow since, but also of the fact that it was in England that you lost your little heart to Tino.'

Sophie returns to Friedrichshof on July 4th and stays there until the 21st. Her departure produces the customary sorrowing letter next day.

'Yesterday I still had you with me. Today all is empty and silent. Mossy walks about with eyes swollen and red with weeping. Parting is simply an agony, and it will take me days to get over it. I came back from Frankfort last night with such a headache, and went to bed with cold wet cloths on my head, but it was no use, I could not sleep, the thought that you both were in the next room and the children upstairs only 12 hours ago, and are now being hurried away every moment farther from me, would not let me rest.

'Today came your dear telegram from Munich. You are right, dearest, to say "cheer up", but I find it very hard to do so. You are still so young, but I feel how fast life slips away, and begrudge the long weeks and months of separation from my own darling child. The uncertainty of life and of all things in this world fills me with terror and anxiety, and I feel I should like to be always near those I love best to protect them from whatever evil or harm *might* befall them.

'You must be at sea now if you embarked early this morning at Venice, May the winds and waves be kind, and may there be no bugs and fleas to make you uncomfortable, and bite the poor children.'

Little Prince George had not, after all, shown himself very keen about his riding, and the Empress's letter on the subject proves her to have been well in advance of her time in the matter of training young children.

'I wonder whether darling Georgie misses his pony, or whether he is glad not to be obliged to ride. I think he is a trifle nervous, like his dear Mama was, but being a boy, that is sure to wear off if one only does not force him, which would be the way to unnerve him quite, and give him a horror of it, which would be very difficult to cure. I think when he gains confidence he will be sure to like it. Nerves are a thing over which one has no control. So many children are dreadfully frightened, but if one is gentle and patient with them, it is quite got over in a little time. A child feels bitterly and is profoundly unhappy when it is misunderstood, and children's little troubles cause them just as acute suffering as our big trials and sorrows do us. Childhood ought to be such a happy time, it never returns.

'I remember what a coward I was as a child over all and everything except the water. I think I had a fairly good nerve when I grew up because my Papa was so kind and patient, and I felt that when he was near nothing could happen to me. If he had scolded and shaken or forced me, I should have been nervous and terrified of him as well. Papa always said he could not bear to think of his childhood, he had been so unhappy and miserable, and had many a time wished himself out of this world. Uncle Fritz Carol's [*Prince Frederick Charles of Prussia — Ed.*] harsh treatment of Fritz Leopold seems to have made that once shy and timid boy into a very unamiable husband and master.

'I always think we grown-up people ought to be *so* careful how we exact obedience from our children. Obedience that is not cheerful or willing only ruins the character. All that nonsense of "breaking the will" is now recognized as making children vicious and false and sly. Training a child's will so that it may trust willingly to the guidance of its elders, and *believe* in their protection, has obtained far happier results than enforcing a dogged obedience, as the child is not convinced that it is wrong but only dreads the consequences of displeasing its elders. But all this we only realize when we are older and have seen something of the world and of character and of childhood.

'For all these reasons I am so much for the "Kinder Garten", and against the dreadful old system of "infant schools", where poor little things were chiefly instructed to sit still and obey like little machines or tiny recruits, which is so utterly the reverse of a child's nature, that wants constant movement and change and liberty, as well as love and kindness, to grow like a young plant in the sunshine.'

Sophie's first letter on her arrival in Athens contains the following request. 'Would you mind, dear Mama, asking your cook to write out the recipe of those delicious sausages we ate one day for breakfast with mashed potatoes.' After dealing with this matter, the Empress passes on to some personal advice to Sophie about her appearance.

'I am so distressed to think you have to go through such frightful heat, my poor Sophie dear, wiping and mopping your face. Do not put on powder, you will spoil your pretty complexion and make it turn yellow, and lose the bloom and freshness. It stops up the pores of the skin and prevents the evaporation from coming through. The more you wash it and rub it with a towel the better for your complexion, as all people can tell you who have made the treatment of the skin and complexion a speciality.

'I hope you will not pinch your dear pretty little waist too much, it is small enough by nature, and it is terribly unwholesome and even dangerous to squeeze one's body, just where lungs, liver, heart, etc., want space, not to speak of the stomach and other internal organs, which get so out of order when they are pressed together. You have such a nice figure that you need not fear spoiling it if you give it easy play as it ought to have. Charlotte and Dona have both done themselves harm by lacing so. To go without stays for some hours a day in summer is so wholesome, especially walking *up* hill, as the lungs and heart are not hindered then. I used always to *ride* and *dance* without stays when I was your age, and I think it was very good indeed, certainly for the circulation. I always took them off for long walks and Alpine tours. You will laugh at your old Mama, but she is right I am sure.

'Ernie and Ducky were here a few days ago. She was looking so handsome, and having her hair gathered off the forehead and put up in natural waves and a loose twist behind suits her wonderfully and shows her pretty young white brow. How I wish my Sophie would adopt that, but she will not, I know, and prefers the great sponge of a fringe on the top of her dear head. Ella also now wears it turned up, and the smartest and prettiest ladies at Romberg have all adopted this fashion, which I think most becoming and a great improvement on the fringe for those who have pretty foreheads and whose hair grows nicely like yours.'

The Duke of Cambridge comes to the district to take the waters. In England, protracted governmental efforts have almost succeeded in forcing his resignation as permanent Commander-in-Chief of the Army.

'Mossy and I paid a visit to Uncle George at Romberg this afternoon. I found him looking aged and bent, and much annoyed about his resignation of the Commandership-in-Chief, which does not seem to be impending quite directly. Still he seems in very good health and seemed as kind and merry and amiable as ever...I trust it is less hot now and that you are all well. Does Georgie play with his jockey cap? and does he like having a handkerchief knotted at the 4 corners on his head? Row that reminded me of you, when you were a child.'

August 26th is one of the anniversaries that the Empress never forgets to dwell upon.

'One more line this morning, my own beloved Father's birthday. Row I look back to the happy day when this used to be the brightest day in the year for us children. Row cruel he should have been taken from us so young. How you would have loved him and admired him. How your dear Papa doted on him and looked up to him, and thought him the best and wisest man alive. How I worshipped him, and what untold grief it was to lose him. He was your Grandpapa Emp. William's *best* and truest friend.
'Yesterday I drove over to Homberg and had breakfast with Uncle Bertie, whom I thought looking very well, his dear kind face wore its beaming and sunny expression, which always warms one's heart. We had a nice little *tête-a-tête* and talked of Tino and you, and London, etc., and he said how they were all so pleased to see you both over there this summer. I rode home through the woods. It was the hottest day we have had, the sun baking but not the least oppressive, the air light and fresh. Uncle Bertie came to luncheon.'

In Germany there are important anniversaries of a different kind to commemorate.

'The celebrations of the anniversaries of the war 1870-1871 are going on everywhere all over Germany, and it is touching to see the great enthusiasm they call forth, though it is in no way done with the wish or intention to hurt the feelings of the French...The Sedan celebrations were really without end. Unfortunately Willy made a speech in which were some passages which I thought inappropriate and imprudent, even dangerous, and of course they have been much commented on. I am afraid they have unnecessarily furnished the Socialists with many a good argument, whereas if the subject of Sedan had been let alone the utterances of the socialist press about it would have been condemned by the whole public, whereas now many a one may feel persuaded to take their part.'

Sophie writes of proposals to improve the drainage and water supply of Athens, a subject that the Empress seizes on to write several letters of advice. In one of them she says:

'Athens increases in size and population, yet drainage and water supply are not properly provided. At present it is done in a sort of "happy go lucky" style, so that I wonder there is not more typhus, small pox, scarlet fever, diphtheria and even cholera, than there is already. The expense becomes double and treble the more the town is allowed to grow *before* the pipes are laid. Perhaps during the time that Tino is Regent he can push this question, the King has tried so often, and not with success.

'What a charming town Athens would be if the water supply were indeed properly organized, and how pretty the road from Athens to the Phaleron might be. I should plant 4 rows of trees on either side, of cypresses, oaks, plane trees, and one of Johannisbrot [*locust bean — Ed.*] that have such fine large glossy leaves and edible beans. Then short-cut hedges of myrtle, acacia and oranges, and outside, a stately hedge of aloes, which looks so handsome. Then one could drive, ride and walk in the shade to the Phaleron from Athens! A row of villas would soon start up both sides, and it would make a delicious promenade.'

Athens is busily making ready for the first Olympic Games to be held in modern times. The Empress has been discussing the Games with various friends, and becomes shrewdly alive to the possibilities of using the event to help open up tourism.

'...as many foreign visitors might come to Athens as go to Rome and Naples, which brings money, and does good in making the country more known. The chief obstacle is that travelling and accommodation is *not* organized in Greece, as it is in Syria even, which has been opened up by "Cook" to tourists, and where one can get about with ease. One so often hears people regret that the journey to Greece for ladies and for pleasure excursions, etc., is so uncomfortable and ill-arranged. No one in the world could remedy this like Cook — you know what wonders he has done in Naples and in Egypt. Time must not be lost, however. The principal thing would be if Tino while he is still Regent, would express a wish to see Cook junior (Cook senior has retired) and tell him that the Government will give what facilities they can and even a little help. Then the thing might be pretty well arranged before March and many people would be only too glad to come. P.S. I hear young Cook is rather a snob, but that does not matter, and perhaps he will be all the more flattered and ready to take up the idea if Tino proposes it to him.'

Returning to the subject in a later letter, the Empress remarks: 'It seems that a good many German societies have been invited to go to the Games ...and no doubt from other countries too. In March therefore, Athens should be swarming with foreigners. I do hope there will be no earthquake.'

A gossipy family letter in September contains both good and bad news.

'I hear that Sandra of Edinburgh and Ernie Hohenlohe [*Prince Ernest of Hohenlohe-Langenhurg — Ed.*], now engaged, are very happy and devoted to each other. In point of fortune and position, of course, the marriage is not a brilliant one, but if they are happy, what does it matter?

'The sad news came yesterday that dear Liko's mother, dear Princess Battenberg, had died of a stroke. ... I am very sorry. I have known her many years and have always liked her very much. Poor Louis is at sea, Liko in England.

'Charlotte has gone off to Roumania again. I do not think it is the place to take little Feo [*Princess Feodora — Ed.*] to, just when she is beginning to come out. But I fear that nothing very wise is ever done by Charlotte.

'May of York is expecting in December. I hear she is very well, which is a great blessing. Alicky, I believe, is expecting in November. I know of no other babies in the family that are expected.'

The Empress's lack of knowledge about forthcoming babies is very quickly made good by Sophie's next letter, which announces good news, though not with absolute certainty. After the initial surprise, her mother writes, 'My poor Sophie, to think of your having had hopes, and now fearing a disappointment.' The uncertainty remains, though there is sufficient confidence for the Empress to write: 'I hardly dare believe in the joy of No. 3 arriving. What happiness it would be for you, and also for me. Think of my seeing Greece again! What happy hours we could spend together.' But gradually, in spite of her mother's optimism, Sophie gives up her expectations.

With this theme, however, the writing turns easily to Sophie's desire to open a maternity home, about which she asks her mother for information, 'if it does not trouble you too much'. The Empress replies with a very long letter indeed, in the course of which she says:

'It is giving me no trouble, I am only too glad to be of use in any way to my own darling Sophie, and glad she should occupy herself with things that are so useful to the poor and the suffering, especially in Greece, where so much still has to be done. I wish indeed you could found a maternity hospital and a child's hospital, also a nursing school which could be combined with both. They would be a great boon to Greece, to the town and the people and also to the doctors. Could not the Government and the town give subventions? Surely ground could easily be found, not far out on the road to Phaleron, where there is not much building going on yet. Space is wanted for a good garden and of course good water is essential. The hospitals should be built on the best and newest principles, *not* smart and costly buildings, but externally quite plain and simple, with the *best* drainage, ventilation, hygienic appliances, steam stoves for disinfecting dirty linen, and electric light for the operation room. As little wood and paint as possible. Stone, tiles, iron and glass to be mostly used.

'I have written to London to ask about the Great Ormond Street Child's Hospital, which is such a fine one, and have also enquired about the newest and best children's wards in India.

'It is a pity you have not got a couple of young Greek doctors who could study children's diseases in England and in Germany — it is really a special branch, and many doctors would be wanted at a child's hospital.'

Sophie asks also how to discourage cruelty to animals, and her mother responds enthusiastically:

'I have written to Uncle Bertie, who has been a member of the Society for Prevention of Cruelty to Animals for many years, and he has given orders for suitable papers, reports etc. to be sent to you straight from London...Indeed, one needs such societies in the south, where people are never taught in their childhood to show kindness to animals. I am sure such a thing is wanted here in Germany too. It makes me sick to see men thumping the poor jaded horses and mules and the gentle oxen.

'How *can* anyone ill-treat a poor beast! People who seem quite good-natured and good tempered do not seem to feel or see how brutal and cruel it is to ill-treat dumb animals.... But if children are never taught that it is wicked and cowardly to do so, and that to give animals pain wantonly is an action a human being, and especially a Christian, should be ashamed of, they will grow up not knowing it. Kindness to animals ought to be taught by schoolmasters and priests.'

The Empress visits Baden, from where she is to take part in the ceremony of unveiling a statue to her husband, as victor of the Battle of Wörth. She writes from the Schloss Baden-Baden, home of her husband's sister, the Grand Duchess Louise.

'Uncle Fritz and Aunt Louise are most kind and try to make me feel at home. Baden is very beautiful as to landscape, etc., but now so "tea-gardeny" and Cockneyfied, and over-run with smart modern buildings that I cannot admire.... The 18th was bitterly cold.

At the little station at Worth, we found Dona, William and [*a list of relations and personages — Ed.*] William got on horseback, and Dona and I drove in a carriage and 4 (shivering with cold) through the villages, along the road to the Battlefield. The country people in their pretty costumes were most civil and cheered all the way. We all took up our places on a bit of rising ground, with the whole of dear Papa's staff on the right of us. When I saw all their familiar faces I could not restrain my tears. After a speech, the drapery fell from the statue amid cheers and the band playing and guns firing. You cannot think how solemn and impressive it was to see the battlefield spread out behind the statue of our beloved one, and so many of the men standing there who had been present at the fierce and terrible struggle. And he who led them gone from us in the flower of his age. What I felt I cannot describe, all my loneliness seemed to come upon me at once. With Henry's help, I laid down a large wreath of beautiful white flowers from Friedrichshof at the foot of the monument. Then came a parade of the troops. The last time I saw the village of Worth was when Papa took me there in 1871, when all was still untouched after the battle, and it looked so dreadful. Now it was the picture of peace and prosperity, and were it not for endless crosses and monuments one would never guess what had happened there 25 years ago.'

From Baden, the Empress goes to spend a few weeks at Trento, one of her familiar resorts in Italy. She writes again from the Hotel Trento.

'You think it will be dull for me here? But as I come here to enjoy the walks and the scenery and the air and the quiet, I shall not mind it being "dull" ...Yesterday evening on returning from a drive I received a telegram from Uncle Bertie and Aunt Alix announcing Maud's engagement to [*Prince — Ed.*] Carol of Denmark. I am delighted, as I am so glad she is going to marry and have a home of her own. We must soon be hearing that Alix has a baby at Petersburg, and then we ought to hear from Sandringham or the White Lodge that May has another.'

Sophie writes of being depressed over the difficulties of getting results from her welfare efforts, and of how the Greeks need somebody like her brother to push them on.

'Your dear letter of the 14th reached me safely yesterday from Berlin. ... I am sorry to hear your Almshouses are in such a mess and that you will have to withdraw your patronage and co-operation. I trust that some day later when it is better managed you can take it up again.

'...My poor Sophie I feel for you having *heimweh* [*homesickness — Ed.*] sometimes, I can so well understand it. It is only since 1888 that I have lost mine. It lasted 30 years! I can well understand that you should regret things improving so slowly and being so behindhand in Greece and so much still to do, but believe me, such a one as William would be no use, but only create confusion. I am sure Tino's will is plenty firm enough when he has the opportunity of showing it, and, nowadays, absolute government is nonsense, it cannot and will not work, but your Greek constitution is not fortunate in its qualities, and in the working. Still one must not forget how young the country is as an independent state and how much progress *has* been made.

'If only that blessed railway were finished and Greece connected with the rest of Europe, you would see how the country would open up and visitors come, and how near us all you would feel. The Orient Express with nice comfortable carriages would run on the line, and Cook could organize some comfortable hotels. It always enrages me that it is so easy to get to Roumania, a country in which I cannot feel any warm interest, and not to Greece, which I love.'

The Empress has frequently suggested that Prince Constantine should have his own villa in the grounds of Tatoi, and now Sophie asks for advice. In a long reply her mother goes into detail of design, building materials, roofs, chimneys and every other point she can think of, generously illustrated with thumbnail sketches. She provides plans of Osborne Cottage, which 'dear Grandmama has been so kind as to send for you', and also those of Friedrichshof Cottage and Sandringham's York Cottage. Her technical suggestions for blending these plans end with, 'but I am not an architect, and this would need to be talked over with a clever one'. She continues, 'all these plans are castles in the air, but they may interest and amuse you, my Sophie darling, and I look at everything when I travel with the view of finding something adaptable to your wants'. She concludes with reference to Prince Nicholas, now in England, 'Should he be going back through Germany, how glad I should be if he could spend a fortnight with me at Berlin. Wedell would be at his disposal for military things, and I would show him all I could of museums, etc.'.

The Letters, occupied largely with descriptions of sightseeing trips — 'a magnificent castle on a steep hill with an enchanting view down the valley of the Adige, how I longed to paint it' — the family gossip — 'Grandmama telegraphed me that she was so thankful Alicky is safely delivered of a little daughter' — are suddenly transformed with indignant outbursts against Turkey over the Armenian massacres.

'Indeed I am more shocked and horrified than I can say about the inhuman shameful cruelty to those poor unfortunate Armenians, it makes me quite savage and my blood boil! Why indeed do the Great Powers not put an end to it? I suppose they are afraid to bring on the whole Eastern Question, and with it a universal war, with still greater bloodshed and disaster, but it is indeed sad that this dread should interfere with energetic and prompt action for stopping such atrocities. The Turkish peasants are I believe quiet, simple and industrious, and do not drink, the soldiers are brave, devoted and obedient, but the governing classes and officials are bad, and the Sultan a poor creature in terror of his life.'

A couple of weeks later, after a talk with the Emperor and with Prince Bernhard, she reveals, 'in strict confidence for Tino and you....'

'William thought matters would remain relatively quiet until after the coronation at Moskow, and then a conflagration might break out...The disturbances in Turkey are supposed to have been secretly stirred up by Russian agents. Of course, the Dardanelles are what Russia wants, and Constantinople...my hair stands on end when I think of what the consequences of all this might be.

'Everyone should be prepared what to do in case the tottery edifice of the Turkish Empire should crumble. It is such a mistake that the Great Powers should never look this Eastern Question in the face, they patch things up whenever there is a flare up, then turn back to their own internal affairs. Russia, and Russia alone, pursues her aims and plans, and has a definite purpose, works on in silence, and when others are paying no attention, her eye is ever watchful to take advantage of an opportunity.'

The Empress returns to Rümpenheim just before her birthday, November 21st, when, once more, 'there was so great a rush and bustle I had not a minute to myself to relapse into the sad thoughts that always fill my mind on that day'. And again, 'William appeared early in the morning as a surprise for me, not for the others, though they only heard of it the evening before. ... I am struggling through a pile of letters and telegrams.'

'I was indeed sorry that our poor dear Sir Henry Ponsonby died on my birthday. How his poor wife and children will grieve. I feel for them so much. Aunt Lenchen's son, Christie [*Prince Christian Victor — Ed.*] has gone to Ashanti with the expedition, and Liko is going to join them immediately. Poor Aunt Beatrice writes in a great way about it.

'I have just received your dear letter of the 23rd for which many kisses and thanks. Fancy Georgie cutting off his hair. I remember a sweet little girl standing on tip toe before her Mama's looking glass, and with a pair of enormous scissors cutting off some very pretty fair curls of which I was very proud. I was horrified when I saw my "curly wig" with her locks shorn off on one side! But I forgave her with many kisses and could not help laughing. I am very glad Georgie tried it on his own head and not on baby Alexander's, whose lovely curls it would have been a 1,000 pities to touch. At least one will be able to see Georgie's pretty forehead now!'

The Empress's next letters are from Victoria's new home, the Schloss Detmald.

'I arrived very early and was most kindly received, all the inhabitants of the place seemed to turn out for the occasion, and there was a grand cheering and waving of pocket handkerchiefs. So far, I have only had breakfast, washed and dressed and trotted with Vicky dear the rounds of the rooms in this old Schloss. It is very interesting, fine and picturesque, not large, but a real old 15th-century building, solid and massive. I like old houses such as this in winter, they have something snug and warm about them, and one feels safe and protected.'

Subsequent letters describe the house and its furnishings, and also trips in the town and local villages. 'Detmald is very picturesque, and interested me very much. In spite of the bad weather, the people were most kind and civil, bombarded us with bouquets, cheered, sang "God save the Queen", and seemed in the best of humours.' [*On the back of this letter there are several pencil drawings, the efforts of a young child. Princess Sophie presumably left it within reach of little Prince George! — Ed.*]

Writing next from Berlin, the Empress gives various items of news, and as Christmas approaches finds herself busily occupied once more with her institutions and gatherings and children's parties.

'Poor dear Uncle Bertie had a little accident out shooting which luckily was not serious, though it might have been, but was, he says, extremely painful. Some powder went into his eye from his gun. Thank God, it was no worse.'

'Yesterday I had a letter from dear Grandmama who says she has seen our dear Nicky at Windsor and that she thought him "charming, so good looking, so gentle and pleasing" which I was delighted at. She also says that May had a very good time, was ill in all 4 hours, and only half an hour in bed, and that the boy is a fine one, and May doing very well. What a blessing! I hear he is to be called Albert, after my dear father and Uncle Bertie.'

'It is so dark here that since a fortnight we have not seen the sun. All day I cannot see without a lamp on my writing table. I cannot see to do a single stroke of drawing in my studio. It is so cold and miserable too. Outside the town the thermometer is 15 degrees below zero. There is thick snow, the sledges are out, and people are running over the ice.

'Goltz Pasha is here from Constantinople. He is leaving the Turkish service now. He thinks there is not much danger of war this winter, but that things may take a different turn in the spring. He came after dinner, with others, I had much interesting talk with him.

'Yesterday, Willy and Dona and the 4 eldest boys came. They are much grown, but very plain indeed, and look pale. I am sure their rooms are too heated...Charlotte's Feo is now happy playing the grown-up young lady. Today P. is taking her out sightseeing, you can fancy Feo's pleasure at walking in the streets!'

The year ends on a mishap to Princess Frederick Leopold, the Empress Augusta's sister, which might have been a tragedy, but provokes a preposterous piece of petty tyranny on the part of the Emperor. On December 30th, the Empress writes:

'Yaya has had a terrible accident. She and her lady-in-waiting went out 2 days ago, no footman with them, and crossed the ice on the Griebnitz See, without even enquiring whether it was safe. About thirty paces from the shore the ice broke and in they went! The water was 3 metres deep, but they clung to the ice, which kept breaking off at the edges, and screamed. They were up to their chests. A man heard them, came to the rescue and fell in too, then the man's son came with a pole, but it was too short, then a ladder was brought, and they were dragged out. In another few minutes they would have sunk and been lost, as they were too numb and exhausted to hold on any longer. They were 20 minutes in the water and Yaya was almost insensible, but has now recovered. She was wonderfully brave and made them pull the lady-in-waiting out first. Was there ever such folly as crossing the ice beyond where it was swept!

'Yesterday evening I was at a church concert which was very good, Joachim played divinely. Dona was there, much upset at her sister's adventure and very angry at her having been so foolish.'

The Empress closes with her customary wishes for the New Year, to which she adds: 'Every day I thank God for the blessings that have been vouchsafed to you. May they be preserved to you, and may you never be called upon to resign them, as I was.' But this was a prayer to which the distant future was not to grant fulfilment.

Chapter Eight – The Letters, 1896

Once the New Year wishes are completed, the Empress writes in successive letters chiefly about the extraordinary action taken by the Emperor over his sister-in-law's accident.

'I hear that Wm. has put Fritz Leopold and Yaya under arrest for not having reported her accident on the ice directly. This really is too much! What a high-handed and autocratic proceeding. I could hope it may not be true, but when I think of 1888, and the cruel 15th of June, and our house surrounded with soldiers, I can believe *anything* and *everything* of him.'

[*Next day* — Ed.] 'Alas it is quite true about Fritz Leopold and Yaya. The soldiers and officers are now removed from their door, but they are forbidden to leave their garden and grounds for a fortnight, or to hold communication with anyone, nor may any one go near them. I really think it too hard. If Fr. L. had committed some misdeed, one could not treat him much worse, but for not announcing his wife's accident sooner (and for often commenting about Wm. and D, which I fear 1000's of others do too) really he does not deserve that. Should it penetrate to the public, I fear there will be much speculation and disapproval of such high-handed measures. I am much distressed about it.'

[*Four days later* — Ed.] 'Poor Fritz Leopold and Yaya still under arrest, and as I foresaw, every sort of extravagant rumour has got about the town, as no one can believe that they are shut up for next to nothing at all. Some people even imagine poor Yaya wanted to commit suicide! I *thought* that such an unheard of measure would create every imaginable "cock and bull" story.'

[*Two days later* — Ed.] 'Poor Fr. L. is still shut up, soldiers in his house, an officer walks behind him in his garden, and one comes every evening to see whether he is at home. They say his lights have to be put out at 8 o'clock (I don't know whether this is true, but I fear it is). How enraged he must be!'

Even this sensation takes second place to the outcry raised in Germany by the Jameson raid in the Transvaal, and the reaction of anger in Britain at the Kaiser's telegram of support to the Boer leader.

'What do you say to this explosion of savage hatred and abuse of England in the German papers! That telegram of W's to Pres. Kruger was really the greatest mistake. I am afraid this Dr. Leyds, President Kruger's Secretary of State, who is here and has constant access to the Foreign Office, had a great deal to do with it and with misleading the German Government...but the Germans have always petted the Boers, because they were enemies of England. Alas, people in England are beginning to wake up to the fact, though the English newspapers do not translate *all* the insulting articles, but only give very short extracts from *some,* and from those that are least violent. I am very careful not to talk about the Transvaal here in the house and do not mention the subject at meals before the ladies, it is much too painful, and my position *too* delicate. Poor Grandmama is miserable about it all, and what *my* feelings are I cannot describe.'

On January 13th, in a gossipy letter, the Empress makes casual mention of the illness of Prince Henry of Battenberg, who has insisted on taking part in the British expedition being staged to stop Ashanti slave raids into the Gold Coast.

'I hear from home that poor Liko has a slight fever, and had to be taken to the hospital ship. How annoying it is, Aunt Beatrice will be in such a way, poor thing...I am to be godmother to Georgie and May's little baby, Albert, which gives me great pleasure...They say Maud is going to be married in June. I suppose you will wish to go to her wedding, so my Sophie it will be a sad summer for me if I see so little of you.

'Whether I can get to England or not just now I really do not know, on account of the storm which the abuse of the German Press and Ws telegram have raised in England. It is a sad experience, and a new one. Hitherto when there was such an ill-feeling here (and there always is, more or less) it was not realized in England and no notice was taken of it, whereas this time there is an outburst of fury at which people here are very much astonished and profess to think quite uncalled for. Newspapers which have never lost an opportunity of a thrust or a hit at England are very much shocked now that England hits back!'

Two days later, Prince Henry's illness is still only a matter for casual mention.

'Tomorrow our Mossy darling and Fischy and the little ones appear. Once more dear voices and little footsteps in the corridor! I shall have breakfast in the dining room again. When I am alone I have no regular breakfast, but only stand a cup of coffee by my side and drink it while I am writing letters or walking about the room, to save time.... Would you mind, my darling, when you write to me, to write a little larger, and the lines not quite so close together, and with a little thicker paper and darker ink, as when I have not my spectacles at hand, I cannot read your dear letters and have to rush for my glasses.... Dear Grandmama telegraphed that Liko is doing well. Still, fever is a horrid thing.

'Yesterday, in the afternoon. Prof. Rontgen gave a little private lecture at the Schloss, explaining his wonderful new discovery of the new kind of invisible rays of light that are not reflected but go straight through anything that is not metal, bone or stone. Then I went to our English service, and in the evening, I had all the ladies of our different institutions and charities. I send you a weekly paper I thought might be of use to you, to keep you informed of what is going on in women's education and in women's work of all kinds.'

On January 18th are held the celebrations of the 25th anniversary of the founding of the German Empire.

'The 18th was a most fatiguing day. The ceremony at the Schloss went off with great order and precision, but somehow one felt no enthusiasm. William read the speech well, but there was no mention of beloved Papa, the one to whom so much was due, and that pained me. The weather was awful, cold and wretched, with all the melting ice and snow steaming up in a dense fog. The next day was the Ordensfest, but I was so dead tired I *struck,* and did not go!

'Last night I went to a little tea and a quiet evening at the Victoria Haus with all my nurses. Pro. Leyden and his wife were there and we were talking of massage in general and he said it was not good for ladies. I liked being there very much, the sisters look so nice in their pretty clean dresses, aprons and caps, and did the honours very well.'

Towards the end of January comes a big surprise from Athens. Sophie's expectations of the previous September having subsided, the subject has since lapsed. Now a letter comes to which the Empress answers,

'Oh, you cracked little Sophie, what have you been about! Certainly I was not prepared for *this* announcement...The stork this time seems to have been a most capricious bird! But if you have felt the movement, I suppose all is right. You are delighted, I am sure, and so am I. Of course I feel very sorry for you to miss the Coronation at Moskow, but to have a sweet baby again will more than make up for the disappointment. Perhaps it will be a girlie, who knows? It would be very nice for you to have one, she would be a companion for you later. Anyhow I must try and come to you, this time it is very difficult to manage as I am patroness of a great charity fair at Frankfort on the 15th of April, and also of the International Art Exhibition to be opened on the 1st of May. Would it be all right if I left on the 16th of April...?'

The Empress then launches into the precautions that Sophie must take, which are continued in the letters that follow, until, three days later, the news comes that Prince Henry's 'slight fever' has killed him.

'I know how much you will sympathize with poor unfortunate Aunt Beatrice and poor dear Grandmama in the dreadful sorrow that has befallen them. How unexpected, how cruel! Poor dear Liko at 36, it is too sad! You know how fond of him I always was, and how nice he always was to me. Think of the sadness at home. Dear Beatrice a broken-hearted widow, and my poor Mama with *no* one to lean on.

'I had a letter only yesterday morning from Grandmama in such good spirits, saying the fever had left Liko, and he was now only weak and would sail directly for Madeira. They had been having theatricals at Osborne, and were looking forward to my coming with Fischy and Mossy. Grandmama was much against Liko going to Ashanti, but he wanted to see some active service, and make himself useful. He was so fond of soldiering, a passionate traveller and seafarer...How handsome and agreeable he was, how keen on his yachting and hunting and all the local Isle of Wight affairs. What a desolate black future for dear Aunt Beatrice, married only 9 years! May her 4 children be a comfort to her.'

For some days her letters dwell on the consequences of this loss to her sister and mother.

'How will they ever be cheerful again at home, when poor dear Aunt Beatrice's loneliness is ever before them and no man of the family in the house, to help in a 1000 little ways. Grandmama at her age, and with all her duties and responsibilities, deprived of the comfort of a happy young menage by her side! She has had enough trouble and sorrow, one would wish to see her old age happy and cheerful. I wish I could be with her, but at best I am a visitor, who leaves again after a short while, and I have a constant sorrow which does not make me so helpful a guest as I should like to be.'

'In 10 days or a fortnight there will be the funeral and the poor things will have to go through harrowing scenes. Poor Auntie has not had a last goodbye, and cannot even have a last look at her dear husband's features, though there is *no* comfort in that, only a racking recollection which haunts one for ever.'

'I have had a letter from dear Mama, which says "Beatrice is an example to all, such patience, courage and resignation. We are well in health, but it is a house of woe." Vicky and I were at the English Church, and they sang the touching hymns, "Abide with Me" and "Thy will be done", and played the funeral march of Chopin on the organ, which always goes through and through me, there is such a wail of sadness in it.'

There is a fresh outburst in the Berlin press over the situation in South Africa, and the Empress writes indignantly.

'The German newspapers go on abusing England in the most wholesale, impertinent and I may say stupid way, very difficult to stand when one has English blood in one's veins. But I can only treat it with utter contempt. The German papers have always done it, and in the 38 years I have been here, I have had ample opportunity of experiencing the amenities of their language, but England has never taken any notice of it. Now it is a revelation to them, and will, I fear, bear evil fruit. The 1000's of Germans who live in our British colonies, and enjoy a liberty that they do *not* have at home, and are prosperous and successful, have now to be sacrificed to the *vanity* of being able to say "We have colonies". I am sorry for William, as it deprives him of sympathies in England which would have been very useful to him. In dear Papa's day, this could *never* have happened. This telegraphing all over the world, and all these rash speeches, were *not* his way.'

Sophie announces that her efforts to found a maternity hospital are at last bearing fruit. The Empress begins, 'I am indeed glad that your idea of maternity and children's hospitals is popular, and will be taken up...I am sure you will get them both in time. I worked away for 20 years before I got my Victoria Haus, and look how flourishing it is now!' A long letter contains practical advice on how to build and staff the hospitals. For matron, she suggests one of her *Victoria Haus* nurses, well qualified and entirely suitable.

'The only drawback is that the girl, who has pleasing manners and a nice appearance and sympathetic expression, has inherited 10,000 marks from an aunt, and my matron fears that when men hear of this she will instantly have offers of marriage, and then all our trouble and nice training might be in vain.

'My Bornstedt Kinderheim does so well now, people are going to imitate it in other parts of Germany. It answers the purpose of a combined creche and kindergarten, and is invaluable for those poor little children who would otherwise be neglected while the parents are busy or out at work. Of course, the children are fetched home at night. The mothers learn from the Victoria Sisters how to wash and dress and look after their children, but there are great difficulties with some parents, who are obstinate and ignorant to a fearful degree.'

The Empress pays a visit to the Palace to which she and her dying husband returned from San Remo on his accession nearly eight years previously.

'Yesterday Mossy and Fischy and I went to Charlottenburg. I had not set my foot there since the 1st of June, 1888, when I left it with my 3 darling girls and beloved Papa, on board the steamer for Potsdam. I have never had the courage to go there, but yesterday somehow I felt I should be able to look at the rooms once more, and show them to Fischy. They are not as we left them...to think what trouble I took to arrange that dear fine old house, and how little they have respected anything we did. How I thought of dear Grandmama's visit, and Aunt Beatrice's, and poor Liko's. How I thought of Henry's wedding and Papa's dreadful illness, of our kind Sir Morell.

'A poor Count. S., whose speech became hoarse a very few months ago, came here last week to Bergmann [*one of the German doctors who had wanted to operate on the Emperor Frederick — Ed.*] who said he had the beginning of the same as dear Papa, and proposed to the Count to operate on him. The operation lasted 2 hours, and yesterday the poor victim died.

'I always feel so thankful we listened to the excellent Sir Morell, and that dear Papa was not murdered in this fashion, though there were some who for their own political reasons and selfish ambitious plans, would have preferred it to be so, and that dear Papa should never have reigned at all. I need not tell you who these people were, as you know them. They tell me that poor Count. S's state after the operation, with half his throat gone, was so dreadful that to die was a mercy and a relief. It is horrible even to think of. If he had been left alone he might have lived for months, and perhaps a couple of years. How I feel for the poor Countess.'

Discussing Sophie's problems of educating her children, the Empress offers firm advice.

'I should be inclined to let them have a governess before they go to a tutor. It makes it far easier for children than going straight from a nursery to a tutor, women are far more clever and patient in giving the first lessons and first training. They understand smaller children so much better than men do, and have the knack of managing them with gentleness. It is also better for the ways and manners and health,

'You will have to be careful when the time comes to choose a tutor...William's boys are good-natured and happy, but I am sorry they have not a really superior tutor instead of a military governor. It is a pity the system is so antiquated, they will be brought up in all the prejudices of their family and their class, which will be made worse later in the regiments and at Court. Of course I am never asked anything, they seldom come to see me, but are always very nice when they do, and I am very fond of them.

'They came to tea yesterday, with Mossy's and F. Leopold's and the 3 Reischach children, and played in the big room afterwards. They made a noise which was indescribable, but seemed very happy and thoroughly enjoyed running and tumbling about. Mossy's little people were not at all frightened by the rough play and loud shouting of the older children. Fr. Leopold's little girl is really beautiful, with such lovely fair curls and big blue eyes.'

Prince Frederick Leopold and his wife have now been released from house arrest, but are still far from comfortable.

'Yaya came to luncheon yesterday. The poor thing is still very troubled and unhappy about the constant interference from Court, in all their affairs. It is really rather hard to bear, and one cannot wonder they rebel against it.'

In this and subsequent letters, the Empress touches on her various activities and interests in Berlin.

'I gave a dinner the other evening to different generals and notables, amongst others. Prof. Virchow, who with a twinkle in his screwed-up eyes, said he felt much inclined to go to the Olympic Games. I tried to encourage him, and if he should do so, I hope that Tino and you will kindly show him some civility. You know how highly Papa thought of him, and he is our greatest professor now. Yesterday evening we had the whole British Embassy to dinner and also a few Germans, Count Hatzfeldt, General v. Werder, etc...This was my last dinner. I have worked very hard this year and shall try to see fewer people this summer.'

'Mossy and Fischy went to the Opera Haus Ball the other night. She was looking like a little rose, and had all her emeralds on that so suit her lovely fair skin. ... I am so thankful she has stayed here with me this winter, it was such an intense comfort and pleasure to have her and her little chicks, which are a constant source of interest and pleasure to me.'

'I went to an exhibition of work of the poor Silesian weavers, who are starving because their trade does so badly, and they will not try to learn another. Now there is an attempt to teach their children wood carving, instead of weaving, and yesterday all the specimens of their carving were exhibited, really very well done, only the patterns are not very varied.'

'I send you some menus and little books of our cookery exhibition which will amuse you. The "School of Gardening for Girls" of which I am patroness did the table decorations. There was a table served according to old accounts of a dinner in the middle ages, the dishes with such funny names in old German. One book is very ingenious, a little cookery book from which children can cook, A girl of 12 years and her little friends made the dishes quite well. There was such a crush and rush — the public nearly squashed us in the corridor of the house where the exhibition was.'

'May I remind you that you promised me your photograph and that of Tino and the children for dear old Mons. Godet, Papa's tutor. He is over 80 and very frail, so one must not put off giving him this pleasure. You know how devoted Papa was to him, and used regularly to send him all new photographs of you all.'

As the time for Sophie's confinement draws nearer, the Empress's thoughts turn more and more frequently to the Athens she will soon be visiting again.

'I am so glad the result of your bazaar was so brilliant. How kind of the King to give you such a nice sum, and what an excellent amount you have raised in so short a time.

'You seem in good health and spirits and that is such a comfort to me. Grandmama writes saying she hopes a doctor would go out with me, for you, but this is out of the question for if I brought a foreigner, I fear there would be a row and a set out at Athens, and it would not be liked!

'Yesterday I was at an exhibition of objects for sick nursing, hospitals, etc., and found one or 2 nice and useful things, also a new English disinfectant, which supersedes all others for daily use, and as it is the safest and most efficacious, I shall bring some to Athens...I thought of bringing my bathing dress and of trying to get sea bathing at the Phaleron, which no doubt would do me good. The mosquitoes are not bad in May, are they?'

Sophie has urged her mother to come out to Greece in time to see the Olympic Games.

'Indeed you can imagine how much I would have liked to see the Games, also how much better in every way it would have suited me to leave Germany a fortnight sooner, but I am bound to stay on account of the tiresome bazaar at Frankfort, which is given under my patronage for the building fund of our Cronberg Hospital. So I cannot leave here before the 17th. Please, please, my Sophie, wait for the darling baby to arrive until I am with you! It is really not my fault that I cannot come sooner.... Athens must now be filling up for the Games, and the guests all beginning to arrive. I suppose the young Grand Duke George is a suitor for Minnie?'

The Empress leaves Berlin for Schloss Rümpenheim at the end of March, Margaret and her family having preceded her. Extracts from successive letters written before she sets out for Greece reflect current events and interests.

'I left Berlin yesterday morning shortly after 7 and arrived here in time for tea. It was bitterly cold, and we had snow and rain all the time. My Mossy darling is well, but looks rather pinched and pensive. There seems to be reason to think she is imitating your example! ...I had a telegram from Willy saying he had enjoyed himself immensely at Naples.'

'How interesting it must have been to see trials for the Olympic Games. But to have such long races is dreadfully dangerous, one might break a blood vessel or overstrain the heart, etc. I hope and trust the man who was so done up has not injured himself for life...Indeed Tino was right to tell the authorities to clean up Athens and make the streets tidy. How charming it must look! How I wish they would water the Athens streets with sea water as they do in so many English towns. It is in no way unwholesome nor does it injure the eyes, whereas dust carries all sorts of germs and irritates the eyes very much and is so bad for the lungs. Why do they not make the experiment with a few watering carts? They would soon see how far preferable it is to the horrid dust, and how it would cool the air.

'Henry and Irene and Toddie [*Prince Waldemir — Ed.*] arrive today. I am going to lend her my best jewels for the coronation at Moskow. Angeli is at Darmstadt painting Ducky. I envy him, she is so handsome that it must be a real pleasure. I admire her still more than her sisters-in-law, Ella and Alicky, lovely though they are.'

'Today, April 6th, the Games will begin. The stadium must look splendid, and altogether the sight be beautiful. I hope and trust the weather will behave itself...Yesterday the telegram from your Mama-in-law came saying dearest Minny is engaged to the Grand Duke George. I hear Minny has been wishing it for some time, so I rejoice for her, dear sweet girl. But oh, what a terrible long way off she will live.'

'We are quite horrified at the death of poor Herr v. Schrader in a duel with that horrid Kotze, who was not wounded at all. Duels are wickedness and folly in my eyes, and this already terrible affair grows worse and worse. Reischach is quite crushed at his friend's fate. My opinion of Kotze remains what it always was, and the way in which he has been shielded and protected throughout by his party, who are all powerful at Court, seems to me very unjust.'

'Since last I wrote, I have seen with pleasure the accounts of the Games and that they seem to be a success. ... I am so glad that a Greek won the running race from Marathon, and can quite imagine the enthusiasm at Athens.'

'I wonder in what way the news of Tricoupis's death at Cannes will affect the situation in Greece. He was unpopular, and yet a remarkable man. He did a deal of harm as well as good, yet he was full of energy and intelligence, and he worked hard. If you think fit, please send a message of condolence from me to Sophie Tricoupis, whom I knew when I was still a young girl, and who must be very unhappy now. I should like her to know that I feel for her in her sorrow.'

After calling in at Nice to see Queen Victoria, the Empress makes her way to Athens, and is there on May 3rd, when, as she had hoped for, a daughter [*Princess Helen, who writes the introduction to this book*] is born to Sophie. There is a description of her during her visit, in E. F. Benson's *As We Were*. 'A quiet comely woman, plainly dressed in black', who would sit for hours on a block of masonry in the Acropolis sketching and painting, watched by tourists who only learned who she was when her secretary. Count von Seckendorff, came with bared head to tell her the *fiacre* had arrived. For the return journey to Trieste after some six weeks in Athens, the *Surprise* is, for once, not available, and the Empress travels by train to Patras to take passage in an Austrian Lloyd Steamer, the *Vorwärts*. Her letter on June 5th begins, 'How dear and good of you to telegraph to me and say cheer up. Oh how I wish I *could,* but the stupid tears *will* flow. I thought my heart would break when I said goodbye to you, but I will not say more of this.' Then after several more paragraphs on the subject, she continues:

'It was very hot in the train, but not unbearable. Here at Patras, when we scrambled into rather a funny little boat, Wedell lost his footing and sprawled into it. The Consul, with white kid gloves, picked him up, and then got knocked over by poor Countess Brühl, who arrived "plump", all of a heap down at Wedell's feet. I am afraid I laughed!

'Oh, you *must* see the exquisite country between Corinth and here, it is so beautiful, greener far than the north, the grass, the trees, the vines, all smelling so sweet, and fields of oleander, with their lovely pink blossoms. The air from the mountains was so pure, and yet scented. Greece is a lovely country! God bless you, my Sophie, once more 1000's of kisses to Georgie and Alexander, and a gentler tiny one to wee Ellene, from your dearest fond and doting Mother. V.'

To travel in an ordinary passenger vessel is a new experience for the Empress. Next day she writes:

'It is very queer to be on board with all these people, but I think it will be quite comfortable. It seems so funny to be on a ship, and yet not be able to walk up and down the deck. I have got a place screened off for me, aft, and there I remain, for the boat is crammed full of all sorts of passengers, including a horse. Some are very dirty...The Captain is a nice civil and considerate man. He has given me his cabin, a slip of a thing, but which has the enormous advantage of being on deck, so that it has good big windows, and I can have all the air I want. The bed was like a stone, but I turned and twisted about, and thought of my Sophie, etc.'

After going ashore at Corfu, where she visits the King's residence — 'I hope your dear Papa-in-law will not think me indiscreet that I was anxious to see *Mon Repos* and the Palace once more', she writes of her interest in some of the furnishings,

'...especially the old Turkey carpets in the Palace, they are grand in colour and design, you will find no better anywhere, and well worth being copied by the School at Athens, where they should work only from the best. Excuse my saying this, but I was so struck with the beauty of these old carpets and they are getting so rare now, and their value is great. I know something about oriental carpets, having hunted for them so much. P.S. Now I am no longer in your house, there is no one to fidget and worry about smells and drains. I am sure I made myself a pest to everyone, but it was necessary for you, as I have not the slightest doubt that Andrea had the typhoid from the abominable drains at the Palace. Pray, pray be most particular, and complain directly you smell anything.'

The trip provides the Empress with further unaccustomed experiences.

'The night before last we were dreadfully disturbed at Brindisi where there was a visitation of the ship on account of the cholera, and a medical officer came on board to inspect everyone, and all the passengers had to bundle out of bed at 2 o'clock at night and appear on deck, and answer to their names. This proceeding I declared *I would not share.* Countess Brühl and Wedell only thrust their heads out of their cabin windows, but our poor servants had to turn out. The noise was something indescribable, screaming, shouting, laughing and vociferating in German, Italian, Greek, French, it was a real tower of Babel. You can imagine what a night I had! ...All the lambskins and goatskins that were shipped smell dreadfully, and I fear my boxes and clothes will have partaken of this fearful odour.'

After the arrival at Trieste, the Empress's letters, apart from advice to Sophie to look after herself and the baby, are occupied chiefly with descriptions of her journey home through the Dolomites and Austria. From Innsbruck, she writes:

'...such magnificent scenery! ...and the Alpine flowers in full beauty, gentian, cowslip and forget-me-nots in great quantities. The drive and walk over the Rolle Pass is very fine indeed, first the wild top of the hill with the great peaks towering above, with a good deal of snow, then the forests, with immense trees and rushing waterfalls, then lower down, the rich pastures covered with grass and flowers, and grazing herds of cows with their tinkling bells. We passed through many pretty villages with quaint houses and churches.'

'Our expedition across the hills succeeded very well, though the first day it poured with rain for hours. I got out of the carriage and walked in the steep places with my waterproof cape and umbrella, but my petticoats were so soaked that they had to be dried by a kitchen fire in a little wayside inn.'

'We stayed some hours at Lindau on the Lake of Constance, which is charming. In spite of the rain, the Burgomaster in a white tie and kid gloves, "frack", and orders, insisted on showing me the town, and we picked our way over the wet slippery pavement. I was dragged right and left, struggling with my umbrella, while poor Countess Brühl panted and gasped behind me, carrying her petticoats very high and, though she had very thin indoor shoes on, which she always *will* wear, stepping into all the deepest and brownest puddles, because she is so short-sighted. Of course the younger generation of the town, having found out I was there, stuck to our heels the whole time. The town library has a good collection of books which I enjoyed looking at. Then we had a little supper at the hotel and returned to our railway carriage.'

Back home at Friedrichshof, the Empress quickly falls into her normal routine and writings.

'Today being Saturday, baby is 6 weeks old, bless the sweet little dimpled thing. What a pet she will soon begin to be. I can hardly believe I am back again.... This dear place is looking very pretty and tidy, and though the landscape is tame indeed compared with what I have lately seen, yet it is so peaceful and neat, and my old Burg looks so well through the window. The rose garden is just perfection.

'I have some new horses, and the dear big one has been sold, I am sorry to say. Today I asked some children to tea, lo in all, belonging to our neighbours. They had chocolate, strawberries, raspberries, cake and bread and butter, were very merry, and played games under the chestnut trees, where your dear little people liked playing last year.

'There was a fete here in the village which would have amused you to see. The little Church has been fresh painted and new bells hung, and as it was the day of the patron saint, there was music and banners and flags flying, and High Mass and a procession. They invited me to go down to look at their decorations — they had put up 3 triumphal arches — so of course I did. It was a gay picturesque sight, and everyone was in the best of humour.

'Yesterday your dear Apapa was here for luncheon and looking wonderfully well, as charming, amiable, young-looking and handsome as ever. The Grand Duke and Grand Duchess of Luxemberg were here too, it was very pleasant.'

The Letters commence to mention the Empress's concern at the continuing troubles in Crete.

'I am always thinking of those unfortunate people and longing to hear that they are freed from the cruel Turkish yoke, but I fear that Europe has but one idea, to smother and stifle all disturbances for fear of provoking war. But it seems a cruel shame not to help the Cretans win their independence. Should you happen to be writing to dear Grandmama after your birthday, do tell her how distressing the condition of the Greeks and Christians on the Island is, one must lose no opportunity of making one's voice heard, it may do good in the end. I always write fiery letters to England about Crete, the situation makes me so very unhappy.'

Shortly afterwards, after noting that 'Grandmama writes that she hopes and trusts affairs in Crete will be satisfactorily settled, but she does not say how', the Empress is stirred to protest about Bismark's warnings against German intervention in the Cretan troubles.

'Did you read what Prince Bismark said about Crete? I thought it disgraceful, as heartless and cynical and unprincipled as possible. But he was always proud of "taking no interest in Eastern affairs, as they in no way affected Germany", forgetting that what affects Europe must always in the end indirectly affect Germany too, and that where the Great Powers can by throwing the weight of their influence into the scale prevent cruelty and oppression and bloodshed, they have the moral obligation to do so. This is called Don Quixotism but it is not, and nations, like individuals, *must* think of helping those in tribulation. Of course the ways and means must be prudently chosen, as politics are a complicated web of considerations, and have to be treated most cautiously.'

The Empress goes to Wiesbaden to return the King of Denmark's visit, then calls to see a maternity hospital, which she describes in detail, 'as it is on a small scale, just what I would wish you to have for Athens...You could so well combine it with a training school for monthly nurses, which is an urgent necessity...Could no one be found who would lend the money?' She continues:

'You will laugh at me, but you do not know how I miss the Greek sunset! I used to look forward to that hour every day and could not take my eyes off the landscape. It was too beautiful.... Last night the moonlight here made me think of that last moon in Athens, when I stood on my balcony watching the beauty of the southern sky and drinking in the perfumed air, and listening to the nightingales and the little owls. And that lovely, lovely view from your children's nursery over the Palace Gardens to the Hymettus!'

The Empress has enlightened views on the provision of libraries for the people, and on women's civil rights.

'Last evening the S's and Dr. D. came to tea, and we had a most animated discussion about "free libraries", which I think such a good thing, but which Reischach thinks quite useless, as people like to sit and drink in the Bierhaus and not read books. My argument was that one should give them the chance of reading at any rate, and that they would often avail themselves of it. Easy and harmless books, also instructive ones, should be provided. We are going to start this here at Cronberg, but of course the people will only be inclined to read in the winter months.

'Willy has gone off to Norway, he did not even wait to see whether the new "Code Civile" for Germany was accepted by Parliament. I hear that it *is*, which is really a blessing, though I do not think it very perfect, women are not fairly treated, there are different rights which ought to have been granted which they enjoy in England. For instance, widows can be guardians of their children in England, but here not without some special arrangement.'

That Sophie should attend the coming wedding of Princess Maud had seemed to be ruled out by the nearness of her recent confinement, but now comes a surprise.

'I was utterly thunderstruck by your telegram yesterday. I thought the idea of a journey this summer was quite abandoned. Of course I am delighted for you and for Tino. I know how much you like going to England and how it amuses Tino, and yet I sat down and had a good cry. The idea of my not seeing you is too cruel when you will be within 2 days journey of me...How surprised you must have been when your Papa-in-law offered you to go to England!'

Princess Sophie and her husband and Prince Nicholas are already on their way and the Empress duly learns of their arrival.

'So many thanks for your telegram just received. Last night after having heard by telegram from dear Uncle Bertie, who is so kind and never forgets me, that you had safely arrived, my thoughts were so much at Marlborough House, picturing to myself my Sophie there amongst all our dear ones. Today you will be going to the fine Greek Church, and no doubt paying a few visits. You know my thoughts are with you every day, every hour...but do *not* trouble to write to me much, I know how tired you will be, and how your time will be taken up, and I do *not* expect it.'

Fondly, and a little jealously, the Empress follows her daughter's participation in the festivities up to the wedding on July 22nd.

'Since I wrote this morning, I have received your dear letter from Marlborough House. Many, many thanks. I am delighted to hear that you liked the wedding so much, and enjoyed your stay in London so thoroughly. And I am thankful and relieved that Sir J. Williams was pleased with your state of health.

'Grandmama has just telegraphed to me that Tino, you and Nicky have arrived at Osborne. I am so glad you will have some days of rest there, and enjoy the Cowes week. I read that you went to see a home for incurable children with Auntie Alix and Thora [*Princess Helena Victoria — Ed.*]. If you have time, the hospital at Ryde would please you much.'

A few days later, the Empress refers to a message brought by one of her personal maids, whom she had sent to London to look after her daughter. She also has another dig at Sophie's fringe.

'Emma gave me your message that you thought you had fewer jewels than the others at the wedding. I cannot quite agree, you may have fewer diamond brooches but such a set of turquoise as *you* have very few people possess, and also such a set of rubies, and the diamond diadem I gave you is very valuable as the stones are *old*. Cape diamonds may be much more effective and large and showy, but not so good and fine. Indeed I wish I had more to give you, but you must wait until I die, or am older and need no longer wear jewels, then I can give you a few more, and be pleased to see them on your dear neck.

'Ernie and Ducky send you their love. It is very nice having them here. She is looking wonderfully handsome with the graceful fashion she wears her hair, in large waves back over the head showing the roots turned back in the middle of the forehead, which is so pretty because one sees that it is a person's own hair. The towsel and fringe like a thick sponge over the forehead suits Aunt Alix but no one else. It spoils Maudie's pretty face, and May wears a wig front, and Charlotte is quite disfigured by it. I hear my Sossie laugh, but she would agree with me if she could only see herself I send a little drawing of it for you — it would suit you so well.'

In August, the Cretan insurrection is again in the news. Russia's obstructive attitude to a solution, and the consequent reactions of the Bismark press again evoke the Empress's ire.

'I do pity your Papa and the Greek government immensely. I think they are most unfairly dealt with, and the question is very badly understood, at any rate at Berlin, where the old Bismark tradition of moulding Germany's attitude towards anything that touches the Eastern Question on Russia's wishes is strictly adhered to as the best way of buying *Russia's* good graces. It is quite a mistake, as the Russians do not care two pence for Germany's support, their policy is to please France, in order to command French money and the French alliance. Thank God the German Liberals are not so wrongheaded, they take a *right* view of the Cretan question, and think the conduct of Russia very bad, which I am sorry to say it is. She seems bent on humouring the Turks at present.

'This is my last letter to England, I fear, as I suppose you will be leaving in 2 days to begin the long homeward journey. If only I could have seen you for a little while. Dear Grandmama writes so pleased with your visit, and so kindly about Nicky, as well as Tino and you.'

But to the Empress's joy, her daughter and Princes Constantine and Nicholas arrange to travel home by way of Frankfort. After a short stay at Friedrichshof, the day of parting once more comes.

'I tried to put a brave face on it as I watched the train gliding away, the smoke curling up in the moonlight, and my own Sophie's head still at the window, until I could see her no more. But then the tears rolled down my cheeks and I turned home with a heart as heavy as lead. I would not get into the same carriage in which we had just sat together, nor drive back the same way. The scene was very pretty with the moon shining on the houses, but the soul and life seemed gone out of everything. Yet I am indeed so intensely grateful for the unexpected treat of having you here for nearly a fortnight when I had quite thought I should not have a glimpse of you!'

The Empress little knows that in a few years' time the world would have telephones, aeroplanes, cinematography, television, when she writes:

'It is a week since we parted, but I am thankful to think your journey is over, and that you are safe at home with the darling children. If there were only a telescope to see you, and a speaking trumpet to speak to you, and a flying machine to fly over to you now and then, the distance and the separation would be bearable.

'I am very glad you saw something of the Munich Exhibition...the Menzel drawings are fine, but if the one you fancied only costs 500 marks then it must be only a pencil sketch, and that, in proportion to your means, I think a large sum. I will see whether he has not a pencil drawing to spare for you some day, he has heaps and heaps...Today, September 1st, is the anniversary of Sedan, and also just 8 years since I saw this place for the first time, and immediately resolved on buying it. Certainly I do not regret having done so.

'What terrible new horrors have been committed at Constantinople! These wretched Armenians, I do feel for them so much, and so must everyone with a heart and human compassion. Why do the Powers allow these massacres? Thank God they have at last shown a little energy over the poor Cretans, who are going to have a constitution, I see, but only after 1000's of unfortunate victims have lost their lives.'

A week afterwards, she writes of visitors from England, the young Duchess of York and her mother.

'Aunt Mary Teck and dear May are staying with me for a couple of days. May has your rooms, it is always a pang for me to see anyone else in them, but you will not mind May using them, I know how much you like her. It is indeed pleasant to have them, especially as everyone here says May is your image. She is so sweet and charming and sensible, and her being like my Sophie drew me towards her. She is in great good looks, and of an evening wears a pink satin gown, which suited her so well. I think people admire her much here. She speaks such nice German and French. Alas, yesterday, it poured cats and dogs, however we attempted to drive to Homberg, as May had never been there, but such a thunderstorm was going on, she did not see much. While I am writing to you the rain is coming down again like a waterspout. The sight of my garden makes me miserable, all my lovely roses with their heads hanging down, quite drowned and washed to bits, all the other pretty flowers crushed flat to the ground.'

Among the Empress's many other visitors are some who amuse her and others who hold her admiration.

'Today I have got to give another dinner. There is a list of 70 people still to be absolved before all my social obligations are finished with. Yesterday, at dinner, we had some very funny people. One gentleman from Wiesbaden came in a tail coat (buttoned up) a white satin cravat and white kid gloves, and one lady in a low gown with a boa round her neck and artificial pink roses. It was rather hard to keep one's countenance, and I remembered the guest at Tatoi, not certain whether he ought to eat the little papers in which the cheese souffle was served!

'A few days ago, we had the pleasure of seeing Sir Arthur Sullivan. He came over from Nauheim and stayed a night here, and played to us charmingly from many of his operettes

'I am trying to persuade the painter Passini to go to Athens, as I think he would make such lovely drawings and pictures there, and find such "motive". I said I was sure you would be much pleased if he came someday. You know what an old friend of Papa and mine he is, since so many years.'

With a thought for Greek financial troubles, the Empress writes:

'I send you a little paragraph out of the *Daily Chronicle*. In general I am very much against lotteries, there is something about them which partakes in an unpleasant way of gambling, but who knows whether the suggestion might not be a practical one in this emergency.

'I also send you two books and a pamphlet which were given me when I attended the opening of the Congress of Medical Men and Scientists at Frankfort. Fischy went with me. The speeches were most instructive, and it was interesting to see all these men of science together, such an illustrious assembly!'

Although the Letters are taken up with so many and diverse subjects, there are few that do not mention Athens and Princess Sophie and her family.

'I am so glad the little pearl necklace for sweet Ellene pleased you. She can wear it until she is quite a big girl, I hope.... How I wish I could see the tiny girlie on your lap and in your arms, and Sweetie carrying his adorable dimpled daughter about! She must be such a joy to you. When you have a photo of this little "Maid of Athens", please send me one. Also the one of you in Greek costume that I have asked for so long.

'How interesting for you that our dear splendid British fleet came to Phaleron Bay. I am sure it was a treat for you to visit Louis's ship [*Prince Louis of Battenberg — Ed.*] the "Cambrian"...Yes, indeed, I am fond of our navy — the

Navy — there is none in the world like it, just as there is no army like the Prussian (German) Army. Of this I am convinced, though our small British Army is most gallant and the officers wonderful, as I am sure you will agree.

'I am so impatient for your new house to be finished. The old one, devoted as I am to it, because I have spent such happy days under your hospitable roof, is getting too small and crammed for you, and it is rather too *bourgeois* to be so close to the street, and to have so much of the dust and noise, and no privacy for getting in and out. To be built *entre cour et jardin* was indispensable for every good house of a gentleman in town, with a nice approach to drive up to the doors...Is anything settled about the stables? Do not have them too close, they will smell so in hot weather. Has the kitchen been begun? To me the work seems to be a little like Penelope's robe, i.e., it does not get on any faster. If one could only get that kitchen-garden out of your Papa-in-Law! I would go down on my knees to him for that! Is there no means of the King's vegetables being grown in another spot?'

Sophie has taken up the fashionable new sport of cycling, and the Empress is a little worried.

'I hope you will be careful when you try the tricycle first, as one gets awkward falls before one knows how to manage it, and I believe it is more difficult for a lady to extricate herself from it than from a bicycle if it overturns. But from both there have been very bad and awkward falls, legs and arms broken, etc. Watch also whether it makes your legs swell or not. In moderation it is a wholesome exercise, but if the least overdone becomes very injurious. Along a flat road it must be very nice.'

Because of the coming confinements of Princesses Margaret and Irene, the Empress gives up her customary autumn trip abroad.

'So I shall go straight to Rümpenheim from here and wait for the event. Then when Mossy is on a fair road to recovery I shall go to Kiel to see how Irene is getting on with her baby, which I trust will be arriving at the same time as Mossy's...I am wondering whether Mossy will have a daughter. Sometimes I think she has symptoms which are different from the last time.

'Victoria Battenberg was here with her 3 children yesterday. Alice is so handsome and one really cannot call her deaf, she is only not very quick of hearing, that is all. She is 11 but as big as a girl of 14. Little Louise is also very pretty, and the boy a fine child.

'The leaves are beginning to turn, and the autumn tints to cover the woods and hills. Lovely as it is, it always makes me sad, as it means that summer is over and that winter, which for me is like an enemy, is approaching, tedious and endless and wretched, with colds, rheumatism and neuralgia and chilblains, dismal dark skies and howling winds, and ice and snow, all of which I do so hate. All nature seems dead and buried under a shroud, and one is more or less of a prisoner indoors with no rides, no walks. I never feel well when it is cold, it seems to take all the life and energy out of me, and I cannot stand the atmosphere of heated rooms, they give me a racking headache.'

The Tsar Nicholas and his wife, after visiting England and France, are now in Germany, attending the Imperial manoeuvres. 'From Breslau I hear that Nicky and Alicky's visit was a great success. My regiment of Hussars is said to have looked very smart indeed in the long cloaks I have had to give them, and which half ruins me!' Now, in October, they are coming to Romberg, and will pay a visit to the Empress, who sees a busy spell ahead of her.

'This week will be a bubbling one. On the 16th Nicky and Alicky's visit, and the laying of the foundation stone of the Greek Church at Homberg. Then on the 21st, William and Dona come for a day, with 17 ladies and gentlemen! It is really terrible to bring such a suite, and most inconvenient to me to have the house so full when Mossy wants to be quiet and undisturbed. Charlotte and Bernhard come on the 17th with little Feo, and the Grand Duke of Weimar on the 19th.'

Her letters of the 16th and 17th October describe the Tsar's visit.

'I can only write in the greatest hurry as I must be off to Homberg to fetch Nicky and Alicky. Fischy goes with me. Since Nicky arrived at Darmstadt there are 40 detectives at Frankfort, 4 have come here to our innocent town of Cronberg and one marched up to the cottage yesterday and asked for information about the road we meant to drive over. Indeed, I am very glad I am not the Tsar, and can go and come as I like without detectives at my heels. Never to be safe is a high price to pay for such a position.'

'All went off very well yesterday, with the exception of the weather which was fiendish. I received Nicky and Alicky at the station at Homberg, which was beautifully decorated with flags and hanging garlands and bouquets. I had to present [*then follows a long list of names — Ed.*]. The ceremony of laying the foundation stone went through well and quickly. I then drove Nicky and Alicky over here, they wished to have the carriage open, though it was awfully cold and blowy. Nicky was so nice and kind, and I think him such a dear. Alicky is looking very happy and blooming — having done away with their fringes does suit her and Ella wonderfully! Here at Friedrichshof it was quite pleasant and everyone seemed at their ease, not stiff or ceremonious. Nicky looked about him and said he meant to copy a good deal. There was just time to plant two trees before they left again by train, and of course I took them to the railway station.

'Today Charlotte and Bernhard and Feo arrived. The latter, poor child, is dressed in clothes fit for the old Empress Augusta, but one must not say a word. Charlotte is looking much too thin, and her face worn and pulled and aged. Bernhard is in very good humour, and though he still says the most extraordinary things when he begins to abuse anyone or anything, his expressions are really so droll one cannot help laughing.'

The Empress goes the next day to Coblenz to the unveiling of a statue to her mother-in-law, the Empress Augusta, whose daughter, the Grand Duchess of Baden, is among the distinguished relatives present.

'It was cold, rainy and windy, but there was no downpour during the ceremony of unveiling the statue, which is pretty good, though the architecture around it is perfectly hideous. Aunt Louise was of course much moved, but notwithstanding made endless "cercles" and held quite a "cour" with everyone who had formerly belonged to the Empress Augusta's household. She talked so long that it began to rain again, and we got wet.'

The Empress is irrevocably tied to the routine of closing Friedrichshof for the winter, and so towards the end of October, she writes:

'This will be my last letter from Friedrichshof this year. I always leave it with a heavy heart as I am so fond of it, and get more and more attached to it as new interests spring up. It is so nice to watch all the things grow that one has planted, and make little changes and improvements here and there. When one goes elsewhere one misses the electric light, the nice pure soft water in such abundance, and many other comforts.... Our public library at Cronberg, which I set going, is working well, the people rush for the books, as I expected. We have already collected 400 volumes. P.S...Yes, I quite agree, letter writing *is* perfectly horrid, and especially when one feels one has *no time!*'

Princess Sophie's new home in Athens is nearly ready, and she announces her proposals for furnishing it.

'Having an agent of M's over to furnish your new Palace *en bloc* is no doubt a good plan, but I am afraid not in all respects. If the furniture is too much alike everywhere, the house easily has the appearance of a hotel or steamer. The charm of a house is, I think, to see that the objects of furniture have been carefully and well selected, and not bought wholesale to save thought and trouble. I think it is more interesting to have things from all sorts of places...I am so glad the foundation stone of your hospital was to be laid the day you wrote. That indeed is a great step, and may the enterprise be a blessing to Athens.'

In November, Sophie is troubled with a spell of children's illnesses. 'I am horrified', the Empress writes, 'to think that your sweet little Alexander should have an attack of croup. I feel so much for you because I know what anxiety one goes through until it is past. I went through such dreadful times with Henry and Charlotte and...' The rest of the letter mainly records who, in the Empress's family, and among her relations, did and did not have croup. A week later a telegram announces that little George has scarlet fever. The reply, and other letters that follow, consist chiefly of instructions on how to handle the illness and how to prevent it infecting others of the family. The Empress concludes: 'Of course, we shall be very careful here about your dear letters, and it was most thoughtful of you to telegraph about them. Today your letter of Thursday the 5th arrived and it was baked in a stew pan with the lid on first before I touched it.'

Meanwhile, things are not going too well at Rümpenheim, where the Empress is now awaiting her daughter's confinement:

'Alas, dear Fischy has been in bed 2 days with a high temperature and pulse and with acute pain in his leg which Dr. H. fears is rheumatic fever. It is most awkward just now. What *shall* we do if dear Mossy is laid up now and Fischy cannot leave his bed? She is most brave and sensible, and does not make a fuss, but one hears her heaving deep sighs, and her dear little face wears an anxious look.'

That same night, November 7th, the birth takes place, and with it an explanation of the unusual symptoms that Margaret had shown.

'...Our Mossy has twins! The first baby was born at 1, but it was evident there was a second. She suffered much before the 2nd was born at 4. Our darling was as brave and as patient as you were. Poor Fischy is in his bed upstairs, and I have to run from one to the other.'

Two days later, the Empress records that:

'Mossy dear now looks most sweet, pretty, and rose and childlike. She and Fischy keep writing one another little notes on slips of paper and I carry them to and fro. I think Mossy has never had such a good recovery as this time. The eldest is to be called Philip after their great ancestor, and the 2nd Wolfgang Moritz, also after ancestors.'

On November 21st, the Empress's birthday, she is able to report that:

'I had a very quiet birthday under Mossy's roof, trying not to dwell on the sad thoughts which pass through my mind on such anniversaries. Just now I feel full of deep gratitude that Georgie and Alexander are so much better, and my Sophie well, and Mossy and her twinnies getting on so nicely, and my poor Fischy at least no worse.... This morning. Mossy was carried, sofa and all, carefully wrapped and covered, up to Fischy's bedroom, and her couch put alongside his bed, and there they remained most part of the day, she highly delighted as you can imagine.'

But Princess Margaret's twins are not the only new grandsons for the Empress to be gratified at, for a week later she writes:

'I thought you would like to read this letter from Henry about Irene and her baby boy. What a splendid short and easy time she seems to have had, thank God. I shall go and see her soon...I have today read in the papers of the shocking storm at Athens, the havoc done, and the lives lost. I am so grieved about it, I cannot say. Dear Athens to be thus visited! For earthquakes one was more or less prepared, but not for this!'

In December, several of the letters deal with disclosures made in Athens about the unready state of the Greek army.

'I am very sorry things are not going with you as they ought. I read the King's message. It seems to me as if you wanted a reorganization of the army.

Tino would be the one to do that. I wish you could get help from our German army, it has such a good organization. Prussian officers in Turkey have improved the army there, and under Sandro, who was such a good soldier, much was done for the Bulgarian army. The English have achieved wonders with the Egyptian army, as you know, and have proved that they *can* organize. Much might be done too for Greece, but *money* is one of the principal requirements! If only those foreign creditors could be satisfied, and their mouths stopped!'

The Empress goes to the Schloss Kiel to spend Christmas there and to see her other new grandson.

'I found Henry looking very well, also dearest Irene. The baby is a fine child, not as pretty as our twins, but larger of course...They give him the pet name of Budge, but he will be christened Sigismund...

'Yesterday Henry took me out to their new estate, Hemmelmark. It is a fine large property, with barns and cow houses, some woods and a good sheet of water, but very damp and low. The house is even rougher and more out of repair than the one you live in at Tatoi. Henry and Irene are quite devoted to the place, and the thought of it being their very own makes them love it, they enjoy perfect liberty there, and live *à la* Robinson Crusoe.

"These strikes at Hamburg are dreadful. I have not the same view of the case as the German Government. I think the pay the workmen get *so* low that I wonder how they can live with their families, and wish indeed they could be given higher wages.'

Before the end of the year, the Empress goes to her Palace in Berlin, from where come the Letters that end the year.

'Only a line in haste to say that I arrived this morning before sunrise. Vicky and Adolf arrived at ii, and Willy and Dona and 5 of the children came to luncheon, and the 2 others later. They were all very jolly and seemed to enjoy themselves. Afterwards I paid my visit to the Schloss and was shown six Gobelins Willy has bought and is much delighted with. They are something like the one I have in the hall at Friedrichshof, but less good. Afterwards I went to the studio to see dear Papa's statue for Wiesbaden. Wm. and Dona were also there and an enormous suite, which was rather awkward, as I could not make many remarks...I congratulate you on sweet baby's first tooth. It is not too late, 7 months is considered about the right time.'

'December 31st. This will be my last letter in this year and when I look back upon all it brought, I think of the time at Athens with a heart full of gratitude, how my darling Sophie was preserved to me and sweet little Ellene given to us...Let me wish you and Tino a happy New Year and may every blessing be yours throughout 1897. May we meet before the year is very old. I suppose you will come to dear Grandmama's Jubilee, and D.V., if we are all alive, I shall go too.'

Chapter Nine – The Letters, 1897

The Empress's output of correspondence to Princess Sophie during 1897 was almost double that of any other year. The reason for this great increase was the Greek war with Turkey, following on the staged insurrection in Crete, When the country that now so strongly held her affections plunged recklessly into a hopeless conflict, she was roused to a flood of letters on the day-to-day military and political excitements, letters so frequent, sometimes several in a day, and so lengthy, that only a fraction of their contents can be reproduced here in addition to the matters with which her writings were normally concerned.

The year began quietly with the usual family gossip. 'I congratulate you on darling Ellene's 2 teeth, and think you may venture to give her a little food now...The heaps of books I sent are for the library of the institution of which you are patroness...I am immensely proud because the German Archaeological Institution (of Berlin, Rome and Athens) have made me an honorary member...' She goes on to describe the customary succession of visitors, from 'William and Dona for luncheon, the children came later' to 'Max of Baden came to tea, he had been to Rümpenheim and found Fischy looking very ill, no wonder considering all he has gone through'. She writes too of her habitual round of visits, the Mausoleum at Potsdam, the Kinderheim at Bornstedt — 'the dear little children in their blue pinafores looked so happy, they came and chatted to me as if I were an old friend' — and the Victoria Haus and other institutions. She continues:

'Here in Berlin it is intensely cold with a constant N.E. wind, nobody seems to care to venture out, and streets are empty except for a few people holding their ears and burying their faces in their collars. When you come here again you will see many changes, but the character of Berlin remains quite unchanged, the public, especially the men, just as ill-dressed. What increases with great rapidity are the restaurants and hotels, the tramways, and now the bicycling. Even since last year there are double the number of bicycles, and it makes driving in the streets no easy matter.

'Yesterday I took a walk with Yaya, she was really so nice, and is an excellent, good creature. She and Fritz L. get on much better together than they did, but there are constant rows between them and the Court, which are very trying, though only on such trifling subjects. ... A few days ago Prince Hohenlohe came to see me, I thought he looked aged and ill, but his mind is as quick and active as ever.

'This will only be a short letter as I am writing in bed. I have a feverish chill this evening and feel so wretched, but I trust a day or two in bed will put me right, so do not alarm yourself, not that you are given to that, because I think you consider your Mama as strong as a horse, and that she never can be ill!'

The Empress has a pleasant reason to write one of her infrequent letters to Prince Constantine.

'Darling Tino, I have today received the Diploma naming me an honorary member of the Hellenic Archaeological Society of which you are President. Your dear signature is on the document and I hasten to express my thanks. Nothing could give me greater pleasure, I consider it an honour of which I am justly proud. Anything that connects my name with your country, and with its glories of the past, is a joy to me.'

At the end of January, the Empress goes to England, and her first letters comic as before from Osborne.

'How I missed Liko, and how saddened the house is without him. Auntie Beatrice seems in very low spirits indeed, but between times when the tears do not flow, she is cheerful and her old self. Dearest Grandmama is looking very well, and seems so, only alas still more infirm. I have not seen her walk at all, and her sight is very bad. She was full of questions about you and Tino and the children and hopes you are coming for the Jubilee. She much wishes to have her grandchildren around her for that occasion. I of course shall certainly come,'

Subsequent letters report meetings with relations and the usual local shopping and other outings. A week afterwards she writes:

'So many thanks for your dear letter written on 25th Jan. (I think you had forgotten that was my wedding day, and Mossy's!) I am *so* glad you are trying to put order and enforce cleanliness and tidiness in the offices downstairs and servants' quarters. If not done *now* the staff will not learn how to get into nice ways before you go into your new house, and you will have much annoyance if that is all messed about.

'May and Georgie are here, and their 2 little children. The eldest, David [*Prince Edward — Ed.*], is such a little love, and talks so plainly and is so forward. I think he is very intelligent, he has a lovely complexion and such fair hair with dark blue eyes. He is a fascinating little child. The second is so bright and jolly and good-tempered and not a bit shy, not a pretty child exactly, though he has delightful little natural curls over his head, and the merriest of smiles. The little ones live quite close to me in the tower rooms, so I have a good opportunity of seeing them...May is expecting another baby in April.

'I send your little girlie a frock of washing silk, which I thought so pretty, also a sash of very soft silk, thinking they might be useful. I bought them at an excellent children's shop in Ryde. I also send a little book to make Tino laugh, which amused me very much.

'I quite agree about French plays. There are some such excellent actors, but the pieces are really quite terrible sometimes, and the subjects revolting. Alas, they translate them into English and German and Italian, and give them everywhere. There is hardly a single modern French play that is proper, it is indeed deplorable. We have also a modern style in Germany which I think shocking, Gerhard Hauptmann and others of his genre...like Ibsen...I think it unwholesome and mischievous.'

In February, Turkish repressions of fresh and serious disturbances in Crete set Greece alight with anger.

'You cannot imagine what a state I am in about Crete. I live on the telegrams which Grandmama is kind enough to let me hear when they are read to her. How alarming this new outbreak...the fire at Canae is dreadful. Here, the fear seems great that your Government will do something precipitate...I cannot help thinking that the King will prevail in making his Ministers prudent and cautious...Excuse me writing all this, but my mind is full of nothing else at this moment.'

The Greek Government sends naval vessels, with Prince George commanding, to lend support to the insurgents.

'Since I wrote this morning, the news have come that dear big Georgie is gone with the gunboats and torpedo boats to Crete. I am all of a shake and a tremble, and I can fancy the agitation you all must be in.... Grandmama is also most distressed and anxious. How one does feel being at such a distance at such times.

'Yours and Tino's telegram [*a protest at Mr. Curzon's anti-Greek speech in the House of Commons — Ed.*] reached me as we were in the drawing-room after dinner. I read it to Grandmama and she will send a copy of it to Lord Salisbury tomorrow morning.

'My anxiety and excitement continue at a white heat. As was to be foreseen, the Great Powers disapprove of the action of Greece, and say they will not have their hand forced. Their laudable desire to preserve peace I understand, but evidently their information about the Turkish provocation is *not* sufficient. What I can put forward of the immensely difficult situation in which Greece is placed, I lose no opportunity of doing, with all the warmth possible. Of what use this is I do not know, at any rate one can but do one's best.'

Anxiety over developments in Greece has not yet become all-absorbing.

'Hardly had I sent off my letter yesterday than I received the photograph of your sweet smiling Ellene. The dimple looks most dear. How I long to see her, she must be such a love. Fancy her making little sounds as if she were going to speak. Has she any hair? Does she attempt to feel her little feet yet or not? ...I am sorry you found the foundling hospital so badly managed, and not clean and tidy, in time I am sure you will be able to improve it. Of course to start things on a proper footing, foreigners are needed to teach, and by degrees the people themselves will learn how it ought to be...I am glad you are going to have a second soup kitchen arranged, it is terrible to have to send people away unserved.

'Georgie and May have left, but their dear little people have stayed on for a short time. Little David is the sweetest dearest little man, rather a nervous child, but so good and obedient and civil, and with a gentle disposition. He and baby and I are the greatest friends, they travel with me to London on the 12th, when I go to Sandringham. I join dear Grandmama on the 15th at Windsor. Of course I grudge every moment away from her, and also from this dear sweet peaceful quiet place, the place I love best of all, but it is a very great pleasure to stay with dear Uncle Bertie,

'I went over Portsmouth Dock two days ago. How much it has grown and developed even in the past few years — 9,000 men at work, mostly earning 30sh. and 40sh. and even 50sh. a week!'

A week later, further news from Crete has made clear the dangers of the situation that Greece is creating.

'The telegram from you last night that Colonel Vassos had landed with troops, and union been proclaimed — it is a bold step, but I am in terror less it should lead to worse difficulties. The Great Powers are furious! That one country should step outside the pale of law and try to redress its grievances in an illegal way — that is their argument, not that the cause is a bad one. Still, as the step has been taken, and the situation is as it is, Greece must not mind the abuse lavished upon her so freely by the Powers. Politics are a rough game, and the purest motives and noblest sentiments get cruelly misunderstood.'

The Powers try to smother the outbreak by naval patrols in Cretan waters and by landing an international force, actions which inflame the Greek temper.

'Grandmama wishes me to tell you how awfully sorry she is for you and Tino and Papa and Mama. She is so anxious and troubled, and as far as she *may,* and as she *dare,* she tries at ways to make peace and to soften asperities and cool down angry spirits, as does Lord Salisbury. He said many sensible and wise things about the Greek Constitution and its imperfections, to which he attributed your financial difficulties, also the impression that the so-called "mob" gets the upper hand, and makes the Government too weak to govern the land properly and direct the policy of the country. The public feeling is very strong here in England for Greece. It is only the Conservatives and their papers who take the other side. These will not believe the Turks have been cruel, and fancy that the Christians have been just as cruel, which of course is nonsense. I wish there were a few good letters written to *The Times* from Athens, describing the real state of things.'

The part taken by British Naval vessels in restraining the Greek insurgents arouses Sophie to bitter reproaches. From Windsor Castle, the Empress writes:

'Indeed I am not angry with any violent expression you have used, when one is in a situation painful and difficult it is too natural. I do not expect measured expressions from you. I do not even use them myself, as my sorrow and excitement know no bounds, and the anxiety has made me quite ill. What I suffer I cannot tell you. I am always afraid of bursting into tears at meals and before everyone...In short, I feel as I did in 1866 and 1870, and as I hoped never to feel again. This bombardment of Crete is too abominable! I was in a rage I cannot describe and Aunt Alix too! Poor Uncle Bertie has a fine time of it between us. Though there is no better Englishwoman than I am, and I am a devoted German too, yet on this occasion I feel more Greek than either! Yet, if there is one nation in the world that understands national liberty, that feels for others, it is just England. She deserves indeed to be loved, and to think that her policy now places her in so false a light *vis-à-vis* of the Greek nation grieves me to the utmost. All humanitarian considerations are laughed at by other Powers, and that England should have them at all is looked upon as so impossible and ridiculous on the Continent, that it is simply disbelieved and regarded as hypocrisy. This you can see every day in the German and French press. And yet it is true, and has often been shown and proved. That it should be *England* that should have had to "warn off" dear Georgie is too distressing.'

The Powers order Greece to withdraw her troops from Crete as a first step towards settling the dispute. The Empress, realizing the headstrong mood of the Greek people, counsels prudence.

'*Can* and *will* Greece accept these conditions, seemingly so unfavourable to herself? I think she would do wisely if she did. Between two evils, choose the lesser evil! The other would be terrible, it would be madness to face it. You know, or do not know, what *war* is! The Greek army is not large or perfect enough to cope with an adversary like the Turk, for though his soldiers be neither paid nor dressed nor fed properly, yet theirs is a big army, and they are no mean soldiers. They would have beaten the *Russians* but for Charles of Roumania's army...Nothing is so costly as war! Greece is beginning to develop and prosper after centuries of oppression and neglect. War would devour her slender means and throw her back.

'Here the day is so fine, the view of Windsor Park out of my window is of peace and serenity. Early spring in England has its own special and caressing beauty, the soft misty distance, the grass like an emerald carpet, the crocuses out, the birds all singing, it is so charming. But I cannot enjoy it. I am too sad and anxious. It is so cruel to have one's heart working one way and one's head the other. Much as I long for the extension of Greece, more greatly do I dread a war which would bring no good. Will Greece be calm enough to listen to the voice of reason? P.S. Please God may my next letter be more cheerful.'

The Emperor William's violent condemnations of Greece, which stir Queen Victoria to protest through her ambassador, provoke Princess Sophie to even more indignant remonstrance.

'Oh my Sophie how well I understand the state you are in! All you say goes to my heart. Pray do not think I suffer less because I am William's mother. He does not know the real state of the matter, and is violently for "order" and the "right" as he considers it, which in his eyes is represented by the Sultan! I cannot approve of what Germany is doing, and of course that will not be considered patriotic. In Berlin I shall have to live with a padlock on my mouth.

'Here I do what I can, even at the risk of being considered meddlesome and dangerous, but I have to be very careful, which is difficult when I am blazing and boiling with indignation. I am told that sentiment and relationship do not count in politics, which is true, of course, but blood *is* thicker than water.

'My poor dear Mama feels very sad and depressed that all this political trouble should take place in the year of her Jubilee, and also the awful Indian famine, and the plague in Bombay. She is already so unhappy about it all that it seems a shame for me to make her still more uncomfortable.'

Refugees from Crete are pouring into Athens, and the Empress discreetly collects funds for their relief. She writes from Buckingham Palace.

'Please, darling Sophie, when you get the money, distribute it as you think right amongst those poor refugees, but say you have collected it from and amongst your friends, as it would not do if it were officially known that I had collected and sent it. I might get into trouble. And please, dear, not a word must be said that Grandmama contributed, nor must the others be named at this moment, as you will understand. Ferdinand Rothschild I saw yesterday, and he also will send a contribution, but begs his name not to be mentioned.

'The Water Colour Institute kept asking me to lend them some sketches to exhibit, but as I had none except those I did at Athens last year, I have lent them. It will seem a curious coincidence, but it is by mere accident that I have nothing else. I brought them to show dear Grandmama, and alas, she cannot see pictures much now, her eyesight is so bad.

'I spent two very nice days at Bagshot Park with dear Uncle Arthur and Louischen. It is such a pretty place, the gardens lovely, and so beautifully kept. But one's heart is so heavy about Greece that one can enjoy nothing. Now the blockade of Crete has been resolved on, it is being carried out. If only all remains quiet in Macedonia! The idea of all those troops, Turkish and yours, massed opposite each other at no great distance is terrible.'

The Empress returns to Berlin for the celebrations of the centenary of the birthday of the Emperor William I, which take place on March 22nd.

'The fêtes were very brilliant, with great noise and bustle, the streets filled with flags and decorations, but there was much that jarred on my feelings. Not once was dear Papa's name mentioned, neither in the speeches nor in the many articles which were published. Bismark was also not mentioned, strange to say, nor Moltke, which I think most odd. The monument to Grandpapa is undoubtedly fine, but there is much that I do not quite like. When the eye has once known Greek beauty and purity of line and perfection of proportion, then one does not quite take to a style something between rococo and naturalism, and heavy and overornamented.

'Here in official circles the whole attitude of Germany to Crete is considered as an effort to prevent Greece from rushing to her doom by bringing down the Turkish hordes upon her, the very thought of which makes my blood run cold. This is Prince Hohenlohe's reason for not helping Greece to get Crete — I told it you already once — this and the desire to save Europe from a general war. P.S. How strange it seems here in Berlin not to see a blade of grass or a green shrub or a flower, after England!'

The Greek Government has not responded to the ultimatum of the Powers, and the tension grows as the Athens populace cries out for war against Turkey. At the beginning of April, Prince Constantine, as Army Commander, is at his headquarters at Larissa, where Sophie visits him.

'How your description of Larissa interested me. Of course, it was wiser to return to Athens, and leave Tino darling to his duties and responsibilities...It is good news indeed that he will try to keep things quiet, prevent the troops from attacking the Turks on the other side of the frontier. My terror was and is that your army is *not* in a fit state — organization, arms, material, etc. — for fighting a big army such as the Turks.

'All yesterday I was immensely busy. In the morning I breakfasted with William and Dona at the Schloss a frois, then I paid a visit to the Roman Catholic Hospital, then I had several audiences. Then the Ratibors [*Duke and Duchess — Ed.*] and Abby [*Prince Albert of Holstein — Ed.*] came to luncheon, and afterwards I went to take leave of Countess Brühl, who is ill, poor thing, then to the Friedrichshain Hospital, and then to the Victoria Haus, where I had a long talk with the Matron about what we can do to send out Sisters if there is war. In the evening, a banquet, at which I felt very wretched, as I had the toothache the whole time.'

The plight of the Cretans does not mend, and in Greece, war fever has mounted to a delirium, which is forcing the hands of the Government and King. The Empress now writes from Friedrichshof.

'The thought of unfortunate Crete is sickening! I have talked until I am hoarse, and written my fingers off, and burnt them very often into the bargain, and done all I can to help..."The Times" irritates me beyond expression so that I can hardly read it, and throw it down on the floor and stamp up and down the room....

'The news seems very disquieting about the "Frei Corps" having passed the Greek frontier, and there having been an engagement. These irregulars may be splendid creatures and well-armed but they are in inconvenience to the army and an embarrassment to the Government and to Tino unless they place themselves under the Command of the regular troops.'

On April 18th, the Empress breaks a letter about 'what I think of the Powers and their means of pacifying and "liberating" the Cretans' to announce that:

"This moment, while I write, I am brought a telegram from William saying, "Just received news of the inroad of Greek army, which has crossed the frontier in 7 columns. Turkey thereupon has resolved to declare war. I fear the worst will come from this most rash and unwise provocation. William." You can imagine with what feelings I read this!'

The rest of a long letter apprehensively examines the dangerous possibilities ahead. During the week that follows, the Letters dwell on little else than the progress of the campaign.

'All day yesterday fighting was going on, and that big Turkish army is prepared for anything, trained on the Prussian system by German officers, it is truly dreadful to contemplate! For how can your army cope with such an antagonist? ...I had a letter from beloved Grandmama, who said "My heart bleeds for you, your anxiety is I am sure, overpowering! If only something could be done as we wish. Heaven protect dear Tino." If only darling Tino's health keeps all right now, and he can get enough to eat, and some sleep and rest in the middle of all dangers. The power of endurance of the Greeks is great and they can live on so little, but so can the Turks, I believe. P.S. 5 of my Victoria sisters have volunteered to be sent out to Greece by the Red Cross. Doctors and material will go with them.'

After a week, disaster has fallen, and the Greek troops centred on Larissa are melting away before the Turkish advance.

'April 25th, my poor sister Alice's birthday — I am writing in a perfect agony of despair. William telegraphed to me that Larissa is taken! Of course, what has happened was only to be expected. Here were overwhelming numbers against a small army, inexperienced, untried, imperfectly organized, and above all not in the hands of the military commander but half dependent on political men in Athens! Beloved Tino managed well to collect his forces and retire in order, and take up fresh positions. To think of all this bloodshed for nothing, it is quite maddening, yet all Greece wished for war!

'How will you manage with all the poor wounded? As the weather is warm you can put up the beds for the wounded out of doors, as I did for many of the Austrians in 1866, and just stretch canvas overhead, with branches of heather or brushwood to keep off the sun. I am so horrified to think there was no chloroform at Larissa and operations had to be performed without. If you still need some, telegraph to Aunt Alix, Grandmama or me.

'Do you hear from the front every day, and know where Tino is? Darling Nicky's battery seems quite to the front, from what our newspapers say, heaven protect him, dear precious boy. We pore over the map of an evening and can talk of nothing else — one feels too miserable. Mossy is always preaching to me "If you make yourself ill with worry, you will do Sophie no good, and only give her anxiety more." That is true, so I will try not to, but it will be difficult.'

The Emperor, who because of his designs for a full understanding with Turkey, has publicly shown a hostile face to Greece, now appears with disconcerting information.

'Yesterday morning I was utterly surprised by a telegram saying that William would be here in the course of the afternoon. Max's father. Prince William of Baden, having died, Willy could no longer stay shooting in the Grand Duchy of Baden, but came on here. He spoke very nicely of Tino and of you. His news and information and his views were rather different to mine. He seemed to think the war was as good as over, that almost the whole Greek army was disbanded, and 10,000 men had vanished no one knew where to. But he considered the state of things at Athens very serious and dangerous, and as your Papa was left without guards or troops to keep order, he had sent a German Ironclad to Piraeus to be ready to protect you, and take you and the children on board in case disturbances should break out and a revolutionary movement attempted. He said he had first meant to telegraph it to you, but fearing you would perhaps not understand it, and send him a refusal (to which he could not expose himself) he had not done so. A Russian and an English ship had also been sent for the same purpose.

'William pities Tino very much and thinks he has been placed in a most difficult position...He persists that *all* the news Delyiannis publishes of the war is *untrue*. He also will not believe that the Turks commit acts of cruelty, and ill-use the prisoners and wounded. He said he had let the Sultan know especially to be kind to the wounded and look after the ambulance and lazarette...He also said he was very sorry the Greek Army was not so well prepared as it ought to have been, and that he would gladly have lent Prussian officers as instructors. This was really nicely and kindly meant.

'I cannot tell you how nervous and frightened I am. Your safety and that of darling Tino and the children, and your parents-in-law is now my first care and anxiety. Is it wise for you all to remain in the town? Would you not be safer where there is no mob? Have you ever thought of having your valuables and jewels and papers packed up and sent on board a German or English ship? We did that in 1866, that is to say we had all ready to send to Konigsberg, and then it was unnecessary.'

But although the war is already lost, the fighting drags on. In Athens, the forces that had pushed the King into leading the country into war now turn against him and Prince Constantine, who relinquishes his command. This sudden unpopularity dismays Sophie but not the Empress.

'To oppose these elements is the duty of a true Patriot, and to risk one's popularity is an act of *courage* in such a moment, and Tino and the King are far too noble and high-minded to think of currying favour with such a wretched lot as those "cafe politicians", who try to stir up ignorant people with their lies and wicked nonsensical rubbish. (In the year 1888 the unpopularity *I* had to suffer from did *not* come from the *lower* orders, but from the higher quarters.) Popularity is a most fickle thing, and it is easy to get up a cry against anyone. I fear it belongs to our position to be exposed to this. All Tino's friends here think he has been used ungratefully, and unjustly, and deeply regret that the odium of disaster which was from the first quite unavoidable should fall on his innocent head.

'My heart is overflowing with tender wishes and blessings for your sweet little Ellene. It is a year since this precious little thing was born and already war is around her...My little Sophie, *you* were one of my "Kriegskinder", at your christening everyone appeared in "Feldanzug" [*field uniform — Ed.*] and the next morning they were gone!

'P.S. Please Sophie darling pray burn all my letters or send them on board an English ship to Auntie Alix, or Thora, to take care of. It is *not* wise or safe to keep papers of any importance by one in such troublesome times. One can never know what may happen. Please listen to my advice.'

After smouldering on for a month, the war ends in an armistice, and the Powers begin to discuss how Greece shall be punished. Meanwhile the antagonism to the Royal Family spreads to Princess Sophie, for the reason that German instructors were stated to have fought with the Turkish army. The dark prospects ahead discourage her, but her mother replies encouragingly.

'My poor Sophie, love, your dear sad letter of the 28th of April, so full of grief and despair arrived yesterday. What can I say to console you? Not that things do not look most gloomy and ugly, because they do. Still, nothing is so bad that it might not have been worse. All nations have had such times of crisis, and yet survived. History teems with them.

'One must remember that as gold tried in the fire comes out brighter and purer still, so those who are noble show their grandest qualities in misfortune. Think of your own country in 1805, trodden underfoot by Napoleon, the foreign usurper, the Army of Frederick the Great beaten, the provinces torn from Prussia, the Royal Family losing *all,* and obliged to fly to Konigsberg and Memel. Even Prussian fortresses capitulated without firing a shot! Think of the French, parading their troops at Potsdam and Berlin, totally crushing Prussia with war contributions, the Prussian women giving their all to turn into money, their wedding rings, even cutting off their hair to sell it. All seemed gone for ever when your Grandpapa was a little boy. But in misfortune the stern resolve was taken to improve and reorganize, and in 1870-1871 Prussia was avenged. Only let Greece be as determined to raise herself, to recover from the blow, and a great future is still before her.

'Your dear letter cost me many tears. The disaster is terrible. The system under which the army and the whole country has been labouring and suffering for years, and none more than the King and your Tino, has broken down, and now something better must be organized...but it is *no use* to spend one's energies in only complaining, one must try to get *out* of the mess. You are Papa's daughter, so I know you will be courageous and patient, as he was, and do your duty as he did. (Do not think me an old preaching tiresome bore, you have not a better and devoted friend than I am.) I have written a long letter to William to do what he can to help, and I bombard my dear Mama with letters and telegrams.

'My darling Sophie, I was very much taken aback and a little frightened to see reprinted in the German papers, quoted from the "Daily Chronicle", what I told you William said. I am so afraid I shall get into a scrape. Please be careful my darling what you say to people of the Press about us here, for you know how very prudent I have to be, and how difficult my position is. P.S. The stuff you wanted for inoculation against that awful Tetanus, of which I saw so much in 1870, was ordered directly and sent off to you from the main factory.'

The Empress's concentration on affairs in Greece is distracted for a while by preparations for the celebration of Queen Victoria's Diamond Jubilee on June 22nd, as also by various family events.

'We shall leave for the Jubilee next week. I go to Windsor and all the others to Buckingham Palace. Today, Georgie and May's little girl is christened at Sandringham, Victoria Alexandra Alice Mary. I hear May was already at different exhibitions and at the Court Ball! I must say I think all that rather soon, as not 6 weeks are over. She has been to London and back, and to the theatre, etc., after 4 weeks, it will make her old before her time. Alicky has another little girl, I fear they will be rather disappointed, they have not even announced it to us. However she is young and there is plenty of time for sons, who I hope will come later.

'Mossy darling is looking very well and in great beauty, only we are both tremendously sunburnt from our early rides. For your dear birthday instead of sending you another present, I send 1000 marks, thinking you may wish to spend them for your Child's Hospital or for getting artificial arms and legs for those who have been amputated, or clothes for the refugees from Thessaly. I wish I could be with you to work at the soup kitchens and the hospitals, or to help make the clothes. P.S. Please do find time to bath in the sea on your way *to* and *from* hospital to avoid infections, and drink a glass of milk with a drop of brandy.'

The Empress crosses to England on the *Victoria and Albert* on June 16th, and writes from Windsor of her mother, whom she finds 'looking well but rather fatigued and dreading all the ceremonies, etc. she has before her', and of meeting the other relations gathered for the occasion.

'I arrived in time for Grandmama's breakfast and then the presents were given. At ii there was a very beautiful, touching and impressive service at St.

George's Chapel, to which we all went. The music was very fine indeed. We all had a family luncheon at 2, after which the others left for London, except Aunt Lenchen, Aunt Beatrice and myself. There was a second splendid service at St. George's but I did not go. I went in the afternoon to Frogmore and the Mausoleum. Every one speaks well of Tino and you, and wishes all these sad events had not prevented your being here.'

Three long letters following the days of the Jubilee celebrations briefly recount the Empress's part in them, but she begins by saying, 'For all the descriptions of the processions and receptions I must refer you to the newspapers, as I could not undertake it!' The letter of June 23rd comes from Buckingham Palace, those of the 25th and 27th from Windsor.

'The celebrations were no less magnificent than 10 years ago, though of course to me the procession could never seem the same without beloved Papa. The thought that dear Eddy, Uncle Louis and Liko were missing, and Tino and you far away, made one's heart ache. The streets were most beautifully decorated, the crowds immense, the enthusiasm great, and the perfect order was marvellous, all so well-arranged and organized. The scene in front of St. Paul's was most impressive, and when the bells pealed out from the dark old Cathedral, and the cheers rang out again, and the sun shone on all the glitter of the escort and carriages and the countless spectators, it was as fine a sight as you could wish to see.

'We all got back to the Palace at exactly the moment expected, and I think there were few accidents. I drove in the carriage with Uncle Alfred, Aunt Louise and the Crown Princess of Naples. How I missed you sitting with the other Princesses, and at dinner and in the evening. Buckingham Palace is like a beehive, the place is so crammed we do not see so very much of one another. I return to Windsor with Grandmama, and all the others stay here, for dinners and fêtes.'

'The drive through Eton from Slough and the arrival at Windsor yesterday evening was perfectly beautiful, one of the prettiest sights I ever saw. Windsor was turned into a garden, and so decorated with flags, stands, festoons, and draperies that one saw nothing but bright colours. The crowds were dense and in the best of humours and smartest of attires. We were dead tired in the evening.

'Yesterday Grandmama received the foreign royalties. Henry, Georgie of York and young August Coburg were present, also Aunt Beatrice and I. All day long there were telegrams to answer and a flood of letters. I read your dear letter to Grandmama, who thanks you so much for it, and is so exceedingly sorry that you and Tino and your children are not here, and feels for you both so much in this sad time of terrible anxiety.'

'Yesterday morning we left Windsor for the Naval Review. The sight was one never to be forgotten, and would have rejoiced your eyes and Tino's and Georgie's. All the beautiful ships in such marvellous order, the quantity of flags, the sea so blue, the sun so bright. The Solent seemed regularly crammed with ships, from Portsmouth and Spithead to beyond Cowes. Nothing can equal the splendour of that Naval Review, the precision with which the line was kept and the ships anchored, the way the British ships were painted and rigged and manned, etc., boats slung, just perfect!'

The Empress's days are packed with a busy round of luncheons, dinners, soirees, garden parties, which she declares very fatiguing. But she finds time to make money for Sophie's fund for the wounded. 'I have realized £30 from the sale of my drawings. It is not a large sum, but it is better than nothing...it is a cheque, which you must sign on the other side, anyone at the British Legation will show you' — and also to make a journey to the

'...Cheltenham Ladies College, an immense one, which you must see someday, beautifully arranged, nearly a 1000 pupils. Cheltenham is a sweet place, one would like to settle in it, and the country is lovely against the blue range of the Malvern Hills, and the Cotswolds. The girls must be very happy there, the teachers seemed charming, and all had an air of brightness, very different from our German girls' schools! I saw the classes at work, and the girls in their fine playground. They gave us luncheon and sang to us.

'Tomorrow we leave dear England. It is always a painful moment as you know, and I feel leaving dear Grandmama more and more now she is growing old. Still I am so glad to have spent this time with her and thankful that all went off so satisfactorily. Grandmama has gone though a deal of fatigue, but she is much gratified by the great loyalty and enthusiasm displayed.'

Back at Friedrichshof, the Empress, after sadly announcing the Detmald judgment, turns once more to Greek affairs.

'Alas the Detmald succession has been given by the King of Saxony against Schaumburg-Lippe and for the Biesterfelds. It is a crushing blow to Vicky and Adolf. That charming home, lovely country and fine houses, position, occupation, future, all gone! Poor Vicky is most unlucky in life, if only she had children she would not mind so much. She and Adolf will now settle in the hotel at Bonn to superintend the furnishing and finishing of their little villa.

'Do not be depressed, my darling. There is no lack of vitality in Greece, but soberness and steadiness of purpose has been wanting in political circles, and *experience* was lacking. Now it has been dearly bought...Things will come right in time, the Greeks are far too intelligent not to see how it saps their strength and energies to be perpetually fermenting the intrigues of political factions in their struggle for office, instead of uniting their labours for the good of the whole country.

'One must try to look forward and not back, though it is well to find out the real causes of disaster and see what mistakes have been made so as to avoid them in future. With men as with nations, to see where one has been wrong is half the battle. Look where the French have been led to by their vanity and self-conceit, and they are not cured of it yet. May the Germans not fall into the same fault, though the danger is not beyond possibility, unfortunately.'

The Empress has frequently asked for photographs of Princess Sophie's children, and at last they arrive. About her own picture, she is moved to one of her rare efforts at deliberate humour.

'What a joy to receive the photographs. The little head of precious Alexander is too duckie, he might sit for an "infant Bacchus!" I wish I could brush the hair back from his brow, as all children in England wear it now. Georgie looks such a little man, and Sweet Ellene, the dearest little cherub! But my own Sophie has her fringe still drawn on her nose in the old-fashioned way that one sees no more, and that spoils her pretty little face.

'A painter is doing a portrait of me for an institution. Till now it is rather dreadful. I look like a sea-sick owl that has been sitting for 100 years on a tree and has a very cross expression. ... It is lovely and quiet here and a fine day. My hay is being gradually carried. It is a fine crop, but one can hardly sell it, as everyone has enough this year.'

The terms of the Greek peace settlement, at last announced, do not please the Empress, but she sends on also the more impartial views of the Prince of Wales.

'It seems the peace *is* made! But what a crying shame to make Greece pay 4 million of £'s. How *can* she? I wish with all my heart the Turks may never see a penny of Greek money, wrung out of a poor country in this extortionate way, and yet I hardly see another way out of it now, and that they should leave Thessaly as soon as possible is so important.

'Uncle Bertie writes to me today saying, "You will have read Lord Salisbury's speech. It explains the recent situation and how everything now depends on Greece paying the war indemnity. I most regret to hear that the Greek Government are so averse to the proposed European financial control. However disagreeable it may be to the "amour propre" of Greece, yet it is the only solution I can see out of the present difficulty. Refusal would only react upon themselves, as the Powers would not be able then to get such good terms from the Porte."'

There are rumours that because of his new-found unpopularity. Prince Constantine will leave Greece for a while. The Empress urges that 'if I were Tino, I would take no notice of this rubbish'.

'In the year 1888, when people talked of my having stolen State papers, and also after the publication of dear Papa's Journal, they said I should have to leave Germany, and even our relations asked me whether I was going to settle at Rome or in England. I said I should do nothing of the kind, and quietly settled here. *Now* people do not even remember the calumnies and lies they spread (though *I* do!). When popular opinion has been led astray the only way is to show people by degrees how mistaken they have been. Of course when there is great excitement, one must wait until it has subsided a bit.

'I see a vile Athens newspaper has now taken to running down big Georgie about the torpedoes aboard his vessel. I should like to torpedo that newspaper! It makes me so savage to hear those I love abused ...and yet I suppose one *ought* to take absolutely no notice.

'In your yesterday's letter you said you wished there was an iron will in Greece, such as William's. An iron will has its advantages when great prudence and knowledge, experience and tact, and a liberal spirit of fairness and kindness go with it, but if sudden rash impulses are carried out, and mistakes are made which have to be undone later, I do not think it an advantage.... Wm. reminds me of new wine which effervesces for a long while before it is really ready and finished and clear, but then it improves in value every year.'

As the Empress sees it, one of the reasons for the unpleasant situation in which Constantine and Sophie find themselves is an ineffective personal staff.

'Your position is not easy to fill and you have so much responsibility and are so much "en évidence" that you ought to be well seconded and supported, and have the best forces around you, people you can trust, and who can put to silence the unjust and impertinent criticism which certain parties put forward. Do think it over, it is more important than you think for the future. You are not private individuals, you must keep in contact with the outer world through men who carry weight with the public, and are able to keep you informed of so much that would escape you. Forgive your old Mama for saying so, it is not from a wish to meddle but from true anxiety to see you as well off as possible. You have such a future before you, and such a part to play.'

Princess Sophie, despite her dejections and anxieties, does not falter in her good works, and is now more accustomed to travel.

'It interests me so much to hear about the hospitals and the poor wounded. How tiresome that the doors in your future children's hospital have been made too high, and above all too narrow. Wide doors are so necessary for moving beds and furniture, etc. Do you think that the way the English nurses worked in your war hospitals opened the eyes of the Greek ladies about nursing? *There* is a great field for good work! Could not some young women of good family go through courses this winter, such as Aunt Alice and I went through, it would draw their attention and interest, especially if you were to give the example, and have the lectures once a week in your own house.

'Fancy your living on board the old Sphakteria, poor old thing, I thought she was condemned. The new yacht is charmingly arranged, but she seems to me so narrow for her length and for her height out of the water, I should fear she would roll terribly. I wonder whether you will find less insects at Agia Marina? The way to be safe from being bitten, I am told, is by sleeping in a linen bag in which one has put a good deal of insect powder. People manage to get on quite well with that in Persia.'

A sidelight is shown on the strained relations between the Prince of Wales and the Emperor.

'My sister Louise will be coming for 2 days before she joins Uncle Bertie at Marienbad. I think he will find it rather dull there compared with Romberg, which he is so used to, but for this year it was quite right for him *not* to come. It would have been very awkward for him when the Court comes for the manoeuvres, as it might have looked strange his leaving 2 days before W's arrival, and I do not think a meeting would have been very agreeable to Uncle just now.

'The other day, I was at an exhibition of bees, honey, wax, and the latest appliances for bee-keeping. It interested me very much. I spoke to a peasant there who regularly makes 500 marks a year from his bees, and I thought to myself, what if people in Greece could be taught the art of bee cultivation on a large scale? ...How dear it must be to hear your little girl beginning to talk. Does she yet say Mama and Papa? How I should like to hear her and cover her with kisses. P.S. I am going out with Dete Reischach and her boys this afternoon, as Vicky and Adolf are out on their "Bykes". Vicky is a very good bicycle rider now. Do you ever try yours?'

In early September, there is a big assembly of important personages at Homberg for the Imperial Manoeuvres that are taking place in the district.

'I have just time to write to you before my morning ride, after which I shall scramble into my things to drive to Homberg. There I shall have to receive Wm. and Dona at the station, and then drive round *outside* the town to the Schloss so as not to spoil their procession by my presence! In the Schloss there will be a luncheon, to which I stay, and then I shall not go down to receive the King and Queen of Italy, but wait in the Schloss and take part in the dinner. I must alas sleep at the Schloss, as the parade is so early in the morning.'

Two days later, though exhausted by her efforts, the Empress finds the energy to send off a long letter.

'It is late in the afternoon and I am dead tired, so you must excuse if I do not write properly. I have had an immense family lunch, for Wm. and Dona, the King and Queen of Italy, the King of Saxony, the Bavarian Princes, Uncle George Cambridge and others. These distinguished guests did me the honour to stay rather long!

'How thankful I was to return here yesterday evening after the noise and discomfort of the old Homberg Schloss, I cannot tell you. The place was as full as an egg! There were a couple of hundred servants running about, bawling at the top of their voices. That poor old Courtyard ringing with the noise of carriages and escorts and companies coming to bring the Standards. I felt most unhappy and déplacée. There had been a grand cleaning and putting in order. New bathrooms, fireplaces, etc. are thought indispensable by the Imperial Hofmarschall when Wm. and Dona spend 2 nights there, whereas they were not considered necessary for me and my family when we lived there four years! Sometimes it does rather make me angry, though it may be foolish to feel this.

'The Parade was *endless*. There were 30,000 men on the field and *two* marchpasts! I drove with the Queen of Italy, and was stiff and cold from sitting so long in one position. Dona rode in uniform, also Ducky, who looked very pretty indeed, she cantered past so daintily.'

After proving that she too is still not past a hard day's riding, the Empress ends her part in the manoeuvres as she began, with big-scale entertaining.

'I rode out to the manoeuvres, really horrible, it poured every 10 minutes. I have never seen the ground in such a state, our horses were almost up to their knees in the sticky and slippery mud. What the poor horses and troops must have endured is not to be described. They were so muddy and wet from head to foot that one could hardly tell one uniform from another. Thick fog covered the whole country, so that very little was to be seen. I came home in the afternoon so drenched and chilled that I took a warm bath and went to bed. Having been up at half-past 5, of course I was tired. In the evening I gave a dinner here for all the Italians. We were 30, and it was not easy to manage. I had to hire 6 shut carriages to bring them up from the station, as I had only 2 shut carriages of my own. The dinner went off all right, but I am thankful it is over, as these sort of receptions are always an anxiety in a country house not intended for court ceremonies. The King and Queen are such easy guests to entertain and so kind. Prince Hohenlohe was here, also the new minister for Foreign Affairs, H. von Bülow. The King and Queen of Italy leave today and I have to go over once more to Romberg to attend a big luncheon and see them off. The Queen told me to send you her best love.'

Despite these demanding activities, affairs in Greece still occupy the Empress's mind, as two letters at this time reveal.

'I am always thinking of dear Greece, and how to help her out of her troubles, and I collect the opinion of those in touch with the political and financial world. All agree that military exploits must not be thought of for a long time, but that the army should be thoroughly trained and organized. The principal thing is to turn the mind of the nation *towards* working at their own development and improvement, and *away* from politics that only excite and madden and make them unfit for other things, *that* is the great task now before their rulers. Also to prevent Athens from being the *sole* preponderating centre of activity. It is the provinces that want the care and the energy, the peasants and country people that want encouragement and help. If *Greek* patriotism and ambition would but take this form, what a country it would soon be. Nature has done so much for you, has given you sun and soil and climate, brains and vitality. It only wants organization and discipline in the method of setting to work.'

'My thoughts are still running on reforms that could be introduced into Greece', she begins the second letter, and after making several suggestions for political reorganization, she turns to the idea of a Women's Association for developing minor industries in Greece.

'I still think it might be possible to form a "Verein" on business principles, its declared object to benefit the country, even at some cost to subscribers. A board of directors of business men...capital or fund formed by subscriptions...assisted by *local* committees of ladies all over the country — their aim, to work various small industries (at very small profit) for instance, bees and honey, of which I wrote, carpet weaving, tile and pottery making, and raising of chickens and turkeys to export eggs to Germany and England (they take hundreds of millions a year). To start work of this kind is not easy, but in such sad times, one cannot sit down with one's hands on one's lap, but must put one's shoulders to the wheel. If your Mama and you would give your names, your patronage and assistance and perhaps Minny too, the influence of the committee would be considerable. I can if you like get a scheme drawn out in detail. I feel sure that something might be done in this way and that it would teach the Greek women to try and work for their country and help the poorer classes, and it would promote a good feeling, and give the Queen and you pleasure and satisfaction.'

This letter crosses one in which Sophie expresses her dejection over how little progress her welfare efforts achieve. In her reply the Empress refers to the engagement of her eighteen-year-old granddaughter, Feodora.

'Of course it must be most grievous and trying to think that all your work for the nation is *so* uphill, and that there is so much ignorance and folly and ingratitude. It is very disheartening. Nations want many long years of good government to establish good traditions and a spirit of earnestness, soberness and work. Greece is young amongst the nations, and has the faults and failings of youth.

'Feo's engagement causes much surprise everywhere. Charlotte and Bernhard seem delighted, especially at seeing Feo so very happy. May she remain so. It is a marriage I really never would have dreamed of. You know more about this Prince Reuss XXX than I do, I have only seen him once. It is of course not an advantageous marriage in point of rank or position, but if Feo is happy, which she really seems to be, and the parents are satisfied, one ought to be glad. I am very glad he is older than she is, and if he is wise and steady and firm, he may do her a vast deal of good, and it may turn out very well, but she has had a strange example in her mother, and so is a strange little creature.'

In Athens the situation is easing a little, and Prince Constantino returns home. Relations are improving between Sophie and her brother, who gives her a decoration for her nursing work in the war. In connection with the unveiling of the Wiesbaden statue to her husband, the Empress receives another kind of recognition, which she regards with a practical eye.

'What a complete joy it is to me to think you are happy again with your Tino at home. May you never be separated again for such a time. How amusing that the sweet little girlie did not know her Papa at first, but now I am sure she is devoted to him. I am indeed delighted you are so pleased about the decoration. I did have it suggested to Willy, and he took the idea up. I am very glad you telegraphed and wrote him. I received the same or something very like it in 1871, but I so seldom wear all my orders, because I have so many, that perhaps you never remarked it.

'The day was beautiful on the dear 18th. Wiesbaden was crammed full of people and gaily decorated. The monument to dear Papa is, I think, a success, also the pedestal. The speeches were short, and only 2 short choruses were sung. I laid a wreath down for you of roses from the garden here, at the foot of the statue.

'I was made Chief of the 80th Inf. Regt., which is at Homberg and Wiesbaden, at which I was very much pleased but rather taken aback, as I have one Regiment already for which I have to pay out a good deal, and I do not know how I shall be able to satisfy two! However it was very kindly meant, and I hear the officers are pleased, which flatters me very much.

'Willy and Dona paid me a visit with the 3 eldest boys, who were very merry and seemed quite at their ease. They wanted to stay a bit with me, but their Mama would not let them! It is a pity that she is so jealous and dislikes their coming near me, but she does, though she is all that is civil and amiable to me. She left with them for Berlin, but Willy stayed the night and left early in the morning.'

At the end of October, the Empress once more reluctantly leaves Friedrichshof for her autumn trip to supposedly warmer climes. She again writes from the Hotel Trento.

'I was wretched to leave my dear Friedrichshof, but I must shut the house up for a bit and give the servants a rest, and also get different repairs carried out...but I find it no warmer here and the leaves no greener. I shall miss my daily rides so much, and the dear comfortable house and garden, and above all the feeling that Rümperheim was close and I could see my darlings often. I am altogether depressed and out of spirits.'

As usual, the Letters are largely taken up with descriptions of trips in the locality, on which she usually takes her sketch book.

'This is a beautiful part of the world. The new hotels are mostly all built by a Greek, educated in Austria, he seems very clever and enterprising, it is a pity he does not work for his own country...We were out all day and had our luncheon in a beautiful spot 4000 feet high, lovely short green turf, where we found a lot of beautiful blue gentians, like little stars. We drove up as far as the carriage would take us, and then walked, rather a stiff climb, and the road rough and steep. I find my legs will carry me anywhere still, and that I do not get tired, but climbing I get dreadfully blown, and the blood hammers in my temples. But I enjoy mountain walks as much as ever I did, the pure air and the beauties of scenery and nature. It gives me intense pleasure to study the lights and shades, and the lines and colours of the hills, stones and vegetation. An artist's powers, and an artist's fingers and training and knowledge, I have not, but I think I have a bit of an artist's eye, and may lay claim in some ways to have an artist's soul in my intense love of nature and the beautiful.

'In sheer beauty *nothing* comes up to the Greek landscape for colour, purity of outline, transparent atmosphere, and everywhere the lovely sea...Wedell says Italy is dethroned in my admiration and my heart since I have become so fond of Greece, and it is quite true!'

The Empress is too modest over her capabilities as an artist, for no less an authority than Lord Leighton declared that her technique was such that she could not be regarded as an amateur, but must be judged by professional standards. Her enjoyment of her visit is broken at the end of October, by news of the death of the Duchess of Teck.

'You can imagine how terribly sorry I am about poor dear Aunt Mary Teck's death. She was the friend of my youth when we were girls together, and though she was 8 years older than I am, I was sincerely attached to her. She was full of brightness and life and such an agreeable companion. She was very popular in England. How her poor children will feel it, and dear Grandmama. How poor Franz Teck will get on I do not know, he is no longer what he was, and wants care and looking after...I heard the news from him, he telegraphed "I am heartbroken". I little thought when I parted from her after the Jubilee I should not see her again, poor dear Mary. What a mercy May has a happy home of her own.'

The Empress's own family is now affected by Germany's ambitions in the Far East, for Prince Henry is nominated to take a naval expedition to China, with the object of seizing the port of KiaoChau. Returning to Rümpenheim in time for her birthday, the Empress writes:

'My birthday passed very quietly. Adolf arrived after breakfast and brought news that upset me very much indeed, that Henry is going to China in about 3 weeks. I know he has for a long time been planning to do some service there, but now Germany seems to want a port in China waters there is an opportunity of sending ships. I wish with all my heart Germany would let alone all these adventurous plans and puerile ambitions, but I cannot help thinking Henry is right for his career to wish to have one more command at a distant station. Of course I feel my son's having to go so far away, very much, though I know that it is a sailor's fate.

'Oh, if my Sigie or my Waldie were only alive, one son to come to me often!

Now I hardly ever have a son to help me or lean on. Instead I look to Tino (whenever I have the joy of seeing him) and to Fischy dear, who is a most kind and good son to me. Bernhard is never near, nor should we perhaps always agree, though he is good in many ways, and Vicky and Adolf have been so hindered from being much with me.'

Princess Sophie is still struggling doggedly with her soup kitchens and other welfare activities.

'I am sorry you did not find the soup-kitchens in good order. Your supervision must be much required...You are right to have made stricter rules, which I hope will be kept to as you wish...As soon as I get home I will enquire about a person to look after a "creche", though you know that day nurseries are far better kept and understood in England. But if it is a Kinderheim you want, as I have at Bornstedt, then I could best find you someone at Berlin...So you have decided on green for the walls of the hospital! I hope it will look nice. I never would choose it myself because it is the colour always used in the old hospitals at Berlin, wretched dark places, their walls had a poisonous look, so I suppose I have a prejudice against it...I shall certainly tell Uncle Bertie how pleased you are to have the Order of St. John of Jerusalem. The St. John's Ambulance Classes are very good I hear.'

Half-way through December, the Empress prepares to leave the Schloss Rümpenheim. 'I am so sorry my stay here is coming to an end. It is so nice and homey, and I am out of the worries and excitements that begin directly I get to Berlin.' From the capital she gives news of various members of the family, including Prince Henry's departure from Kiel, and of her many welfare duties. She writes thankfully of the signing of the peace in Greece, and concludes her letter:

'I am indeed glad to hear that peoples' eyes are beginning to open about Tino dear, and the folly and prejudice and untruths beginning to dispel.... God bless you, my own Sophie darling, and 1000 best wishes to Tino dear, who is a hero and martyr in my eyes, and I pray, "Oh Lord God arise — confound his enemies — and make them fall. Confound their politics — frustrate their knavish tricks, etc." ... (in the words of our British anthem).'

On December 22nd, she writes of the death of the Chancellor's wife.

'In the evening, alas. Princess Marie Hohenlohe died, after an illness of 3 days. I went to see poor Prince Hohenlohe directly, and found him in deepest grief, but he was very touching, so gentle and resigned. It is so affecting to see an old man's tears. He was very fond of his wife and she had many splendid qualities, so upright and straightforward. To me she was always most nice, and I liked her very much, for she was kind and warm-hearted. It is hard for the poor widower to have all his work and responsibilities with this sorrow at home.

'I saw the Victoria Haus sisters who had been in Greece and they told me how kindly you had received them. They wore tiny Greek flags as brooches that they had bought at Athens. I think if your Mama could send them a wee bit of white and blue ribbon, with a drachma or small silver Greek coin, to wear as a war medal, they would be immensely pleased.'

Christmas passes quietly, and the year ends on a note of hope for her daughter's future in Greece.

'Please God, Greece will be sensible in time, and learn from her misfortunes, and matters will mend. I shall think most tenderly of my Sophie with many an ardent wish and prayer — that she may be protected, and fresh joys and blessings be added to her home and life, and that she may be spared all the bitter trials and sorrows her Mama has been through, and that her Tino and her children may be preserved in health and strength for the good of their country, their happiness and prosperity.

'P.S. Since writing I have received your dear letter of the 17th with joy, with darling little Georgie's bookmarker and sweet Alexander's cross and Georgie's first little letter. You can imagine what precious treasures these are to me.'

Chapter Ten – The Letters, 1898

After expressing her customary wishes and hopes for the New Year, the Empress describes how, 'for 2 days, I am overrun with audiences, visits, and business of all kinds...I had to give a large dinner last evening, 4 Ambassadors, some Ministers and Court officials and a few professors'. And at Potsdam, when she goes to see her husband's mausoleum, she is forced to take a step into the past. Never since her husband's death had she set foot in the Neue Palais, which to her is still Friedrichskron.

'Only fancy, I called yesterday at the door of Friedrichskron! It was to see Dona, who is ill, and cannot come to Berlin for another week. I could not stay away from the Mausoleum longer, and to go to Potsdam and *not* enquire after her would not have done. I just went upstairs and into our little blue breakfast room, luckily not into my own sitting room, *that* I could not have stood. Time seemed not to have moved since 1888. With an aching heart and trembling legs, I walked away from that dear door for the first time since 10 years. Luckily, all the gentlemen were out shooting, and the place was quite silent, and no one saw me, which was a great relief. I shall not do it again, it upset me dreadfully. If I had not had Mossy and Fischy with me, I should never have plucked up the courage.

"This morning, Charlotte and Feo and Prince Reuss appeared. I need not describe him to you, as you know him. It seems the wedding is now settled for September at Breslau. The Duke of Meiningen will give his granddaughter

30,000 marks for the trousseau and 25,000 marks a year, which for him is a large sum, and for them of course is not very grand, still it is better they should begin in a small way, someday as an only child Feo will be very rich. Charlotte is looking ill, I think, but especially because she covers her face with powder. She used to have such a fresh rosy complexion and that is quite spoilt by this white stuff.

'Poor old Mr. Gladstone has been very ill at Cannes and I have written to ask after him, he is very old now and it is sad to think he should suffer so much from violent neuralgia. I know what an agony it is.'

In Athens, the Crown Prince's report on the army's failure in the war coincides with proposals for military reorganization, and for the future administration of Crete.

'Yesterday evening I read with deep and painful interest in "The Times" part of Sweetie's report. It is so clear and good. What a trying thing it must have been for him to write down the details of misfortunes he could and would have prevented had the army been put into the right condition beforehand. I shall never understand why he was not more seconded by sea. Surely in the Greek General Staff the whole plan for a campaign against Turkey, with the part the fleet should take, ought always to be ready and constantly worked at and corrected and modified.

'I see in the papers there are going to be Austrian instructors for the Greek army, and I am very sorry to hear it. From what I have seen lately of the Austrian soldiers, they seemed to me a sorry lot, ill-dressed, ill-drilled, ill-set-up. I used to watch them exercising every morning, it was anything but businesslike. Could you not get anyone from Wurtemberg or Saxony who could indirectly take advice from excellent General v.d. Goltz? Really, our soldiery here *is* superior to the Austrian and the French. Organization, training drill, instruction is best in Prussia I am sure, and next best in Wurtemberg.

'The newspapers put forward dear big Georgie's name as Governor of Crete. How far and away the best solution that would be...It is the first sensible and proper thing that has been done since the war began. My dear Mama was the first to propose it last year, as you know, but whatever England proposed was usually thrown out by the others out of pure foolish suspicion and jealousy.'

The Empress is concerned over Prince George's possible financial liabilities as Governor. 'I can imagine how difficult a position it would be for our dear Georgie, and how little money he must have to get on with there. I wish he would marry a rich wife.' Then, after listing several eligible princesses, she adds: 'But they are all Catholics, and difficulties would have to be got over. I know no Princesses at this moment in Germany that have any money...'

Princess Sophie has another spell of depression over things in general, to which her mother replies:

'Poor Sophie dear, you are very despondent and much depressed about matters in Greece. How well I understand it! You say people have no moral education whatsoever, and I suppose you are right. It is so in a still higher degree in Roumania, Serbia, Bulgaria, also in Spain and Portugal. In the 3 former, as in Greece, it is the consequence of the long Turkish rule, and that cannot wear off in half a century.

'You say no one comes to Athens that you invite. If you knew how many people would like to go until they find how badly the ships run, and many other difficulties. If the journey were better organized and easier you would have more visitors than you care for. If only that blessed railway could be arranged! You do not know the enormous difference it would make. There are so many people who dread the sea.

'I could not help smiling about your smart butler, I am sure his dress shines forth amongst the others, though I must say I thought your people in the house (*not* the stables) very nicely dressed, cravats and coats, etc. Of course in livery, people never can look really well with moustaches, and that is universal in Greece, as it once was here.'

In remarking on the 40th anniversary of her wedding, and in a subsequent letter on her first arrival in Berlin, the Empress indicates, without comment, the easing relationship between her and her eldest son and his wife.

'How nice it was to receive your dear letter yesterday on my wedding day, 40 years ago. What joy and happiness that day brought to me and how sad and bitter to think that all is gone. Looking back and longing for what is no more is a pain that I trust and hope you may never know. Thank God at least this dear anniversary is brightened beyond words when I see Mossy and Fischy so happy, both looking well thank God, and with their little darlings. Mossy looks about 15, too pretty with her dear child's face, and sweet expression which she had always kept since she was a baby, and her graceful little figure. I gave a dinner last night to Wm. and Dona, Aunt Marianne, Fritz Leopold and Yaya.

'Yesterday Dona asked me to come over to the Schloss to the Crown Treasury to advise her about the making up of jewels and ornaments, of which there are some still unused and unset. I told her how she could employ them, and have more ornaments to wear. They showed me some newly arranged apartments at the Schloss. They have bought a quantity of old furniture and tried to arrange them like Friedrichshof. The things are very fine, and the splendid thick walls and deep windows make a fine ground to work upon, but somehow or other the effect and arrangement are not quite a success.'

'Yesterday it was 40 years since I arrived at Berlin. The town sent me a kind and civilly worded address of congratulations. To me it appeared a sad anniversary, or rather that thinking of those former days and hopes and contrasting them with the present seems so bitter. Mossy, Fischy, Irene and Willy brought me some lovely flowers. We three lunched at the Schloss with

Wm. and Dona.

'I have just been to look at some portraits by the Hungarian artist Laszlo, they are not at all bad. Of course not like Angeli, but pretty in their way. Uncle Bertie has had an excellent sale of his "Shire" horses, they have realized £12,000. I always want Tino to have a stud at Manolada to breed horses for the peasants and farms, and for the army. But I suppose it requires money from the State to start such things...I am so glad to hear of a depot of Greek industry being opened in London.'

Princess Sophie has appealed for help over her troublesome soup-kitchens, and thanks her mother for arranging to send an expert over to Athens.

'I saw today the person who is going out to you for the soup kitchen, Frau M. She is nice and quiet, about 50 I should say, and has a lot of experience as to management, expenses, etc. She was afraid that it would be an unseasonable time to go to Athens as she heard that the Church feasts were very strictly kept, and she was wondering what the poor were in the habit of cooking and eating at these times. She had got it into her head that the Greeks live on melons, and that she ought to take out a machine to cut the melons up. I could not help smiling...But I am too pleased whenever I can do the smallest thing for you, or in the way of helping your undertakings. All these matters naturally have to be taught and learnt at Athens, where there is no tradition and very little money, it is not to be wondered that they do not work properly.

'I am so glad to read in the newspapers that the loan for Greece is arranged and guaranteed by England, France and Russia. It is a shame that it is not guaranteed by Germany too. How much opposition there seems from Russia to Georgie's candidature to the Governorship of Crete. But I trust it will succeed. Oh, how I should rub my hands and dance about with joy! But I fear it is not at all settled yet and "there is many a slip twixt the cup and the lip". I rarely even hear a piece of really good news, so I cease to believe that anything I sincerely wish for will come to pass.'

In Athens, public anger over the army's shortcomings in the war has produced a crop of military trials.

'What you say about the trials in the army and navy at Athens is quite true, they are distressing and disgraceful. There is but one thing to say, that though it is grievous and painful to every patriotic heart to see one's "linge sale lavé en publique" yet it is better if the evil is to be eradicated that all should come out. It strengthens the hands of reform and makes it more easy to insist on changes. A clean sweep will have to be made of the old army elements that mix in politics. If Tino could only take it in hand, i.e., lay before his father and the government and the chambers a really prepared plan of what he thinks ought to be done. I look to him to take the initiative and put the army and navy on a sound footing. Of course, reformers are not popular for the time being, are attacked and maligned in every sort of way, naturally enough, as all wrong-doers are against them, but one must make up one's mind to that and do one's duty fearlessly that good may come. *Not* in a brusque and violent way, but with as much calm and justice as possible, taking into account how many people are at fault more from ignorance and want of training than from bad intentions or wicked design.'

The Empress's interest in Sophie's new home is revived by news that the work is to be completed.

'I am indeed glad the money is voted for your house at last, so that it can be got on with. What you say about putting the kitchen under the ballroom seems to me a very good and sensible plan. Only if I remember correctly this space is low, which would make the kitchens very hot for the poor cooks. Then you would have to see that the kitchen smell did not come into your bedroom and dressing-room window. If only the King would surrender his kitchen garden. Cannot you and Tino propose to rent it of him? It would make such a difference to health and comfort and independence to have a bit of a garden of one's own...As for oil pictures of dear Papa and me, I must certainly give them to you some day for the new house. A couple of large ones of Tino and you should also be painted at once.

'P.S. I can well imagine you find it difficult to persuade your servants to part with their moustaches. They no doubt do not see how ugly it looks in livery. We had also great difficulties *here* when we married! The old Empress Augusta's and ours were the only people that were shaved, now of course it is adopted at all the Courts here.'

The Emperor William's two eldest sons, William and Eitel Frederick pay their grandmother a visit, and of them she writes:

'The eldest is not at all good-looking, but he has something decidedly attractive and interesting, and will have, I think, a distingué appearance. The second is so fat and ugly and ill-grown, he might really not belong to the upper classes at all! I suppose this will all change, but at present it is distressing. He is a very good boy, I believe. I think it such a pity they are so completely brought up by officers, and have all the prejudices and ideas of the average Prussian, nothing a little wider or more liberal or more cosmopolitan. It is the very style that I tried to guard against with your brothers, and with some success until they were 14 or 15, and then they were plunged into military Junker influences and opinions which they took up almost with fanaticism, but which I *most* disagreed with, and which seem to me to have done great harm here. Wm's boys will have a fairer chance in one way than my two eldest had, as no one will be so anxious to get them in antagonism to their parents. We were helpless to prevent this as we were *not* the masters.

'Poor Fritz Leopold shows himself very little, alas they do not get on very well with the Court, where the elder sister is very fond of meddling and interfering with the younger, and tantalizing and educating her, which of course makes the younger couple fume and storm and chafe. The footing on which the 2 sisters are since the ice accident row 2 years ago is cold and distant, and the little cousins hardly ever meet. Yaya's children are quite charming and the little girl so gentle, such pretty manners and ways, a lovely child with a complexion like a rose. It would amuse you to see this younger generation, alas so fast taking the place of others...'

At the end of February, King George narrowly escapes assassination while driving with Princess Marie.

'Hardly had I sent off my letter this morning than I saw a telegram in the papers that an attempt had been made on the King's life, and I did not believe it. Then I received your telegram. Thank God that no harm was done, and one cannot be grateful enough for this merciful and miraculous escape. Such dreadful things, alas, happen in every country, but never yet in Greece, and it is so unlike the Greeks in general. I am sure it will be a shock to poor Mama's nerves. Minny too must be quite upset. It seems a horse and coachman were wounded, and Papa had jumped out of the carriage, and two men lying in a ditch had fired 7 shots...Thank God you were not also in the carriage, nor Tino nor the children. Pray tell Tino how grateful I am that his Father's precious life has been preserved. I am sure the horrible attempt will call for the loyalty and sympathy of all right-thinking people.'

The King's escape preoccupies the Empress for some time, and successive letters refer to it. In early March, she receives Sophie's account of the affair.

'It makes one shudder to think of the danger Papa and Minny were exposed to. A perfect volley of balls! No doubt his courage in getting up in the carriage disconcerted the men. These wicked newspapers have a deal to answer for. The constant abuse must mislead ignorant people and sow the seeds of discontent and disaffection. I am all for liberty of the Press, and where it does not exist the dangers are far greater, but one is disgusted at the creatures without conscience who never pause to think what mischief their inflammatory rubbish works. How gratifying is the feeling of loyalty that has risen to the surface to show what the people really think. As a thunderstorm clears the air, so do I trust this awful affair on the Phaleron Road will bring many people at Athens to their senses, and make them see what would become of the country if it were left to the rule of demagogues who think only of being in power and nothing else.'

The feeling of loyalty to the King evoked by his escape is not unanimous.

'What a shame that the deputies should not have passed an address of congratulations to Papa unanimously and that some should get up a story of the attempt being an arranged thing! It is really too bad. I wish the King would make a stronger use of all the Powers the Constitution gives him, and that the ministers were more courageous and energetic. As you say it *could* all be so good in Greece. That beautiful little country, the most interesting and poetical in the world, with a past like none other. That gifted, fine and noble race, that fine climate and sea-girt land. It does seem wrong it should be in such a state through lack of order and proper government. Copying the French so much has done a lot of harm, you had better copy the English and the Germans!

'This is the anniversary of Grandpapa's death, now lo years ago already. I am sure you will not likely forget the day, and our hurried journey back from the sunshine and blue sky of San Remo to the snow and ice of Charlottenburg and Berlin, and the dreadful days that followed.

'That my stupid neuralgia has caused me to miss seeing the rehearsal of "Macbeth" by the English company (in the morning and incog.) is a great disappointment to me. Mr. Forbes Robertson is an excellent actor, no doubt you saw him in London. Yesterday I was at a lecture at the Polytechnic Institution which was very good indeed, on light and electricity, etc., with very interesting experiments. William and Dona and all the Court were there, though I expect a good many did not understand a word.'

The Empress now pays a visit to Princess Irene at the Schloss Kiel.

'I miss Henry here more than I can say, it is so quiet and silent in the house, and seeing his empty rooms and things is so sad. Irene is very well and cheerful, as are the 2 children. There is actually a wee bit of blue sky to be seen today, though I suppose it will be hidden in a few minutes, the sun does not seem to exist here. The torpedo boats are screaming (the sirens) in the harbour. There was a launch here yesterday, and Irene christened the ship, a small one. That Admiral Tirpitz was here for the occasion, he is a clever man, and does well in his position in the Reichstag, although the work is not what he is used to.

'Here is a little ship you drew as a child which I have always carried about with me. Please give it to your Georgie and put it in a tiny frame. What a pity you do not continue your drawing. I am very glad that little Georgie is learning the bicycle. Children learn so easily, are not easily giddy, and when they fall they do not hurt themselves as much as grown up people. Do you keep up your tricycle? I hope so, as I am sure it is good exercise. Vicky and Mossy and Adolf are very good bicycle riders indeed, and Fischy is learning now...I do so long to see sweet Ellene, though I fear she would be afraid of me in my black gown. How it amuses me to hear you say she has some little likeness with me. I hope she will be far more like her lovely other grandmama, the dear Queen.

'I am very glad Frau. M. is of use and shows how to economize in the running of the soup kitchens. I expect that the lower classes are the same in every country, they would rather starve than eat anything that is new to them and they are not accustomed to. Here it is impossible to get them to eat fish, except smoked and salt herrings. They might buy other fish very cheap and make a good dinner of it, but one cannot persuade them. In Scotland they will not touch cocoa, in Ireland they refuse what is not a potato in some shape or form.'

Early in April, the Empress moves to Bonn and stays with Princess Victoria, whose house, since its enlargement, is called the Palais Schaumberg.

'Yesterday morning we had an hour and a half to wait at Cologne and I spent it, as you may imagine, in the Cathedral. It is one of the wonders of the world as to size, but is very bare, and the material has something cold compared with the heavenly cathedral of Milan. Still there is so much of interest to see, and the treasure room is full of wonderful things, jewels, relics, chalices, crucifixes, etc. I am going again soon, for the older one grows the better one learns to understand and value art in all its branches, at least so it seems to me.

'Vicky and Adolf met me at the station and brought me here. I am the first guest in the new wing. The house would just enchant you now, it is just like a pretty English country house. There is not one *large* room, so she could never give parties, dinner or dances, but that they had done on purpose, as they did not want to be continually entertaining. All is in such good taste. Vicky has collected some charming pieces of furniture and has not a single ugly object about. The house looks unpretentious from outside, but so nice, white with green shutters and a grey roof, with English chimney pots. But hot air heating besides (i.e. hot water) and no double windows in consequence. I think you and Tino would be quite delighted. As you are busy with your own house I thought these details would interest you. Yours is of course twice the size, and alas there is no nursery here. P.S. If you could only send me a box of those little fluffy acacia flowers like balls, that have such a delicate perfume, it is just the time now I think. I love putting them among my fresh linen in the cupboards, the sweet smell reminds me of Greece.'

The Empress has periodically referred to developments in the Far East, where Russia had gained possession of Port Arthur, and Germany, with the backing of her naval expedition under command of Prince Henry, of Kiao-Chau.

'The mass of the public here and the less thinking politicians are quite delighted that China has ceded this Kiao-Chau for 50 years to Germany on a lease, and of course they say that Germany will never leave it again. I do not think England need mind Russia being at Port Arthur so much, only I wish she were stronger at Hong Kong, because of the close proximity of the French. The poor Chinese will not like all these foreigners coming to settle down upon them. Still it will be an advantage to the world later if China is opened up to civilization and her vast resources turned to some account.

'Alas, Russia is so insincere in her policy and protestations that one never knows exactly what she is driving at, her diplomats are so cunning. Trade, commerce, railways, etc., cannot develop without freedom and the principle of liberty, and this Russia has not got, and is too blind to see how their system cramps their resources and keeps down all the vital sources of real power and prosperity. They go on increasing their already almost unlimited territorial extension, but do not seem to know what to do with the countries they seize and join to their gigantic but very unhappy Empire.

'The German navy bill has passed, I am not altogether happy and enthusiastic about it, as I think other things want the money still more in Germany, that will now have to wait, alas. Of course England does not like it ...but the abuse poured on England by the German Press day by day about everything and on every occasion is quite extraordinary. I fear it leads to a distressing conclusion in England, which is that she has no greater enemy than Germany and no more bitter foe than William. This is not the case to that extent, and if it has the effect of making England draw nearer to other Powers it will indeed be sad for both our countries. The whole Chinese business seems to me dangerous. The Slav element seems everywhere to threaten to overflow and overrun the world, while the Germanic element, instead of resisting this, is divided because Germany is so jealous of England and anxious to thwart her.'

With the easing of political tensions in Athens, Princess Sophie and her husband plan to visit their relations in Germany, Britain, Denmark and Russia.

'Oh what joy it will be when the telegram comes that you are allowed to travel! I think I shall go off my head with joy, and especially so if we can drink Georgie's health as Governor of Crete, and give 3 hearty ringing cheers for him! William and Dona come here tomorrow evening for an hour or 2, then he leaves for Dresden for the King of Saxony's Jubilee. Charlotte is very busy making preparations for Feo's wedding, her trousseau and getting ready a little house they have had to buy at Frankfurt a.d.O. [*on the Oder — Ed.*], one of the dullest, ugliest and most tiresome places in Germany. Reuss's Regiment is quartered there.

'I learn that poor Mr. Gladstone has a cancer in his nose and palate, and suffers so much that he prays to die. Is it not sad? The pain was long thought to be neuralgia. He is not long for this world, I fear...I read about the trial of the men who made the attempt on the King's life. No doubt it is right and just they should be condemned to death, and yet it has something awful.

'This moment I received your dear telegram that you are coming. What a joy untold! I will send this scribble to Venice. Till our meeting, there will be not much sleep for me.'

Sophie and her husband arrive with the three children and the dachshund, Blackie, and make a long stay at Friedrichshof, during which, on May 19th, Mr, Gladstone dies. Leaving their children behind, Princess Sophie and Prince Constantine go to Berlin, to improve their relations with the Emperor.

'My surprise was great on hearing that you want your little Georgie at Berlin, but I have arranged all for his journey as you wish. If there is an opportunity I should be so glad if he could be taken to the Mausoleum and see his beloved Grandfather's grave. It would be nice to think he had been there. I am so glad your visit is a success and a pleasure, and is going off well. I think it will be good in so many ways for the future. If only Tino has an opportunity of explaining to William how desirable it would be to have a Greek officer now and then to serve in a German regiment, and to have a few instructors out for your army.

'Before you leave Berlin, will you not consult Reischach about the little presents to be given, etc.? As your Mr. P. is quite new to that kind of work, perhaps Reischach's advice might be of use.'

After a further spell at Friedrichshof, Princess Sophie and her husband set out at the beginning of July for England. In her Letters, the Empress now uses Ellene's pet name, Sitta, which is taken from her brother Alexander's efforts to say 'Sister'. The name is to stay with her all her life. Alexander's pet name, 'Tootseyman' also appears. While in London, staying at Marlborough House, Sophie is enjoined by her mother, with typical thoughtfulness: 'Do not forget to send for your dear kind Nana, and Emma and Moddy and Miss Green, all anxious to catch a glimpse of you.' These are former nurses and servants. The next letter goes to Windsor

'You are at Windsor now, my dear old home, most likely living in the rooms I always have, the rooms Papa and I had on our wedding day, which in consequence I love so much. I suppose you will go to the Mausoleum at Frogmore for morning service I hope you will visit Eddy's monument at St. George's Chapel (Wolesey Chapel). ... I am thankful you found Grandmama so well. She is indeed wonderful. She telegraphed to me that she was so happy to have you both, which of course gave me great pleasure. I am glad you have had this opportunity of seeing her, and wish the expense had not been too great to take the darling children,

'Your dear little people are very well. Sweet Sitta has hardly cried at all. Georgie and Alexander ask me so many questions that I hardly know what to answer. "What do you wash your ears with, Grandmama?" "Why have you been an English girl?" "Do you know the names of all the servants? Do you not forget them?" "Why does a strange man come and pick the cherries off your trees?" "If he dies, will the cherries belong to you again?", and so on! "Tootseyman" gets handsomer every day!

'I can imagine how dear old London amuses you, it is such a universe in itself. I read in the newspapers that you have been to the theatre with Aunt Alix and Victoria, and hope you liked it. I hope you enjoyed the State concert, too. I am sorry that Lord Salisbury was silent and pre-occupied when you sat near him, but the times are very anxious and he has enough on his hands. ... I forgot to say before you went that I wish you could manage to see Sir Richard Wallace's collection which he left as a museum for the nation. Also, if you could see Waddesdon, Ferdinand Rothschild's estate, I am sure you would like it very much. Also Alma Tadema's house. P.S. Kiss dear Grandmama's hand for me, please, with tender, respectful love.'

Describing her rounds of entertainment, Sophie mentions that London society women use make-up.

'It interested me so much to hear of all you have been doing in London. I do not wonder you are tired. I always think a "season" in a big town with the late hours, toilettes, visits, dinners and parties, and just going about, most terribly exhausting. Worse even at Berlin because one never could get away from the suffocating stoves and gaslight in the crowded ballrooms without even a window open.

'It is indeed a pity that Ladies *will* paint and powder, and dye their hair. I think it so ugly. Formerly in England it was quite the exception, whereas at Paris everyone did it, and in Italy and Austria it was quite the habit, now alas it has been adopted in London, which I greatly regret, as English ladies had such beautiful hair and complexions. In the country I do not think they do it at all.... I am glad you will see Waddesdon and Knole. If you go to the Isle of Wight on no account neglect going to see the little sailors' home at Cowes for old sailors and their families.

'Prince and Princess Pless (i.e. Hans Heinrich and his wife, Daisy) are here for a day and a night. She is looking perfectly lovely. I can only stare at her! Her beautiful fair hair so charmingly done, and her skin and complexion so brilliant that she would really light up a room. She has such a merry good-natured expression, and pretty dimples. In short, she is difficult to surpass. (She was a Miss Cornwallis West, as perhaps you know.)'

Sophie and her husband visit Waddesdon with the Prince of Wales, who unfortunately slips down the stairway and breaks a kneecap.

'Your letter arrived yesterday evening with details about Uncle Bertie's horrid accident, which makes me quite miserable. Poor dear Uncle! What pain it must have been at first, but I do trust as surgeons are so skilful nowadays that the leg will not remain stiff. I cannot say how much I feel for him. You know all my fondness for him.

'Yesterday was the fair in Cronberg and your darlings went out in 2 carriages and drove through the fair, and were much interested by the "carousel" (merry-go-round). They are in unabated spirit. I think Georgie will have a talent for drawing, if he is taught. Sitta looks like a dear little boy, with her short hair. She hugs a dolly in a faded green dress and takes it to bed with her. Alexander likes playing with newspapers to anything else, folding them up and making parcels of them, looking extremely busy all the while. They all send you their love and many kisses and are very anxious to know when you are coming back. P.S. Georgie dictated the words of the telegram to you this morning.

'I see to my joy that this will be my last letter to you in England and you will be here on Tuesday. Should I not be at the station to receive you, you will know that it is not my fault, I could not upset my arrangements with the Empress of Austria [*who is staying in the district — Ed.*] it would have been too uncivil. She asked me to come on Sunday, but I had to say I could not come on account of our "Schutzenfest" [*local festival of riflemen — Ed.*] so I cannot put it off a second time, I fear, without being impolite.'

Princess Sophie is staying at Friedrichshof when, on July 30th, Bismark dies peacefully in his sleep. As with Gladstone's death, there is thus no letter to reveal the Empress's thoughts on the passing of her old adversary. Towards the end of August, the children are again left behind while Sophie and her husband make their visit to Moscow.

'How pleased I was to get your dear telegram, and to know you are safely at your journey's end. I do hope you were not too done up with all that shaking for so many hours. But the Imperial Train has very comfortable carriages, and in Russia (on the broad gauge) the line always seems smoother, besides they do not go so fast. I am sure your dear Mama-in-law was delighted to have you again and Andrea and Christo to see you. I trust you found Tino's beloved Grandmama well. Now you will have visits to pay and churches to see, as well as what you can of the town, which is so curious and unlike anywhere else, with all the gilt cupolas and onion-shaped tops to the towers. It is sure to strike you very much, though snow and ice are Moskow's real and most characteristic garb...Fancy dear old Blackie in Moskow!'

The Empress's next letter, dated September 4th, mentions a fall from her horse, the effects of which were afterwards believed to have precipitated the dread disease to which she was to succumb three years later.

'What a joy to receive your dear letter written in the train, and then from Moskow. All your impressions of the journey interest me so much. Is it not strange how the moment one passes the German frontier and gets into Russia, one is in another world. There is something so squalid and sad, suggesting poverty and loneliness, about the landscape and population, so much in contrast with the enormous wealth of the Imperial Court, the money and jewels, the almost reckless extravagance with which some things are carried out, and presents lavished on people. [*The rest of the letter is in the writing of Princess Margaret — Ed.*] Mossy dear is kind enough to continue this letter for me as my right hand is painful and must be kept quiet for a day. The Grand Duchesses have a "luxe de toilette" which is far beyond what is necessary, and are loaded with jewels. Still, they have such immense means at their command that they can do it easily. The comfort and order and tidiness in their houses leaves much to be desired, but so many prefer it, and think themselves more "ungeniert" [*free and easy — Ed.*] in a wild confusion than where there is care and method.

'Georgie is overjoyed with the "shop" you brought him, and all three play with it and are quite absorbed in the charms of this new toy. I tried to draw Georgie in chalk, but with scant success, and made a sketch of Tootseyman in charcoal. P.S. I stupidly came off my horse this morning and it trod on my hand, but it is only bruised and strained, and nothing broken.'

From Moscow, Sophie returns to Germany on her way to Copenhagen, where the Danish Royal Family are assembling for the 80th birthday of the Queen, 'Amama', who is, however, sinking into her last illness. The Empress sends the children to meet their parents on their arrival at Berlin.

'I have just received your dear telegram from Berlin. I am so glad you breakfasted with William, and so grateful you were given such a good reception...Yes, Berlin looks quite nice when the trees are out, not so terribly dark, monotonous and melancholy and ugly as when I have to pine away there during the dreary winter.

'How I miss those little people, I cannot say. Adored little Sitta got great friends with me at last, let me carry her and kiss her and take her up. I hope all the unknown faces will not upset her and make her shy and frightened. Georgie has derived benefit in many a way from his stay here. He has learnt German, and the bicycle, and has got on a bit with his riding though I do not think he cares for it much. He is so thoroughly truthful, honest and trustworthy, which is an immense comfort.

'I had a telegram from your Amama in answer to mine, so I hope and trust she is better. I hear that Georgie and May and little David are at Copenhagen too...My hand is much better today, though I have a little lump on my forehead, and my right arm is rather strained, and neck and shoulders hurt. It was indeed a mercy nothing happened, as it might have been an awful accident. My head was close to the horse's hoofs, my habit was fast on the pummel of the saddle. A lady is quite helpless in such a position.'

The Empress's next letter is taken up entirely with the news of the assassination of the Empress of Austria on September 10th. In the course of it she writes:

'Yesterday evening the most awful news reached us by a "Wolff's Telegram" that the sweet Empress of Austria had been murdered at Geneva, stabbed by an anarchist. Oh, I have no words to say how dreadful I think it! Poor dear soul. So harmless and kind, she would not have hurt a fly. And she was *so* unhappy. I only saw her the other day, and was so pleased to have paid her a visit. She was once the most beautiful woman in Europe. Even now, the figure and the walk and carriage were unchanged, only the grand hair was thinner and the beautiful complexion lined. How devoted she was to Greece, she talked a long time to me about it the other day.

I was very fond of her, and to me she was unchangingly kind since 1862.

'Unfortunate Emperor! His only son, Rudolf, died a violent death by his own hand. His brother, the Emperor Maximilian, murdered in Mexico, His sister-in-law burnt to death last year in Paris [*the Empress Elizabeth's sister. Duchess of Alençon, killed in the charity bazaar catastrophe — Ed.*]. And now the wife he loved and admired so much and was so proud of, killed in this way in the year of his Jubilee. Is it not fearful?'

The impact of the tragedy persists in the Letters over several days. Sophie has now arrived in Copenhagen.

'You are again in a large family party and very glad to meet many relations again. The news of Amama sounds very anxious still. I hope she will be able to see your dear children, so that the journey was not in vain for them. I am so very glad that May should see them, and that you can see dear little David.

'The weather here is beautiful, not too hot, bright and sunny, the air fresh and balmy as if it came from the sea. We have excellent melons and pears. I wish I could send some to you. I had a ride this morning again, but I cannot yet get a glove on my right hand, it is still painful.

'This awful tragedy of the poor Empress of Austria makes me quite ill, so shocked and horrified I am, and so do I grieve for her husband and daughters. I cannot help thinking constantly of her, who was once so beautiful that she seemed a dream, now an inanimate form, pierced by the dagger of a madman or fanatic. Woe untold!'

The Empress travels to Breslau for the wedding of Princess Feodora, the first of her grandchildren to be married, and the only one she was destined to see married.

'The journey was very fatiguing as I was not feeling very well...Breslau is such an ugly stiff mountain town, the modern part, though the old part is interesting and has some fine buildings. It is sad for me to see it again without beloved Papa, we were here several times together. You and Tino are badly missed, as you were anxiously hoped for. All the wedding guests arrived yesterday, Feo has received many presents and some very fine ones. Yesterday I was all over the place, seeing the hospitals and a few churches and the museum. In the hospital I saw one or 2 nice appliances which might be well worth your copying, I will write them down for you.

'I think Charlotte looking worn, Bernhard very flourishing, and little Feo very happy and quite unconcerned, not the least agitated, just as if she were going out for a walk or a drive, and in the words of the Mikado, "Life was a joke that had just begun". Evidently the young people are very fond of each other.

[Later] 'The wedding is just over. Feo looked very nice in her wedding gown, which was low and of white satin, trimmed with myrtle and orange blossom and Venice lace. She wore a wreath like yours, and Charlotte's wedding veil, which I put on for her, and my diamond pins in her hair. The ceremony in the church was very short and the music very good, also the clergyman's address, which was brief and well put, which is so rarely the case. Crowds lined the streets and cheered most warmly and kindly. Afterwards there was a big luncheon, very long and tremendously noisy.

'My thoughts are with you my darling, day and night. The horrible death of the poor dear Empress of Austria weighs upon one like some dreadful nightmare. Thank God, the end was so sudden that she never knew exactly what had happened.'

Bismark's newspaper henchman, Busch, has published a book on the dead statesman, containing every criticism he had ever made against members of the Royal Family.

'We are indignant at the book of Moritz Busch. One had hoped that now Prince Bismark was in his grave, lies and calumnies would cease. Instead, all the spite and gossip which he always spouted has been faithfully collected and printed, whether with his consent before he died or not, one cannot know. To speak as he did of the Royal Family, always to detract from them and to make himself appear in contrast as the one patient and wise man, oppressed with cares and difficulties and his work for his country, that was always his way. How he courted popularity in certain circles, and swallowed honours and money, etc., and went on constantly complaining that he was not enough appreciated. His vanity and ambition were as insatiable as his despotism was unlimited.

'Ihne and the sculptor Maison are here, the latter is to do dear Papa's monument at Berlin, and this afternoon I am to see the models. Not until 1903 will the monument be unveiled. *That* would be a time for us all to be together! Heaven knows what may not happen before then...Your Amama was worse yesterday, from what I hear. How very sad it is.'

The Empress now goes to England, and on September 29th, writes from Buckingham Palace.

'On arriving here I heard the sad news that your dear Amama has passed away. She lived to a great age, and it was vouchsafed to her to pass her last days on earth surrounded by all her dear ones, and go to her rest in her own home and in the midst of her family. This thought must console all those who will now deeply mourn and bitterly miss her. To me she was always most kind since I saw her for the first time with her children in June 1861. My thoughts are so much with you all.'

After a few days in London, she joins her mother and other members of the family at Balmoral. She refers disapprovingly to the Emperor William's visit to Turkey and Palestine.

'Dear Balmoral is looking very pretty. Of course it is sad for me to see it again after 14 years — I was *not* lone then. I found beloved Grandmama very well. We went over to Mar Lodge today, where we saw Uncle Bertie, Louise and Fife, Victoria, May, and Frank Teck. Georgie and May's little ones are here, little David full of questions, such a dear little man.

'Yesterday was poor Liko's birthday and as Aunt Beatrice wished to be away from the house, we went a drive across the lonely hills and moors. Not a human being did we meet. The rocks and sky and heather and brown grass stretching far away, are exactly like parts of Attica.

'I am unhappy about Willy and Dona's journey to Constantinople and Jerusalem. All this coquetting with the Sultan and supporting his abominable rule is against the interests of progress and civilization and liberty. It may bring some advantages in a commercial sense to Germany but it does her harm in ways which are serious. The moment is so inopportune, when almost all countries are so unsettled!'

Since April, the Empress has frequently touched on the events of the Spanish-American war. She is glad that 'Cuba will be delivered from Spanish rule, which was most cruel and iniquitous' but is 'so sorry for the Queen Regent, who tries to preserve peace and finds it very difficult'. The war has ended successfully for the United States. In early October, the Empress's sharp eye spots a business proposition.

'Have you seen that Spain has been selling her vessels to the Spano-American Republics? It would not be too late I am sure to sell the Greek ones to some state or other, even China and Japan, and have newer smaller ones. Do tell Tino again, one must be keen and on the alert in these things or one misses good opportunities that do not return.

'It has been very cold here these last 2 days but very fine. Dear Uncle Bertie is established in the little cottage close to the house, and seems to improve daily. I shall stay here until the end of the month, and then go for a day to Lord Rosebery's house at Edinburgh, then to the Duke of Buccleuch's Drumlanrig Castle and from there to London, until I join Grandmama at Windsor.'

King George sends the Empress a letter of appreciation for her interest in Greek welfare and her help in her daughter's good works.

'I received such a nice letter from your Papa-in-law and I sent him a few lines this morning. I ventured to say at the end that I hoped Tino would find work worthy of him at Athens, and the means of actively serving his country, and gaining the popularity he so justly deserved. I hope this remark will not be ill-taken, but I feel so strongly how important it is that the Dynasty are not silent and idle spectators of what is going on, but can and do influence the affairs of the country and further the interests of the nation to its moral and material advantage by helping in every good public work, and pushing on improvement and progress in small things as in great, and thus teaching and educating people by their example, which is as important in its way as great political questions. May you and Tino never lose heart and energy and interest, and strive to rouse the people to good and useful things for which by their natural intelligence and quickness they are so eminently fitted. Never give way, never be beaten! You have plenty of pluck in you, and I hope plenty of ambition for Greece, and where there is a will there is a way, and heaven will send a blessing on your efforts.'

While Sophie is travelling back to Athens, the Empress pays her visits to her friends in Dumfriesshire and West Lothian. She is pleased and impressed with the several stately homes at which she stays... 'quite regal in splendour, yet there is no show or fuss'. She concludes her last letter from Drumlanrig Castle before returning to London.

'I wish you could see these homes, the happy family life, not like the fashionable sets in big towns, but examples of what country homes should be, kind and good and considerate to all around. In short, "homes", and not only grand "establishments", which one may admire and wonder at but which do not make one *happy* and comfortable, such as these...To my satisfaction I can tell you that not *one* of all the young ladies I saw at Dalmany, Gosford, Hopetoun or here were painted, powdered or laced or got up or wearing fringes, but fresh and lovely as English and Scottish maidens should be in the bloom of health and youth.

'It is too tantalizing to think that on your return journey you were so near Friedrichshof and I not there to welcome you. I am sure you found Rümpenheim so pretty, clean and comfortable. Although I once got abused and laughed at and stormed at for being "house proud", yet it has been of some use in Germany, and my children have been imbued with the spirit of it, and sought to carry it into their homes, and make them cheerful and tasteful, wholesome and tidy! One can live like Diogenes if it is inevitable, but that rich people should not try to keep their homes in good order I cannot understand...Helen Aosta (Orleans) has a son, how pleased they will be, there seemed no chance for a long while.'

Sophie is now back in Athens. On November 11th, the Empress writes from Buckingham Palace.

'How relieved I was to get your dear telegram that you had arrived safely and had a good passage. I was very uneasy, as we had such constant gales and when I heard the wind howling, I trembled in my bed, thinking of you and the children at sea.

'Dear Lady Ponsonby is in town and went shopping with me yesterday. It amused me so much to see the Lord Mayor's Show on the 9th. I went to see it from Coutts' Bank. Tomorrow I go to Windsor. I am sending a little smock (pinafore or can be worn without a dress) for Sitta, a sweet blue. I saw it in the Art Needlework School in Sloane Street and thought it so pretty that I could not resist buying it. I thought she would look such a Duck in it, and could put it on to play and romp in the nursery, as it is strong.

'Politics are indeed in an anxious state. It seems all will be peacefully settled with France over Fashoda, but no doubt the danger is still there. Here, people are very quiet, but anxious and serious, they know not what the future may bring, but wish to be ready for all eventualities. Our Fleet is splendid, and though our army cannot compare with the German — the *precision* and organization of the latter, the quickness of handling, the drill and armament, are unequalled — and though small by comparison with the German and the Russian, it is better in many ways than the French, Austrian and Italian, and in the point of *bravery*, and of the intelligence and independence of the officers, and the *spirit* that pervades the whole force, we are inferior to none.'

Princess Sophie, at last moving into the new house, is upset because it is still not completely ready, and because the furniture from London disappoints for the reasons her mother had warned her about months before.

'I can well imagine that it annoys you that the house is still backward. How I was kept waiting with Friedrichshof for months and weeks! We were often driven nearly wild. Then the things ordered did not fit, and there were such floods of letter writing and telegraphing, then the agonizing bills, so as you see, building and arranging is not done by magic, or without untold trouble and annoyance, and a deal of patience! One's nerves and temper get sorely tried. You used to laugh at me and now you see yourself.

'I am indeed distressed to read of your annoyance and disappointment at the furniture. M's stuff is excellent in quality, but as for taste and shapes one can never trust to a firm, one must choose oneself. I think you always want a stock of useful practical comfortable furniture in a new house, and not of any particular taste, then one puts the carefully chosen things among them, and arranges so that they should not clash. But the 1st year you can never expect a house to look quite as you would wish. When all your pictures are up and your books and knick-knacks arranged, and the pieces of furniture you had in your old house, I am sure you will by degrees make it very pretty. But do not be disheartened, and do not lose patience.'

Princess Sophie is also not very happy about the cottage in the Tatoi Estate which the King allows them to use.

'It is really wretched you should be without baths and W.C. and the conveniences one ought to have, even in a simple cottage. Would not the King give up to you altogether the other little house, which is better built, and let you add on to it? If that will not do, you will have to arrange yourself a small country house elsewhere, perhaps at Manolada, ever so simple, comfortable, clean, wholesome and roomy. You should not be uncomfortably lodged, it makes your life so much harder to be struggling with "les petites misères de la vie" which poison one's existence and sap one's strength for overcoming the serious trials one has to bear.'

In mid-November, the Empress joins Queen Victoria at Windsor Castle. 'I found dear Grandmama very sorry to leave Scotland, which I understand so well.... Grandmama has 2 ostriches and some kangaroos that have been given to her and are down on the farm.'

'How glad I am that you have seen the new Ministers and think them nice. I hope you and Tino will see them often and get to know them and that they have confidence in him...If Tino could only gather round him the best men of the army, and also see the best heads in the country, and remain in constant touch with public life, have some sphere of influence, and use his rare gifts for the good of his country. I do so want him to become in himself a "pillar of the State" he will someday be called upon to rule over. I want him too to have success and satisfaction after he has suffered so much injustice and ingratitude. Help him, like a good and admiring and helpful, faithful little wife, whenever you can. P.S. I am so glad Sweety now wears spectacles while reading, it will rest his eyes. That straining and frowning was so bad for him.'

At last the Powers agree that Prince George shall become Governor of Crete.

'So big Georgie *is* appointed for Crete! How glad he will be, and all of you. Everybody here is so pleased that it has been settled at last. I am sending a few lines, which I hope you will give him before he leaves...To see his arrival would be interesting. I should love to be there to shout "Zito", which I would do with all my might. I hope he will have a good doctor with him, and also some friends, as he will feel very lonely. Now, in time, there is every prospect of the Island joining Greece altogether, only one must be prudent and cautious.

'I have been reading all the reforms proposed by Zaimis [*the new Greek prime minister — Ed.*] in answer to the King's letter. They seem very good to me and I can only hope that they will be accepted and carried out. It really seems to me as if things were going a little better in Greece. What an immense blessing it would be...Greece must show she is in right and good earnest with her reforms, and gain the good opinion of the rest of the world, and I am sure all will go right then.

'...Lord Kitchener has been staying here for a couple of days. He met big Georgie at Cairo some years ago, and said of him, "he is a splendid fellow", and that gave me great pleasure.'

The Empress describes a day in London in early December.

'Yesterday I had a very busy day in London. There was not an atom of smoke or fog, I suppose because it was blowing so hard from the south. In the morning I looked for things for Xmas. I went into some shops, Kensington way, and saw no end of things which would have done for your house, all real and *old*, and very pretty and not at all dear! These shops are quite small and not fashionable, all in the Brompton Road, and most tempting, indeed so tempting that I could hardly trust myself to remain longer, and went to the new Depot of the Greek Industries. The ladies and gentlemen there were most nice and civil, and seemed pleased to see me. The choice of carpets and stuffs seemed very good to me. I bought a few pieces, and arranged for some things to be sent for Grandmama to choose from. I thought I might perhaps be doing a little good, and that you would wish me to go there, so I went.

'Then I went to lunch at Lord and Lady Clanwilliam's with their charming daughters. In the afternoon I visited the Great Ormond Street Hospital for Children to see the new wards which had been made since I was last there. I found it the *perfection* of sweetness and good air and order, neatness and cleanliness and comfort. The nurses so nice and so well dressed. The poor little darling children all contented and quiet, and not shy or frightened. Afterwards I went to the German Governesses' Home, which gets on very well and does a great deal of good.'

Princess Margaret and her husband and children are paying a visit to Athens.

'Pray thank your Papa-in-law for kindly telegraphing Fischy's and Mossy's arrival to me. Now that you have your Mossy (*my* Mossy — *our* Mossy) with you, you can chatter with her as much as you like. You will be up to fine tricks together, I can just imagine.

'I just received your very short letter, the first from your new house. Let me send you best wishes for your "house warming". May you spend days of peace, happiness and prosperity there, free from anxieties, illness and sorrow. Indeed I know what it is to get into a new house, one cannot find one's things, and chimneys, water, electricity, all do not work properly...As the water appears so brown to you in the glasses, I hope you do not drink it until it has been analysed. I wonder whether you have brooms and brushes and dustpans from England to keep the place clean and spotless, which is the secret of healthiness and comfort, at least *I* think so — and it is your mission to teach that in Greece.

'Charlotte wrote to me that she had been to see Feo and that she found her very well and happy, but that she had quarrelled with her son-in-law about different things. I fear she does not like him at all, which is very sad, as she has only the one. Perhaps however that will all settle down later. I am certain he will never be half as rude to her as Bernhard has so often been to me, and yet I am very fond of him in spite of it all.'

After a brief stay at Sandringham the Empress goes to Osborne, where she passes Christmas and the New Year.

'Dear Grandmama has asked me to stay a little longer so I shall remain for another week at Osborne, and probably not arrive till mid-January at Bordighera, where I shall be under the name of "Grafin von Cronberg"...Aunt Louise and Lome and Aunt Helen are coming here for Xmas. The house will be very full. Grandmama sends you both her best love and Xmas wishes. I sent you an almanack as Xmas card, which I hope you will like.

'We have a lovely day to-day, and yesterday evening the sunset was as you children used to say "like an Xmas card"! So lovely! The thrushes are singing and rooks cawing, as if it were spring; the Park and the enormous trees, and the long, long stretches of green turf that make one long to scamper over on a good horse.

'Dear Aunt Alix has just telegraphed to me the death of Ferdy Rothschild. I am inexpressibly shocked. I liked him so much and he was a great friend of Uncle Bertie's. He made such a good use of his truly regal fortune, and was a very cultured man. I saw him walking in Bond Street only the other day.

'Now your big Georgie is at Crete, and has already been enthusiastically received. He telegraphed so nicely to Grandmama who was much pleased. ... By the time this reaches you, it will be Xmas Eve. How I shall think of my darlings and the children's joy and excitement!'

In her last letter of the year, on the 31st, the Empress mentions her visit to the Portsmouth Sailors' Home, whose work and organization she describes in some detail.

'Yesterday I went over to Portsmouth to see the beautiful Church of which I had laid the foundation stone in 1887. You, Vicky and Mossy were with me. Afterwards I went to Miss Weston's great Sailors' Home of Rest, and opened the new "Diamond Jubilee" block of buildings, and went over the whole place, which is so admirably arranged. What a comfort and boon to the sailors! It is beautifully kept, as clean as possible, and such excellent air. The restaurant, billiard room, recreation hall, baths, etc., so nice. They pay 6 pence for their cabin, with charming bed, 4 pence for a hot bath, 3 pence for a cold bath, 1 penny for a cake or bun...excellent meat, vegetables, puddings, etc., at moderate price...1000 sausages were eaten in 2 or 3 days!

'We returned in the "Alberta", a lovely passage after the sun had set, the sea like mother-of-pearl, and 1000's of gulls flying about.'

Chapter Eleven – The Letters, 1899

During her Portsmouth visit, the Empress had sought information about her scheme for washing down the Athens streets with seawater, and one of her first letters of the new year is to Crown Prince Constantine.

'Darling Tino, I am sending off detailed information about the use of seawater which I have received from the Mayor of Portsmouth today. I hope it may be of some use to you. Your Papa often said he thought it a pity there was such a prejudice against watering the town of Athens with sea water. You will see that *here also* there were prejudices, but that these have been overcome. The old idea that the road became sticky and the tyres of carriages rusty is *quite* mistaken.'

The Empress also obtains particulars of windmill pumps, which she sends on through Sophie.

'Will you please tell Sweety that I am sending out information, printed papers, etc., about the pumps and windmills for raising water, which I hope will perhaps be suited to application in Greece. Tino will think I have gone mad on the subject of sea-water for the streets, windmills, railways, etc. Indeed my head is always running on your railway to Salonica. It would make an untold difference to Greece. When one thinks how railways are being pushed into the wilds of Africa, and now in China, one wonders that yours has not been done long ago.

'I send you a tiny tract which the St. John's Ambulance Society, of which you are a member, are printing for the public, to enlighten the ignorant a little on different subjects.

'Fancy your having snow! We have not seen any yet here, and I am very thankful indeed for it. How does Blackie feel in the new house? Has he got accustomed to it, has he his basket in Tino's room, as usual?'

The Empress prepares to leave Osborne for Bordighera. She permits herself a smile at two of the servants of her suite, and refers to some pictures which a painter friend. Professor Schrödl, who lives near Friedrichshof, has supplied for Sophie's new house.

'By the time you receive this I suppose I shall be at Bordighera, which Emmel calls "Portischera", while Gossmann talks of the "Schindelmann Border", meaning the "gentleman porter" at Buckingham Palace.... Yesterday we had a most beautiful sermon from the Bishop of Ripon, really a joy to hear. His gentle and impressive voice touches one, his language is so fine, and the thoughts so devoted. He is really the kindest and best of human beings, and lives only for others. We are all so fond of him.

'I am so glad Fischy likes your water colours. You have really a very good beginning of a little modern gallery of good things, 2 sea-pieces, 2 landscapes, a flower piece and 2 heads. Now you ought to have a good picture of animals, and one of architecture, and one of still life. ... I am very sorry you think the Schrödl pictures look less well than they did at Cronberg. The light in your house is no doubt very strong. I always think Schrodl's colouring a little heavy and opaque, the purity in the light wanting, also the depth and transparency in the shadows, at which Angeli is great. But Schrödl is a clever artist, the drawing is good, and often I think the arrangement pleasing. The flesh tones in his pictures are often a little leaden. You know how difficult it is for portraits to succeed and how rarely one is quite satisfied.'

The Empress's departure is delayed, and in writing from Buckingham Palace on January 13th, she refers to one of her gentlemen-in-waiting, who is ill with neurasthenia.

'This was the day on which I ought to have arrived at Bordighera, but when we wanted to start yesterday morning the gale blew so furiously that the channel service was suspended and we had to give it up. Of course, I am not sorry to be kept a few days longer in England, though it is provoking, as my rooms are taken at Bordighera and being paid for. But I made the best use of my time yesterday and went to see the splendid Rembrandt Exhibition, which was most interesting, and then the Burne Jones Exhibition, which is a very fine one.

'Poor Conte is still very weak...it will be months before he will be fit for work again. You can imagine how awkward it is for me, as fond as I am of Wedell, he is absolutely no use to me, and I have to see to all myself. Reischach will stay part of the time with me at Bordighera, but not long, as I must have someone at Berlin to look after the Hofmarschall affairs, money, house and other servants. It will end with my having to take a fourth gentleman, which is a great encumbrance and expense, merely because Wedell cannot do the work, and I cannot say to the poor man, "make way for one who can and *will* work". If he were efficient, three would be more than enough, but now all the work falls on 2, and if one of them is taken ill I am put to the greatest inconvenience. Wedell is so loyal and attached, and means so well, that I cannot possibly offend him by saying he is only an ornament. To have to do business with him is trying beyond words.'

Writing next from the Hotel Augst, Bordighera, the Empress refers to the Christmas presents she had sent to Athens.

'If you like the medals, which I thought so pretty and sent for from Paris, pray keep them yourself, and wear them on your watch chain and I will get something else for the children. Did Tino receive the little silver jug? A real old English ale jug, I thought you could use it for cold milk or lemonade or claret cup.

'This hotel is really very nice, new and clean. It has electric light! A great big white house with balconies, on the side of a hill covered with Aleppo pines. In front is an olive grove, which has been converted cleverly into a garden by adding palms and aloes, and cryptomerias and roses, a deal of heliotrope and some lovely jessamine trailing on the walls. The views are lovely, towards Ventimiglia, Mentone, Cap Martin and Monaco...I do not do much drawing here, but have begun a water-colour of the rocks and a little beach, with a small church and a strip of blue sea.

'The moonlight last night was bright as day, but there are no dear little owls here, whose pretty cry I loved to listen to in the night at Athens, in the Palace gardens. Nor do I hear the pitter-patter of the goats' feet early in the morning just after sunrise and the tinkle of their bells. But mules and donkeys one sees in plenty, unfortunate animals, theirs is indeed a hard life. The people hereabouts behave pretty decently to the poor beasts, though yesterday I did see one to my horror with a broken leg, dragging a heavy cart. Does the society for preventing cruelty to animals make good progress in Greece?

'Potteries seem to flourish here in all the little valleys. I wish you had a private one at Tatoi, *if* the clay is to be obtained, it looked like it if I remember rightly. It would be such a pleasure reviving the old forms and patterns, such as the heavenly vases in the Athens museum. Women can do the painting and glazing quite well, I have done it myself, do you remember my taking lessons? ...Have Mossy and Fischy visited the English and American Archaeological Schools yet? I am sure they would like to see them.'

Princess Sophie has a fit of depression at the apparent futility of her husband's efforts to introduce reforms in Greece.

'What you say about no reforms being possible or thought of makes me quite miserable. One must *not* sit down and twirl one's thumbs, and wait for misfortune to overtake one, and then accuse fate and providence! To fall into a fatal apathy and indifference and discouragement would be losing the battle beforehand which you mean to win! I would go on and on in some way or another until attention is paid to Tino, and he is listened to. Has your Papa-in-law no confidential friend to whom you both could speak? Of course it would do no earthly good if I wrote to him, or I would do it directly. It would be so easy for him to put me off and say I was a stranger and understood nothing about the situation in Greece, and ought to mind my own business.'

Young Prince Alfred, son and heir of the Duke of Edinburgh and Saxe-Coburg-Gotha, who has been sickening with a disease for some time, dies early in February.

'I am sure you feel deeply for poor Uncle Alfred and Aunt Marie in their overwhelming grief. Those poor unhappy parents! What must their feelings be, with their life and future so bound up with their son! I am so miserable about it. Poor dear young Alfred, to think his life should be cut off so soon. That he should have died without one of his family near him is too sad, too tragic. I hope and trust the poor dear boy's end was peaceful and painless, but it is cruel to think of. The *only* son!

'When one has been through what I have, the sorrow of those one loves sinks deeper into one's soul and makes all the sorrows of the past wake up again and seem so near and so recent. I am sure you can understand this with your kind and feeling heart. I love my brothers, so that the thought of *their* sorrow and grief is great pain to me, quite apart from the fact of a young person's death always being sad and unnatural.

'Today is the anniversary of Papa's operation. Do you remember that terrible day? How eternally grateful I feel to poor dear Uncle Louis. How good and kind and really brotherly he was to me on that day. ... I am exceedingly sorry to hear of poor Count Caprivi's death. He was a man in whom I had great confidence and for whom I had much respect. You remember him, I am sure.'

Answering Sophie's enquiry, the Empress tries to explain the delicate subject of the cause of Prince Alfred's death.

'I knew how shocked and grieved you would be at the death of your poor cousin. It is indeed terrible, terrible. You ask about the cause. It is true that he was giddy and wild, as many young men alas are, and that he contracted an illness, of which I know next to nothing, as I have never asked or heard anything about it, one dislikes thinking about it, and still more speaking or writing about it. This was neglected, and the poor boy led a dissipated life besides. Potsdam! — *that* was not the place for him. He was too inexperienced and heedless and giddy to resist temptations, bad examples, etc. Is it not all too miserable! I loved that boy, there was something irresistibly taking about him. He was one of those who are not fit to take care of themselves, not from evil disposition but from weakness of character.'

The famous actress, Madame Elenora Düse, visits Athens, and makes a conquest of the Royal Family.

'I am very glad you saw Madame Düse and that your parentsin-law received her, and that your father-in-law gave her a bracelet. I hope she will return when the new theatre is finished, and inaugurate it with a really good piece. I never saw her on the stage, but believe from what I hear from those who really understand, that she is the best actress living, with most genius and most taste — greater than Sarah Bernhardt, only in another style. I know she is a charming and sympathetic, gentle and intelligent person with a sweet attractive voice and manner, and with a very interesting and expressive countenance, because she once came to see me and spent an hour with me, I am delighted she had a success at Athens. Her character is said to be as good and respectable as Madame Bernhardt's is the reverse.

'How interesting that you heard Madame Düse recite from Gabriel d'Annunzio. He is a man of marvellous talents and gifts as an author, alas his writings are sometimes marred by being *so* the reverse of proper and pure and moral that one is *quite* horrified. His descriptions of nature are beautiful, almost unequalled. They say he has a deep-seated passion for Mme. Düse.'

The Empress mentions the Italian Forestry Controls, which when later adopted in Greece as the result of Princess Sophie's urgings, brought much benefit to the country.

'It is a pleasure here to see, far inland, how the hills, so bare 16 or 20 years ago, are now all covered with pine woods again. The Italian government passed very good "Forest Laws" some 20 years ago, and furnished seed and also guardians to the communes. So there is constant supervision, only a certain number of trees can be cut and at a certain age, and the goats, sheep and cows are not allowed to graze *everywhere*. I was wishing this could have been in Attica too. The hills here were just as bare 30 years ago!'

Princess Sophie asks for advice on planting the space in front of the new palace. The Empress, whose knowledge of garden design is wide and practical, launches into a long and detailed examination of all the possibilities, of which short extracts are given.

'For trees, none are more beautiful than mimosa and acacia, also Japanese medlars. Plant 2 or 3 "Cedrus Deodarus", it is so much in use in India, and should do very well in Athens. Palms, orange and lemons— but they get straggly if not looked after — and laurels, the "Laurus Nobilis" would do, other kinds want more water. Have bougainvilleas and Banksia with bright scarlet flowers...different sorts of Bignonias, red and orange would do on the pergola, and over the house too, they keep the heat from the walls...ribbon grass stuck between bits of stone as a border to a shrubbery...

'Turn a bit of ground into a carpet of wild flowers, not planted regularly as in a flower bed — wild hyacinth, every kind of narcissus, jonquil, daffodil, wild anemone, wild tulip, which is tall and red, some violets to perfume the air, bunches of yellow daisies and white...cascades of geraniums to hang over walls or from large pots...large red earthenware pots and glazed green ones do make a terrace and garden look pretty, especially in the South...they are mostly made near Florence, at Imprunata. Someday when a Greek vessel returns half empty from Italy it could bring you a cart-load, they are not at all dear.

'You should get the pretty illustrated paper called "Country Life". It contains so much information and such charming pictures of fountains, vases, gardens, flowers, and would I am sure be of use to you.'

The elections which have recently been held in Greece have resulted in an anti-Delyiannis combination headed by M. Theotokis coming to power.

'I am so thankful the elections have been satisfactory, it shows that the opinion of the country has undergone a salutary change. I am sure that Tino's reports had something to do with the defeat of the Delyinists. I do hope Tino will be able to have an *influence* on Theotokis and get him to assist in so many important matters.

'Tomorrow I attend a meeting held by the Bishop of Gibraltar for the Mission to Seamen, of which there is a branch at Athens and the Pireaus. In the newest report, your dear mama-in-law's kindness to a British sailor is touchingly mentioned. Should her name be again mentioned tomorrow, of course I shall rise, to show my respect.

'I shall go over once more to the hospital [*for consumptives — Ed.*] at San Remo. Not to the town, that I could not bear. The poor Russian gentleman who I went to see there and hoped was getting better, died alas 2 days ago. I was so sorry, he seemed a nice young man. I sent him some flowers and gave him a "drinking cup", as he was too weak to sit up and drink comfortably. Poor soul, only 30, and 2 more dear things have died since I saw them the other day. They are sent out to the south much too late, when it can do no good.'

Queen Victoria comes to stay at Nice, and the Empress pays her a visit, with other members of the family, among them the Princess of Wales, who is touring the Mediterranean in the Osborne.

'I was at Cimiez yesterday with dear Grandmama. I thought her looking very well, perhaps a little pale. She said how much she hoped to see your dear children someday. Beloved Aunt Alix was there, and Uncle Bertie, his dear kind face is always sunshine to me. He always enjoys being here so much.

'I do not like Nice at all, and think living there must be anything but pleasant, though the hotel in which dear Grandmama is staying is splendid, with immense rooms and every comfort and luxury. But, oh, how *I* prefer to exist in quiet simple Bordighera, where one has the woods and mountains in immediate neighbourhood, and is so near the sea, and out of the way of smart people. Today, sweet Aunt Alix was here to see me, so dear and good of her to come over from Villafranca bay. She *hopes* to be able to pay a tiny visit to Athens, but of course she cannot quite tell yet.

'William wrote to me he was delighted with Cecil Rhodes whose visit to Berlin was a very good thing. He is certainly a man who strikes and impresses everyone by his powerful mind and character, his genius for organization, his coolness and energy and keenness.'

One of the subjects which Rhodes discussed was the alliance which the British Government had recently offered to Germany, and about which he was enthusiastic. But the German Government distrusted British motives. The Empress now prepares to leave Bordighera. Princess Sophie has written consoling words on the anniversary of the death of her brother, Waldemar.

'I am very busy packing, gathering and putting my things together, alas. I shall be very sorry to leave Bordighera, which I like very much, though of course I shall be pleased to get a glimpse of Florence and Venice and Trento again, as I am devoted to these places as you know.

'So many thanks for your words about our beloved Waldie. But I cannot think that "all is for the best" that happens! The ancients used to say, "Those that are loved by the Gods die early", but I cannot quite agree with this, though I have been through life's bitterest woe. Many a life that is taken is never to be replaced, the loss an irreparable misfortune. But I do think that we should try to take what comes with resignation, courage and patience, that we should try to make the best of what is *left* to us of our lives and our powers and our happiness, and that we are doing right in making this effort, hard as it is.'

After a brief stay in Florence, the Empress moves on to Venice, where the busy round of visits and visitors is high-lighted by the arrival of the *Osborne* - 'I had tea with Aunt Alix on board, it seems she *will* pay you a visit - Oh that I could have remained on board and gone with them, alas, I cannot, but must go home.' She then goes on to Trento, from where she writes on April 23rd.

'Here it is so cold that one is glad of a winter wrap, and has a blue nose in spite of it! I went to Levico, the village where the celebrated waters come from. Now a German company has been formed to reorganize the watering place, as the properties of the springs are considered so wonderful for different diseases, and weakened health in general. What a pity that a company does not form to exploit the hot baths in Greece for rheumatism. Many people would be glad to go there, but the arrangements are most primitive, no good hotel, nor restaurants, people have to make their own beds, etc., and the baths themselves are not comfortable. In a volcanic country like Greece there are sure to be many valuable springs not yet turned to account.

'It is really splendid of Mdme. Syngros to have given lo million towards the water works for Athens. She deserves the thanks of her fellow-townspeople for evermore. I hope the rest of the money may be raised in some way.'

Back home at Cronberg, the Empress, writing at the beginning of May, tells that 'Dear Friedrichshof is looking in best trim, but alas the weather is like winter, so icy-cold...Dear Vicky and Adolf are here. I am sure you are delighted to have dearest Aunt Alix and cousins and enjoy seeing the dear *Osborne*. How pleased I am Fischy's tour was such a success, and that he looks so well.'

A newsy letter half-way through the month reveals nothing of the shadow of disease that has crept into the Empress's life during the past few weeks.

'By the time this reaches you, you will have parted from Mossy darling, and she set out on her homeward voyage. It was so nice for you both to have been together for so long a time — you will miss her frightfully at first. Auntie Alix seems to have been much pleased with her visit to Crete and to have found dear big Georgie in good spirits. I read a long account in the "Times" about the Greek finances which rather comforted me. Things really seem to be going better, thank God If only there could be strict honesty in the administration, all might be better still. I am sure Theotokis sees this too.

'Yesterday William and Dona were here for tea. They brought a *swarm* of people with them, which was not to my taste. Dona's hair is growing as grey as mine, but as her face is young it suits her very well. We had a large tea laid out in the big dining room, and everyone seemed very hungry. Strawberries and cream rapidly disappeared!

'I had my first ride this morning and found it very enjoyable, on a new horse though, and all the roads are cut and ploughed up by the carting of wood and stone while the ground was soft. Reischach is gone to look for horses to England and will be at Uncle Bertie's sale of "Hackneys" at Sandringham. I have a gentleman here, on trial, as a 4th Gentleman, a young Herr von S. of the Garde du Corps. He is of a very good family, with excellent manners, not exactly lively or amusing, but I fancy will suit very well. It is dreadfully difficult to find the right person as you know, and one is thankful to find anyone who cares to come, and seems to take an interest in what he has to do. He is a good rider, which is a great advantage.'

Two days later, on May 16th, her letter gives a clue to hidden trouble, for she rejects an invitation to visit her mother.

'At Wiesbaden yesterday I joined William at a luncheon at the Military Casino given him by the "Gersdorff" Regiment, of which I am "Chef". I went there as a surprise for him. After the luncheon I went to the Cronberg Schloss to pay Dona a visit. We took a drive afterwards, Dona, Vicky and I and the 2 children. I was really dead tired on arriving here again last night. The strain of keeping up conversation and being amongst so many people for so long is very fatiguing.

'It is a very great disappointment to me not to go to England for the 80th birthday of beloved Grandmama, particularly as she so kindly invited me, and Uncle Bertie urged me so. But I am not quite well, and the fatigue, etc., after I have not been home long, besides many another reason, made it impossible for me to manage, so I had to give it up to my very great regret.'

The 'many another reason' that held back the Empress from attending an event to which she would normally have flown with eagerness and devotion is that she had just received her death sentence. Her doctor had confirmed that she was suffering from the same disease that had killed her husband.

Her Hofmarschall, Baron von Reischach, records in his memoirs how she calmly told him of this news, not in order to seek sympathy but to ask him to reduce her public engagements. She said that all her life she had prepared herself physically to resist illness, and that she expected to live another ten years. As her physician-in-ordinary was growing old, she appointed a second doctor. Dr. Spielhagen of Cronberg, but Reischach pressed her also to consult

Facsimile of First Page of Letter Quoted Opposite

a specialist. Professor Renvers of Berlin. He told Reischach that had she disclosed her symptoms six months earlier, she might have been saved, but now no operation was possible. She had only two years to live.

From now on, the Empress, knowing that she was doomed, but hoping at first to hold the disease at bay — 'I shall enjoy having my children and grandchildren for a long time', she told Reischach — faced her dread future fearlessly, endured her agonies with fortitude, and never ceased to keep up her active interest in all that affected her family and the three countries she loved.

During the visit of the Emperor, she had disclosed her condition, but bound him to secrecy for reasons which the Letters later explain. No letter has been found to show that she then also informed Princess Sophie, but she may have done so towards the end of May, for Sophie quite unexpectedly sets out for Friedrichshof.

'My joy and surprise are boundless, your dear telegram has just arrived saying you were just leaving. But who is coming, you and Tino and the children? Pray let me know from Venice. I hope to be quite well by the time you come, but I have lumbago from the violent wind and cold weather.'

Princess Sophie arrives at the beginning of June with the children, but without her husband, and stays until early September. The Empress's sadness at separation is as deep as ever, but she expresses it less emotionally than before, and for the first and last time in the Letters, ends with a quoted prayer.

'Now the much-dreaded parting is over, and I hope and trust you have got over it. As for me, I am more utterly wretched than words can say. The sight of your empty rooms without your dear face and voice and self, and without all the things that betoken your dear presence, without dear Blackie, made my tears flow again most bitterly. The darling children, too. Georgie so sensible and such a companion already, my beautiful Tootseyman, and precious little Sitta, with her bewitching dimples and sweet round person. Most bitterly I shall miss them. Goodbye, goodbye once more, oh *hateful* word, cruel invention.

'"The Lord bless thee and keep thee.

The Lord let the light of his countenance shine upon thee, lift up his countenance on thee, and give thee his Peace."'

The Empress's desolate mood persists in her next letter.

'Oh my own child, I am still so sad. None but Mossy and Dete. R. feel for me and understand my deep depression. What shall older ones do who are tired and weary, and who have been sorely wounded in life's battles, who have lost their helpmates and comfort, whose future has passed into other hands, who have lost their illusions, and whose hearts are full of disappointment? One wants buoyant spirits indeed not to give way to depression.

'Last night how I missed the children, little sweet Sitta with curl papers and her little plaits like tiny tails all over the back of her head, and in her pink and white dressing gown. The beloved little brothers in their blue ones. ... I did not tell you that when I said goodbye to dear Blackie, when I went downstairs, he turned his head and looked at me with his big brown eyes as if he could have *spoken,* and in his expression one seemed to read the thought "perhaps you will never see me again at Friedrichshof". I felt ready to cry, dear faithful wise old animal.'

But it is not long before she is distracted by her indefatigable interest in current affairs. A visit by the King of Bulgaria provokes comment on the need for Balkan unity.

'Yesterday, Ferdinand of Bulgaria made himself very amiable, and said he had the greatest sympathies for Greece and was very anxious to be on the best of footings, whereas he feared it was impossible ever to get on with the Servians. He said he regretted that the Greek element carried on so much agitation in Bulgaria, to this of course I made no reply. Ferdinand of Roumania, who is at Wolfsgarten, declares that affairs in Bulgaria are in a very bad and dangerous state, and that it is Ferdinand of B's fault, who has made great mistakes.

'I do think it would be good if your Papa-in-law once went and saw the King of Roumania and also Ferdinand at Sophia. I am glad the Prince of Montenegro went to Athens. All these states ought to stick together as much as they can, as they are neighbours. It is true their interests are very conflicting at times, but still it is not impossible to smooth away some of the difficulties and differences that keep them apart, and they have a common interest both in resisting Turkish oppression and staving off an invasion from the north.

'Goodbye my own Sophie darling, I must rush off and dress. Remember me to Messie [*Miss A. Contostavlos, Princess Sophie's lady-in-waiting — Ed.*] and say all that is kind to Edith and Ellen [*two of Princess Sophie's servants — Ed.*]. The pain is very bad at times...'

In France, the verdict has gone against Dreyfus, despite the exposures of corruption in French public life.

'I had a letter from dear Grandmama, dreadfully upset about Dreyfus' condemnation and she thinks it wicked and abominable. It certainly produces an immense sensation. Who can ever trust and believe those generals again after forging, lying, swearing false oaths, etc. I am sorry for all reasonable and nice Frenchmen, who must feel so distressed and humiliated at this shameful affair, and so grieved at the abominable mess their poor country has got into...if true patriots they will not allow their country to become the prey of wolves and jackals.

'I am very fond of the French, so I grieve at it, but they are going down as a state and a nation. Morality, justice, order, etc., are in a state of disorganization...Europe would be like a face without eyes if we were to lose France, and what the French have done for civilization, the knowledge and talent they have accumulated, are too valuable and indispensable for us other Teutonic races for it all to be wasted, but if they do sink lower and lower, it is their *own* fault, and *not* that of foreign enemies...They are politically incapable of understanding true liberty...Their government and administration, army, etc., are a very bad example to everybody, and teach a lesson which should be read and not forgotten...Goodbye my own sweet Sophie, you will think your Mama very prosy and tiresome, I know.'

The Empress mentions the deteriorating political scene in South Africa, and shows, by her reference to her illness, that she has no conception of what suffering lies ahead of her.

'I am dreadfully afraid we shall have war with the Transvaal. The sacrifice for England will be awful, but I do not see *how* one can make more concessions to Kruger, and allow him to promise a thing one day and retract it the next....

'I am in bed again with stupid lumbago, which is the greatest bore, and hurts me dreadfully at every movement. I tried to ride but found it too painful, and moving about is wretched, so I have to stay in bed, the greatest trial I know, when there is a good deal to be done and one is the head of a house. My other pains were very bad again yesterday. Having two sorts of pain at once is rather much! My plans have been much in discussion, and I have been advised not to go to Berlin, Bonn, Kiel and England but to the South. This distresses and disappoints me beyond words. What will all my institutions at Berlin say, that expect me, want me and wait for me?

'I have been thinking so much of Corfu. I do not want to be an expense to you in any way, so you must say straight out to me whether it would be of great inconvenience to you if I came in February. If I am well enough. But of course I do not know whether carting over some of your household there would not be very expensive. I could pay that if you wish. I know how heavy all your expenses are. What would you say to that? You must think it over quietly, and tell me so that I can talk to Reischach. If you think better *not,* you have but to say, my precious one, and your old Mama will make other arrangements.'

Princess Sophie's letters at this time, while showing her worry and concern at her mother's illness, dwell also on her own unrewarding existence. The Empress, forgetting her troubles, sends a long letter of encouragement.

'My poor Sophie dear, it makes me miserable that you are so depressed and low-spirited. It worried me to think of that wet pocket handkerchief! I wish I could cheer you up, my darling, and make things seem brighter and more cheerful around you. The short time I was there, I did so love Tatoi and Athens, and I have always a longing to get back, but we are different and have different tastes, all the discomforts and imperfections are nothing compared with the joy of looking at that sky, those hills, that colouring, those rocks and plants, but then you know I live (3 quarters) with my eyes, and as you do not paint, of course all these joys are lost upon you.

'One comfort is that all the neglect and untidiness *can* be put straight and should be. Think of all the valiant English ladies, that in the wilds of India, in tiny hill stations far away from towns, in Australia, South Africa, the backwoods of Canada, etc., manage to make themselves comfortable English homes (for their husbands and children) and force civilized habits and some sort of method and order to follow them wherever they are, and in whatever climate they may have to live...

'I think Missy of Roumania more to be pitied than you...The King is a great tyrant in his family, and has crushed the independence in Ferdinand so that no one cares about him, and his beautiful and gifted little wife, I fear, gets into scrapes, and like a butterfly, instead of hovering over the flowers, burns her pretty wings by going rather near the fire!

'When one has had a happy home and childhood and has lived amongst many friends, of course it is a terrible wrench to give them up. My Sophie darling, my own love, you must feel that wherever you are you have your mother's love and sympathy with you, who understands all your feelings, and would wish to help you in everything. God has been very good to you. He has given you a husband, dear and good, clever and handsome, children of which you may well be proud, and to bring up well and in the right way, so that they may do their duty and make others happy, and be useful to their country.

'The Greek people are splendid, I admire them more than I can say. I think with Mr. Rodd [*later Lord Rennell — Ed.*] that the Greek peasant is the born gentleman of Europe. Of course the upper classes, with all their intelligence, are not at present what they should be, the spirit of duty, self-sacrifice, steadfast work, order, conscientiousness and honesty, does not prevail as it should, their training has not educated them for the service of their country. The great work of improving, reorganizing, etc., is left to Tino, and I trust you will be his help and comfort and support. If you only manage to have a *little* centre of civilization around you, and show how things ought to be, it will *spread.* 'Example is better than precept", and people who have never seen how things ought to be, cannot be expected to know. Greece is worth fighting and suffering for, and what you *can* do, is to find the people who *will* help you to make your ideas known, and to draw out the good and useful qualities of others. Quite alone one cannot get on and succeed.

'Do not forget darling that you have many a nice success to be thankful for. In lo years, much has been done. You say yourself your Palace looks nice, and that the military hospital is in good order. I am sure with steady work, patience and perseverance, all will transform and improve. Changes can only come gradually, and slowly. All sudden and violent shocks are artificial and destructive, and bring a bad reaction with them. Look at *France,* plunged from one system into another, a series of convulsions have *shaken* her to the foundations, and *when* will she ever regain her equilibrium and steadiness? She has had a century of unrest and change, and this was preceded by a century of misgovernment by the upper classes. They did the harm, and the consequences now fall on every one. In Greece you are still suffering from the effects of the Turkish rule. Countries and states are not made in a day, and *long* and *many* are the struggles they have to go through.'

Returning to the subject in her next day's letter, the Empress draws on her memories of her own early struggles in Berlin.

'I must tell you, when I was a young thing, 40 years ago, Berlin was an awful hole. No drainage, fearful pavements, awful smells. I spent the first year without W.C, baths or water to be got at, no cupboards for my clothes, my things had all to remain in boxes. The servants horrified me by their dishonesty and impertinence, their rough, untidy, dirty ways, their disobedience. A lady was nothing, not to be listened to. My Hofstaat [*Court household — Ed.*] quarrelled and made my life a torment. The tyranny of my parents-in-law was not to be described, the people one saw one could not trust, and they were most spiteful and unkind. I had to conquer my bit of independence bit by bit. Beloved Papa's position was very difficult, and I did all I could to help and support him, and slave for him. I was hated and abused and persecuted for it, as the old Prussian conservative party did *not want* the influence of the liberal-English wife, and opposed it at every turn. Then for years the interference with *all* we did. We had no liberty, *you* thank God have plenty. You are beloved. Then came the long years when we were trodden down under the iron heel of Bismark, it often was a "purgatory", the intrigues that raged around us. When the time came for us to be able to be of real use to the country, death snatched away all. All this I only say to show you that others have had their difficulties too, and that you must not lose heart.

'Now, Berlin is a very fine city, the Schlosses that were pigsties are put in order, not with the taste I should approve of, and with unnecessary expense, but at any rate Lynker and Eulenburg learnt in our house how things ought to be kept. Trained servants who know their work are still very scarce, and many are still very bad, but it has all improved. The army is splendid, the administration good, the navy progressing, industry grows apace, also trade, and material development is great. Science flourishes, art not as it *should,* but alas in politics, in true liberty, in individual independence and dignity, things go badly. There is a deep-seated dissatisfaction among the lower orders. Socialism grows every day, as the labour question is not studied and treated in the proper way, alas. I fear W. is unpopular and very badly advised often, and I own it makes me very anxious. When I think of dear Papa's patience and wisdom, of the enlightened ideas he had, and of his constant plodding and working, reading and studying things, I grieve and grieve to think the fruits of so much serious and conscientious devotion are lost."

Princess Sophie describes the inadequacies of the villa in the Tatoi grounds, of which her family has the use.

'...I well understand that the state you found the house was *not* edifying. Your description reminds me exactly of what Friedrichskron used to be like between 1860-1870. 1000's of dead bats I found in one big empty room, and bugs by the 100. The beds I begged all to have burnt, but they were not. W.C's and water there were none. You can hardly have an idea! How furious the royal Hofmarschalls were with me when I rowed and complained and begged for money and reforms. Now William and Dona live there in comfort and cleanliness, where their parents were more or less only encamped for years. Every drop of water was fetched for every bath and for the kitchen, etc., by soldiers, a battalion of men. It took me over 30 years by degrees to get that old Palace into working order, and then I had to leave it, and had spent much of my own money on it.

'At Bornstedt, when we first took it, no farm servant had *ever* had a mattress or sheets or blankets! They never undressed to go to bed, but kept on their clothes and enormous leather boots! — never washed and had no place to have meals, but sat and ate any where in the yard, stable or on the staircase. Papa and I changed all that! The school was a disgrace, the church too, and the churchyard was scandalous, all the graves trodden over, the monuments broken and thrown down, one tangle of weeds and nettles. We put all that in order again. I only say this to comfort you. In those days I never saw any cleanliness or order out of England except in Holland, and Ostfriesland, and the north of Bavaria in the mountains, where I was surprised to see clean floors, clean kitchens, bright copper, clean window panes, snowy linen, tidy beds, flowers in the windows, etc., and yet there the people are poor.

'Of Royal castles, the only clean ones were Gotha and Coburg and Hesse and Brunswick, where the servants were tidy. All the rest were as you saw at Aunt Vera's and in Denmark. Dresden and Weimar were awful. The servants quite terrible everywhere, dishonest, greedy, grasping, dirty, familiar and impertinent, ill-dressed, ill-mannered. *Worst* of all at Carlsruhe and Baden, where I used to stay for weeks every year, and where I used to have an insight into German Court and Palace Life behind the scenes which filled me with dismay, the cheating and stealing that used to go on. I was just as horrified as you are.'

Sophie comments on how fortunate her mother is in her beautiful smooth-running home.

'Indeed I do appreciate my dear Friedrichshof, am always impatient to return to it and distressed to leave it. It cost so much time and thought and money and work to get it to its present condition, and is so difficult to keep it as it ought to be. Alas, very few servants of any of my guests take the least care of my things, and are very messy and untidy in their rooms. I shall have to fresh paper several. They have completely spoilt the new blotting books and ink stands I brought from England this spring, and are altogether most careless. I have to have my eyes everywhere. I know what a privilege it is to have such a nice home, and am anxious to keep it so, I can assure you.

'We have just returned from the simple little ceremony of opening our Cronberg hospital. The weather was really tolerable for once. All the committee and all the colony of Cronberg were present. After a little speech the building was declared opened, and we went all through the house and visited the rooms.'

Subsequent letters continue with encouraging proposals and urgings, together with a warning about a foreign financier who aims to float a company to build the Larissa railway.

'I am very glad there is a better Mayor of Athens now, you should see him often and try to interest him in all the important hygienic questions, etc., and charities, you could do a lot of good...I hope the water question will be taken in hand without swindlers and speculators making a mess of it and ending in disaster. The same I hope with the railways.

'Please tell Tino (in confidence from me) I have heard the King is being approached by X. about the railway to Larissa...I fear your papa-in-law believes in him, he ought to be warned...X. is considered a man who does not shrink from "sharp practice"...I am very sorry to have to say so, but I would never enter into an agreement with him...Please burn my letter.

'I send you 3 numbers of the "Agricultural Times" for women, which Lady Warwick has sent me, as I thought it would interest you. About the dairy keeping of cows and goats, and about the poultry, the articles are very good...One day you could turn Tatoi into a paradise. A couple of good Scotch gardeners, one for the fruit and one for the flowers, and the wives to look after the milk cows and poultry. Oh how beautiful one could make it! Such a fine property, all the roads made already. I should have a larger house built, in country style, and you could have friends staying there, and many a pretty cottage could be built to *let* in the summer to nice people. You would not complain then of its being lonely.'

The trouble in South Africa again looms darker, and from now on most of the Letters make some reference to it.

'Aunt Helen has been staying with me, and leaves today. She is in very low spirits, as her Christie leaves for South Africa on Friday to join his Regiment, and she will only just get home in time to say good-bye to him...The Transvaal danger makes me most unhappy. The spite and rudeness of the German Press knows no bounds, and the abuse and sneers lavished on England. Three hundred Germans in arms going to join the Boers! I want to know why the Boers, who are Dutch intermarried with the wild tribes of South Africa, are considered of closer kin to the Germans than the English, who are Anglo-

Saxons. Everyone knows that the *one* country Holland hates and dreads *is* Germany.

'Missy of Roumania has been staying at Wolfsgarten, and Alicky of Russia. Mossy will have told you all about our visit. I thought Missy a dream of beauty, I have seldom seen so lovely a creature, so graceful and with such a complexion and hair. She is a perfect picture. They want her to go back to Roumania for her confinement. If I were her Mama I would implore the King to let her stay here.

'Alicky's little baby, Marie, was very good in my arms, where she remained for a quarter of an hour, she cooed and smiled and looked about. The eldest, Olga, is a big fine girl, without being pretty, but has lovely hair. The second little one, Tatiana, looks pale and delicate and very serious, a sweet little girl, however.'

Following on another visit by Professor Renvers, the Empress reluctantly prepares to leave Friedrichshof for the warmer south.

'I am horrified to think Sweety dear had a sore throat and fever and I do hope and trust he is all right again. It is so easy to get a bad chill after having heated oneself on a bicycle. I hope he will not do it again, i.e. sit at a window without changing his clothes after cycling.

'Renvers has been here and found the local affection in a better state than he expected...and fancies that if it remains dormant I shall have much less pain. Of course the repeated attacks of pain have pulled me down a good bit, and for *that* he insists on my going south sooner than I had wanted. Here, I feel *near* my Mossy and not distant from Vicky either. I had wanted to spend Xmas quietly with them and the children, and arrange a nice Xmas for all the poor around here.

'I am very glad the question of forming a society for rewooding the hills and plains in Greece is going to be gone into seriously. It would be a pity to plant only *one* sort of tree. It ought to be a mixture of evergreen, oak, aleppo and other pines, including the umbrella pine (pinus Italica) and cedar and cypress.

'It must have been nice taking a bicycle ride with Tino and Andrea, and I can imagine how difficult it must be to keep up with these 2 young men with their long legs. For a lady almost impossible!'

King George of Greece has again come to the district to take the baths and waters, and he pays a call. There is mention of the prolonged engagement between the Grand Duke George and Princess Marie, who has not been able to make up her mind whether to go through with the marriage.

'Hardly had I sent off my letter yesterday than I had a telegram that your Papa-in-law was coming here. He arrived at 3 and stayed till after supper. He was most kind, and in the best of spirits, and said he had arranged the town house at Corfu so that I could go there if I liked. We talked of Nicky's prospects and big Georgie's, and also, quite casually touched on Minny's difficulties. The King did not seem to know which way it would end, whether she would or would not take Russian George, and he did not wish to influence his daughter one way or another. I was so glad that the King had asked to go and see William. I consider this a very good thing, and I am sure you will also. About Greek affairs I purposely said nothing, fearing to appear meddlesome.

'Our Cronberg hospital is filling, and begins to look businesslike...My lumbago is awful! I am obliged to call out when I move or turn. I can walk, going up and downstairs is painful, and getting in and out of the carriage much more so. Is it not a bore!'

On October 9th, the Transvaal Republic issued their peremptory ultimatum, which amounted to a declaration of war.

'The war in the Transvaal has really begun! It will be dreadful I fear. What bloodshed there will be! I am so sorry for poor dear Grandmama to have this grave anxiety, this terrible trouble at her age and when she longs for peace. It is a tremendous business for the British Government; 5 Millions of £ (100 millions of Marks) have been spent already on sending troops there. Fancy having to ship a whole army to a distant land! If the poor Boers fare badly they will have to thank Germany (not exactly the government but the Colonial Verein, telegrams, etc.) for having made them think themselves what they are not, refuse to keep their engagements, and rely on support which they will not be able to get.'

The Empress writes next from Rümpenheim, her first stop on the journey to the South. The dread scourge from which she is suffering tells one of her close friends.

'I am so deeply distressed at my dear kind Marie Munster's death. I cannot tell you how much I feel it, she has been such a true and faithful friend to me. When I saw her at Bordighera she had a place like mine, smaller and less painful. Alas, she was persuaded to have an operation performed...it was pronounced to have been successful! I find it hard to believe that kind dear friend of so many years is gone, carried off by the same disease in a few months, which, thank God, with me, under the proper treatment, shows signs of being arrested for the moment.

'I *thought* my Sophie darling would be pleased at her Papa-in-law and Nicky having been to Berlin. I was only afraid that William and Dona might not have been as civil and kind as they should. I heard Dona was inclined to be stiff (just like her) but it wore off later. I believe William had no talk on politics with Papa, which I am sorry for, but Papa saw Bülow for 2 hours. Anyhow it is a mercy that the ice was broken. This visit will, I trust, have softened many edges and smoothed down ruffled feelings.

'I am so glad you are in a more cheerful and hopeful mood, and no longer so depressed. My darling Sophie I quite understand it. You can say what you like to me, you know I will never misunderstand. Being older and more experienced and having struggled and suffered so much in my life, I may be of some use to you, in comforting and cheering you up when you feel low and tired and downhearted.'

At the end of October, the Empress is writing from the Imperial Hotel at Trento.

'Yesterday I went to pay a visit to the Count and Countess W. at their old interesting castle not far from here, Castel Ivano. Anything more magnificent than the view and the landscape I never saw. The gigantic mountains rising up 1000's of feet, so steep and sheer, rugged and grand, and at their feet the valley, the slopes and lower hills covered with Spanish chestnut, oaks, pines, larches. The vineyards, fields of maize, lovely green turf, really indescribable. The air pure and crystalline, and the sun like summer, and a deep blue sky! The pretty picturesque villages, and people so nicely dressed and looking so respectable and pleasant. I was wrapt in admiration.

'My lumbago is as bad as ever. I am in perfect tortures sometimes, and cannot prevent the tears running down my cheeks. I have to be helped in and out of bed. I cannot turn at all. The pain goes into my ribs and down into my body. I have a double rope tied to the end of my bed to help me to raise myself and catch hold of when I want to turn. Oh! I am so sick and weary of this pain, and it depresses me so. Dressing is so difficult. I can walk pretty well, and my appetite is not bad, but I have to take constant drugs to dull the pain, which of course is *not* good. I am afraid I am a great bore to my staff.

'Henry will return somewhere about the 19th of February, and I hope to see him when he arrives, therefore if I manage to get to Corfu it would only be directly after. Reischach has taken a villa for me, called "la Marigola", for 3 months, Dec, Jan., and Feb. at Lerice, on the gulph of La Spezzia, a quiet and secluded spot, no town near and very good for yachting, I believe. The "Loreley" could be close by.'

The Empress bravely dismisses her condition as a bore. It was as well that she did not know that she was to be in almost constant and ever worsening agony until her death twenty-one months later. From now on, most of her letters contain some reference to her suffering, at first with a note of hope.

'Thank you darling for all you say about my health. I hope indeed that the chief place shows signs of remaining dormant and hardening...You must *not* however think the disease is permanently cured, this is *not* possible, but if it can be kept under it need not endanger my life or shorten my days as it would have done had it continued to develop rapidly. I am sure all your good wishes have helped me. The lumbago is still very bad, but now Spielhagen tries electricity and massage, a little stronger and a little longer each day, and in about a fortnight it ought to tell.

'You speak about going to take the sacrament. My own Sophie darling, as far as I am concerned you have never in word or deed done anything to ask pardon for, only given me pleasure. But it is right and good to think over all we do, and try to improve in every way, as long as we live on earth. A blessing is sure to rest on the conscientious endeavour to do what is right and live up to the highest standards, with the example of Christ before us, and struggle with the faults and weaknesses of our nature which so readily lead us into error. Life is a great puzzle and a great mystery, and slips away very fast!'

During King George's recent visit, the Empress had asked him to take back a surprise Christmas present for Sophie, but she gets it too soon, and does not understand.

'The fan was to have been on your table at Xmas, and I begged your Papa-in-law to keep it till then. It was the fan I used on all smart occasions, dearest Papa gave it to me just before we were married. I meant to leave it you in my will, then I thought it a pity it should remain in its case so many years unused, as I no longer carry coloured fans of an evening. I am sorry it came sooner than Xmas but it does not matter so long as you are pleased. I was very fond and proud of that fan and valued it very much, and shall be delighted to think that you use it.

'The weather is intensely cold. Thick icicles hang from the rocks, and in the shade the ice does not thaw all day. In spite of this, the sun is so hot by day that one has to walk at midday with a parasol and cannot bear heavy clothes, whereas mornings and evenings one is glad of a fur wrap. Yet the tiny lambs are on the grass, and there are still roses in many gardens.

'I went out today, and was able to do a little shopping. Driving does not hurt me. I bought a beautiful old bronze bell for the English church of St. George's at Venice, and have dedicated it as a humble memorial of the officers and men of our army and navy who have fallen in South Africa. It is a tiny tribute of affection, sympathy and admiration for my beloved countrymen, but of course quite private, and will not appear in the papers. ... I am sending you a yellow bed-cover for a single bed (half silk, half cotton) it will wash or clean. I thought it so bright and pretty that you might like to have it. You said once you had not many bedspreads and this one seemed rather uncommon, indeed it is more like your Greek stuffs.

'How very tiresome and disappointing for you that your Children's Hospital cannot be opened yet, that the debts are large. We too have debts on our Cronberg hospital, which is only for lo beds, and I know how immensely expensive all good hospital arrangements are.'

At Queen Victoria's invitation, the Emperor William and his wife and two sons have been visiting England, where their stay does much to remove the hard feelings aroused among the public by the Kruger telegram. In London and at Windsor the Emperor and von Bülow confer with British ministers on the proposed alliance. The Empress presumably knows of this, but refrains from mentioning it.

'Grandmama and dear Uncle Bertie write much pleased and satisfied with the way Wm. and Dona's visit had gone off. This is a great blessing and I am very glad...I have also had a letter from Willy, delighted with his visit. All the English papers have been so nice, so courteous and civil and in such good taste, whereas I grieve to say our German press is more rude and spiteful and insolent about England, the war, the visit, than ever, it gives me a perfect fever to read them. Of course, this wicked rubbish is not convenient for the German Government, which wants now to be on the best terms with England on account of its colonial plans, etc. Yet on the other hand it finds that this Anglophobia is one of the chief impulses for moving people to vote money for the extension of the fleet...It seems that Russia has been working hard to persuade Germany and France to join her in taking measures against England, but luckily it does not suit the interests of Germany, so the German Government will not join.

'Indeed the Transvaal war is distressing, but it seems all going on as satisfactorily as one can expect. Now I hope the Ladysmith garrison will be able to hold out until Sir Redvers Buller's forces can come up. I think we can be most proud of the achievement of carrying so many 1000's of men across the sea to fight in a distant land. I do not fancy it was ever done before. You have read of Lord Methuen's success no doubt and how splendid the British Infantry behaved, our dear sailors and our Highlanders are *such men!* And all the others too.

'Poor Lady Salisbury's death is very sad, I am extremely sorry. Just now, with the war, it is most sad for him, when he wants all his energies, it will be an awful blow to him, they were so devoted to each other.'

At the beginning of December, the Empress moves to her villa, La Marigola, on the Riviera di Levante. The yacht, *Loreley*, has arrived for her use.

'I send you some photos of our villa and grounds. It is an old stone house, quite small, with vaulted lower story and balconies...the staircase and floors are all marble, like in the old Genoese houses...the villa stands high, and there is a wood of pines and ilexes down to the road.

'Our little trial trip on board the "Loreley" was very amusing, in spite of my being more or less of a helpless cripple and suffering so much pain that I often did not know what to do. The poor little "Loreley" was tossed and rocked about like a cork, as the smallest motion causes her to roll. Of course, I was very sick. We arrived in the afternoon in the harbour of dear Portofino, looking as lovely and green as ever, the trees immensely grown. We went up to the Castello Brown for tea, it all looked so pretty and comfortable, and we scrambled early to bed. The next morning we went Up to the Villa Carnarvon. There is but little altered. There were your rooms, Mossy's and Vicky's and dear Papa's. You can understand what my feelings were. Nature as smiling and unchanged, as rich and beautiful as ever, and our dear one swept away.'

Extracts from successive letters portray the Empress's struggles to cling to her normal life and interests, despite the burdens of her illness.

'Yesterday we had a lovely drive and walk down to La Spezia. Holly and gorse like in England grows all over the hills, mixed with the myrtle and arbutus, pines and beautiful ilex and also caroub trees. It is a very wooded country, and yet it reminds me much of Greece, the formation and height of the hills, etc. Wedell has gone off to Florence for a few days to try a cure for his rheumatism. I think he makes a mistake to try this at this time of year, but it was better to let him have his own way. His rheumatism has not lasted a fortnight yet, and mine will soon be 9 weeks! I had a letter from Henry, so annoyed that I am not going to Irene, which I was sure he *would* be. He is vexed at coming home earlier too, I think! They have made him Vice-Admiral, which is rather too soon it seems to me. I wish they would give him the command at Kiel. I am sure that would be the nicest thing for him. Irene's time is approaching, between Xmas and the New Year one might have news. Poor little Missy's time is also very near. One cannot think of her without pity and anxiety. Altogether they are in such a mess in Roumania, that one feels sorry for them indeed.'

'My lumbago was such agony yesterday that Dr. Spielhagen gave me a morphine injection, which made me most sick and wretched, but did not take away the pain. The electric current is employed every day. I am told I must have patience!

'It is *so* nice and good of you to say you will send something for our poor wounded heroes. It would be so much appreciated, even if only a small contribution. Some cigarettes would be the very best thing, and some wine. "Turkish delight" is rather too sweet, I hardly think they would care for it. But I know that everything gives pleasure. I am knitting my fingers off to send some things.'

'The news of the war prevents my closing my eyes at night, I am so worried and distressed, so unhappy to think of dear Grandmama's sorrow at all the losses and anxiety. One must be prepared for reverses...Mistakes have certainly been made, but it requires to know every detail before one can judge correctly of what might have been done. These 3 poor besieged towns, Ladysmith, Kimberley and Mafeking, make one so unhappy, what they must be enduring now that relief is deferred! I remember well the days of the Indian Mutiny, where our sorrows and troubles were greater still, and the danger more serious, but we got the better of all difficulties at last, and in Africa, in the end, we shall manage it, in spite of the present triumph of our enemies, the joy of the Germans, the delight of the French and the Russians. It is very hard to bear their taunts and jeers, the spiteful ill-natured lies. Oh, if I were a man, how I should like to knock a few people down!'

'Every blessing for you and yours this Xmas morning! My thoughts are with you and I long for many kisses. Our little party yesterday evening was peaceful and bright and quiet...How sad to think of Xmas in England and the Transvaal, and in many houses in Germany where dear ones have lately died.

'I have a letter from dear Grandmama. She does not seem in alarm about the Transvaal, disturbed and unhappy as she is. Grandmama was so touched and pleased when I told her you were going to send some cigarettes and wine to the wounded. She said she would thank you herself. Vicky has sent some nice "tarn o'shanters" (caps) and Mossy, socks. My own box will be sent in a couple of days.'

'My pain becomes more and more acute. All I am doing in the way of cures and remedies is absolutely no use. Yesterday afternoon I found it impossible to stand up or sit down, and screamed when I made the slightest movement. Dr. S. who is very strong, had to carry me to bed, and there I remain for the present, having small doses of morphine to keep down the pain. To be a useless helpless log is really wretched. My patience is nearly worn out, I assure you. Excuse my writing, so bad.

'How touching that some Greeks have actually volunteered for the English Army to help in South Africa! I cannot say how much pleasure it gave me to read this, nor how nice I thought it.'

At the end of her last letter of 1899, the Empress renews a request which she has been making periodically ever since Princess Sophie first went to Greece.

'I am now completely in bed, and have to be washed and waited on like a baby. The smallest movement makes me scream with pain! Nice state of things! It is a great help having Vicky dear here. This acute state of the attack can surely not last for ever.

'I am very glad that proper congratulations for your Papa-in-law's birthday were sent from Berlin. Altogether, thank God, many a thing has improved, and many a cause of uneasiness and unpleasantness for you has been removed. Dear big Georgie's 1st year in Crete is over, and one may say has been successful and a great credit to him. How I wish he could marry and be less lonely. I am sure you are sad at the Duke of Westminster's Death, he was a true friend of Greece. A noble man, charitable, generous, openhanded and public-spirited, making the best use of his fine position and enormous fortune. One of his sons is gone out to S. Africa.

'Goodbye my own Sophie darling. God bless you and Tino and the darling children. I suppose this is my last letter in this year, and this century! I part reluctantly from the year in which we spent such a happy time together, and the best thing the coming year can bring me is that we should meet again soon. May I soon cease to be the helpless object and bore I am now. P.S. Will you not once have yourself photographed for me in a Greek costume? Even if it be not the Court costume. One could borrow a real one for you to be photographed in. It would give me so much pleasure.'

Chapter Twelve - The Letters 1900-1901

A letter early in January explains why the Empress does not wish the news of her illness to be made public.

'...a long conference with Renvers. He is not alarmed about me one bit. Thank God my brain and heart, etc., are *quite* sound, but the one evil is there. Still it may be got the better of by an otherwise healthy body, and though it does undermine one's constitution and is an element of hidden danger, yet it *need not* with any absolute certainty shorten my days.

'You may speak to dear old Sabba [*Princess Sophie's doctor — Ed.*] about me if you like, but it *must* remain an *absolute* secret. To have all the world know it would be to make my life utterly *wretched*, and deprive me of all peace and independence. You know how indiscreet people at Berlin are. I am not much loved, so I should not like to have people most likely *rejoicing* over my misfortune and speculating on my coming decease before it is necessary. At Berlin in certain circles, when anyone is ill, they instantly conclude that they are dying and act accordingly, pay no more attention to them. Did we not see enough of that in 1888! *No,* I want to remain mistress of my actions and have no one interfere about my health or in my private affairs. That is also why I am quite glad to be in this out-of-the-way place, as all gossip and curiosity is cut off.

'I hope in my next letter to tell you that I am really better. After 13 weeks of pain I think I am entitled to *some* improvement. Excuse my untidy writing, as I am lying down. There are still heaps of Xmas and New Year letters to answer, so difficult from bed and sofa, and in such a helpless state. A chair to carry me in will arrive in a day or 2, the same one I took to Athens for you and you *refused* to be carried in or even to try! It was the one I had from London for dear Papa, and which he liked so much at Charlottenburg. It has been lent to several invalids since.'

In spite of her incapacitated condition, the Empress clings to the hope that she will soon be fit enough to travel to Greece.

'I am delighted with the card with the photo of your Palace. Oh, how I *long* to be there with you. Come I will as soon as I can wring the permission from the doctors. It is the one wish of my heart. I am not in a fit state yet, but will see how I am the 2nd half of February.

'As for my condition, it is much the same. I spend the day lying on the sofa, or sitting in an armchair with many cushions. Breakfast I am obliged to have in bed, and tea in my room. Writing to you does not tire me, and is only a great pleasure, still I have a good deal more to write than I like. I dictate some letters to Detta Perponcher [*a lady-in-waiting — Ed.*] Conte reads to me in French. I study the "Times" and the Italian papers, and *those parts* of the German ones that do not make me *mad* with their insolence and rudeness, and I do an immense deal of crochet and knitting for the sick and wounded in S. Africa. Vicky dear sits with me a great deal.

'I suppose you know that Victoria Battenburg and May are expecting babies, so with Ducky's, Irene's and Missy's, Grandmama will have 5 new babies to welcome in 1900. Goodbye, my own most precious Sophie, best love to all at the Palace and 1000 kisses for the dear children.'

In Athens, memorial services and demonstrations have taken place in sympathy for British casualties in South Africa.

'How very kind and good of the Greeks to show their sympathy to England. It makes me love them all the more. Dear things! Dear Grandma wrote to me today and says, "I am so touched at the Greeks having volunteered for us, and being so friendly." How delighted I am to think that giant Georgie is with you again. His heart is as big as his body, which is saying a great deal, and he is what the Americans would call "a rattling fine fellow". Please give him my love. I hope that the ball at the Palace will go off well, and I shall be indeed grateful for a little photo of yourself in the Greek costume which you wear. I have been asking for this photo for 10 years, so that I think I have been patient, and there has not been great alacrity in listening to my supplications!

'The good news has arrived from Kiel that dearest Irene has a little boy. How glad and thankful and relieved I am that she is over her troubles, and that it is a boy. I think she and Henry would have preferred a little girl, but one or 2 will I hope follow later to keep their brothers company. Missy has a little girl, born in the old Schloss Friedenstein at Gotha. I am glad she is there and not in Roumania at this moment.'

Although during the past ten years, Sophie has developed from a girl into a woman, she has rarely disagreed with her mother's views. But now she takes up the reasons for secrecy, to which goes the reply:

'My own Sophie, you say I ought to forgive everyone, but indeed I do with all my heart. I bear no malice, but I also have no illusions, my experience of 42 years has taught me that. The ill will so many bear my country is also extended to me, and at Berlin most people totally misunderstand me, and I am not to their taste. I have met with ingratitude and unkindness and disloyalty untold but I am not unforgiving, I assure you, far from it. I should not like people at Berlin to know I am ill. My own friends would be sad and sorry, and also many a one among the townspeople, but the rest would be only too pleased to get rid of me! That was shown, written and said too plainly in 1888 for me to forget or misunderstand it.

'Pray, my darling do not think it disturbs my peace of mind or makes me feel revengeful towards these people, it does not, I assure you. I am merely quite certain as to how much or how little sympathy I can count on, and do *not* deceive myself. Prejudice and ignorance are so often the cause of dislike and enmity, and so it is here. To explain and convert people is not possible, so one must take things as they are and make the best of it. I have never done them any harm, and have *tried* to do what good I could, but as for *pleasing* them, it is impossible. It is not my fault, but the fault of circumstances, which I had against me ever since I set my foot there in 1858, as a young girl only anxious to please, and be pleased with everybody. It was my *misfortune.* Had dear Papa been spared to reign for 10 or 20 years, things would have changed very much in that respect, as I would have had the *possibility* of rendering many a service which has been denied me, the means and the opportunity not having come to me.

'How sad for poor May to have lost her father, Franz Teck. For him poor man it can only be looked upon as a happy release, for he was in a pitiable state and hardly knew anyone or anything any more. Poor Aunt Ada [*Duchess of Augustenburg — Ed.*] is extremely ill, and yesterday the news sounded very serious.'

The Letters contain frequent comments on the progress of the Boer War, and on the hostile attitude of the German and other Continental newspapers.

'I have thought all along that a regular army with so much infantry was quite out of place there, and that volunteers and picked mounted rifles would be far better, left to fight the Boers in their own fashion, bit by bit driving them back and tiring them out, and taking as much time as they liked. One would have lost far fewer men and had less trouble and expense, but of course that is only my idea. How Napoleon's army suffered from the Spaniards hiding behind rocks, and firing at the soldiers from heights! ...Sir Charles Warren has managed to take one of the most important Boer positions, "Spion's Kop", and I hope and trust they may be able to reach Ladysmith. Every day the foreign papers spread false reports of reverses, lost battles. Never a word of hope or encouragement, it makes me so *savage*!

'Now poor dear Aunt Ada has died, and Dona seems in great grief, and to feel her poor Mother's death even more than I expected. I am so truly sorry, she was an old friend of mine since our young days, she was 3 years older than I am. She was so kindhearted and good-natured, and very pretty in her youth.'

The German training corvette, *Gneisenau,* pays a courtesy call on the Empress. Later, British warships also appear with a similar purpose.

'The weather has been fiendish! I never left the house for 2 days. As it happened, I was specially bad with pain, not only in my back, but in the old place. Yesterday in the midst of the awful weather, the "Gneisenau" appeared at daybreak, and anchored here, just off Lerici. Alas, I could not go on board, and our house was too small, and I too unwell to give the officers a dinner, so they all came up after luncheon and I spoke to them. Today the weather abated somewhat, and I begged Vicky to go on board in my name, which she did with great difficulty. After lunch she went to La Spezia in the steam launch and bought chocolate and cigarettes as a present for the middies and the boys. Then I joined her in the launch, and we steamed round the "Gneisenau" that was heaving up and down in the swell, and the Captain came down the accommodation ladder and I called across to him how very sorry I was not to be well enough to scramble up on board, and that I wished them a good voyage, and thanked them for the nice flowers they sent me.'

Sophie had recently inquired whether German army doctors could be lent to the Greek Army, and the Empress's reply had not been encouraging. She now explains.

'With respect to what I said of Army doctors: The Prussian ones used to be a little too fond of thinking every ailment feigned, and when the poor soldiers screamed during an operation (a smaller one) they were punished by having *half* their food taken away. I used to think they were most harshly and unkindly treated, more like prisoners than soldiers. That is a little better now, but there is room for improvement. The food was abominably bad, and the administration of the Lazarette was *not* very good or very honest. That too I hear is rather better. I think it right you should know this. In our English naval and military hospitals, the tone is much better, the men are more kindly treated, and they have *nurses* (not allowed in Germany, Papa always meant to introduce it).'

Prince Henry, on his way home from the Far East, calls at Spezia in order to see his mother.

'Henry arrived looking wonderfully well and in good spirits, very anxious to get home to his wife and children and see the new baby. Unfortunately when he arrived I was in bed with one of my worst attacks of pain and could not get up to receive him. I am better now, however, but had to have 2 injections of morphine. Fortunately he did not say disagreeable things to me on the subject of the war or of England, as I am so afraid of "flaring up", which I do *not* wish to do, but one gets so exasperated with the German press that it is enough to make a saint swear!

'The news of the war is most distressing and I fear the business will be long, and will try the patience and endurance of the troops out there, and the anxious expecting public at home! The Government will have a most difficult time, and it is very hard for dear Grandmama, but she neither loses her nerve nor her confidence, and feels that in the end the difficulties will be mastered. But at what cost! ...Greek sympathy is indeed most gratifying to think of. Our German papers are just as mad about it as they were against England. Mostly it is the work of Dr. Leyds and his bureau at Brussels, they carry on a regular "propaganda" on the foreign press to influence the public mind against England, and are very clever about it...How like Elsi of Weimar to take Dr. Leyds into her railway carriage, and Uncle of Weimar to give him an audience. They shall hear something from me if I meet them again! ...How distressed I am that Tino has such toothache and a swelled cheek, it is so painful.'

There are now few Letters that do not contain some mention of the Empress's illness, and of the sufferings she endures only with the relief of frequent morphine injections. These paragraphs make painful reading, and only a few of them are here included. A succession of extracts from the Letters over the next few weeks needs no explanation or commentary.

'Mama's physician, Sir Francis Laking has come to pay me a visit. It is a great comfort to me, and I can tell him about my sufferings. He thinks much the same of my case as Renvers. He thinks I should not move or travel now. I should much like to go to England later, perhaps when *you* come, and enjoy our all being there together. Grandmama *must* see your children and Mossy's, it would be so sad if they had no remembrance of her later when they grow up.

'I hope your concert went off well for the institution for poor boys to teach them a trade. Have you ever given a concert in your house yet? I suppose music would sound very well in your ballroom, both singing and orchestral music. ... I am so glad you have had some golf, and that you liked it, and that even the King had tried it. People say it is a very good exercise.

'There is a splendid man-of-war here in harbour, the "Caesar", one of our new British ships. She is really magnificent. I managed to go on board her and sit in the captain's fine large cabin for a bit. P.S. William, Henry and Charlotte do *not* know that Sir Fr. Laking has been to see me. I say nothing about it. My recollections of 1888 are *too* fresh in my mind.'

'I send you a letter from Countess Brühl about my Greek protegee, Flora Spirla, who is to become an opera singer, if possible. You will see that another year's subvention is required to finish her, I feel that I can hardly spend any more money on her without depriving other people of help which is so necessary for them. [*The Empress subscribed regularly to over forty philanthropic institutions.* — *Ed.*]. I believe that Syngros left money for the encouragement of Greek music, and training of musicians. Can you not procure the sum necessary for Flora Spirla to have one more year at Berlin? It would be a pity if the girl's training stopped half-way.'

'You and Tino and the King will have rejoiced with me at the relief of Ladysmith. Thank God for that, it was a blessing indeed. What those poor creatures endured, what suffering and privations, is not to be told! I trust Mafeking will soon be relieved, and thereby place another first-rate man, Col. Baden Powell, at Lord Roberts' disposal. The German, French and Russian papers in *general* now loudly clamour for *peace!* They urged on the Boers and helped on the war, and now they wish to save them from the consequences of their own folly. I hope England will turn a deaf ear, and settle the business once and for all.'

'You will have heard dear Grandmama is not going to Bordighera. She says that the abuse the French, German and Belgian press have heaped not only on England but also on herself would make it disagreeable for her, etc., which one so well understands. Instead she is going to Ireland, which will give great pleasure and do a lot of good. Grandmama and Uncle Bertie most kindly invite me over to England, and as soon as I am able to move about with ease again, I shall try to go. My other troubles I can hide, but this I cannot, and you understand one's not liking to show oneself in so helpless a condition. It would be sad to be in such a plight in England.

'I took a 3-hour trip on board the "Loreley" to Leghorn and spent the night in the harbour there. Yesterday morning we took carriages and drove to Pisa to see the Duomo, which is so fine...I would have enjoyed our tiny expedition very much had not the pain been so acute again, making every movement a torment.

'Dona and Willy's eldest boy has gone to live at the Stadt Schloss for his "Officer's Examination". It seems so strange that *young* Willy should be 18 now. I cannot imagine why they make such a dreadful fuss for his coming-of-age, the Emperor of Austria going to Berlin, etc., all the splash is enough to turn the poor boy's head, make him conceited and taken up with his own importance. He will go into the 1st Garde Regt. I only hope it will do him no harm, it did his Papa no good!'

'I must now try and do a little drawing and painting, as the weather promises to be fine at last...I try hard to learn Greek all alone by myself. Every morning in bed I learn words by heart, but my memory is very bad, and when one does not *hear* a language one picks it up slowly...The new French play by E. Rostand, "L'Aiglon", is not a success, I hear. I have read it, but do not very much care for it. Madame Sarah Bernhardt is said to act her part extremely well, but it seems too unnatural for her to represent a fair youth of 18.

'I venture to remind you of how much I want a photo of you in the Greek Court dress you wore on the 1st of January. They say that drops of water at last make a hole in a stone, so perhaps by dint of asking and begging I may someday succeed in getting the photograph.'

'Three days ago the British cruiser "Astoria" came here most civilly on my account. I was much touched and pleased, and went on board to a little luncheon of 7 people, which I managed to accomplish without much difficulty, as it was very smooth and I was helped up and down. The Captain was Capt. Paget, our Ld. Alfred Paget's son! ...Please excuse this dreadful writing but I am lying down, and it is so difficult to find a position which is convenient for writing and not painful.'

'I cannot say what an intense joy, relief and happiness it is to me to hear that the Bill about Tino's Army Reform had passed. *What* a blessing it will be! I was so delighted that I telegraphed to you. Do tell Sweetie how I rejoice. It will give him a deal of work, but he *can* do it, and will do it so *well.* I only hope he will be well seconded and supported. Theotokis has really been as good as his word and proved the best Minister you have had. What a tremendous task for Tino!

'Is it true that lovely Corfu is going to be turned into a Monte Carlo? It will bring money, but in the shape of poison! It will fill the Island with the scum of society, and certainly ruin the inhabitants. What I saw of Monte Carlo last year filled me with disgust, the lovely landscape spoilt with vulgar artificial gardens and smart buildings in very bad taste, a very temple of dissipation and vice. *How* it would spoil Greek society, who love what is rather frivolous and smart and fashionable. Cannot something else be invented to attract people to Corfu, some baths or cure?

'You will be pleased, I am sure, that May has a 3rd boy. The more the better, *I* say! ...Uncle Bertie is off to Copenhagen with Aunt Alix for Apapa's birthday. ... I have given up going home to Friedrichshof next week, as I shall not be fit to travel and it would be too humiliating to be carried in and out of the train, I should feel too much ashamed, and then it is desperately cold in Germany just now. I am very bad with pain today...'

'You can imagine my horror yesterday at hearing that dear Uncle Bertie had been fired at by a young Belgian anarchist. Thank God he escaped unhurt and his precious life was preserved. These dastardly attempts are too dreadful, thank God they mercifully rarely succeed. What a shock for dear Grandmama and cousins. I was all of a tremble when I heard.'

'I am so anxious to know how your picture is getting on with this French artist. ... I wonder whether my Sophie has disfigured her pretty forehead and nice-shaped head by that sponge or muff which she puts on, quite making her head out of proportion. I know you do not agree with me, but I am vain of your appearance and if you made your head look smaller instead of bigger it would be as pretty again (Do not be angry with me, please, I mean no offence!) I can quite imagine that Sitta will not keep quiet. Sweet Sitta with her eyes like drops of dew, so transparent and light, and deep set like those of her beautiful Grandmama Olga. I am sure the artist admires her. Frenchmen, artists especially, have such quick perception and true appreciation of beauty in any shape or form. Indeed, if I were as rich as people imagine I should send for Bouguereau to paint you and the 3 dear children, on a large picture, and offer it to Tino, but it would be out of the question except for Rothschilds.'

'Renvers is here, he is satisfied, which does not diminish the wretchedness of my condition but must reassure and comfort you. Do not worry about me my darling. Of course if there had been any real alarm about my health I should not have hesitated to send for you and Vicky and Mossy. As you can imagine, anxiety and distress are one thing, danger and alarm another. If my life is spared another few years, and the evil does not take the form of indirectly affecting me as it has done the last 6 months, I may look forward to going to Greece several times again. *If* the evil limits itself! To go on suffering as I have done, I *really* think I could *not* stand.

'Dear Grandmama has had a splendid reception at Dublin, and seems very happy in Ireland. I do hope your Papa-in-law's earache is better, please ask in my name how he is.

'How glad I am to hear your child's hospital is at last opened. I must congratulate you with all my heart. I am quite excited and delighted at the thought that this good work of yours has at last been set going.

'I am so pleased you are encouraging embroidery making. But I think it a mistake to copy Italian, French and German patterns. They ought only to be Greek, and distinctly Greek. Some person ought to be commissioned to search the Greek provinces, towns and villages, and also the Islands, and even the great Greek colonies in Sicily, to find samples of real Greek patterns. A careful collection ought to be made, and the girls taught to work fine old patterns in truly national style. If I were you, I would start a little collection. The Queen of Roumania did it, and it has been very successful.'

The Empress's condition improves sufficiently for her to return to Friedrichshof. She arrives at Frankfort on April 20th, and is given an affectionate welcome.

'I was so overcome with joy to see my angel Mossy again, looking like a rose, and so much "en beauté". She came to Heidelberg to meet me, and the darling children, and Fischy, Vicky and Adolf were at Frankfort Bahnhof, and got into our carriage.

'My dear Friedrichshof is so charming. It looks so tidy, clean, well-kept and in apple-pie order. It seems as if I had never been away, though it is sad indeed to be wheeled about in a chair like an old, old lady, and carried up and down stairs like a child, *here,* where I have always been so active. I only hope I shall keep well and not have another fearful attack, like the 3 I had in Italy.

'I am quite delighted to hear that there is a chance of something being done for Flora Spirla...It is cold, but a slight veil of green is creeping up the hillside, and over the fields, and the apples, pears and cherry trees are coming into blossom...The Duke of Argyll has died, and now Lome is Duke of Argyll. It will seem strange to me to call my sister Louise by a new name.'

From now on, the Empress is seldom without the company of one or other of her numerous circle of relations and friends.

'William was here all day yesterday, arrived early and went away after dinner. He thought me looking very well. I only wish I felt so. Vicky and Adolf, Mossy and Fischy helped me to do the honours. I managed to keep about all day, only resting on the sofa (the red sofa in the sitting room which my Sophie even slept on at Potsdam in 1888, when I used to hear her rustling like a little bird in a nest before she settled down to sleep).

'I had a charming visit from dear Maud and Charles of Denmark and a short one from dear Georgie of England. He was much pleased with his visit to Berlin, and got on very well indeed with Willy. I saw Charlotte and Bernhard yesterday. I could alas do but little in the way of mending matters with Feo. I spoke to Charlotte about my health for the first time, and told her that I reckoned on her silence and discretion, which she promised and I hope will keep.'

Princess Marie of Greece, whose hesitations have led to a long break in her engagement, now makes up her mind. 'I was indeed surprised to hear of dear Minny's re-engagement', the Empress writes. 'May she be happy and never repent it.' Barely a week later she notes that:

'Today is our dear Minny's wedding. Certainly a more beautiful place and season could not have been imagined than May in Corfu to be married in. To have to leave the sunny south, where a free people rejoice in the blessings of liberty, for the gloomy north, where alas there is still so much oppression, must indeed be very hard...Darling little Sitta will now be the only unmarried Greek princess!

'Henry and Irene and the 2 children are with me. We do not mention the war, as dear Henry is very opinionated, and does *not* understand the question, and so easily loses his temper in discussion that I always avoid it. I cannot convince him, as it would take far too long a time, and I should have to say many an unpleasant thing about Germany, which would put him in a fury, so I am silent.'

For several weeks the Letters have contained eager references to Princess Sophie's plans to visit Friedrichshof. She arrives halfway through May, accompanied by her husband and the children. After a couple of weeks, she and Prince Constantine go to Berlin, and stay in the Neue Palais at Potsdam. There are no letters to show the Empress's reactions to the relief of Mafeking on May 17th, but on June 6th she writes:

'Thank you so much for congratulating me for the entry of our troops into Pretoria. Here people pass it over in complete silence, or hardly allude to it, or with half a sneer. It has only one effect, to make one feel oneself a perfectly rabid "John Bull" at times, which otherwise one would not.

'Your sweet darlings are very happy and very good, and keep asking after Papa and Mama continually. I think Tootseyman's heavenly eyes have grown bigger, and Sitta's sweet dimples more bewitching, her little mouth and her smile more dainty, she is such a little duck. Tomorrow they are going to the Frankfort Zoological Gardens. Yesterday, Mossy's dear little people were here and they were very merry all together, but very harmonious. Aunt Anna also came to tea and was looking very well (for her).

'Darling, I long for you to be back so much. But I know you are enjoying yourself in the home of your childhood, the house where you were born and christened, though fate has banished your mother from it. How bitterly I rebel against fate sometimes, I cannot say! It does seem so cruelly unjust that all should have come as it did.'

After another stay at Friedrichshof, Sophie goes towards the end of July to Scheveningen in Holland, while her husband crosses to England for Cowes Week and to see his relations. On July 29th, King Humbert of Italy was assassinated. 'The poor dear King of Italy's death is a perfect nightmare' the Empress writes, 'he was always kindness itself to me and all my children.' But her sorrow is overwhelmed by the far greater loss two days later of her brother, the Duke of Edinburgh and Coburg.

'I can only say that I am quite crushed with this grief and that my tears are for ever flowing anew. It is all so sudden, I cannot believe my darling brother is gone. I cannot understand it at all yet. He had a sore throat it seems, and in June it was discovered that it was cancer of the root of the tongue. Details I have none. It is all one grievous piteous mystery to me. And I shall see him no more.'

Writing to Prince Constantine, who is staying with the Prince and Princess of Wales, to congratulate him on his birthday, the Empress exposes the deeper fear that her brother's death had raised for her.

'...I am so heartbroken at my darling brother's loss, and feel so unwell that all seems *dark* around me...Dearest Tino, my beloved brother's death is an awful blow to me. I did not know his state. No one said anything was the matter, I cannot understand how such a disease could develop between June and now, and become dangerous to life *so* quickly. It is fearful! ...Give my love to all the dear ones at Marlborough House.'

To Princess Sophie the Empress shows what is in her heart about her own sufferings.

'I am so miserable about Uncle Alfred I can hardly fix my thoughts on anything else...I suppose one must consider it a mercy that he was taken before he knew of his illness, and was spared long and cruel sufferings...My tears flow bitterly when I think of the dear companion of my childhood, and the unchanging affection between us. Now it is silence and a great blank....

'You do not seem much charmed with Scheveningen, but I hope the sea air will be beneficial all the same. Your darlings are very well and in good spirits. Georgie was so delighted with his birthday presents. Sweet little Sitta follows him about, admiring his presents, but without any envy or jealousy, with true sisterly devotion. Excuse this miserable scribble, but I am in a hurry and must dress, a thing I dread as it is so painful to stand.'

After a further stay at Friedrichshof, Sophie and the family leave for Athens on August 27th.

'Before crawling into bed and ending this sad day, I must scribble a line. No one knows what parting from you means to me. I shall lie awake and in tormenting pain, but thinking of you and Tino, your future, your work, your opportunities, and praying God to enlighten you and show you the right way, that you may leave those sweet children an inheritance to be proud of. You can both be the *blessing* of your country, and that is a proud and inspiring thought.

'You know my great anxiety to be of help in anyway I can. The few years it may be God's wish I shall spend on earth, I long to be useful to you and Tino, your children and your country. You know and feel that, I am sure. I will plod away at my Greek, and try in time to be able to read, in that way I shall be very near you with my thoughts, as I *always* am in everything I do or see and hear.'

A visit from her brother a fortnight later helps to cheer her up. The old Burg in Cronberg is being restored on her initiative and largely at her expense.

'Yesterday Uncle Bertie came for luncheon and remained for tea. We went to look at the Burg, The roof is finished, also the paving of the courtyard with big irregular stones. Not much more will be done this year. Dear Grandmama and Uncle Bertie are so much for my going to England at the beginning of November, but Renvers is much against it. I hope to persuade him. Here the weather is splendid, bright sunshine, air like crystal, the distance very blue and the smoke rises straight in the air. Oh, how nice a good ride or good long walk would be, but none of that can I have now.

'Do not thank me, my darling for your stay. It is *I* that thanks you for coming and shedding the light and joy of your dear presence on your mother's house.

'The Transvaal has been pronounced a British Colony, thank God, I am so delighted. It will be an immense advantage to South Africa, and England will at last have done what she ought to have done long, long ago. The mistake of *not* doing it we have paid for very dearly, by a long and expensive war and heavy sacrifices and the loss of so many valuable lives.'

The Empress's condition worsens again, and from now on, with the increasingly severe attacks of pain, her physique begins to suffer, and her morale to flag. Towards the end of September she writes:

'How interesting to go and see the marble quarries of the Pentelikon. I trust it will develop and become a source of prosperity. Do not forget that Papa and Tino and you have promised a block from there for the Friedrichskirche Mausoleum, for *my* tomb, whenever the time comes...I have been very bad these last few days. You have no idea what pain I suffer when the spasms come on. They do so sometimes every two hours and last a good half-hour or 3 -quarters. I can only scream and groan, and nothing gives relief. I asked the doctor to sleep in the house so as to be able to have him *quick* in the night. All the promises that the pain would soon wear off have *not come true!*

'Ducky and Missy came over here 2 days ago. The latter I thought more lovely than ever, she was very quiet and seemed quite unconcerned.... Little Feo is still here, extraordinary little person, she reads to me a good deal, but so fast that I have difficulty in understanding it. The weather is quite perfect, my second crop of hay is all but in. P.S. I was so pleased Uncle Bertie's horse "Diamond Jubilee' won another race.'

A few days later, for the first time, she mentions the thought of release from her sufferings.

'The Empress Eugénie has most kindly offered me her charming villa at Cap Martin for the winter. If I had been well I should have accepted it gladly. Her kindness touches me so much, it is just like her. She does not stop to ask whether it will do her good or harm in the eyes of her Party in France, but follows the dictates of her kind heart.

'I am still quite in bed. Never have the spasms been so frightfully violent as these last days. If somebody had put me out of my misery I should have felt intensely thankful. I had to have morphia every 2 hours in the night. When will it improve? All the time I am longing to go out, and to be down and about again, but with these pains it is impossible.

'Charlotte and Bernhard arrived last night. It is so tiresome for them, poor things, that I am laid up. I fear she has not kept that dangerous little tongue of hers in order, but has been talking about my health. It is really too bad when she swore she would not..., Has Tino's motor car arrived? I must say it rather strikes terror to my heart when I hear of all the accidents so constantly occurring with these things,'

The Empress has an exceptionally bad attack, and for the first time in her illness, is frightened. She writes in pencil on October 20th.

'Oh, my child, I am so thankful to be alive, as I can live in the hopes of seeing you and Sweetie and the children again. But oh, I was *so* near gone, and *felt* going. I cannot speak of it all to-day, but will do so later when I am stronger. It is all so horrible...It is rather naughty of me to write, I know, and I do not quite think it would be allowed, but the longing to write to you is beyond control. Besides, though terribly weak, so weak that I can hardly hold the pencil, I am getting better.

'How glad I am your journey with Tino was such a success and so interesting. May it be the first of a series of such journeys. The people must feel that Sweetie has his eyes and his ears everywhere, *watches* over his people, is ready to *lead* and advise and *help* them. He will soon have the right influence and be so popular...Yes, it is right about Mossy dear. Of course it makes me anxious and nervous until it is all well over, but I am very pleased all the same. Perhaps it will be a little Sophie!'

Writing on Sophie's wedding anniversary, October 27th, the Empress calls down blessings, but her own world grows more and more baneful.

'May God bless you both, and your darling children and send you many long and happy years of usefulness and success. Thank God great happiness has been granted you in a dear husband and sweet children. Life is *never* easy, it is a struggle at best, but the hours of sunshine, and the blessings vouchsafed, make up for what is pain and sorrow.

'My own Sophie, I am going on well in most respects, but the *terrible* nights of agony are worse than ever, no rest, no peace. The tears rush down my cheeks when I am not shouting with pain. The injections of morphia dull the pains a little for about a quarter of an hour, sometimes not at all, then they rage again with renewed intensity, and make me wish I were safe in my grave, where these sufferings were not. So my nights are spent! The electricity does no good, nor poultices (hot), nor ice-bags, nor embrocations, *nothing, nothing!* It is fearful to endure. My courage is quite exhausted, and this morning I cried for an hour without ceasing.

'I bear this martyrdom hoping to live on a few years more, and see you happy, and the children grow older. I should be cheerful when the pain leaves me a little peace, were it not for all the cruel things that happen. Every day brings some sad news. This death of poor dear Christie of typhoid at Pretoria has given me a dreadful shock. Aunt Lenchen's grief makes my heart bleed. He was her *idol,* and gave her such joy, and proved such a good steady boy...Poor Grandmama, this is her 3rd grown-up grandson she has lost.

"Then the death of dear old Mons. Godet, Papa's much-loved tutor, to whom I was so attached, grieves me much. I send you a letter from the widow to me, which is very touching, perhaps you would send her a word of condolence through Messie...then also my friend, Prof. Max-Muller...it is *so, so* sad!'

Inevitably, almost every letter contains a description of the Empress's sufferings, mostly too harrowing to reproduce. But though physically she is helpless, her mental energy remains unimpaired, and she clings determinedly to her interests, as is shown by the following extracts from lengthy letters over the next two months. From now on the letters are written in pencil, except when dictated.

'A new excellent life of dear Papa has appeared by a historian, a Dr. A. Philipson. I have had nothing to do with it, nor do I know the author. Please ask Tino to read this biography, it will show him what a life of trials and struggles poor dear Papa's was. What a life of self-sacrifice and often disappointment and insuccess, but still how noble and how useful! His position was terribly difficult, and the calumnies and enmities, the attacks and intrigues, under which he had to suffer as Crown Prince, quite wore out his health. He was so sensitive, and felt so deeply the injustice of his fate. This book is quite a surprise to me, but a pleasing one after all the *lies* of the disgusting *vile* Bismark memoirs, Busch, etc.'

'How is Tino's work getting on? Is he very busy? I hope Nicky and Andrea will not be left unemployed, there is so much serious work to do in the country, and the example must be set by the Royal Family, to whom others will then look more and more. The future of Greece depends on the energy with which the reigning house devote themselves to the task of *helping* on the nation in every way. The Constitution, if rightly understood, does *not* prevent it.

You do your duty thank God, and it is appreciated even now, which must be a satisfaction to you in spite of the toil and uphill work and great difficulties you have to contend with.

'Today I send you a little book, hints for young mothers about the treatment of their babies. I thought if you had it translated into Greek, it would be useful for distribution amongst Greek mothers who do not know much on the subject, though the beautiful darkeyed babies *do* seem to flourish...I have read with very deep interest and not a little excitement about the work of the British Archaeological School in the excavations in Crete. Wonderful!'

'I have been in bed *six weeks* today. We have passed from summer to autumn, almost winter without my perceiving it. Of course I have plenty of time to think and think, and my thoughts are *not* cheerful. My legs are shrunken and fallen away to nothing, a mere skeleton. The agony is as bad as ever, the nights are a torture. In 24 hours I do not get 2 hours sleep. The pain is too frequent, too violent, like ever so many razors driven into my back. The tears and groans all night long drive me utterly mad. I often think I should put an end to myself if I only could. Oh, I cannot bear it any longer! Pity me! I do not think anyone can suffer much more.'

'Your house in town must be quite charming, and will become more and more so every year. It must be a heavy expense to you to have to furnish it yourselves, and to have to correct the mistakes the architect made. I well know how expensive it is to establish a house properly, and how many unforeseen expenses have to be met. Still by degrees and not doing all at once you will succeed...I am sorry for you having to change your cook, but when they once begin to drink it is no use keeping them. I am very glad your little dinner went off" so well, all the same. I am so pleased you had a flower show, and that you think people are beginning to care for flowers and gardens. Athens ought to be buried in flowers, like Mentone, Bordighera, everything should grow there with a little care and trouble.'

'Please thank Sabba, Messie, ...and all who have thought of me. It is a sad way of spending my 60th birthday, in bed, feeling weak and ill, and off" and on in great pain. But letters and telegrams in perfect avalanches arrive, and more flowers than I can possibly find vases for. I have had charming presents. I am not feeling happy about dear Grandmama. She has not been very well, and was rather feeble. It worries me very much, considering her age, and makes me feel my being so helpless and not being able to fly to her.... Mossy is severely scolding me for not ending this scribble, so I must close.'

'I cannot write much today as my right hand is bandaged, and my left one so swelled that alas, I had to have my wedding ring sawn off my finger with a little saw. To be without my wedding ring for the 1st time since 1858, when dear Papa put it on the finger of his bride of 17, in the Chapel Royal at St. James! It seems so dreadful to have it broken in two, and taken off by force, but it had to be.

'...I heard from Alicky, and she says Nicky is going on well, and she too is pretty well, and expecting a baby.... Fancy your darling Sitta growing so immense. She will be a young "Valkyr". I shall be very proud if I live to see her — perhaps Queen of England, or rather Princess David of York?'

'Mossy is kind enough to write for me, writing being difficult with my stiff and aching hand. No doubt you are already thinking of Xmas. So am I, here on my bed. It is a tremendous business, so many institutions to think of. I am sending a tiny cloak for Sweet Sitta, and a little brooch to wear and some silver for Georgie and Tootseyman. For you and Tino, an Empire bronze clock of very original pattern, and for you alone 3 table covers, you said you had not many.

'It is disgraceful what a fuss is being made in Germany about that nasty common old thief of a Kruger. Luckily not by William or the Government. [*The Emperor refused to see President Kruger — Ed.*] It is only because people consider him the enemy of England. That is enough to make any wretch a hero in the eyes of the Germans, they fall easy prey to the lies and intrigues of the Boer Committee, Dr. Leyds, etc'

'I have had 2 nights without as much as closing my eyes for two minutes. I am quite overcome with the pain and can do nothing but cry, which is foolish indeed, but one cannot help it, one is so worn out with struggle and suffering. Still, I have so many comforts I must not complain. You can imagine how pleasant it is to have a well-warmed, lit and ventilated house in illness, and how convenient to have the hot and cold water.'

'Fancy my surprise and delight at having a visit from dear Aunt Beatrice, who had come to Frankfort for a couple of days. What a joy and comfort for me. Alas, she leaves again for England on Monday, and has come to say goodbye to me today. She sends you her best love. Today, as the weather was sunny and fine, I was carried down on the terrace for a moment. Auntie. B. went with me.

'I am so glad your idea of replanting and rewooding the waste places in Hellas has met with so favourable a reception and become popular, and that your tree-planting ceremony went off so well, and such interest seemed to be taken. Trees ought to be planted on national fete days, the Day of Independence, your birthday. Papa's and Tino's...If a little botany and gardening were taught in the schools, the idea of replanting the devastated woods would spread much faster.

'I am often in very low spirits and shed many tears, but sometimes when I feel a trifle better I am full of hope, and think of a possible future and better days, though I well know that I cannot be cured, and that my life can never again be what it was. This must be accepted, but I do not find it easy, I assure you.

'Aunt Marie Edinburgh came over from Darmstadt to see me. You can imagine what a sad meeting it was. I had not seen her since poor little Alfred's death, and now this terrible loss. She was very nice and kind...though she hates showing her feelings in general, she did not conceal from me how much she suffered...She brought Little Bee with her, who has grown to my taste into a very strikingly pretty girl, with a beautiful figure, and looks very piquante.

'I am sure you are inexpressibly shocked at the loss of the "Gneisenau". You had been on board several times and knew the officers and captain. What a disaster! I had seen them all only in January.' [*The vessel sank during a gale, at Malaga, with the loss of fifty lives — Ed.*]

'It is Xmas Day, and although my right hand is so swelled and so stiff that the fingers will hardly hold the pencil, yet I must try and write myself. I am feeling very poorly with the constant fever. Every afternoon I have myself taken downstairs to look at our presents and watch the sweet children in their innocent joy, playing about the Xmas Tree. This cheers me *so* much. Our servants, our workpeople and the poor of Cronberg are all much pleased with their presents. It was a tremendous business to get all ready. Tomorrow at 11, Pastor E. from Offenbach comes to give me the Sacrament as I cannot go to church. Mossy will take it with me and some of the household. Goodbye, my own Sophie darling. I can write no more as I am in great pain at this moment.'

'How you made me laugh about the serving at Court, and the poor lady fainting in her neighbour's lap. Serving will have to be drilled, and hard, like everything else, it does not "come natural", I fear, especially on the Continent, where I have seen so many funny things in that way.

'You will laugh at me I know, and think me very foolish, but I do so often wish you had a gentleman of your own who could manage your money and charity affairs. Your business will increase from year to year, and I fear soon be beyond what the faithful Messie and yourself together can manage. I hardly like to offer any advice on the subject for fear of meddling, still I wish you had some one to help you in all you have to do.'

'I am beginning the New Year very badly, fever and pain torment me increasingly, the swelled legs, hands and joints are perfectly miserable. My life is not worth having. The thought of seeing you so soon again cheers and comforts me more than I can say...I trust I may improve, unless some horrible new complication comes to prevent my regaining my strength and the use of my limbs...Excuse this short letter but I am feeling so very uncomfortable that I can dictate no more.'

'This (Jan. 7th) is your [*Orthodox Church — Ed.*] Xmas day I believe, may your darling children enjoy it. I hope you will let Sitta wear the little brooch I sent her. May her bewitching dimples, when she grows up, not create so much commotion in the world as Helen of Troy's beauty once did, tho' I am sure your little Maid of Athens will win many admiring looks...P.S. I have been 17 weeks in bed today. My poor legs are only 2 straight bones — how they are ever to carry me again, I do not know.'

'Most loving thanks for your dear letter of the 7th just arrived. I am so glad the tree was so nice at the Palace and wish I could have seen the children's eager excited faces. How most kind of the King to give you a miniature of me, I am much touched, and think it very kind of him, certainly we shall look for a frame together. I am so sorry that the table cloths seem not to have arrived yet. I had so hoped they would have come in time for Xmas.'

The Empress has become increasingly worried over her mother's health. 'How I wish I could see her soon, I long to be with her, but am a stupid useless thing, like a log of wood!' After the 'miniature' letter there is silence for nearly a fortnight. On the evening of January 22nd Queen Victoria breathes her last. Until now, despite her discomforts and swollen hands, the Empress's pencilled handwriting had been as firm as ever before. But the straggling lines in the letter of the 23rd show how prostrated she is by her mother's death.

'Words cannot describe my agony of mind at this overwhelming sorrow. Oh, my beloved Mama! Is she *really* gone? Gone from us all to whom she was such a comfort and support. To have lost her seems *so* impossible — and I far away could not see her dear face or kiss her dear hand once more. It *breaks* my heart. My Sophie darling, you have lost a most dear and kind and sweet Grandmama, who was ever so full of love for you all, taking an interest in all that concerned you. What a Queen she was, and what a woman! What will life be to me without her, the wretched bit of life left to me, struggling with a cruel disease? How her affection and sympathy used to cheer and help and comfort me. Now all that is gone. My dear home in England, my home no longer. The feeling is immense in England, and well it may be. Every Englishman has lost almost a mother and a friend. In the bitterness of my grief I must admit that it was a mercy she did not suffer pain, and that she had no long illness, a peaceful end, that she was not stricken with infirmity and obliged to have a Regency. All that was spared to her, and to us. That she went to her rest in dear Osborne is what I feel she would have wished herself.'

Prince and Princess Constantine go to London for Queen Victoria's funeral, then come to Friedrichshof, where they stay until the beginning of March. The Empress's first letter on March 7th, like all that follow, is again in her usual firm handwriting, though sometimes the blurred pencilling is barely decipherable.

'I know you have forbidden me writing and I have promised to obey, but one little line I must send you to say how my thoughts are with you on the journey. How I miss you I cannot say, nor how grateful I was for your visit, my own pet. You were so sweet to your Mama and so patient with her, sacrificed so much time to her and read so much, and it was such a joy to have you. This is Easter Day, and I send you every possible greeting and loving wish. I am spending it miserably in my bed, in great pain and torture. Irene has just arrived, Henry comes this evening. I am going to have some eggs hidden in the garden for Mossy's dear little people...I hope the 2 rose plants which I promised Tino for your garden arrive all right. Have you seen all the funny and mostly very incorrect pictures in the illustrated papers about dear Uncle Bertie's visit here?'

It was during this visit that the Empress secretly gave King Edward's secretary, Sir Frederick Ponsonby, her letters to Queen Victoria, which he published twenty-seven years later. He describes the Empress, when he sees her in her sitting-room, looking 'as though she had just been taken off the rack after undergoing torture'.

Extracts from selected letters show how the Empress kept her mind and interests active, in spite of her ever-growing weakness under almost continuous anguish. Only a few of her constant references to her illness are given here. During these last months, she comes to realize that there is no hope.

'Today I have no one to dictate to, so I must write with my own stiff, painful, awkward hand. How I envy your seeing the fragments of the glorious statues whose beauty has arisen again from the depths of the sea, from centuries of oblivion. Yes, the sense of beauty need never die out in Greece. Nature is so beautiful and tradition so strong. In my eyes the type has remained much unchanged, in spite of migrations and the floods of foreign elements which ravaged the country.

'The house is undergoing a "spring cleaning", the carpets are taken up bit by bit and beaten, and the floors polished, the curtains shaken and brushed. As I cannot get away, it must be done while I am in the house. It has been for so many months half hotel, half hospital. I had thought of going to Baden-Baden for a month, in the hopes a change might do good, but have given it up. I also do not think I shall get to the Isle of Wight now in Spring, as I had so much hoped, I am still too weak.'

'How truly glad I am to hear of the female prison being such an improvement on the former one, and such a success.... Dear Lady Ponsonby has been here with Maggie [*her daughter — Ed.*], and leaves again in 2 days. Henry, Irene and the 3 children are coming next week. The house will be full again. I am happy to say Mossy's nurse comes tomorrow, so I shall feel less nervous. It is a terrible trial to me to think I shall not be with her, and cannot be of use to her, sweet child.'

'How *nice* is the success of the soup kitchen! In time, people's baths and peoples' libraries must follow. Wholesome food for their bodies and their minds, *and* cleanliness will do a deal of good. Will you dear, when you next come, bring me some of the soap that is made either in Cephalonia or Zante, with olive oil? It is so excellent for washing linen.

'I had a very bad night again, nothing could calm or relieve the raging pain. I could only scream and moan and groan. The first morphia injection took no effect, the 2nd one given about 2 o'clock *did,* and I had peace, and a little sleep till 5, when the pain came on again. Oh, it is so awful to bear, I am so weary of the constant tearing pain.'

'Henry and Irene and the children are here, all looking very well. Toddie grown and much stouter. Budgie not so cross as he used to be, and the baby I cannot judge of, as he screams and cries violently the moment he sees me.

'...I think it so nice of little Georgie to ask you whether I was an orphan now. The thought is so natural...What would you say if you could look out of the windows here and see the thick drifting snow eddying and pelting as it did in January, and now it is April!'

'It is such a pleasure to have sweet Aunt Alix here, she is so kind and dear and gentle and quite touching in her goodness to me, and admirable in the way she fills her new position, with such true tact and good sense. No other would I have liked to see at the head of our dear old home, and bearing the name so sacred to us. It is very kind of her to spare a few days to come and see me. I am very loth to part with her, as you can imagine. We talk together as well as we can, I with my weak voice, and in pain, though I fear she does not quite hear or understand all. Her deafness has rather increased.

'Vicky dear returned to Bonn yesterday, where she is preparing to receive William, who stays with her a couple of days. I miss her so much. Dear kind Victoria Battenberg is staying with me. Such a comfort. She reads to me and we chat, when I am able...Do not distress yourself about my writing in my own hand. I promise you I will not tire myself, and it gives me pleasure to write to you, as long as I have a hand to write with.'

'Renvers is satisfied in many respect that the disease has not seized upon the inner organs, but he understands how dreadful and piteous is the state of suffering and weakness I am in, and hopes to get it to improve.

'How charming that Sitta helped her Grandpapa in the distribution of prizes at the Stadium, she must have looked sweet indeed, and is beginning the fulfilment of public life very early. Dear Aunt Lenchen's visit is a great comfort to me, she reads to me and looks after me most kindly. William was here yesterday, looking very well, I thought. Aunt Beatrice will be here about the 9th or 10th May.

'We have had 2 or 3 days of beautiful weather, the trees and bushes are beginning to come out. Cuckoos and swallows have arrived, and I believe a nightingale! The primroses are beginning to flower in the garden and the daffodils are out.'

The Empress is weakening, and her letters are less and less frequent. It becomes obvious that the end cannot be far away. Princess Sophie prepares to set out once again from Athens, accompanied by her husband and the children. The Empress writes on the anniversary of Queen Victoria's birthday, May 24th.

'This was once such a proud day for me, one of brightness and rejoicing. Now those days are dear memories, and *she* is gone whom we loved to try and please and cheer on this her birthday...I am so glad Tino had a good reception everywhere on his tour. These trips *can* only do good! Missolonghi must be beautiful. Did you go to Manolada? I do wish Andrea would come here into the German army for a little while, it would be so useful for him.

'Excuse my writing so little. The pain has been unbearable. The | Bishop of Ripon has been staying with me with his wife. He gave me the Communion this morning, a perfectly simple and short service. Kisses to the darling children, best love to Sweetie. The place is looking lovely just now, the azaleas one blaze, also the rhododendrons, glycerias, tulips, iris, and all the foliage in brightest green.'

Two days later, when the Empress next writes. Princess Margaret has given birth once more to twin boys.

'I have been terribly bad these last 3 days and nights. I think the agony must have reached its climax, as I simply could *not* endure more. I think I shall lose my reason sometimes, so acute is the pain...The joy of seeing you will I trust do me good.

"The Congress of Doctors must have been interesting. I am glad Tino has brought some Venetian "Coats of Arms" from Nauplia. I remember seeing beauties on the old town wall and before a large gateway (arch), and heard with regret that both had been pulled down. Mossy is doing well, and her little ones too — I must not betray what they are to be called. The dear four eldest were here for a moment this afternoon and were very good.'

On June 3rd, the Empress writes, as she unknowingly says, her last letter — the last of all those many she has written year by year to Princess Sophie.

'My own Sophie darling,

'If the newspapers are to be trusted, this will be my last letter, as they say you leave on the 9th. You will be glad to leave the heat. Here it was very hot for some days, and made all the spring flowers which came with a rush, fade and go off directly. Now we have the roses beginning.

'I have been terribly bad these last few days. The attacks of pain so violent, the struggle for breath so dreadful, when in bed or lying down, most distressing...I manage to struggle through the day, I know not how, and am much out of doors, lying down, my arm hung up in a cushion, and my head too. Of an afternoon I have a drive.

'What joy it will be to see you and Tino and the sweet children. If you are only not bored. All else I will speak to you about when we meet. I hear darling Mossy and the twinnies are doing well, thank God. I suppose they will be christened here in the house. Goodbye my own darling, God bless you.

'Ever your devoted, fond and doting, suffering

'Mother, V.'

Chapter Thirteen - Aftermath

The Empress had two months yet to live, two months of excruciating agony relieved only by repeated morphine injections. Her general condition weakened, her face, which until the end of 1900 had not greatly altered, became thin and pale. But until a week or so before her death, she was, though despondent, still able to write and still interested in all that was happening in the world.

During the last few days, at the beginning of August, the members of her family, not only her own children and grandchildren but some nieces and nephews and others, assembled sadly at Friedrichshof. The Emperor and his wife arrived thirty-six hours before the end. He was one of those who sat continuously by the bedside, and was with her when she died in the early evening of August 5th.

It was an irony that the two who were dearest to her, who had rewarded her love with their own deep devotion, who had watched over her for months, and stayed at her side without a break during the previous weeks, were not with her at the last moment. 'My sister Sophie and I', wrote Princess Margaret to the Editor shortly before her own death at Friedrichshof in 1954, 'had just gone into the garden to have a rest when we were called back, and we were too late to be present when she actually breathed her last.'

It has often been asked whether there was a reconciliation between the Empress and her eldest son during these last hours of her life. The Letters show that the tensions between them eased a good deal after she had taken up residence at Friedrichshof. To the Editor's question, 'Was there a final reconciliation between the Empress and her three eldest children during the last phase?' Princess Margaret wrote, 'Yes, to a certain degree'.

The devotion that the Emperor William showed at his mother's deathbed, however sincere, did not prevent his repeating at Friedrichshof the scenes that Friedrichskron had witnessed in 1888. With a few hours of her death, her home was under guard by troops while special police searched every room. If they were looking for letters, those to Queen Victoria had already been taken to England by Sir Frederick Ponsonby, and those to Sophie were safely in Athens.

The Empress had faced her approaching end fearlessly. A fortnight before she died, she dictated to Reischach her instructions for her funeral. There should be no post-mortem, no embalming, no photographs and no lying-in-state at Friedrichshof. The coffin, she said, should be closed and taken to Cronberg Town Church, until it could be moved to Potsdam. 'Anyone who pleases may visit the church.' At her burial she wished the Court Chaplain 'to say a short prayer, but on no account is he to make a speech'.

After two days, her body was taken to Potsdam and buried in the Mausoleum by the side of her husband. It was strange perhaps that just as he had died in the same year as his father, so she died in the same year as her mother.

Her carefully pondered testament disposed of every item of her fortune and belongings. Friedrichshof, the lovingly created home she had enjoyed so briefly, and most of its contents went to Princess Margaret. Every piece of her jewellery, silver, art treasures and other valuables was allotted specifically to members of her family. There was a gift to each of her employees, and to those who had long been close to her.

So ended a life begun with hope and happiness, passed in struggle, contumely, disillusionment and sorrow, and running its course after prolonged physical suffering. Yet much as we must pity the Empress for the agonies she endured before death released her, perhaps we should not regret, for her sake, that she died at what we should today regard as the not very advanced age of 60.

For had she lived as long as her mother, she would have witnessed happenings that she might have found even more cruel to bear than physical pain. She who belonged to her mother's age, the Victorian era, would have seen her accustomed world, resting on the monarchical structure that largely dominated Europe, the three great dynasties of the Hohenzollerns, the Habsburgs and the Romanoffs, disappear like the blown-out flame of a candle.

She would have seen her eldest son lead his and her country into a suicidal war against her beloved England, a war that shattered the Empire her husband had helped to create. She would have seen him precipitate the struggle between Europe and the Slav Russia that she always feared, by plunging Europe and indeed most of mankind into disaster so great that a second world war and the cold war of today have not yet sighted the end of it.

She would have seen him abdicate and flee to Holland, and the rest of her family in Germany sink into comparative obscurity and exile. In Russia she would have seen her niece, Alicky, and Nicky and their children, brutally murdered by Bolshevik revolutionaries, as well as scores of other Russian relations and friends, among them Ella, who, widowed already by a nihilist, was flung cold-bloodedly to her death down a mine-shaft.

The Empress's oft-repeated prayers for Sophie and Tino and their children, as for Mossy and hers, brought them no blessings. It seemed instead as if a curse lay on all her house, for most of her children met disaster — and few of her grandchildren found lasting happiness.

Had she lived on, her heart would surely have broken over events in Greece. She would have seen 'dear Papa-in-law', King George, assassinated, and 'darling Tino, as dear to me as my own son', after only a few years on the throne, driven with Sophie and the children out of his country by France and Britain. A few years later, she would have seen them both, and Queen Olga also, dying in bitter exile, Sophie from the scourge that had killed her father and her mother.

In Germany, had the Empress lived even longer, she would have seen her 'Mossy, looking like a little rose', who had already lost her two eldest sons in her brother's war, reduced by Hitler's war to living in a cottage by the gates of a transformed Friedrichshof that had become a club for American officers. And with what anguish and compassion would she have seen 'Vicky, looking so regal', left a childless widow in 1916, making a crazy marriage thirteen years later with a young Russian adventurer, and dying in the same year, in mortification and penury, after he and her fortune had vanished.

And what of some of the others whose names appear so often in the Letters? 'Ernie and Duckie' divorced: Feo, 'that strange little creature', unhappy in her marriage, willing herself to die: 'Big Georgie', forced by intrigue and revolt to give up his governorship of Crete: Andrea, narrowly escaping execution by the Greek revolutionaries that dethroned his brother for the second time: Minny, widowed by the Bolsheviks, and ending her days in exile: 'Tootseyman', succeeding his father as King, marrying morganatically, dying in early manhood: 'Sitta, such a little sweet', marrying 'Missy's' first son, ('poor little man') Prince Carol, a union that ended in disaster, as did also 'little Georgie's' marriage with, Carol's sister, Elizabeth....

But the tale of infelicity is long enough to show that it was as well the Empress did not live to a great age. She did her best to prepare her younger daughters and their families for the future, just as she tried to guide everybody she loved or liked along the paths she thought they ought to follow. But a contrary fate was too strong for most of them, just as it had been too strong for her.

Yet in spite of the limits that circumstances and events placed on her authority, she did make her mark on Germany, especially in the spheres of culture and welfare, and as she points out in the Letters, on the way of domestic life. On Greek affairs, she exercised an indirect influence. She may have done so even in political matters by her encouragements and exhortations of the young and inexperienced Prince Constantine. She certainly did in the development of welfare and social services. The many good works, from hospitals to afforestation, for which Queen Sophie is gratefully remembered in Greece, were mostly inspired by her mother, as the Letters show.

But there were a few matters on which no amount of prompting or even pleading could produce results. There is, for example, no record that Princess Sophie ever went to Manolada. Nor did she give up her fringe. Nor, apparently, did she ever send her mother that photograph in Greek costume. There were limits even to the Empress's powers of persuasion!

In such small things as these, as well as in those immeasurably more important affairs on which she gave her sometimes unwanted ideas and advice, the Empress displayed that urge which had inspired her all her life, and which she never could subdue — the urge to help others, to better them, to guide them towards those material, moral and social standards that she had first imbibed in England.

There were many, especially in Germany, who regarded these efforts as meddlesome. But in the light of all that has happened since, we know now that not only were most of her views and judgments sound and long-sighted, but her aspirations were in tune with the inevitable march of political and social progress.

It was not the Empress Frederick who was always in the wrong in the autocratic, reactionary Germany of those days. With her husband and that liberal-minded minority of whom she was the leader and symbol, she was in many ways another visitor to a Country of the Blind, the only one with eyes to see.

Bibliography

In compiling Chapter One and the commentaries to the Letters, the Editor has sometimes referred to the following books:

Letters of the Empress Frederick. Edited by Sir F. Ponsonby.
The Letters of Queen Victoria. Third series, 1886-1901, edited by G. E. Buckley.
The Empress Frederick. A Memoir (Anon).
The Empress Frederick. Princess C. Radziwell.
Under Three Emperors. Baron Hugo von Reischach.
Queen Victoria's Relations. Merial Buchanan.
Further Letters of Queen Victoria. H. Bolitho.
My Early Life. Kaiser William II.
My Memoirs. Kaiser William II.
Reflections and Reminiscences. Prince Bismark.
Memoirs. Prince Chlodwig of Hohenlohe-Schillingfürst.
Behind the Scenes at the Prussian Court. Princess Friedrich Leopold of Prussia.
Reminiscences. Princess Marie of Battenberg.
Life and Times of Princess Beatrice. M. E. Sara.
Mary Ponsonby. Edited by M. Ponsonby.
The Daughters of Queen Victoria. E. F. Benson.
As We Were. E. F. Benson.
The Kaiser and his English Relations. E. F. Benson.
The War Diary of the Emperor Frederick. Translated by A. R. Allinson.
Frederick the Noble. Sir Morrell Mackenzie.
Kaiser William 11. Emil Ludwig.
The Kaiser. J. von Kürenberg. Bismark. Emil Ludwig.
Edward VII. Sir Sidney Lee.
The Downfall of Three Dynasties. Count Egon Corti.
Royal Cavalcade. Erica Beal.
She Made World Chaos. E. F. P. Tisdale.
Queen Victoria. Works by E. F. Benson, Sir Sidney Lee, L. Strachey., E. Sitwell, R. Fulford, H. Bolitho, Sir F. Ponsonby.
Contemporary files of *The Times.*

www.ingramcontent.com/pod-product-compliance
Lightning Source LLC
Chambersburg PA
CBHW032040090426
42744CB00004B/76